OUR LADY

PAPAL TEACHINGS

OUR LADY

Selected and Arranged

by

THE BENEDICTINE MONKS OF SOLESMES

Translated by

THE DAUGHTERS OF ST. PAUL

ST. PAUL EDITIONS

IMPRIMATUR:

✠ **His Eminence, Richard Cardinal Cushing**

Archbishop of Boston

May 31, 1961

Library of Congress Catalog Card Number: 61-14934

Printed in the U.S.A. by the DAUGHTERS OF ST. PAUL
50 St. Paul Ave., *Jam. Pl., Boston 30, Mass.*

Acknowledgments

The Daughters of St. Paul are deeply grateful to Reverend John H. Collins, S.J., for his careful reading and improvement of this translation.

❀

Grateful acknowledgement is given to *National Catholic Welfare Conference News Service,* and *Catholic Truth Society* of London, for kind permission to use translations of a number of addresses and documents as indicated in the Index on pp. 572-591; also to *The Pope Speaks* Magazine, *Catholic Documents,* and *Papal Documents on Mary,* by Doheny and Kelly.

PREFACE

Among the Old Testament figures of Our Lady is that of the "Garden Enclosed." "My sister, my spouse, is a garden enclosed, a garden enclosed" (a).

In the 17th century St. John Eudes, echoing the thought of other spiritual authors, wrote: "The Garden of the Beloved is the Heart of her whom He loves; the Heart of Mary is the Garden of Jesus." To explain why the Beloved twice calls her a Garden Enclosed, the Saint gives as a reason: "it is closed to sin, closed to the world and to all that is not God" (b).

Previous to the author of The Admirable Heart painters, engravers and makers of artificial flowers had employed their talents in representing concretely the beautiful Marian symbol which Pius IX took pleasure in mentioning in the Bull Ineffabilis.

Little by little theologians, renowned guides in the spiritual life and even the Pontiffs themselves have revealed for us the flowers from that garden: Mary's divine Motherhood, her Virginity, her Immaculate Conception, her bodily Assumption into heaven, and many others not as yet plucked from the garden, yet none the less rare.

For a long time those flowers were not gathered together in a bouquet. Hence, it has been difficult to catch their scattered fragrance. The Fathers of Solesmes, however, by their selections from Papal pronouncements, have made this possible.

Papal pronouncements, in whatsoever way communicated, are the Church's supreme teaching. Apart from ex cathedra definitions, they remain the teachings of the Bishop of Rome, the successor of St. Peter, who received from Christ our Lord an unique mission in the domain of teaching. Later in this book the reader will meet with texts upon this subject. We may mention a few here, because from awareness of this fundamental principle the collection herein of pronouncements on Our Lady derives all its value.

In his Encyclical Ad Cœli Reginam (October 11, 1954) Pius XII reminded us that in Marian teaching, as well as in the whole of Christian doctrine, "for everyone the norm closest to the truth and the one universally to be accepted is the

(a) Cant. 4:12.
(b) Oeuvres choisies, 7, 122-123.

living Magisterium of the Church which Christ founded for the purpose of clarifying and explaining the truths contained only obscurely and as it were implicitly in the Deposit of Faith." In his allocution before five hundred members of the hierarchy on October 30, 1950, two days before proclaiming the dogma of the Assumption, and most of all in his Bull Munificentissimus Deus containing the definition, the Pope stressed the importance of that same Magisterium, which "sustains and directs" Christian faith. In his letter Testem Benevolentiæ (January 22, 1899), Leo XIII had also declared: "the promptings and urgings of the Holy Spirit are most frequently felt and recognized only with the unerring help and guidance of the external Magisterium." That Magisterium is ordinarily expressed by the Bishops of the entire Church. However, all are agreed that its most authoritative voice is that of the Sovereign Pontiff.

Listen again to the words of Pius XII. The Bull Munificentissimus Deus, speaking of the feast of the Assumption, emphasizes the fact that it is "the Holy See, the inheritor of the mission entrusted to the head of the Apostles, of strengthening the brethren in the faith," which "in virtue of its authority makes the feast more and more solemn." About one hundred years before (1854) the Bull Ineffabilis had restated that authority in strong terms: "the Church of Rome is the Mother and Mistress of all the churches." She has "pre-eminence and sovereign authority; she is the center of Catholic truth; in her alone the Deposit of Faith is inviolably guaranteed; from her all other churches must receive the faith as handed down. . . . As a matter of fact, our Lord, Jesus Christ Himself with divine power conferred on the Sovereign Pontiffs in the person of the Prince of the Apostles the responsibility and the supreme power of feeding his lambs and sheep, of strengthening their brethren and of ruling the universal Church." The Pope of the dogma of the Assumption, in his allocution delivered soon after the proclamation, could say that in his voice the vast crowd assembled in front of St. Peter's and the world-wide audience listening on radio had heard "the voice of the centuries, in fact, the voice of eternity."

A summary of the preceding statements show us that we must pay strict attention to all Papal teachings. We cannot but gladly welcome what in these pages those teachings afford us on the subject of Mary.

Everything that touches on faith is of concern to the "Shepherd" of Rome. We like to think that especially dear to him is anything that touches on Mary. In the life of individuals,—among them in the life of those who have been a success with God, the saints—in the life of religious institutes and of Christian nations, in the work of the missions, the Church's crowning labor, Mary, almost visibly, has a role in the sanctification of souls and in the welfare of society itself like to that of him who, being officially in charge of that same salvation and world welfare feels it incumbent on himself to give himself to that charge with everything in his power. His spiritual responsibilities force on him the duty of making Mary's influence known to all again and again and with ever-increasing accuracy. It scarcely need be said that he has an even still better motive. Recent studies in theology, harking back to St. Ambrose and St. Augustine and certainly to St. Paul and St. John, insist on the similarity between Mary and the Church. They call each "the City of God." Should we be surprised, then, that the Head of the Church often fixes his gaze gladly on Mary, the prototype of the Church, and that he directs towards her the gaze of the Church's children? Certainly, the sure way to be a "child of the Church" is to be a "child of Mary."

In view of these plain truths, it is evident that the science of Mary, when it is, if we may say it, in the hands of the Popes, turns to love of her. The reason is that in the hands of the supreme Shepherd, far from remaining purely speculative, it cannot but become "pastoral."

As a consequence, in the following pages devotion to Mary derives quite naturally from the theology of Mary and from the "devotions" to be proposed, because that theology is the first directive means of nourishing devotion. To cite a single example, easily the most striking because it has been made the object of numerous encyclicals of Leo XIII, it is beyond doubt that the devotion to the Rosary (a) has sprung from the distressful pastorals of that Pontiff. When we place him in the historical setting of the twenty-five years of his pontificate, when we come to know the incidents of that long period, incidents that were often tragedies, we see that this learned Pontiff showed himself in his encyclicals first and last a Shepherd. Let one but be willing to read with pencil in hand; he will

(a) Cf. Prayer.

— 11 —

recognize the richness of the doctrine woven into them. "To be an enthusiast," wrote Fr. Faber, "it is sufficient for devotion to the holy Virgin to be theological." Reciprocating, we may add: "to be an enthusiast, it is sufficient to the theology of Mary not to omit devotion." How true it is that in the Papal teachings doctrine and devotion (and "devotions" too) go hand in hand. Fortunate, then, is he who attends and brings others to their classes.

Still, one difficulty arises. Even if, in the Garden Enclosed, as is the case of the one on which we look out as we write these pages and find everything formal—the fountain, the lilies, the rose-tree—, even if in their teachings about Mary the Popes have with equal care marked off her privileges, it remains that it is not so easy to recognize those privileges in their teachings. How indicate in them the ancient plantings, how foresee tomorrow's blooms, how discover the successive and additional nuances of thought issuing from a primitive stock? The present collection gathers together only some of the documents covering some two hundred years. But in the Church's life two hundred years is a long period of time, especially when it is a matter of the theology of Mary, which has literally come to flower only since the preparation of the definition of the dogma of the Immaculate Conception. Therefore, it was necessary that the plan of the Garden be so arranged that each one might be able to recognize all its Marian riches which the Popes have found therein.

We owe a debt of gratitude to the Monks of Solesmes for having undertaken the task of research and for the layout of the Garden. The paths are clearly marked out, they are even carefully gravelled; one cannot become lost. No one need be surprised at this. As a matter of fact, we know that, since the noteworthy productions of Dom Gueranger in behalf of the definition of 1854, Solesmes has a glorious Marian tradition. Nevertheless, through the reading of this volume, which he will love, every child of Mary will have an additional motive for sincere gratitude towards the renowned Abbey.

Le Mans, August 22, 1957

Feast of the Immaculate Heart of Mary

Marcel-Marie DUBOIS
Archbishop of Besancon

INTRODUCTION

HOW THE DOCUMENTS ARE PRESENTED

At the head of each document is found
  a title, to facilitate understanding,
  the type of document,
    the "incipit" if the text is taken from a written document
    the address and the date of origin;
in the body of the text:
  subtitles for the longer citations.
  in italics in parentheses, a brief summary of those
    portions of the original document not cited in the
    text, because not referring directly to the subject
    being treated.

HOW TO USE THIS VOLUME

To find the texts relating to a given question:
  look first in the alphabetical index or else directly in
  the analytical index, where the numbers in heavy print
  refer the reader to the papal texts.
To clarify a text by placing it in its context in the development of the thought of the Popes, or by comparing it
  to parallel texts: the numbers in italics, given in parentheses in the margin of the text, refer to the analytical
  index, which in turn summarizes briefly the lines of
  papal thought and indicates the relative texts.

THE NUMBERING OF THE TEXT

The numbers in heavy print, refer to the paragraphs of the
  papal pronouncements, given in chronological order
  in the text.
The numbers in italics, given in parentheses, refer to the
  divisions of the analytical index.

CONTENTS

INDEXES

PAPAL DOCUMENTS

BENEDICT XIV

(1740-1758)

PROFESSION OF FAITH

Apost. Const. *Nuper ad Nos*, March 16, 1743.

(Profession of faith prescribed for the Maronites.—Adherence to the Ecumenical Councils.)

I venerate and accept the Ecumenical Councils . . . and the third in their number, the first Council of Ephesus. I believe all that was defined by it in its ancient condemnation of Nestorius, namely, that by the ineffable and impenetrable union of divinity and humanity in the one person of the Son of God the one sole Jesus Christ was constituted for us and that in consequence the Blessed Virgin is truly the Mother of God . . .
. . . In like manner I venerate the seventh in their number, the second Council of Nicea, and I believe in all that was defined in it against the Iconoclasts, namely, that we must accept and preserve the images of Christ, of the Virgin Mother of God and of all the Saints and pay them the honor and veneration due to them (a).

1

(24, 153)

THE FIRST MARIAN CONGREGATION

Apost. Const. *Gloriosæ Dominæ*, September 27, 1748.

The Church's devotion to Mary

Our apostolic exhortations, which aim at inflaming all Christian hearts with religious zeal and devotion towards Our Lady, the glorious Mother of God, may appear altogether superfluous. It is evident that Marian cultus and devotion are founded wholly on the manifest will of God

2

(24, 125)

1a Cf. Denzinger, 1462 and 1466.

and the genuine spirit of the Church, and that they are practiced faithfully to the great advantage of the faithful. Indeed, Almighty God enriched the Blessed Virgin with the gifts of His grace more abundantly than He enriched any other creature. He chose her from all mankind and at the word of an angel elevated her to the ineffable dignity of Mother of God. He adorned her with more radiance of glory than any other work of His hands. Because of all this the Catholic Church, formed and nourished in the school of the Holy Spirit, has always professed to render humble tribute to her as the Mother of her Lord and Redeemer, as the Queen of heaven and earth. The Church has encompassed this most loving of Mothers, entrusted to her by the last words of her dying Spouse, with expressions of filial homage and devotion.

3
(103,
123-
124) She is accustomed in the midst of public calamities and the storms stirred up by the powers of hell to seek refuge in her help as in a port safe and secure. The Church knows that it is due especially to Mary that heresies have been engaged in battle and overcome all over the world. Mary is the gracious Esther, so beloved of the Supreme King of kings that He grants her, for her people's salvation, not only the half of His kingdom, but nearly all His empire and power. She is that courageous Judith, the valiant woman to whom the God of Israel granted victory over all the enemies of her Land.

4
(46,
138) The Church, through the words of all the Fathers, recommends her sons to have recourse in all their difficulties and dangers to Mary, the mystical Ark of Alliance. In her the secret mysteries of our reconciliation have been accomplished and the sight of her reminds God of his covenant and causes Him to be mindful of His mercy. Mary is that heavenly stream which brings to the hearts of wretched mortals all God's gifts and graces.

Marian devotion of St. Ignatius

St. Ignatius, when for the greater glory of God he in-   5
creased the army of the Church militant with new legions (175)
enrolled under the standard of the most holy name of
Jesus Christ, was mindful of all these privileges and of
still others. Foreseeing the great battles facing him and
his Society, he very wisely deemed it necessary to secure
the most powerful help of the Blessed Virgin Mary for
the salvation of his Society and that of others. For this
reason, after leaving his father's home and having conceived in his heart great projects and made up his mind
to enter the Sacred Army, he fell at the feet of the Virgin
and under her auspices entered the difficult way of perfection. Later, having chosen his first companions, he decided to gather them together into a Society, which he
did in the Church of Our Lady of Montmartre in Paris.
There, with them, he bound himself by a solemn vow and
there, as on a solid rock, he placed the first foundation of
his Institute.

It was his custom to decide or undertake nothing of   6
importance until after first invoking the name of Mary. (175)
He wished to give her as an example to his followers so
that in their difficulties in the performance of their ministry they would expect God's help above all through her
intercession, and that in the dangers to which they would
be exposed in the cause of religion they might be sure to
find a refuge and a rampart against the enemy in this most
strong Tower upon which a thousand bucklers hang (a).
Thus when to every land and sea, before kings and peoples,
they brought the adorable name of Jesus, they never failed
also to proclaim in every place the name of His Mother.
With the light of faith and their holiness of life, they at

6a Cf. Cant. 4:4.

the same time and in a marvellous manner spread the cultus and love of the Virgin Mother in every region of the two Continents.

The Work of the Congregations

7
(135, 151)
In addition the Sons of St. Ignatius are known as the creators of a wise and excellent institution widely diffused. As one of the many works carried on by their Society in which they continue to make themselves so useful to the Church, they devote their lives to the education of youth. When they dedicate themselves to the formation of youth in religion and in the arts they also take care to unite their charges in associations or Congregations dedicated to the Blessed Virgin, the Mother of God. After consecrating their students to her cultus and service they teach them under the guidance of her who is the Mother of love, of fear of God, and of light to ascend the path of Christian perfection and to aim at eternal salvation. One can hardly imagine the great value of this pious and praiseworthy association, endowed with such abundance of salutary rules, adapted to the various conditions of its members and guided by its directors with efficiency and prudence.

8
(135)
Certain members of the Congregations, faithful to the state of innocence and piety embraced from their tender years under the patronage of the Blessed Virgin, succeeded admirably in preserving in that state throughout life, and even unto final perseverance, the high moral level of a Christian and a client of the Virgin.

Others, helped by the most gentle Mother of God, to whose cultus they vowed themselves in this association, abandoned the seductions of vice which held them miserably back in the way of iniquity which they had entered. They were converted and began to lead a sober, just and pious life in which, sustained by the holy practices of the Congregations, they happily persevered.

Finally, some others, thanks to a filial and long-prac-
ticed devotion to the Mother of God, elevated to the
highest degree of divine love, willingly and heartily laid
aside their possessions and the vain and transitory pleasures
of this world and entered into the holier and safer life of
Regulars. Crucified to Christ on His Cross by means of
religious vows, they consecrated themselves wholly to the
work of their own perfection and the salvation of their
neighbor.

(*Privileges granted by preceding Pontiffs.*)

CLEMENT XIII

(1758-1769)

ABOVE ALL PRAISE

Apost. Const. *Cum primum,* January 27, 1761.

From the time that by the disposition of God's will 9
We were raised in such troubled times for Christianity We *(135,*
never have ceased to ponder and plan what could best *138)*
contribute to the promotion and propagation among the
faithful of the cultus of the holy and glorious Mary ever
Virgin, so that she with special watchfulness might obtain
for Us and for the whole Catholic Church the grace and
favor of Christ, her Son, the supreme Head of the Church.

Still, the homage and the signs of veneration paid on
earth to increase the glory of this creature, privileged
above all creatures, come out of the mouth of the Most
High and having the chief rule in every nation (a), will
always suffice to satisfy Our desire. Therefore, We eagerly
seize the occasions presented to offer her new tributes of
honor. We rejoice exceedingly that the most powerful
King a short time ago expressed on this subject intentions
which agree so admirably with Ours and that he now
zealously solicits a further increase in this cultus.

(*Concessions of an Office and a Proper Mass, following the request of the King of Spain.*)

9a Ecclus. 24:5, 10.

PIUS VI

(1775-1799)

AN APOSTOLIC DUTY

Apost. Const. *Apostolici muneris,* November 29, 1777.

The apostolic office which the infinite bounty of God **10** entrusted to Us imposed upon Us the duty of dedicating *(11,* Ourselves from the outset to the work of promoting for *126,* the glory of God and the edification of the faithful the *138)* cultus and veneration of the Blessed Virgin Mary in the very best way that faith will suggest to Us. In the number of her graces and privileges Mary excels all other creatures by far, and now from heaven she protects and favors us poor mortals in a very special manner. She was torn by sorrow during the cruel Passion of Christ.

(*Concession of the Office and of the Mass of Our Lady of the Seven Sorrows.*)

THE PROPHECY OF EMMANUEL

Apost. Const. *Divina Christi Domini voce,* September 20, 1779.

(*Condemnation of the book: Nouvel essai sur la prophétie de l'Emmanuel, by John Isenbiehl.*)

It was a great scandal to Catholics to hear it asserted **11** that the prophecy of the birth of Emmanuel from the Vir- *(2,* gin (a), although announced by all the prophets, did not *3,* either in the literal or the typical sense refer to the virginal *20,* birth by the Mother of God, nor to the true Emmanuel, *88)* Our Lord Jesus Christ. And when St. Matthew expressly declared (b) that this well-known prophecy was fulfilled in

11a Isaias 7:13ff.
11b Matt. 1:22-23.

this admirable mystery of mutual love, that mystery was not understood as the fulfillment of the prophecy but rather as a simple remark or suggestion of the Evangelist.

For this reason the faithful were moved to anger in seeing both Sacred Scripture and Tradition, conserved for us with the unanimous agreement of the Fathers, so boldly attacked.

(*Recourse of German Bishops to the Holy See.— Condemnation of the book.*)

PIUS VII

(1800-1823)

THE SORROWS OF OUR MOTHER

Letter *Id Officii debent,* to the Bishop of Cagliari, January 9, 1801.

Certainly, it is the duty of Christians towards the Blessed Virgin Mary, as children of so good a Mother, to honor unceasingly and with affectionate zeal the memory of the bitter sorrows which she underwent with admirable courage and invincible constancy especially when she stood at the foot of the Cross and offered those sorrows to the Eternal Father for our salvation. **12** *(44, 116, 168)*

How appropriate then the injunction which the saintly Tobias laid on his son with regard to his mother: "For thou must be mindful what and how great perils she suffered for thee" (a).

What refuge and what consolation can we not promise ourselves and hope for from the Virgin Mary, when in our adversities we ourselves spontaneously desire to take part in her anguish and in her sorrows! Where can we find a greater stimulus to excite our hearts to that sorrow so justly wished for by God in order that He may grant us His mercy, than in the loving and continuous meditation on Mary's sorrow?

(*Concession of the Feast of Our Lady of the Seven Dolors.*)

A MOTHER'S PRAYER

Apost. Const. *Tanto studio,* February 19, 1805.

The zeal and love of the Blessed Virgin Mary have such influence in obtaining God's help for us that, just as through her God came down to earth, so through her man **13** *(37, 48,*

12a Tob. 4:4.

49, mounts up to heaven. But just as man's iniquity often calls
52) down God's indignation, God's Mother is the rainbow of
the eternal covenant for the salvation of mankind. For,
while the prayers of those in heaven have, it is true, some
claim on God's watchful eye, Mary's prayers place their
assurance in a mother's right. For that reason, when she
approaches her divine Son's throne, as advocate she begs,
as handmaid she prays, but as Mother she commands (a).

(*Acknowledgment of Our Lady of Grace as the Patron
of the City of Carmona.*)

MARIAN SHRINES

Apost. Const. *Quod divino afflata Spiritu,* January
24, 1806.

14   Inspired by the Holy Spirit, the Blessed Virgin Mary,
(125, Mother of God foretold that all generations would call her
152, blessed (a). We witness the fulfillment of this prophecy
154) not only in the course of the first centuries of Christianity
when churches were built and altars erected all over the
world in her honor but also now when owing to the daily
increase of the piety of the faithful towards our most
lovable Mother, and owing to the ardor of an ever-
increasing devotion to the dispenser of all graces, these
testimonies of veneration continue to multiply under our
own eyes. Owing to the inscrutable wisdom of God, certain
places were specially singled out where the intercession
of the Blessed Virgin produced wonders to such an extent
elsewhere unknown.

Almighty God, Who must be adored in spirit and
truth over the whole earth, wishes to answer more promptly

13a *Reliquorum namque coelestium incolarum preces divinæ
benignitati dumtaxat, Mariæ vero preces materno etiam
cuidem jui innituntur. Quare ad divini Filii sui thronum ipsa
accedens, Advocat petit, Ancilla orat, Mater imperat.*
14a Luke 1:48.

and abundantly in one place rather than in another the prayers of His sons who invoke Him. Thus, while He distributes His gifts and breathes where He wills, He often grants by the wondrous design of divine providence greater favors to those who implore with greater fervor and perseverance the intercession of the Mother of God before one image rather than before another, in one shrine rather than in another.

(It is the case of the Virgin venerated in the monastery of the Servites of Florence.—Concession of privileges.)

PIUS VIII

(1829-1830)

THE PATRONAGE OF OUR LADY

Apost. Const. *Præsentissimum sane,* March 3, 1830.

No one who with confidence has had recourse to Mary **15**
has failed to experience the power of her patronage. She *(31,*
is our Mother, the Mother of pity and of grace, the Mother *48)*
of mercy, to whom Christ our Lord in His dying breath on
the Cross entrusted us, in order that, as He implores His
heavenly Father for us, she may likewise entreat her Son
in our behalf. With good reason, then, certain confraternities, such as that of the Third Order of Servites, have
honored her with fervent piety under various titles, or in
her mysteries, and have placed themselves humbly under
her protection and patronage. Equally with good reason
we must count among such confraternities those which
venerate her in a special way under the title of Mary,
Mother of Sorrows.

(*Concession of privileges.*)

GREGORY XVI

(1831-1846)

TOWARDS THE DEFINITION
OF THE IMMACULATE CONCEPTION

Letter *Summa quidem animi*, to the Archbishop of Prague and to the Bishops of Bohemia, April 23, 1845.

It caused us great joy to receive your letter of February 2, last filled with a deep sentiment of submission and respect. By so acknowledging, O Venerable Brethren, your special devotion and that of the entire Bohemian realm to the Most Blessed Mother of God, the Virgin Mary, you declared that for you nothing seemed more preferable nor desirable than to see her unanimously honored and acclaimed as having been conceived without original sin. **16** *(65, 159)*

We heartily approve in the Lord such holy desires and We make it known to your fraternities that out of Our great veneration and love towards the Virgin Mother of God and Our most sweet Mother, We have already promised with all our heart that on the feast of her holy Conception in our Papal Chapel in Our very presence, and likewise in all the other churches of our venerable city, the Conception of the Blessed Virgin will be declared immaculate and the Feast will be inserted in the Calendar of the Roman Clergy. **17** *(62, 158)*

Certainly it is not with less interest that We generally accede to the requests of those who desire to render the same homage to the Immaculate Conception of the Virgin be it in the Preface of the Mass proper to her Conception, be it in the Marian litanies and in other public prayers. **18** *(60, 130, 134, 138)*

Seeing the decrees of Our Congregation of Rites, annexed herein, you will easily understand that We willingly acceded to your desires which aim especially at increasing and intensifying their devotion daily more and more in your dioceses.

Continue therefore, O Venerable Brethren, what you are already doing, with ever-increasing zeal to excite and animate the faithful entrusted to your care to devotion towards the Blessed Virgin. Guided by her they will not go astray; aided by her prayer they will not despair; protected by her they will be safe. Do not cease however, to supplicate insistently this most beloved Mother of grace and mercy to help and support by her powerful intercession with her Son Our weakness, weighed down as We are by the very heavy solicitude for all the Churches in such troubled times for Christianity.

(*Blessing.*)

PIUS IX

(1846-1878)

PREPARATION OF THE DEFINITION

Encycl. *Ubi primum*, February 2, 1849.

No sooner had We been elevated to the sublime Chair   **19**
of the Prince of the Apostles and undertaken the govern-   *(29,*
ment of the universal Church (not, indeed, because of Our   *62,*
own worthiness but by the hidden designs of Divine Provi-   *65)*
dence) than We had the great consolation, Venerable
Brethren, of recalling that during the Pontificate of Gregory XVI Our Predecessor of happy memory, there was in
the entire Catholic world a most ardent and wondrous
revival of the desire that "the most holy Mother of God—
the beloved Mother of us all—the immaculate Virgin Mary
—be finally declared by a solemn definition of the Church
to have been conceived without the stain of original sin."

Both to Our Predecessor and to Us this most devout
desire was clearly and unmistakably made manifest by the
petitions of illustrious prelates, esteemed canonical chapters, and religious congregations, notably the renowned
Order of Preachers. These appeals vied with one another
in the insistent request that official permission be granted
for the word *Immaculate* to be used publicly and to be
added to the sacred liturgy, particularly in the Preface of
the Mass of the Conception of the Blessed Virgin (a).

First episcopal requests

With the greatest sympathy We accede to these re-   **20**
quests as did Our Predecessor. Moreover, Venerable Breth-   *(62,*
ren, many of you have sent letters to Our Predecessor and   *65)*
to Us begging, with repeated insistence and the greatest
enthusiasm, that We "define as a dogma of the Catholic
Church that the Most Blessed Virgin Mary was conceived

19a Cf. above, No. 16.

immaculate and free in every way from all taint of original sin."

Nor do we lack today eminent theologians—men of intellectual brilliance, of virtue, of holiness and sound doctrine—who have made their subject and its holy conviction so luminously clear that many are now wondering why the Church and the Apostolic See have not yet accorded to the Blessed Virgin that honor which the widespread piety of Christian people so fervently desires to be accorded to the Most Holy Virgin by a solemn decree and by the authority of the Church and the Holy See.

21
(60,
65,
158)
Welcome, indeed, and full of consolation have such requests been to Us. From Our earliest years nothing has ever been closer to Our heart than devotion—filial, profound, and wholehearted—to the Most Blessed Virgin Mary. Always have We endeavored to do everything that would redound to the greater glory of the Blessed Virgin, promote her honor, and encourage devotion to her. Accordingly, from the very beginning of Our pontificate We have most fervently directed Our energies and Our thoughts to this matter of such great importance. Nor have We failed, through humble and fervent prayers, to beg Almighty God to enlighten Our mind with His heavenly grace in order that We might know what We should do in this matter.

Protection awaited from Our Lady

22
(37,
46,
121)
Great indeed is Our trust in Mary. The resplendent glory of her "merits, far exceeding all the choirs of angels, elevated her to the very steps of the throne of God" (a). Her foot has crushed the head of the old" serpent. "Set up between Christ and His Church" (b), Mary, ever lovable and full of grace, always has delivered the Christian people from their greatest calamities, ever rescued them from ruin.

22a St. Gregory, *De Expositione in librum I Regum,* c.1. M. 7. p. 176.
22b St. Bernard, *Sermo in cap. XII Apocalypsis.*

And likewise in our own day, Mary, with the ever merciful affection so characteristic of her maternal heart, wishes, through her efficacious intercession with God, to deliver her children from the sad and grief-laden troubles, from the tribulations, the anxiety, the difficulties, and the punishments of God's anger, which afflict the world because of the sins of men. Wishing to restrain and to dispel the violent hurricane of evils which, as We lament from the bottom of Our heart, are everywhere afflicting the Church, Mary desires, to transform Our sadness into joy.

The foundation of all Our confidence, as you know well, Venerable Brethren, is found in the Blessed Virgin Mary. God has committed to her "the treasury of all good things, in order that everyone may know that through her are obtained every hope, every grace, and all salvation. For this is His will, that we obtain everything through Mary" (a).

**23
(37,
39,
129)**

Preparation of the definition

Accordingly, We have appointed certain priests of recognized piety and theological learning, and several cardinals of the Holy Roman Church renowned for their ability, piety, wisdom, prudence, and knowledge of the things of God; and We have directed them to make, carefully and thoroughly, a most diligent examination into this most important matter and then to provide Us with a full report. By such means, We feel that We are following in the clearly marked footsteps of Our Predecessors and that We are emulating their example.

**24
(65)**

Wherefore, Venerable Brethren, We send you this communication that We may effectively encourage your admirable devotion and your pastoral zeal and thus bring it about that each of you, in such manner as you see fit, will arrange to have public prayers offered in your dio-

**25
(62,
65)**

23a St. Bernard, *Sermo de Acquæductu.*

cese for this intention—that the most merciful Father of all knowledge will deign to enlighten Us with the heavenly light of His Holy Spirit, so that in a matter of such moment We may accomplish what will redound to the greater glory of His holy name, to the honor of the the Most Blessed Virgin, and to the profit of the Church Militant.

We eagerly desire, futhermore, that, as soon as possible, you apprise Us concerning the devotion which animates your clergy and your people regarding the Immaculate Conception of the Blessed Virgin and how ardently glows the desire that this doctrine be defined by the Apostolic See. And especially, Venerable Brethren, We wish to know what you yourselves, in your wise judgment, think and desire on this matter.

And inasmuch as We have already granted to the clergy of Rome permission to recite the special canonical hours in honor of the Conception of the Blessed Virgin recently arranged and published instead of what is contained in the common Breviary, We likewise, by this present letter, grant to you, Venerable Brethren, the faculty, if you wish to use it, of permitting the clergy of your own diocese to recite, licitly and validly, the same canonical hours of the Conception of the Blessed Virgin now in use with the clergy of Rome. This may be done without obtaining further authorization from Us or from the Sacred Congregation of Rites.

(*Replies awaited.—Blessing.*)

REASON FOR OUR HOPE

Encycl. *Exultavit cor Nostrum,* November 21, 1851.

(*Prayers requested on the occasion of the Jubilee.*)

26
(49,
51)
So that God may more easily hear our prayers and supplications, let us lift our eyes and hands to the Blessed Mother Mary, Immaculate Virgin. We could not find a

more powerful protectress or one more irresistible before God. She is for us the best of Mothers, our safest confidant and in fact the very motive of our hope: she obtains all she asks for and her prayer is always heard.

(*Conclusion.*)

LAST CONSULTATION
BEFORE THE DEFINITION

All. to the Consistory, December 1, 1854.

In the midst of the many grave sorrows and trials which afflict Us, the most benevolent Father of all mercy and the God of all consolation is about to bestow on Us and the entire Church the greatest possible joy. Indeed, Venerable Brethren, the long-desired and most happy day on which We shall, with the Supreme authority of Our Office, define the Immaculate Conception of the Blessed Virgin Mary, Mother of God, is already drawing near. **27** *(48, 66, 107)*

Truly, nothing in this life could make Us more happy. For this decree will serve to increase and to foster, ever more and more on this earth, the honor, the glory, and the veneration of that most glorious Virgin who, exalted above the choirs of the angels and the countless legions of the saints, never ceases in heaven to make most efficacious intercession with her Son for all the faithful on earth.

Well do you know how, day after day, love and veneration toward the Immaculate Conception of the holy Mother of God have steadily grown in the Catholic world; and how eagerly the Church and Our Predecessors have gloried in preserving, fostering, and promoting that same love, veneration, and teaching. As you know, not only the bishops of the Church but even the heads of civil governments have repeatedly requested that the Immaculate Conception of the Holy Mother of God be defined by the Apostolic See as a dogma of Faith. **28** *(60, 62, 65)*

29
(65)   In view of the fact that similar appeals had been made to Our Predecessor of happy memory, Gregory XVI, as well as to Us from the very beginning of Our Pontificate, We have fervently directed Our efforts and Our thoughts to this matter. But wishing to act with studious deliberation in a matter of such importance, We established, as you recall, a special commission, composed of several members of your august body, and We appointed a number of priests, both secular and religious, eminently learned in theology to examine this matter most carefully and submit their conclusions to Us. Then, on February 2, 1849 (a), from Gaeta, We sent to all the Bishops of the Catholic world an Encyclical Letter, requesting them to inform Us by letter concerning the devotion of their clergy and people toward the Immaculate Conception of the Mother of God, and, especially, what they, the bishops themselves, thought on this matter and what they desired.

30
(65)   Having been assured—and, indeed, with great joy to Our heart—by the report of the aforementioned commission and by the reply of practically all the bishops, as well as by the responses of all theologians, that such a definition was so ardently desired of Us, We have directed that the original of an Apostolic Letter be drawn up and sent to you.

Today, therefore, to bring this matter to a conclusion, We, following the custom of Our Predecessors and most humbly imploring Divine Light, kindly inquire:

Does it, therefore, please you that We issue the dogmatic decree on the Immaculate Conception of the Blessed Virgin Mary?

(Having obtained all responses, Pius IX announces December 8 for the solemn definition.)

29a Cf. above, No. 19 ff.

THE IMMACULATE CONCEPTION

Apost. Const. *Ineffabilis Deus,* December 8, 1854.

God Ineffable—whose ways are mercy and truth, **31** whose will is omnipotence itself, and whose wisdom *(21-* "reacheth from end to end mightily, and ordereth all *23,* things sweetly"—having foreseen from all eternity the *70-* lamentable wretchedness of the entire human race which *73)* would result from the sin of Adam, decreed, by a plan hidden from the centuries, to complete the first work of His goodness by a mystery yet more wondrously sublime through the Incarnation of the Word. This He decreed in order that man who, contrary to the plan of Divine Mercy had been led into sin by the cunning malice of Satan, should not perish; and in order that what had been lost in the first Adam would be gloriously restored in the Second Adam. From the very beginning, and before time began, the Eternal Father chose and prepared for His only-begotten Son a Mother in whom the Son of God would become incarnate and from whom, in the blessed fullness of time, He would be born into this world. Above all creatures did God so love her that truly in her was the Father well pleased with singular delight. Wherefore, far above all the angels and all the saints so wondrously did God endow her with the abundance of all heavenly gifts poured from the treasury of His divinity that this Mother, ever absolutely free of all stain of sin, all fair and perfect, would possess that fullness of holy innocence and sanctity than which, under God, one cannot even imagine anything greater, and which, outside of God, no mind can succeed in comprehending fully.

Supreme reason of the privilege: the divine maternity

And indeed it was wholly fitting that so wonderful a **32** mother should be ever resplendent with the glory of most *(27,* sublime holiness and so completely free from all taint of *54,* original sin that she would triumph utterly over the an- *68,*

70) cient serpent. To her did the Father will to give His
only-begotten Son—the Son whom, equal to the Father
and begotten by Him, the Father loves from His heart—
and to give this Son in such a way that He would be the
one and the same common Son of God the Father and of
the Blessed Virgin Mary. It was she whom the Son Himself chose to make His Mother and it was from her that
the Holy Spirit willed and brought it about that He should
be conceived and born from whom He Himself proceeds (a).

Liturgical argument

33
(27,
62,
68,
73,
75,
141)

The Catholic Church, directed by the Holy Spirit of
God, is the pillar and base of truth and has ever held as
divinely revealed and as contained in the deposit of
heavenly revelation this doctrine concerning the original
innocence of the august Virgin—a doctrine which is so
perfectly in harmony with her wonderful sanctity and
preeminent dignity as Mother of God—and thus has never
ceased to explain, to teach and to foster this doctrine age
after age in many ways and by solemn acts. For this very
doctrine, flourishing from ancient times, deeply rooted in
the souls of the faithful, and wondrously propagated in
the Catholic world through the efforts and zeal of the
bishops, was made very clear by the Church when she did
not hesitate to present for the public devotion and veneration of the faithful the feast of the Conception of the

32a *Et quidem decebat omnino, ut perfectissimæ sanctitatis
splendoribus semper ornata fulgeret, ac vel ab ipsa
originalis culpæ labe plane immunis amplissimum de
antiquo serpente triumphum referret tam venerabilis mater,
cui Deus Pater unicum Filium suum, quem de corde suo
æqualem sibi genitum tamquam seipsum diligit, ita dare
disposuit, ut naturaliter esset unus idemque communis Dei
Patris et Virginis Filius, et quam ipse Filius substantialiter
facere sibi matrem elegit, et de qua Spiritus Sanctus voluit
et operatus est, ut conciperetur et nasceretur ille, de quo
ipse procedit.*

Blessed Virgin (a). By this most significant fact, the Church made it clear indeed that the Conception of Mary is to be venerated as something extraordinary, wonderful, eminently holy, and different from the conception of all other human beings—for the Church celebrates only the feast days of the saints.

And hence the very words with which the Sacred Scriptures speak of Uncreated Wisdom and set forth His eternal origin, the Church, both in its ecclesiastical offices and in its liturgy, has been wont to apply likewise to the origin of the Blessed Virgin, inasmuch as God, by one and the same decree, had established the origin of Mary and the Incarnation of Divine Wisdom. **34** *(12, 23, 59)*

Ordinary teaching of the Roman Church

These truths, so generally accepted and put into practice by the faithful, indicate how zealously the Roman Church, mother and teacher of all churches, has continued to teach this doctrine of the Immaculate Conception of the Virgin. Yet the more important actions of the Church deserve to be mentioned in detail. For such dignity and authority belong to the Church that she alone is the center of truth and of Catholic unity. It is the Church in which alone religion has been inviolably preserved and from which all other churches must receive the tradition of the Faith (a). **35** *(61)*

The same Roman Church, therefore, desired nothing more than by the most persuasive means to state, to protect, to promote, and to defend the doctrine of the Immaculate Conception. This fact is most clearly shown to the whole world by numerous and significant acts of the Roman Pontiffs, Our Predecessors. To them, in the person **36** *(61)*

33a Cf. above, No. 16.
35a Cf. St. Irenaeus, *Adv. Hæreses*, book III, c. III, No. 2.

of the Prince of the Apostles, were divinely entrusted by Christ our Lord, the charge and the supreme care and the power of feeding the lambs and sheep; in particular, of confirming their brethren, and of ruling and governing the universal Church.

Cult of the Immaculate

37
(60,
62)
Our Predecessors, indeed, by virtue of their apostolic authority, gloried in instituting the feast of the Conception in the Roman Church. They did so to enhance its importance and dignity by a suitable Office and Mass, whereby the prerogative of the Virgin, her exception from the hereditary taint, was most distinctly affirmed. As to the cult already instituted, they spared no effort to promote and to extend it either by the granting of indulgences, or by allowing cities, provinces and kingdoms to choose as their patroness God's own Mother, under the title of "The Immaculate Conception." Again, Our Predecessors approved confraternities, congregations, and religious communities founded in honor of the Immaculate Conception, monasteries, hospitals, altars, or churches; they praised persons who vowed to uphold with all their ability' the doctrine of the Immaculate Conception of the Mother of God. Besides, it afforded the greatest joy to Our Predecessors to ordain that the feast of the Conception should be celebrated in every church with the very same honor as the feast of the Nativity; that it should be celebrated with an octave by the whole Church; that it should be reverently and generally observed as a holy day of obligation; and that a Pontifical Capella should be held in our Liberian pontifical basilica on the day dedicated to the Conception of the Virgin. Finally, in their desire to impress this doctrine of the Immaculate Conception of the Mother of God upon the hearts of the faithful, and to intensify the people's piety and enthusiasm for the cult and the veneration of the Virgin conceived without the stain of original sin, they

delighted to grant, with the greatest pleasure, permission to proclaim the Immaculate Conception of the Virgin in the Litany of Loreto, and in the Preface of the Mass, so that the rule of prayer might thus serve to illustrate the rule of belief. Wherefore, We Ourselves, following the procedure of Our Predecessors, have not only approved and accepted what had already been established, but bearing in mind, moreover the decree of Sixtus IV (a), have confirmed by Our authority a proper Office in honor of the Immaculate Conception, and have with exceeding joy extended its use to the universal Church (b).

The Roman doctrine

Now inasmuch as whatever pertains to sacred worship is intimately connected with its object and cannot have either consistency or durability if this object is vague or uncertain, Our Predecessors, the Roman Pontiffs, therefore, while directing all their efforts toward an increase of the devotion to the Conception, made it their aim not only to emphasize the object with the utmost zeal, but also to enunciate the exact doctrine (a). Definitely and clearly they taught that the feast was held in honor of the Conception of the Virgin. They denounced as false and absolutely foreign to the mind of the Church the opinion of those who held and affirmed that it was not the Con-

38 (17, 60, 62, 141)

37a C. A. *Cum præexcelsa Feb.* 28, 1476; Denz., No. 734.
37b Decree of the Sacred Cong. of Rites; Sept. 30, 1847.
38a This has been the constant care of the Popes, as is shown by the condemnation of one of the propositions of Anthony de Rosmini-Serbati: (Cf. Denzinger 1891-1930). This is how the 34th proposition runs (Denzinger, 1924): "*Ad præservandam B. V. Mariam a labe originis, satis erat, ut incorruptum maneret minimum semen in homine, neglectum forte ab ipso demone, e quo incorrupto semine de generatione in generationem transfuso, suo tempore oriretur Virgo Maria*". Decree of Holy Office December 14, 1887 (ASS 20, 393). Denz. no. 1924.

ception of the Virgin but her Sanctification that was honored by the Church. They never thought that greater leniency should be extended toward those who, attempting to disprove the doctrine of the Immaculate Conception of the Virgin, devised a distinction between the first and second instant of Conception and inferred that the Conception which the Church celebrates was not that of the first instant of Conception but the second. In fact, they held it was their duty not only to uphold and defend with all their power the feast of the Conception of the Blessed Virgin but also to assert that the true object of this cult was her Conception considered in its first instant. Hence the words of one of Our Predecessors, Alexander VII, who authoritatively and decisively declared the mind of the Church: "Concerning the Most Blessed Virgin Mary, Mother of God, ancient indeed is that devotion of the faithful based on the belief that her soul, in the first instant of its creation and in the first instant of the soul's infusion into the body, was, by a special grace and privilege of God, in view of the merits of Jesus Christ, her Son and the Redeemer of the human race, preserved free from all stain of original sin. And in this sense have the faithful ever solemnized and celebrated the Feast of the Conception" (b).

39
(60,
62,
141)
Moreover, Our Predecessors considered it their special solemn duty with all diligence, zeal, and effort to preserve intact the doctrine of the Immaculate Conception of the Mother of God. For, not only have they in no way ever allowed this doctrine to be censured or changed, but they have gone much further and by clear statements repeatedly asserted that the doctrine by which we profess the Immaculate Conception of the Virgin is on its own merits entirely in harmony with the ecclesiastical cult; that it is ancient and widespread, and of the same nature as that

38b Apost. Const. *Sollicitudo omnium ecclesiarum*, December 8, 1661.

which the Roman Church has undertaken to promote and to protect, and that it is entirely worthy to be used in the Sacred Liturgy and solemn prayers. Not content with this they most strictly prohibited any opinion contrary to this doctrine to be defended in public or private in order that the doctrine of the Immaculate Conception of the Virgin might remain inviolate. By repeated blows they wished to put an end to such an opinion. And lest these oft-repeated and clearest statements seem useless, they added a sanction to them.

Papal sanctions

All these things Our illustrious Predecessor, Alexander VII, summed up in these words: "We have in mind the fact that the Holy Roman Church solemnly celebrated the Feast of the Conception of the undefiled and ever-Virgin Mary, and has long ago appointed for this a special and proper Office according to the pious, devout, and laudable instruction which was given by Our Predecessor, Sixtus IV. Likewise, We were desirous, after the example of Our Predecessors, to favor this praiseworthy piety, devotion, feast, and cult—a cult which is in keeping with the piety unchanged in the Roman Church from the day it was instituted. We also desired to protect this piety and devotion of venerating and extolling the Most Blessed Virgin preserved from original sin by the grace of the Holy Spirit. Moreover, We were anxious to preserve the unity of the spirit in the bond of peace in the flock of Christ by putting down arguments and controversies and by removing scandals. So at the instance and request of the Bishops mentioned above, with the chapters of their churches, and of King Philip and his kingdoms, We renew the Constitutions and Decrees issued by the Roman Pontiffs, Our Predecessors, especially Sixtus IV (a), Paul V (b),

40
(60)

40a Apost. Const. *Cum præexcelsa*, Feb. 28, 1476; *Grave nimis*, Sept. 4, 1483; Denz., No. 734, 735.
40b Apost. Const. *Sanctissimus*, Sept. 12, 1617.

and Gregory XV (c), in favor of the doctrine asserting that the soul of the Blessed Virgin, in its creation and infusion into the body, was endowed with the grace of the Holy Spirit and preserved from original sin; and also in favor of the feast and cult of the Conception of the Virgin Mother of God, which, as is manifest, was instituted in keeping with that pious belief. So We command this feast to be observed under the censures and penalties contained in the same Constitutions.

41
(60)
"And furthermore, against all and everyone of those who shall continue to construe the said Constitutions and Decrees in a manner apt to frustrate the favor which is thereby given to the said doctrine, and to the feast and relative cult, or who shall dare to call into question the said sentence, feast and worship, or in any way whatever, directly or indirectly, shall declare themselves opposed to it under any pretext whatsoever, were it but only to the extent of examining the possibilities of effecting the definition, or who shall comment upon and interpret the Sacred Scripture, or the Fathers or Doctors in connection therewith, or finally, for any reason, or on any occasion, shall dare, either in writing or verbally, to speak, preach, treat, dispute or determine upon, or assert whatsoever against the foregoing matters, or who shall adduce any arguments against them, while leaving them unresolved, or who shall disagree therewith in any other conceivable manner, we hereby declare that in addition to the penalties and censures contained in the constitutions issued by Sixtus IV to which We want them to be subjected and to which We subject them by the present constitution, We hereby decree that they be deprived of the authority of preaching, reading in public, that is to say teaching and interpreting; and that they be also deprived ipso facto of the power of voting, either actively or passively, in all elections, without the need for any further declaration; and

40c Apost. Const. *Sanctissimus* June 4, 1622.

that also, ipso facto, without any further declaration, they shall incur the penalty of perpetual disability from preaching, reading in public, teaching and interpreting, and that it shall not be possible to absolve them from such penalty, or remove it, save through Ourselves, or the Roman Pontiffs who shall succeed Us.

"We also require that the same shall remain subject to any other penalties which by Us, of Our own free will,—or by the Roman Pontiffs Our Successors, (according as they may decree)—shall be deemed advisable to establish, and by the present Constitution we declare them subject thereto, and hereby renew the above Decrees and Constitutions of Paul V and of Gregory XV.

"Moreover, as regards those books in which the said   **42** sentence, feast and relative cult are called into question   *(60)* or are contradicted in any way whatsoever, according to what has already been stated, either in writing or verbally, in discourses, sermons, lectures, treatises and debates—that may have been printed after the above praised Decree of Paul V, or may be printed hereafter We hereby prohibit them, subject to the penalties and censures established by the Index of prohibited books, and ipso facto, without any further declaration, We desire and command that they be held as expressly prohibited" (a).

Testimonies of the Catholic world

All are aware with how much diligence this doctrine   **43** of the Immaculate Conception of the Mother of God has   *(64,* been handed down, proposed and defended by the most   *69)* outstanding religious orders, by the more celebrated theological academies, and by very eminent doctors in the sciences of theology. All know, likewise, how eager the bishops have been to profess openly and publicly, even in

42a Alexander VIII, Apost. Const. *Sollicitudo omnium Ecclesiarum,* December 8, 1661.

ecclesiastical assemblies, that Mary, the most holy Mother of God, by virtue of the foreseen merits of Christ, Our Lord and Redeemer, was never subject to original sin, but was completely preserved from the original taint, and hence she was redeemed in a manner more sublime.

The Council of Trent

44
(59,
61,
63)
Besides, we must note a fact of the greatest importance indeed. Even the Council of Trent itself, when it promulgated the dogmatic decree concerning original sin, following the testimonies of the Sacred Scriptures, of the Holy Fathers, and of the renowned Councils, decreed and defined that all men are born infected by original sin; nevertheless, it solemnly declared that it had no intention of including the blessed and immaculate Virgin Mary, the Mother of God, in this decree and in the general extension of its definition. Indeed, considering the times and circumstances, the Fathers of Trent sufficiently intimated by this declaration that the Blessed Virgin Mary was free from the original stain; and thus they clearly signified that nothing could be reasonably cited from the Sacred Scriptures, from Tradition, or from the authority of the Fathers, which would in any way be opposed to so great a prerogative of the Blessed Virgin (a).

Testimonies of Tradition

45
(18,
61,
And indeed, illustrious documents of venerable antiquity, of both the Eastern and Western Church, very forcibly testify that this doctrine of the Immaculate Con-

44a Sess. V, Can. 6; Denz. 792.—*Declarat tamen hæc ipsa sancta Synodus, non esse suæ intentionis, comprehendere in hoc decreto, ubi de peccato originali agitur, beatam et immaculatam Virginem Mariam Dei genitricem, sed observandas esse constitutiones felicis recordationis Sixti papæ IV, sub pœnis in eis constitutionibus contentis, quas innovat.*

ception of the most blessed Virgin, which was daily more   *63)*
and more splendidly explained, stated, and confirmed by
the highest authority, teaching, zeal, knowledge, and wisdom of the Church, and which was disseminated among
all peoples and nations of the Catholic world in a marvelous manner—this doctrine always existed in the Church as
a doctrine that has been received from our ancestors, and
that has been stamped with the character of revealed
doctrine. For the Church of Christ, watchful guardian
that she is, and defender of the dogmas deposited with
her, never changes anything, never diminishes anything,
never adds anything to them; but with all diligence she
treats the ancient documents faithfully and wisely; if they
really are of ancient origin and if the faith of the Fathers
has transmitted them, she strives to investigate and explain
them in such a way that the ancient dogmas of heavenly
doctrine will be made evident and clear, but will retain
their full, integral, and proper nature, and will grow only
within their own genus—that is, within the same dogma,
in the same sense and the same meaning.

Interpreters of the Sacred Scriptures

The Fathers and writers of the Church, well versed in   **46**
the heavenly Scriptures, had nothing more at heart than   *(63,*
to vie with one another in preaching and teaching in many   *70,*
wonderful ways the Virgin's supreme sanctity, dignity, and *71,*
immunity from all stain of sin, and her renowned victory   *123)*
over the foulest enemy of the human race. This they did
in the books they wrote to explain the Scriptures, to vin-
dicate the dogmas, and to instruct the faithful. These
ecclesiastical writers in quoting the words by which at
the beginning of the world God announced His merciful
remedies prepared for the regeneration of mankind—words
by which He crushed the audacity of the deceitful serpent and wondrously raised up the hope of our race,
saying, "I will put enmities between thee and the woman,

between thy seed and her seed" (a)—taught that by this divine prophecy the merciful Redeemer of mankind, Jesus Christ, the only begotten Son of God, was clearly foretold; that His most Blessed Mother, the Virgin Mary, was prophetically indicated; and, at the same time, the very enmity of both against the evil one was significantly expressed. Hence, just as Christ, the Mediator between God and man, assumed human nature, blotted the handwriting of the decree that stood against us, and fastened it triumphantly to the cross, so the most holy Virgin, united with Him by a most intimate and indissoluble bond, was, with Him and through Him, eternally at enmity with the evil serpent, and most completely triumphed over him, and thus crushed his head with her immaculate foot (b).

47
(59,
63,
68,
74)
This sublime and singular privilege of the Blessed Virgin, together with her most excellent innocence, purity, holiness and freedom from every stain of sin, as well as the unspeakable abundance and greatness of all heavenly graces, virtues and privileges—these the Fathers beheld in that ark of Noe, which was built by divine command and escaped entirely safe and sound from the common shipwreck of the whole world (a); in the ladder which Jacob saw reaching from earth to heaven, by whose rungs the angels of God ascended and descended, and on whose top the Lord Himself leaned (b); in that bush which Moses saw in the holy place burning on all sides, which was not

46a Gen. 3:15.
46b *Quo circa sicut Christus Dei hominumque mediator, humana assumpta natura, delens quod adversus nos erat chirographum decreti, illud cruci triumphator affixit; sic Sanctissima Virgo, arctissimo et indissolubili vinculo cum eo conjuncta, una cum illo et per illum, sempiternas contra venenosum serpentem inimicitias exercens, ac de ipso plenissime triumphans, illius caput immaculato pede contrivit.*
47a Cf. Gen. 6:9.
47b Cf. Gen. 28:12.

consumed or injured in any way but grew green and blossomed beautifully (c); in that impregnable tower before the enemy, from which hung a thousand bucklers and all the armor of the strong (d); in that garden enclosed on all sides, which cannot be violated or corrupted by any deceitful plots (e); as in that resplendent city of God, which has its foundations on the holy mountains (f); in that most august temple of God, which, radiant with divine splendors, is full of the glory of God (g); and in very many other biblical types of this kind. In such allusions the Fathers taught had been prophesied in a wonderful manner the exalted dignity of the Mother of God, her spotless innocence and her sanctity unstained by any fault.

In like manner did they use the words of the Prophets **48** to describe this wondrous abundance of divine gifts and *(63)* the original innocence of the Virgin of whom Jesus was born. They celebrated the august Virgin as the spotless dove, as the holy Jerusalem, as the exalted throne of God, as the ark and house of holiness which Eternal Wisdom built, and as that Queen who, abounding in delights and leaning on her Beloved, came forth from the mouth of the Most High, entirely perfect, beautiful, most dear to God, and never stained with the least blemish.

The Annunciation

When the Fathers and writers of the Church medi- **49** tated on the fact that the Most Blessed Virgin was, in the *(63)* name and by order of God Himself, proclaimed full of grace (a) by the Angel Gabriel when he announced her

47c Cf. Exod. 3:2.
47d Cf. Cant. 4:4.
47e Cf. Cant. 4:12.
47f Cf. Ps. 86:1.
47g Cf. Is. 6:1-4.
49a Luke 1:28.

most sublime dignity of Mother of God, they thought that this singular and solemn salutation, never heard before, showed that the Mother of God is the seat of all divine graces and is adorned with all gifts of the Holy Spirit. To them Mary is an almost infinite treasury, an inexhaustible abyss of these gifts, to such an extent that she was never subject to the curse and was together with her Son the only partaker of perpetual benediction. Hence she was worthy to hear Elizabeth, inspired by the Holy Spirit, exclaim: "Blessed art thou among women, and blessed is the fruit of thy womb" (b).

Mary compared with Eve

50
(27,
63,
76-
79)
Hence, it is the clear and unanimous opinion of the Fathers that the most glorious Virgin, for whom "He who is mighty has done great things," was resplendent with such an abundance of heavenly gifts, with such a fullness of grace and with such innocence, that she is an unspeakable miracle of God—indeed, the crown of all miracles and truly the worthy Mother of God; that she approaches as near to God Himself as is possible for a created being; and that she is above all men and angels in glory. Hence, to demonstrate the original innocence and sanctity of the Mother of God, not only did they frequently compare her to Eve while yet a virgin, while yet innocent, while yet incorrupt, while not yet deceived by the deadly snares of the most treacherous serpent; but they have also exalted her above Eve with a wonderful variety of expressions. Eve listened to the serpent with lamentable consequences; she fell from original innocence and became his slave. The most Blessed Virgin, on the contrary, ever increased her original gift, and not only never lent an ear to the serpent, but by divinely given power she utterly destroyed the force and dominion of the evil one.

49b Ibid., 42.

Biblical figures

Accordingly, the Fathers have never ceased to call the **51** Mother of God the lily among thorns, the land entirely in- *(63)* tact, the virgin undefiled, immaculate, ever blessed, and free from all contagion of sin, she from whom was formed the new Adam, the flawless, brightest, and most beautiful paradise of innocence, immortality, and delights planted by God Himself and protected against all the snares of the poisonous serpent, the incorruptible wood that the worm of sin had never corrupted, the fountain ever clear and sealed with the power of the Holy Spirit, the most holy temple, the treasure of immortality, the one and only daughter of life—not of death, the plant not of anger but of grace, through the singular providence of God growing ever green contrary to the common law, coming as it does from a corrupted and tainted root.

Explicit affirmations . . .

As if these splendid eulogies and tributes were not suf- **52** ficient, the Fathers proclaimed with particular and definite *(39,* statements that when one treats of sin, the holy Virgin *63,* Mary is not even to be mentioned; for to her more grace *68-* was given than was necessary to conquer sin complete- *75,* ly (a). They also declared that the most glorious Virgin *109)* was Reparatrix of the first parents, the giver of life to pos- terity; that she was chosen before the ages, prepared for Himself by the Most High, foretold by God when He said to the serpent, "I will put enmities between thee and the woman" (b)—unmistakable evidence that she has crushed the poisonous head of the serpent. And hence they affirmed that the Blessed Virgin was, through grace, entirely free from every stain of sin, and from all corruption of body, soul, and mind; that she was always united with God and

52a Cf. St. Augustine: *De natura et gratia,* c. 36.
52b Gen. 3:15.

joined to Him by an eternal covenant; that she was never in darkness but always in light; and that, therefore, she was entirely a fit habitation for Christ, not because of the state of her body, but because of her original grace.

... of a supereminent sanctity

53
(23,
55,
63,
68)

To these praises they have added very noble words. Speaking of the Conception of the Virgin, they testified that nature yielded to grace and, unable to go on, stood trembling. The Virgin Mother of God would not be conceived by Anna before grace would bear its fruits; it was proper that she be conceived as the first-born, by whom "the first-born of every creature" would be conceived. They testified, too, that the flesh of the Virgin, although derived from Adam, did not contract the stains of Adam, and that on this account the most Blessed Virgin was the tabernacle created by God Himself and formed by the Holy Spirit, truly a work in royal purple, adorned and woven with gold, which that new Beseleel (a) made. They affirmed that the same Virgin is, and is deservedly, the first and especial work of God, escaping the fiery arrows of the evil one; that she is beautiful by nature and entirely free from all stain; that at her Immaculate Conception she came into the world all radiant like the dawn. For it was certainly not fitting that this vessel of election should be wounded by the common injuries, since she, differing so much from the others, had only nature in common with them, not sin. In fact, it was quite fitting that, as the Only-Begotten has a Father in heaven, whom the Seraphim extol as thrice holy, so He should have a Mother on earth who would never be without the splendor of holiness.

54
(63,
71)

This doctrine so filled the minds and souls of our ancestors in the Faith that a singular and truly marvelous style of speech came into vogue among them. They have

53a Cf. Exod. 31:2.

frequently addressed the Mother of God as immaculate, as immaculate in every respect; innocent, and verily most innocent; spotless, and entirely spotless; holy and removed from every stain of sin; all pure, all stainless, the very model of purity and innocence; more beautiful than beauty, more lovely than loveliness; more holy than holiness, singularly holy and most pure in soul and body; the one who surpassed all integrity and virginity; the only one who has become the dwelling place of all the graces of the most Holy Spirit. God alone excepted, Mary is more excellent than all, and by nature fair and beautiful, and more holy than the Cherubim and Seraphim. To praise her all the tongues of heaven and earth do not suffice.

Everyone is cognizant that this style of speech has passed almost spontaneously into the books of the most holy Liturgy and the Offices of the Church, in which they occur so often and abundantly. In them, the Mother of God is invoked and praised as the one spotless and most beautiful dove, as a rose ever blooming, as perfectly pure, ever immaculate, and ever blessed. She is celebrated as innocence never sullied and as the second Eve who brought forth the Emmanuel. **55** *(61, 62)*

Preparation for the definition

No wonder, then, that the Pastors of the Church and the faithful gloried daily more and more in professing with so much piety, religion, and love this doctrine of the Immaculate Conception of the Virgin Mother of God, which, as the Fathers discerned, was recorded in the Divine Scriptures; which was handed down in so many of their most important writings; which was expressed and celebrated in so many illustrious monuments of venerable antiquity; which was proposed and confirmed by the official and authoritative teaching of the Church. Hence, nothing was dearer, nothing more pleasing to these pastors than to venerate, invoke, and proclaim with most ardent affection the **56** *(61, 63)*

Virgin Mother of God conceived without original stain. Accordingly, from ancient times the bishops of the Church, ecclesiastics, religious orders, and even emperors and kings, have earnestly petitioned this Apostolic See to define as a dogma of the Catholic Faith the Immaculate Conception of the most holy Mother of God. These petitions were renewed in these our own times; they were especially brought to the attention of Gregory XVI, Our Predecessor of happy memory, and to Ourselves, not only by bishops, but by the secular clergy and religious orders, by sovereign rulers and by the faithful.

57
(65, 66)
Mindful, indeed, of all these things and considering them most attentively with particular joy in Our heart, as soon as We, by the inscrutable design of Providence, had been raised to the sublime Chair of St. Peter—in spite of Our unworthiness—and had begun to govern the universal Church, nothing have We had more at heart—a heart which from Our tenderest years has overflowed with devoted veneration and love for the most blessed Virgin—than to show forth her prerogatives in resplendent light.

That We might proceed with great prudence, We established a special congregation of Our Venerable Brethren, the cardinals of the holy Roman Church, illustrious for their piety, wisdom, and knowledge of the sacred sciences. We also selected priests, both secular and regular, well trained in the theological sciences, that they should most carefully consider all matters pertaining to the Immaculate Conception of the Virgin and make known to Us their opinion.

The mind of the bishops

58
(65)
Although We knew the mind of the bishops from the petitions which We had received from them, namely, that the Immaculate Conception of the Blessed Virgin be finally defined, nevertheless, on February 2, 1849 (a), We sent an

:8a Cf. above No. 19 ff.

Encyclical Letter from Gaeta to all Our Venerable Brethren, the bishops of the Catholic world, that they should
offer prayers to God and then tell Us in writing what the
piety and devotion of their faithful was in regard to the
Immaculate Conception of the Mother of God. We likewise
inquired what the bishops themselves thought about defining this doctrine and what their wishes were in regard
to making known with all possible solemnity Our supreme
judgment.

We were certainly filled with the greatest consolation **59**
when the replies of Our Venerable Brethren came to Us. *(65)*
For, replying to Us with a most enthusiastic joy, exultation
and zeal, they not only again confirmed their own singular
piety toward the Immaculate Conception of the most blessed Virgin, and that of the secular and religious clergy and
of the faithful, but with one voice they even entreated Us
to define with Our supreme judgment and authority the
Immaculate Conception of the Virgin. In the meantime We
were indeed filled with no less joy when, after a diligent
examination, Our Venerable Brethren, the cardinals of the
special congregation and the theologians chosen by Us as
counselors (whom We mentioned above), asked with the
same enthusiasm and fervor for the definition of the Immaculate Conception of the Mother of God.

Consequently, following the examples of Our Prede- **60**
cessors, and desiring to proceed in the traditional manner, *(65)*
We announced and held a consistory, in which We addressed Our Brethren, the cardinals of the Holy Roman
Church. It was the greatest spiritual joy for Us when We
heard them ask Us to promulgate the dogmatic definition
of the Immaculate Conception of the Virgin Mother of
God (a).

Therefore, having full trust in the Lord that the op- **61**
portune time had come for defining the Immaculate Con- *(59,*

60a Cf. above, No. 27 ff.

66)   ception of the Blessed Virgin Mary, Mother of God, which
       Holy Scripture, venerable Tradition, the constant mind of
       the Church, the desire of Catholic bishops and the faithful,
       and the memorable Acts and Constitutions of Our Prede-
       cessors, wonderfully illustrate and proclaim, and having
       most diligently considered all things, as We poured forth
       to God ceaseless and fervent prayers, We concluded that
       We should no longer delay in decreeing and defining by
       Our supreme authority the Immaculate Conception of the
       Blessed Virgin. And thus, We can satisfy the most holy de-
       sire of the Catholic world as well as Our own devotion
       toward the most holy Virgin, and at the same time honor
       more and more the only-begotten Son, Jesus Christ our
       Lord through His holy Mother—since whatever honor and
       praise are bestowed on the Mother redound to the Son.

The definition

62   Wherefore, in humility and fasting, We unceasingly
(58,   offered Our private prayers as well as the public prayers
59,   of the Church to God the Father through His Son, that He
66,   would deign to direct and strengthen Our mind by the
69)   power of the Holy Spirit. In like manner did We implore
        the help of the entire heavenly host as We ardently in-
        voked the Paraclete. Accordingly, by the inspiration of the
        Holy Spirit, for the honor of the Holy and undivided Trin-
        ity, for the glory and adornment of the Virgin Mother of
        God, for the exaltation of the Catholic Faith, and for the
        furtherance of the Catholic religion, by the authority of
        Jesus Christ our Lord, of the Blessed Apostles Peter and
        Paul, and by Our own: "We declare, pronounce, and de-
        fine that the doctrine which holds that the most Blessed
        Virgin Mary, in the first instant of her Conception, by a
        singular grace and privilege granted by Almighty God, in
        view of the merits of Jesus Christ, the Savior of the human
        race, was preserved free from all stain of original sin, is

a doctrine revealed by God and therefore to be believed firmly and constantly by all the faithful (a).

Hence, if anyone shall dare—which God forbid!—to think otherwise than as has been defined by Us, let him know and understand that he is condemned by his own judgment; that he has suffered shipwreck in the faith; that he has separated from the unity of the Church; and that, furthermore, by his own action he incurs the penalties established by law if he should dare to express in words or writing or by any other outward means the errors he thinks in his heart.

63
(20)

Hoped for results

Our soul overflows with joy, and Our tongue with exultation. We give, and We shall continue to give, the humblest and deepest thanks to Jesus Christ, our Lord, because through His singular grace He has granted to Us, unworthy though We be, to decree and offer this honor and glory and praise to His most holy Mother. All Our hope do We repose in the most blessed Virgin—in the all fair and immaculate one who has crushed the poisonous head of the most cruel serpent and brought salvation to the world; in her who is the glory of the prophets and apostles, the honor of the martyrs, the crown and joy of all the saints; in her who is the safest refuge and the most trustworthy helper of all who are in danger; in her who, with her only-begotten Son, is the most powerful Mediatrix and Conciliatrix in the whole world; in her who is the most excellent glory, ornament, and impregnable stronghold of the holy Church; in her who has destroyed all heresies and snatched the

64
(120,
121)

62a *Declaramus, pronuntiamus et definimus doctrinam quae tenet beatissimam Virginem Mariam in primo instanti suæ conceptionis fuisse singulari Omnipotentis Dei gratia et privilegio, intuitu meritorum Christi Jesu Salvatoris humani generis, ab omni originalis culpæ labe præservatam immunem, esse a Deo revelatam, atque idcirco ab omnibus fidelibus firmiter constanterque credendam.* Cf. Denz., 1641.

faithful people and nations from all kinds of direst calamities; in her do We hope who has delivered Us from so many threatening dangers. We have, therefore, a very certain hope and complete confidence that this most blessed Virgin will ensure by her most powerful patronage that all difficulties be removed and all errors dissipated, so that Our Holy Mother the Catholic Church may flourish daily more and more throughout all the nations and countries, and may reign "from sea to sea and from the river to the ends of the earth," and may enjoy genuine peace, tranquillity and liberty. We are firm in Our confidence that she will obtain pardon for the sinner, health for the sick, strength of heart for the weak, consolation for the afflicted, help for those in danger; that she will remove spiritual blindness from all who are in error, so that they may return to the path of truth and justice, and that there may be one flock and one shepherd.

65
(49)   Let all the children of the Catholic Church, who are so very dear to Us, hear these words of Ours. With a still more ardent zeal for piety, religion, and love, let them continue to venerate, invoke, and pray to the most blessed Virgin Mary, Mother of God, conceived without original sin. Let them fly with utter confidence to this most sweet Mother of mercy and grace in all dangers, difficulties, needs, doubts, and fears. Under her guidance, under her patronage, under her kindness and protection, nothing is to be feared, nothing is hopeless. Because, while bearing towards us a truly motherly affection and having in her care the work of our salvation, she is solicitous about the whole human race. And since she has been appointed by God to be the Queen of heaven and earth, and is exalted above all the choirs of angels and saints, and even stands at the right hand of her only-begotten Son, Jesus Christ our Lord, she presents our petitions in a most efficacious manner. What she asks she obtains. Her pleas can never be unheard.

TIMELINESS OF THE DEFINITION

All. to the Consistory, December 9, 1954.

(Present difficulties and errors.)

God will assist the Church and hear our appeals if Mary, the most Blessed Virgin Mother of God, whose exemption from the stain of original sin We joyfully defined with the aid of the Holy Ghost and in your enthusiastic presence, intercedes for us. It is truly a glorious privilege and one which singularly becomes the Mother of God to have been preserved free and safe from the universal disaster of our race. The greatness of this privilege will be a powerful means of confuting those who deny that human nature was corrupted by the first sin and who exaggerate the forces of reason in order to deny or lessen the benefit of Revelation. Finally, may the Blessed Virgin, who conquered and destroyed all heresies, uproot and destroy this dangerous error of Rationalism, which in our unhappy times not only afflicts and torments civil society, but more deeply afflicts the Church.

66
(27,
66,
123)

QUEEN AND MOTHER

Encycl. *Quanta Cura*, December 8, 1864, on modern errors.

That God may more readily listen to our prayers and supplications, to yours and those of the faithful, let us in all confidence choose as advocate before Him the Immaculate and most holy Mother of God, the Virgin Mary. She has destroyed all the heresies of the world. She is our most loving Mother; "all mild and most merciful, she shows herself within reach of every prayer; most kind, she takes to herself all our needs with profound love and tender pity." In heaven as Queen at the right hand of her only Son, clothed in golden raiment and all manner of jewels, there is nothing she cannot obtain from Him.

67
(40,
101,
107,
123)

THE SUPPORT OF THE SHEPHERDS

All. to the Consistory, February 22, 1867.

(Opposition of the Italian state in the appointing of bishops.—Damage suffered by Dioceses.)

68
(119,
121,
167)
Indeed it is a serious and a sad affair to have to appoint bishops at such a time when public matters cause great upheaval. What is to be done under the circumstances? Will they cause us to draw back in our decision? Far from it! The workers will flow to the vineyard planted by God and irrigated by the blood of His Son. Let them go to cultivate it in the name of Jesus Christ and expect singular help from Him; let them go and trust in the patronage of the Mother of God, who will uphold them with her most powerful support. Because she is the Seat of Wisdom she will fill the shepherds with the gift of intelligence, and at the same time as Refuge of Sinners she will easily lead back many sheep that have strayed; as Comforter of the Afflicted she will pour oil on the wounds of the unfortunate; as Help of Christians she will grant them the respect and filial devotion of many. Thanks to her, shepherds will find in the docility and affection of all a lightening of their heavy burdens and a comfort in their struggle against God's enemies and the powers of darkness, who are doing all in their power to take possession of the evangelical field and bring it to ruin.

(Decision to appoint bishops notwithstanding governmental opposition.)

THE VIRGIN PRIEST

Letter *Cum purgaturus,* to Msgr. Van der Berghe, August 25, 1873.

69
(44,
If Our Lord has permitted this great persecution which rages against the Church to purify His field, to arouse

sluggish souls, to lead back the people, and especially the clergy, to primitive sanctity of life, to a more fervent piety and to a more fruitful spirit of sacrifice, it is certainly Our duty to second such a wise design of Providence and dutifully cooperate with it so as to brush aside more promptly those scourges which restrain us from obeying His divine laws. In order more perfectly and more securely to fulfill this duty of Ours, We cannot find a more powerful help than the patronage of the Mother of God nor a more perfect and efficacious example than the conduct of Mary. As a mirror without blemish, she reflects, more than any other creature, the sanctity of God. She was so closely united to the sacrifice of her Divine Son, from the virginal conception of Jesus Christ to His sorrowful Passion, that she was called by some Fathers of the Church, Virgin Priest (a).

130, 134, 165)

(*Congratulations to the author of "Marie et le Sacerdoce."*)

STABAT MATER

All. to the Catholic Circles of Rome, September 20, 1874.

(*A coincidence: the feast of the harvest and its caretakers, while Rome entertains its despoilers.—A second coincidence.*)

The coincidence which interests us more and which must be of comfort to our soul is the fact that the anniversary of September 20 (a) falls this year on the same day as the liturgical commemoration of the Dolors of the Mother of God. And while the Church venerates this great and sorrow-laden Woman, we must follow her, imitate her, and be encouraged by her example. In fact she did not say,

70
(116, 131)

69a Cf. No. 258.
70a Taking of Rome by Piedmontese troops, Sept. 20, 1870.

as did the mother of Ismael (b), that she had not strength
to assist at the death which threatened her Son; but as a
courageous Woman she ascended the summit of Golgotha
and at the foot of the Cross she gathered from the lips of
her Divine Son that testament which comforts, teaches,
and renders the Man-God Master of Truth even from the
Cross.

71
(116) Therefore Mary most holy *was standing* (a) with head
raised at the foot of the Cross and while she heard the
blasphemies of the soldiers, the ugly jokes of the Pharisees,
the insults of the priests, *standing,* and with her eyes
turned to her Divine Son, she felt her courage redoubling,
even in the fullness of her sorrows. *Standing!* The sword
was piercing the side of the Crucified Lord, and she
remained a motionless onlooker, not as weaklings who
were assisting at the desolating tragedy as if it were an
exhibition but as a woman meditating, suffering and hoping. At this sight the words of the aged Simeon came
back to her: that that dear child would be a sword of
great sorrow which would pierce her mother's heart (b).

72
(117) Mary most holy *was standing* and she stood firmly at
the foot of the Cross until the consummation of the great
catastrophe. Finally, she retired, and in the midst of the
darkness, willed by God to declare to the world nature's
mourning, she came down with sure step from Calvary
and without fear betook herself to her quarters where we
can piously believe that her dear Son was the first to
comfort her with His presence; and in explaining the
fulfillment of the great mystery it is to be believed that
He revealed to her the future triumphs of the Church,
whose beginning it was right that Mary should have seen.

73
(131) Therefore let us raise our eyes to the Mountain and
profit from the example of strength given by the Immac-

70b Cf. Gen. 21:16.
71a John 19:25.
71b Cf. Luke 2:35.

ulate Virgin, who knows how to suit the event to our
enfeebled powers. We also are sorrowful spectators of
this bitter war and of the torments which the Church
must suffer, this Church which sprang from the open side
of Jesus Christ on Calvary.

(*Duty of all of opposing impiety with religious instruction and praise of God.*)

With Mary at the foot of the Cross

Do not assist at functions that are intended to placate **74**
God as if you were assisting at some spectacle, *tamquam* *(131)*
ad spectaculum (a). The spectators on Golgotha were
reproached on account of their indifference. But do you
assist at this scene as Mary most holy assisted at it. She
concentrated on her sorrow and at the same time meditated on what was taking place and on the words that fell
from the lips of her Divine Son. We may apply to her here
the words: *Mary kept in mind all these things, pondering
them in her heart* (b).

Let us also ponder his words and summarize the fruit
of our reflections in the words: *Agere et pati* (To act and
to suffer).

Take action against the many who call evil good and **75**
good evil. Take action against the monster that is now *(116,*
trying to tear all to ruin; let us do what we can to repel, *131)*
with the help of God, a monster which is the epitome of
all vice. And if, to fight against him, it is necessary to act,
it is equally necessary that we train ourselves patiently
to endure the effects of his poisonous vengeance. *Agere
et pati.*

Blasphemies, insults, derisions must not upset us: we
must remain firmly and constantly at the foot of the Cross.

74a Luke 23:48.
74b Luke 2:19.

After Mary most holy had assisted at the great sacrifice, she descended the mountain, returned to her retreat, walking steadily amidst the dense darkness which miraculously covered the whole earth. We too must watch our steps and walk safely amidst the darkness produced by errors, by false principles, by the spirit of immorality, and retreat into the silence of our heart.

Our attitude toward triumphant error

76
(117) It is to be believed, as I have already said, that Mary, alone and abandoned, was at the end consoled by the sight of her Beloved. For us, too, the Cross is our only defense. Those who could help us are either the fallen ones, the enemies, or the indifferent. Let us therefore turn to Him, Who by His death effaced the condemnation from our brows. He consoled His most Holy Mother in the sorrow and abandonment in which she was plunged. And will He not also console His Vicar, although unworthy, and all those who are with him?

77
Ah! yes! Let us all, at the foot of the Cross, pray to Him with Mary to console us. May He also purify His Church of certain stains which are not hers, but belong to this or that member of the Church.

But let the enemies of the Church who rejoice over all that is happening and who trust in certain possibilities (near or distant, God alone knows), let them know that the Pharisees and their friends also rejoiced over the death of Christ as if they had obtained a triumph, unaware that that death was the beginning of their complete overthrow. Meanwhile let us be patient and listen to the voice of God Who through His Prophet says to us: *Potum dabis nobis in lacrimis in mensura* (a). Let us pray God with confidence hoping that the measure is filled to the brim and the bitter cup be soon drained.

77a Ps. 79:6.

But as in all things we must submit our will to God's **78**
will having asked Him to deliver us from present evils, *(173)*
let us ask Him to free us from future evils through the
intercession of her whom the angel greeted as full of grace.

Oh, yes, blessed Virgin, I pray you for myself, for all
here present, and for all those who are united to me to
assist us now and keep us firm and strong in our resolutions. We pray you to assist us at the moment of our death
when our cold and trembling lips pronounce your name
with languid voice. May you with your most chaste Spouse
gather in those souls who desire naught else but to praise
and bless God forever and ever. *Quando corpus morietur,
Fac ut animæ donetur, Paradisi gloria* (a).

THE LAST WORDS OF OUR SAVIOR

All. to pilgrims from Savoy, September 15, 1876.

(*Need for suffering.*)

What a great comfort it is for us to reflect that we, **79**
represented by St. John, were placed under the protection *(31-*
of Mary as our Mother on Mount Calvary at the foot of *32)*
the Cross! This morning we read in the Holy Mass the
last words that Jesus Christ pronounced on that throne
of pain and love: *Mulier, ecce filius tuus* (a). Let us therefore invoke this Mother of Sorrows, this mother who
ardently desires to see multiplied the number of children
who love her Jesus. Let us beseech her to give Us the
strength and constancy to live the remainder of Our days
in the faithful exercise of Our duties, and in the firm will
always to defend the sacred rights of the Church.

78a Sequence, *Stabat Mater*.
79a John 19:26.

LEO XIII

(1878-1903)

EFFICACY OF THE ROSARY IN HISTORY

Encycl. *Supremi Apostolatus,* September 1, 1883.

The Supreme Apostolic Office which We discharge, **80**
and the exceedingly difficult condition of these times, *(134,*
daily warn and compel Us to watch carefully over the *135)*
safety and welfare of the Church, the more so seeing that
the calamities which she suffers are great. While, therefore, We endeavor in every way to preserve the rights
of the Church and to obviate or repel present or contingent dangers, We constantly seek for help from heaven
—the sole means of effecting anything—that Our labors and
Our care may obtain their wished-for object.

We consider that there can be no surer and more **81**
efficacious means to this end than by obtaining through *(108,*
devotion and piety the favor of the Virgin Mary, the *135)*
Mother of God, the guardian of our peace and the minister to us of heavenly grace, who is placed on the highest
summit of power and glory in heaven, in order that she
may bestow the help of her patronage on men who through
so many labors and dangers are striving to reach that
eternal city.

Now that the anniversary of manifold and exceedingly great favors obtained by a Christian people through
the devotion of the Rosary is at hand, We desire that the
same devotion should be offered by the whole Catholic
world with the greatest earnestness to the Blessed Virgin,
in order that by her intercession her divine Son may be
appeased and moved to compassion toward us in the
miseries which afflict us. And therefore, We determined,
Venerable Brethren, to despatch to you this letter in order
that, informed of Our designs, your authority and zeal
might excite the piety of your people to carry out our
wishes.

Our Lady, help of the Church

82
(28,
41,
121)

It has always been the habit of Catholics in danger and in arduous times to fly for refuge to Mary, and to seek peace in her maternal goodness, which shows that the Catholic Church has always, and with justice, put all her hope and trust in the Mother of God. She who is associated with Him in the work of man's salvation has favor and power with her Son greater than any other human or angelic creature has ever obtained or ever can obtain (a). And, as it is her greatest pleasure to grant her help and comfort to those who seek her, it cannot be doubted that she will deign, even anxiously, to receive the aspirations of the universal Church.

83
(123,
154)

This devotion, so great and so confident, to the august Queen of Heaven has never shone forth with such brilliance as when the militant Church of God has seemed to be endangered by the violence of widespread heresy, by intolerable moral corruption, or by the attacks of powerful enemies. Ancient and modern history and the more sacred annals of the Church bear witness to public and private supplications addressed to the Mother of God, to the help she has granted in return, and to the peace and tranquillity which she has obtained from God. Hence her illustrious titles of "Help of Christians," "Consolation of the Afflicted," "Our Power in War," "Queen of Victory," "Queen of Peace." And among these is specially worthy of note that familiar title of the Rosary by which the signal benefits she has gained for the whole of Christendom have been solemnly commemorated.

82a *Revera primævæ labis expers Virgo, allecta Dei Mater, et hoc ipso servandi hominum generis consors facta, tanta apud Filium gratia et potestate valet, ut maiorem nec humana nec angelica natura assecuta umquam sit, aut assequi possit.*

The victories of the Rosary

There is none among you, Venerable Brethren, who **84**
will not remember how great was the trouble and grief *(123)*
that God's holy Church suffered at the close of the twelfth
century from the Albigensian heretics, the offspring of the
later Manicheans, who filled the south of France and
other portions of the Latin world with their pernicious
errors, and carrying everywhere the terror of their arms
strove far and wide to rule by massacre and ruin.

Our merciful God, as you know, raised up against **85**
these bitter enemies a most holy man, the illustrious father *(142,*
and founder of the Dominican Order. Great in the integ- *148)*
rity of his doctrine, in the example of his virtue and by
his apostolic labors, he dauntlessly attacked the enemies
of the Catholic Church relying not on force of arms but
in that devotion which he was the first to introduce under
the name of the Holy Rosary and which was disseminated
through the length and breadth of the earth by him and
his followers.

Guided, in fact, by divine inspiration and grace, he **86**
foresaw that this devotion, like a most powerful weapon *(148)*
of war, would be the means of putting the enemy to
flight, and of confounding their audacity and mad impiety. Such was indeed its results. Thanks to this new
method of prayer—when adopted and faithfully carried out
as instituted by the holy founder, St. Dominic—piety,
faith and unity began to return; the projects and devices
of the heretics to fall to pieces. Many wanderers also returned to the way of salvation, and the wrath of the
impious was restrained by the arms of those Catholics
who had determined to repel their violence.

The efficacy and power of this devotion was also **87**
wondrously exhibited in the sixteenth century, when the *(142,*
vast forces of the Turks threatened to impose on nearly *146,*
the whole of Europe the yoke of superstition and barbar- *148)*

ism. At that time the Supreme Pontiff, St. Pius V, after arousing among all the Christian princes zeal for the common defense, strove, above all, with great ardor to obtain for Christendom the favor of the most powerful Mother of God. So noble an example offered to heaven and earth in those times rallied around him all the minds and hearts of the age. And thus Christ's faithful warriors, prepared to sacrifice their life and blood for the welfare of their faith and their country, proceeded undauntedly to meet their foe near the Gulf of Corinth; while those who were unable to join them formed a band of pious supplicants, who called on Mary and as one saluted her again and again in the words of the Rosary, imploring her to grant victory to their companions engaged in battle. Our sovereign Lady did grant her aid; for in the naval battle near the Echinades Islands the Christian fleet gained with no great loss to itself a magnificent victory, in which the enemy was completely routed.

88
(148) And it was to preserve the memory of the favor thus granted that the same most holy Pontiff desired that a feast in honor of Our Lady of Victories should keep in memory the anniversary of so memorable a struggle, the feast which Gregory XIII dedicated under the title of "The Holy Rosary."

Similarly, important successes were in the past century gained over the Turks at Temesvar in Hungary, and at Corfu; and in both cases these engagements coincided with feasts of the Blessed Virgin and with the conclusion of public devotions of the Rosary. And this led Our Predecessor, Clement XI, in his gratitude to decree that the Blessed Mother of God should every year be especially honored in her Rosary by the whole Church.

Papal tributes to the Rosary

89
(142, Since, therefore, it is clearly evident that this form of prayer is particularly pleasing to the Blessed Virgin, and

that it is especially suitable as a means of defense for
the Church and all Christians, it is not at all surprising
that several others of Our Predecessors have made it their
aim to favor and increase its spread by their urgent ad-
monitions. Thus, Urban IV testified that "every day the
Rosary obtained fresh blessings for Christianity." Sixtus IV
declared that this method of prayer "redounded to the
honor of God and the Blessed Virgin, and was well suited
to ward off impending dangers," and Leo X that "it was
instituted to oppose pernicious heresiarchs and heresies";
while Julius III called it "the glory of the Church."
St. Pius V said that "with the spread of this devotion the
meditations of the faithful have become more ardent and
their prayers more fervent, and they have quickly become different men; the darkness of heresy has been dissipated, and the light of Catholic faith has broken forth
in renewed glory." Lastly, Gregory XIII in his turn pronounced that "the Rosary has been instituted by St. Dominic to appease the anger of God and to implore the
intercession of the Blessed Virgin Mary."

143,
148)

Urgency of recourse to Mary

Moved by these thoughts and by the example of Our
Predecessors, We have deemed it most opportune for
similar reasons to institute public prayers and to endeavor
by adopting those addressed to the Blessed Virgin in the
recital of the Rosary to obtain from her Son Jesus Christ
a similar aid against present dangers. You have before
your eyes, Venerable Brethren, the trials to which the
Church is daily exposed: Christian piety, public morality,
nay, even faith itself, the supreme good and beginning
of all the other virtues, are daily menaced with the greatest
perils.

90
(142,
168)

Nor are you only spectators of the difficulty of the
situation, but your charity, like Ours, is keenly wounded;
for it is one of the most painful and grievous sights to

91
(123,
144-

147)   see so many souls, redeemed by the blood of Christ, snatched from salvation by the whirlwinds of an age of error, precipitated into the abyss of eternal death. Our need of divine help is as great today as when the great Dominic introduced the use of the Rosary of Mary as a balm for the wounds of his contemporaries. That illustrious saint indeed, divinely enlightened, saw that no remedy would be more efficacious against the evils of his time than that men should return to Christ. who "is the Way, the Truth, and the Life," by frequent meditation on the salvation obtained for us by Him, by seeking the intercession with God of that Virgin to whom it is given to destroy all heresies.

92   He therefore so composed the Rosary as to recall
(145,   the mysteries of our salvation in succession; and the sub-
146)   ject of meditation is mingled and, as it were, interlaced with the Angelic Salutation and with the prayers addressed to the God and Father of Our Lord Jesus Christ. We, who seek a remedy for similar evils, do not doubt therefore that the prayer introduced by that most blessed man with so much advantage for the Catholic world will also have the greatest efficacy in removing the calamities of our times. Not only do We earnestly exhort all Christians to give themselves to the pious recital of the Rosary publicly, or privately in their own home and family, and so unceasingly, but We also desire that the whole of the month of October this year be consecrated to the Holy Queen of the Rosary.

(*Practical dispositions.*)

93   And do you, Venerable Brethren, as you have at heart
(146,   the honor of Mary and the welfare of human society, be
154)   the more diligent to apply yourselves to nourish the piety of the people toward the great Virgin and to increase their confidence in her. We believe it to be part of the designs of Providence that in these times of trial for the Church the ancient devotion to the august Virgin should

live and flourish in the greater part of the Christian world. May now the Christian nations, roused by Our exhortations and inflamed by your appeals, seek the protection of Mary with an ardor growing greater day by day; may they cling more and more to the practice of the Rosary, to that devotion which Our ancestors were in the habit of practicing, not only as an ever ready remedy for their misfortunes but as the very badge of Christian piety. The heavenly Patroness of the human race will receive with joy these prayers and supplications, and will easily procure that the good shall grow in virtue, and that the erring shall return to salvation and repent, and that God, who is the avenger of crime, moved to mercy and pity, will deliver Christendom and civil society from all dangers, and restore to them the peace so much desired.

Comforted by this hope We raise, with all the strength of our soul, Our most fervent prayers to Our Lord, so that by the intercession of her in whom He placed the fullness of every good, He may shower on you, Venerable Brethren, the most abundant graces.

(*Blessing.*)

"QUEEN OF THE MOST HOLY ROSARY"

Apost. Letter *Salutaris ille,* December 24, 1883.

(*Joy of the Pope for the welcome given his invitation to prayer.—Efficacy of the Rosary.*)

And among them, as We have insisted in Our Encyclical Letter, is this weighty reason, that the Rosary was instituted chiefly to implore the protection of the Mother of God against the enemies of the Catholic Church, and, as everyone knows, it has often been most effectual in delivering the Church from calamities. **94** *(123, 148)*

(*Exhortation to the daily recitation of the Rosary.*)

95
(145) To the honor, therefore of Mary, the august Mother of God, for a perpetual remembrance of the prayer for her protection offered among all nations to her most pure heart throughout the month of October; as an enduring testimony of the unbounded trust which We put in Our loving Mother, and in order that We may day by day, more and more obtain her favorable aid, We will and decree that in the Litany of Loreto, after the invocation, "Queen conceived without original sin," shall be added the suffrage, "Queen of the Most Holy Rosary, pray for us!"

IN PRAYER WITH MARY

Encycl. *Superiore anno,* August 30, 1884.

96
(129) Last year, as each of you is aware, We decreed by an Encyclical Letter that, to win the help of Heaven for the Church in her trials, the great Mother of God should be addressed in prayer by means of the most holy Rosary during the entire month of October (a). In this We followed both Our own desire and the example of Our Predecessors, who in times of difficulty were wont to have recourse with increased fervor to the Blessed Virgin, and to seek her aid with special prayers.

Men have responded to that wish of Ours with such fervor and unanimity that it is more than ever apparent how real is the fervor of the Christian peoples, and how great is the trust everywhere placed in the heavenly patronage of the Virgin Mary.

97
(46,
126) For Us, weighed down with the burden of such great trials and sorrows, We confess that the existence of such intensity of public piety and faith has been a great consolation, and even gives Us new courage for facing, if that be the will of God, still greater trials. Indeed, from

96a Cf. above No. 92.

the spirit of prayer which is poured out over the "house of David and the dwellers in Jerusalem" (a), We have a confident hope that God will at length let Himself be moved and have pity upon the state of His Church, and give ear to the prayers coming to Him through her whom He has chosen to be the dispenser of all heavenly graces.

For these reasons, therefore, as the same causes still exist which impelled Us last year, as We have said, to stimulate the piety of all, We have deemed it Our duty again this year to exhort the people of Christendom to persevere in that method and formula of prayer known as the Rosary of Mary, and thereby to merit the powerful patronage of the great Mother of God. Inasmuch as the enemies of Christianity are so stubborn in their aims, its defenders must be equally resolute and dauntless, especially as the heavenly help and the benefits which are bestowed on us by God are usually the fruits of our perseverance. It is good to recall to memory the example of that illustrious widow, Judith—a type of the Blessed Virgin—who curbed the ill-judged impatience of the Jews when they attempted to dictate to God a day for the deliverance of His city (a). The example of the Apostles should also be born in mind, who, awaiting the supreme gift of the Paraclete promised to them, persevered unanimously in prayer with the Mother of Jesus.

98
(117,
124,
146)

For it is indeed an arduous and exceedingly important matter that is now in hand: to overcome the ancient and insidious enemy, Satan, now increased in power; to win back the freedom of the Church and of her Head; to preserve and secure the fortifications upon which depend the safety and well-being of human society. Care must be taken, therefore, in these days of sadness for the Church, to preserve the holy custom of reciting the Rosary of Mary,

- 99
(144,
147)

97a Zach. 12:10.
98a Cf. Judith 7:23-25; 8:10-15.

particularly because this method of prayer is arranged to recall all the mysteries of our salvation, and so is eminently fitted to foster the spirit of piety.

100   With respect to Italy, it is now most necessary to
(134, implore the intercession of the most powerful Virgin by
143) means of the Rosary, since a sudden and unexpected misfortune is threatening us—nay, rather, is upon us. The Asiatic cholera has by God's will crossed the boundary within which nature seemed to have confined it, and has spread through the crowded shores of a French port, and thence to the neighboring districts on Italian soil. To Mary, therefore, must we fly—to her whom rightly and justly the Church calls the dispenser of salvation, the helper, and the deliverer—that she, graciously hearkening to our prayers, may grant us the help sought, and drive far from us the unclean plague.

(*Practical dispositions.—Exhortation and prayers for the peace of the Church.*)

PROTECTRESS OF ROME

Letter *Più volte,* to the Cardinal Vicar, October 31, 1886.

101   Several times during the course of Our Pontificate
(124, We have made known Our predilection for the devotion
148) of the Holy Rosary and the great trust We placed in it during the present grave necessities of the Church. In Our Encyclicals, We abundantly emphasized the reasons for Our predilection and Our trust, and the same reasons impelled Us to prescribe, until further notice, the continuation of the pious exercises of the month of October in honor of the glorious Virgin of the Rosary. It is a great consolation to Our soul to learn that this devotion flourishes in many places, both in public and private, and that to many it brings precious fruits of grace and salvation.

We believe that We never have done enough to promote this pious practice among the faithful. We wish to see it ever more widely diffused so that it may become the truly popular devotion in all places at all times. This desire grows more ardent in Us as the times become darker and more hostile for the Church and as We increasingly realize the need of extraordinary divine aid. The audacity of the sects, increased through the favor or the connivance which they meet everywhere has no longer any limit, and in a thousand ways does all that it can to dishonor and outrage the Church, the only power that can fight such sects and which has always fought them. The Church, a divine work to whom her Founder promises every security, does not fear for herself, but rather because of the damage that is being done to souls is incalculable, a great number of which fall miserably into ruin. These considerations urge Us to have constant recourse to God and to the great Virgin of the Rosary, the most potent help of Christians, whose power the forces of hell with fear and trembling acknowledge.

(*Regulations for the daily recital of the Rosary in the churches of Rome dedicated to Mary most holy.*)

With all good reason We order special prayers for Rome. It is right that Rome, seat of the Vicar of Jesus Christ, particularly favored by Divine Providence and singularly devoted to Our Lady, should lead all other cities in religious manifestations and be an example to all. Moreover, here, in the person of her Supreme Head, the Church suffers more than elsewhere; here, at the center of Catholicism, the strength of enemies is directed, and the satanic hate of sects aims especially at Rome. And so, Rome has more reason and greater need to place herself under the protection of the august Virgin and to merit her patronage. And We do not doubt that the piety of

102
(137, 158)

the Romans fully supports our intentions which aim both
at the good of the whole Church and at the safety of
Rome.

(*Blessing.*)

THE VICTORIES OF THE ROSARY

Letter *Vi è ben noto*, to the bishops of Italy, September 20, 1887.

103
(46,
121,
148)
It is well known to you how much trust we have
placed, during these calamities, in the glorious Virgin of
the Rosary for the salvation and prosperity of Christian
people and for the peace and tranquillity of the Church.

We recall how, during times of great trouble, pastors
and the faithful were always accustomed to invoke with
confidence the glorious Mother of God, the most powerful
help of Christians, in whose hands all graces are placed.
We are equally persuaded that devotion to the Virgin under
the title of the Rosary brings help in the very special
needs of our times. Therefore We wish this devotion to be
everywhere revived and to be more firmly established
among the faithful all over the world. To this end We have
devoted all Our efforts and Our care.

*(Timeliness of the Rosary in Italy and in Rome to
drive away the assaults of the wicked. Unite to prayer
the frank profession of faith and the example of a fervent
Christian life.)*

104
(143,
148)
To obtain Our request We place Our lively and firm
hopes in the ever glorious Queen of the Rosary, who from
the day she was invoked under this title has shown herself ever more ready to succor the Church and the Christian people in their need.

105
(123,
154,
Already on previous occasions we recalled such glories
and the striking triumphs secured over the Albigenses and
other powerful enemies, glories and triumphs which always

redound not only to the benefit of the persecuted and   *176)*
afflicted Church, but also to the temporal prosperity of
peoples and nations.

Why could not such marvels of power and goodness
on the part of the great Virgin be renewed in our present
needs in favor of the Church, her Head, and of the entire
Christian world, provided the faithful could on their part
renew the splendid examples of piety given them by their
forebears in similar circumstances?

And therefore, to render ever more propitious toward   **106**
Us this very powerful Queen, We intend to honor her   *(141)*
evermore under the invocation of the Rosary, and to
increase her cultus.

And thus, at the start of the present year We decreed
that the Solemnity of the Holy Rosary be raised to the rite
of "Double of the Second Class" for the whole Church.
For that same purpose we earnestly desire that the Catholic people of Italy with particular fervor of devotion at all
times, but more especially during the month of October
next, should address themselves fervently to her motherly
heart, beseeching her for the exaltation of the Church and
the Apostolic See, the liberty of Christ's Vicar on earth
and public peace and prosperity.

(*Conclusion.—Blessing.*)

THE SPOUSE OF THE BLESSED VIRGIN

Encycl. *Quamquam pluries,* August 15, 1889.

Although We have already many times ordered spe-   **107**
cial prayers to be offered in the whole world in order that   *(49,*
the interests of the Church be insistently recommended to   *124)*
God, none will think it surprising that We consider the
present moment opportune for again impressing this duty
on souls.

During periods of stress and trials, especially when the powers of darkness seem able to attempt the ruin of all for which Christianity stands, it has been the custom in the Church to plead with special fervor and perseverance to God, her Author and Protector, having also recourse to the intercession of the saints, and chiefly of the Blessed Virgin, the Mother of God, whose patronage has ever been the most efficacious. The fruit of these pious prayers and of the confidence placed in the divine goodness has always, sooner or later, been made apparent.

108
(168)   Now, Venerable Brethren, you know well the times in which we live. They are scarcely less deplorable for the Christian religion than were the days most full of misery to the Church in times past. We see faith, the root of all the Christian virtues, lessening in many souls; We see charity growing cold, youth growing corrupt in thought and act, the Church of Jesus Christ attacked on every side by open force or craft, a relentless war waged against the Sovereign Pontiff, and the very foundations of religion undermined with a boldness which grows daily more intense. These things are, indeed, so much a matter of common knowledge that it is needless for Us to expatiate on the depths to which society has sunk in these days, or on the designs which now occupy the minds of men. In circumstances so unhappy and difficult human remedies are insufficient, and all that remains is to beg for assistance from the divine Power.

109
(129,
134)   This is the reason why We have considered it necessary to turn to the Christian people and urge them to implore, with increased zeal and constancy, the aid of Almighty God. As the month of October draws near, already consecrated by Us to the Virgin Mary under the title of Our Lady of the Rosary, We earnestly exhort the faithful to perform the exercises of this month with even more piety and constancy than hitherto. We know that there is sure help in the maternal affection of the Blessed Virgin, and We are very certain

that We shall never place Our trust in her in vain. If on innumerable occasions she has displayed her power in aid of the Christian world, why should We doubt that she will now renew the assistance of her power and favor if humble and constant prayers are offered on all sides to her? Nay, We rather believe that her intervention will be the more marvelous as she has permitted Us to pray to her for so long a time with special appeals.

But We have another object, Venerable Brethren, which We know you will promote with your customary piety and fervor: in order that God may deign to accede to Our requests and mercifully and quickly hasten to the aid of His Church, We judge it to be of the greatest value that the Christian people should continually invoke with great piety and trust, together with the Virgin Mother of God, her chaste spouse, the blessed Joseph; and We regard it as most certain that this will be very pleasing to the Blessed Virgin herself. **110** *(175)*

(Devotion to St. Joseph.)

The motives for which St. Joseph has been proclaimed Patron especially of the Church—and for which the Church looks for singular benefit from his patronage and protection —are that Joseph was the spouse of Mary and that he was the putative father of Jesus Christ. From these relationships have sprung his dignity, his holiness, his glory. In truth, the dignity of the Mother of God is so lofty that no creature can rank above it. But as Joseph has been united to the Blessed Virgin by the ties of marriage, it may not be doubted that he approached nearer than any-one else to the eminent dignity by which the Mother of God so nobly surpasses all created natures. For marriage is the most intimate of all unions, which essentially imparts a community of gifts between those joined together by it. Thus, in giving Joseph the Blessed Virgin as spouse, God appointed him to be not only her life's companion, **111** *(113, 175)* the witness of her virginity, the protector of her honor, but also, by virtue of the conjugal tie, a participator in her sublime dignity.

(*St. Joseph, help and support of Jesus and Mary.*)

112
(33,
43)
Now the divine household which Joseph ruled with the authority of a father contained within it the beginnings of the Church. From the very fact that the most holy Virgin is the Mother of Jesus Christ, she is the Mother of all Christians, whom she bore on Mount Calvary in the supreme throes of the Redemption; and Jesus Christ is, in a manner, the First-Born of Christians, who by adoption and Redemption are His brothers.

For such reasons the blessed Patriarch looks upon the multitude of Christians who make up the Church as confided especially to his trust—this great family spread throughout the world, over which, because he is the spouse of Mary and the father of Jesus Christ, he holds, as it were, a paternal authority. It is, then, natural and fitting that as the blessed Joseph ministered to all the needs of the Family at Nazareth and surrounded it with his protection, he should now cover with the cloak of his heavenly patronage and defend the Church of Jesus Christ.

(*Patronage prefigured in Joseph of the Old Testament.—St. Joseph, model for fathers and workingmen.— Prayer to St. Joseph.*)

THE PERFECT MEDIATRIX

Encycl. *Octobri mense,* September 22, 1891.

(*Necessity of prayer.*)

113
(25,
37,
46)
The eternal Son of God, about to take upon Himself our nature for the saving and ennobling of man, and about to consummate thus a mystical union between Himself and all mankind, did not accomplish His design without obtain-

ing the free consent of her who was to become His Mother. She was the representative of all mankind, according to the illustrious and learned opinion of St. Thomas, who says that, "in the Annunciation was awaited the consent of the Virgin standing in the place of humanity" (a). With equal truth it may be said that of the great treasury of all graces given to us by Our Lord—"for grace and truth came by Jesus Christ"—nothing comes to us except through the mediation of Mary, for such is the will of God (b). Thus, as no man goes to the Father but by the Son, so no one goes to Christ except through His Mother (c).

Powerful and merciful intermediary

How great are the goodness and mercy revealed in this design of God! What a boon to the frailty of man! We believe in the infinite goodness of the Most High, and we rejoice in it; we believe also in His justice, and we fear it. We adore the beloved Savior who generously gave His blood and His life; but at the same time we dread the inexorable Judge. Thus do those whose actions have disturbed their consciences need an intercessor mighty in favor with God, merciful enough not to reject the cause of the desperate, merciful enough to lift up the afflicted and the broken to loving trust in the divine mercy. Mary is this glorious intermediary. She is the mighty Mother of God. But—what is still sweeter—she is gentle, exquisite in tenderness, and of a limitless love and kindness. As such God

114
(31,
35,
40,
82)

113a Summa Theologica, III, q. 30, a. 1. *Per annuntiationem exspectabatur consensus Virginis, loco totius humanæ naturæ.*

113b John 1:17.

113c *Ex quo non minus vere proprieque affirmare licet, nihil prorsus de permagno illo omnis gratiæ thesauro, quem attulit Dominus . . . , nihil nobis, nisi per Mariam, Deo sic volente, impertiri: ut, quo modo ad summum Patrem, nisi per Filium, nemo potest accedere, ita fere, nisi per Matrem, accedere nemo possit ad Christum.*

gave her to us. Having chosen her for the Mother of His only-begotten Son, He taught her all a mother's feelings that breathe nothing but pardon and love. Such Christ desired that she should be, for He consented to be subject to Mary and to obey her as a son does a mother. As such He proclaimed her from the cross when He entrusted to her care and love the whole of the race of man in the person of His disciple John. And as such does she prove herself by her courage in gathering the heritage of the enormous labors of her dying Son, in accepting freely the office of Mother towards us all.

Confidence of Christians in Mary

115
(29,
31,
37,
129)

The plan of this most loving mercy, realized by God in Mary and confirmed by the testament of Christ, was understood with the utmost joy by the holy Apostles and the earliest believers. It was the belief and teaching of the venerable Fathers of the Church. Christians of every generation received it with one mind; and even when literature and tradition are silent, there is a voice that breaks from every Christian heart and speaks with all eloquence. Nothing is needed other than divine faith which, by a most powerful and yet sweet impulse, moves us toward Mary. Nothing is more natural, nothing more desirable, than to seek a refuge in the protection and the loyalty of her to whom we may confess our designs and our actions, our innocence and our repentance, our torments and our joys, our prayers and our desires—all our interests. All men, moreover, are filled with the hope and the confidence that petitions which might be received with less favor from the lips of unworthy men, will be accepted by God when they are recommended by His most holy Mother, and will be favorably heard. The truth and the sweetness of these thoughts bring to the soul an unspeakable comfort. But they inspire all the more compassion for those who, being without divine faith, do not honor Mary and do not have her for their

Mother. And Our heart is sad because of those who, although of the household of the Faith, dare to accuse the devout of excessive or exaggerated veneration toward Mary, gravely offending thereby the filial piety of children toward their mother.

Urgency of recourse to Mary

This storm of evils in the midst of which the Church struggles so strenuously reveals to all her pious children the grave obligation which binds them to pray to God with perseverance and the way in which they may make their prayers more effective. Faithful to the example of our pious ancestors, let us have recourse to Mary, our holy Queen. Let us with one heart entreat and beseech Mary, the Mother of Jesus Christ and our Mother: "Show thyself to be a Mother; cause our prayers to be accepted by Him Who, born for us, consented to be thy Son" (a). **116**
(51)

Now, among the various devotional ways of paying honor to the Blessed Virgin, some are to be preferred, inasmuch as we know them to be most powerful and most pleasing to our Mother. For this reason we especially mention by name and recommend the Rosary. Common language has given the name "crown" to this manner of prayer, which recalls to our minds the great mysteries of Jesus and Mary united in joys, sorrows, and triumphs. The contemplation of these august mysteries, considered in their due order, gives to faithful souls a wonderful strengthening of faith, protects them against error, and fortifies their souls. The thoughts and memories of those who thus pray, enlightened by Faith, are drawn toward these mysteries by the sweetest sentiments of devotion, are absorbed in wonder at the work of the Redemption of mankind, achieved at such a price and by such great acts. **117**
(147)

116a Hymn *Ave Maris Stella*, verse 4.

118
(147)
The soul is filled with gratitude and love before these proofs of divine love; its hope is strengthened and its desire is increased for those things which Christ has prepared for such as have united themselves to Him in imitation of His example and by participation in His sufferings. The prayer is composed of words proceeding from God Himself, from the Archangel Gabriel, and from the Church, full of praise and high desires; and it is renewed and continued in an order at once fixed and various; its fruits are an ever new and loving devotion.

Victories of the Rosary

119
(122,
123,
146,
148)
Moreover, we may well believe that the Queen of Heaven herself has granted a special efficacy to this mode of supplication, for it was by her command and counsel that the devotion was begun and spread abroad by the holy Patriarch Dominic as a most powerful weapon against the enemies of the Faith in an epoch not unlike our own and, indeed, of great danger to our holy religion. The heresy of the Albigenses had both covertly and openly penetrated many countries; and this evil offspring of the Manichaeans, whose deadly errors it reproduced, was the cause of stirring up against the Church the most bitter animosity and virulent persecution. There seemed to be no human hope of opposing this fanatical and most pernicious sect when timely succor came from on high by means of Mary's Rosary. Thus under the favor of the powerful Virgin, the glorious conqueror of all heresies, the forces of the wicked were overthrown and destroyed, and the faith of many was insured.

120
(126,
146,
148,
154)
All kinds of similar instances are widely recorded, and both ancient and modern history furnish remarkable proofs of nations saved from peril and winning blessings from its use. There is another striking argument in favor of this devotion: from the moment of its institution it was quickly welcomed and used by all classes of society. In truth, the

piety of the Christian people honors by many titles and in multiform ways the Mother of God, who alone among all creatures has the glory of such exalted prerogatives. But this title of the Rosary, this form of prayer which seems to contain a final pledge of affection, and which epitomizes in itself the honor due to our Lady, has always been highly cherished and widely used in private and in public, in homes and in families, in the meetings of confraternities, at the dedication of shrines, and in solemn processions. Indeed there seems to be no better means of conducting sacred solemnities, or of obtaining protection and favors.

The Rosary satisfies the needs of the Christian soul.

Nor may We permit to pass unnoticed the special providence of God displayed in this devotion. For through the lapse of time religious fervor has sometimes seemed to diminish in certain nations, and even this pious method of prayer has fallen into disuse; but piety and devotion have again flourished and become vigorous in a most marvelous manner when, through either the grave condition of the state or through some pressing public necessity, general recourse has been had—more to this than to other means of obtaining help—to the Rosary, so restoring it to its place of honor. But there is no need to seek for examples of this in past ages, since we have in the present times an outstanding instance of it.

In these times—so troublous (as We have said before) for the Church, and so heart-rending for Us—called by Divine Providence to govern her, it is still given Us to note with admiration the great zeal and fervor with which Mary's Rosary is honored and recited in every place and nation of the Catholic world. And this circumstance, which assuredly is to be attributed to the divine inspiration and direction of men, rather than to the wisdom and efforts of individuals, strengthens and consoles Our heart, filling Us

121
(146)

with great hope for the ultimate and most glorious triumph of the Church under the patronage of Mary.

(*The efficacy of prayer: even when God seems to put
off hearing us, and even when injustice seems to triumph.
—Penance and prayer.—Exhortation* [a].)

POWER AND BOUNTY OF MARY

Encycl. *Magnæ Dei Matris,* September 8, 1892.

122
(76,
125,
126,
158)

As often as the occasion arises to stimulate and intensify the love and veneration of the Christian people for
Mary, the great Mother of God, We are filled with wondrous satisfaction and joy, both because the matter is of
prime importance in itself and profitable in countless ways,
and because it perfectly accords with the inmost sentiments of Our heart. For the holy reverence for Mary which
We experienced from Our tenderest years has grown
greater and has taken firmer hold of Our soul with
advancing age.

As time went on, it became more and more evident
how deserving of love and honor was she whom God
Himself was the first to love, and to love so much more
than any other that, after elevating her high above all the
rest of His creation and adorning her with His richest gifts,
He made her His Mother. The many and splendid proofs
of her bounty and kindness toward Us, which We remember with deep gratitude and which move Us to tears,
still further encourage and strongly inflame Our filial
reverence for her. Throughout the many dreadful events
of every kind which the times have brought forth, always
with her have We sought refuge, always to her have We
lifted up pleading and confident eyes. And in all the
hopes and fears, the joys and sorrows, that We confided

121a Cf. ahead, No. 309.

to her, the thought was constantly before Us of asking her
to assist Us at all times as Our gracious Mother and to
obtain this greatest of favors; that We might be able, in
return, to show her the heart of a most devoted son.

When, then, it came to pass in the secret design of **123**
God's providence that We were chosen to fill this Chair *(50,*
of St. Peter and to take the place of the Person of Christ *108,*
Himself in the Church, worried by the enormous burden *158)*
of the office and finding no ground for reliance in Our own
strength, We hastened with fervent zeal to implore the
divine aid through the maternal intercession of the ever
blessed Virgin. Never has our hope, We are happy to acknowledge, at any time of Our life but more especially
since We began to exercise the Supreme Apostolate, failed
to bear fruit or bring Us comfort. Thus encouraged, Our
hope today rises more confidently than ever to beseech
many more and even greater blessings through her favor
and mediation, such as will profit alike the salvation of
Christ's flock and the greater glory of His Church.

It is, therefore, a fitting and opportune time, Venerable
Brethren, for Us to urge all Our children—exhorting them
through you—to prepare to celebrate the coming month of
October, consecrated to our Lady as the august Queen of
the Rosary, with the fervent and wholehearted devotion
which the necessities weighing upon Us demand.

(*Present evils: ignorance, error, vices.—The remedy.*)

Now, to appease the offended majesty of God and to   **124**
bring that health of soul so needed by those who are sorely *(146)*
afflicted, there is nothing better than devout and persevering prayer, provided it be joined with a love for and
practice of Christian life. And both the spirit of prayer
and the practice of Christian life are best attained through
the devotion of the Rosary of Mary.

The well-known origin of the Rosary, illustrated in   **125**
celebrated monuments of which we have made frequent   *(123,*

(135,
148)

mention, bears witness to its remarkable efficacy. For, in the days when the Albigensian sect, posing as the champion of pure faith and morals, but in reality introducing the worst kind of anarchy and corruption, brought many a nation to its utter ruin, the Church fought against it and the other infamous factions associated with it, not with troops and arms, but chiefly with the power of the most holy Rosary, the devotion which the Mother of God taught to our Father Dominic, in order that he might propagate it. By this means the Church triumphed magnificently over every obstacle and provided for the salvation of her children not only in that trial but in others like it afterward, always with the same glorious success. For this reason, now, when human affairs have taken the course which We deplore, bringing affliction to the Church and ruin to the State, all of us have the duty to unite our voice in prayer, with like devotion, to the holy Mother of God, beseeching her that we too may rejoice, as we ardently desire, in experiencing the same power of her Rosary.

Titles by which we invoke Mary
when asking her to hear our prayers

126
(39,
40,
47)

When we have recourse to Mary in prayer, we are having recourse to the Mother of mercy, who is so well disposed toward us that, whatever the necessity that presses upon us, especially in attaining eternal life, she is instantly at our side of her own accord, even though she has not been invoked. She dispenses grace with a generous hand from that treasure with which from the beginning she was divinely endowed in fullest abundance that she might be worthy to be the Mother of God. By the fullness of grace which confers on her the most illustrious of her many titles, the Blessed Virgin is infinitely superior to all the hierarchies of men and angels, the creature who is closest of all to Christ. "It is a great thing in any saint to have grace sufficient for the salvation of many souls; but to have enough to suffice for the salvation of everybody in the world is the greatest of all; and this is found in Christ and in the Blessed Virgin" (a).

It is impossible to say how pleasing and gratifying to her it is when we greet her with the Angelic Salutation, "full of grace"; and in repeating it do we not fashion these words of praise into a crown of devotion for her. For every time we say them, we recall the memory of her exalted dignity and of the redemption of the human race which God began through her. We likewise bring to mind the divine and everlasting bond which links her with the joys and sorrows, the humiliations and triumphs of Christ in directing and helping mankind to eternal life.

It pleased Christ to take upon Himself the nature of man, and to become thereby our Brother, in order that His mercy to us might be shown most openly; for "it behooved Him in all things to be made like unto His brethren that He might become a merciful and faithful high priest before God" (a). Likewise because Mary was chosen to be the Mother of Christ, our Lord and our Brother, the unique prerogative was given her above all other mothers to show her mercy to us and to pour it out upon us (b).

Besides, as we are debtors to Christ for sharing in some way with us the right, peculiarly His own, of calling God "Father" and possessing Him as such, we are in like manner indebted to Him for His loving generosity in sharing with us the right to call Mary "Mother" and to cherish her as such.

127
(22, 39, 41)

128
(29, 31, 40)

126a St. Thomas Aquinas, *Super Salut. Ang.*, c. I.
127a Hebr. 2:17.
127b *Mariæ non aliter, ex eo quod Christi Domini ejusdemque fratris nostri electa est mater, hoc supra matres omnes singulare inditum est, ut misericordiam nobis proderet, effunderet suam.*

While nature itself made the name of mother the sweetest of all names and has made motherhood tne very model of tender and careful love, no tongue is eloquent enough to put in words what every devout soul feels, namely, how intense is the flame of affectionate and eager charity which glows in Mary, in her who is truly our mother, not by nature but by the will of Christ.

129
(47,
83,
128)
Nobody knows and comprehends so well as she everything that concerns us: what help we need in life; what dangers, public and private, threaten our welfare; what difficulties and evils surround us; above all, how fierce is the fight we wage with the ruthless enemies of our salvation. In these and in all other troubles of life her power is most far-reaching. She has the most ardent desire to bring consolation, strength, and help to every race of children so dear to her.

Accordingly, let us approach Mary confidently, wholeheartedly beseeching her by her motherhood which unites her so closely to Jesus and at the same time to us. Let us with deepest devotion invoke her constant aid in the prayer which she herself has indicated and which is most acceptable to her. Then with good reason shall we rest with an easy and joyful mind under the protection of the best of mothers.

The Rosary nourishes Faith

130
(147)
To this commendation of the Rosary which follows from the very nature of the prayer, We may add that the Rosary offers an easy way to penetrate the chief mysteries of the Christian religion and to impress them upon the mind.

(Faith in Christian life.)

131
(25,
100,
101)
To ward off the exceedingly great dangers of ignorance from her children, the Church, which never relaxes her vigilant and diligent care, has been in the habit of looking for the staunchest support of faith in the Rosary of Mary.

And indeed in the Rosary with the most beautiful and efficacious prayers arranged in an orderly pattern the chief mysteries of our religion follow one another, as they are brought before our mind for contemplation. First come the mysteries in which the Word was made flesh and Mary, the inviolate Virgin and Mother, performed her maternal duties for Him with a holy joy; then come the sorrows, the agony and death of the suffering Christ, the price at which the salvation of our race was accomplished; finally follow the mysteries full of His glory: His triumph over death, the Ascension into heaven, the sending of the Holy Spirit, the resplendent brightness of Mary assumed into heaven, and finally the everlasting glory of all the saints in heaven united with the glory of the Mother and of the Son.

This sequence of wonderful events the Rosary fre- **132** quently and constantly recalls to the minds of the faithful, *(148)* and presents them almost as though they were unfolding before our eyes, thus flooding the souls of those who devoutly recite it with a sweetness of piety that never grows weary, impressing and stirring them as though they were listening to the very voice of the Blessed Mother explaining the mysteries and conversing with them at length about their salvation.

It will not, then, seem too much to say that in places and nations in which the Rosary of Mary retains its ancient honor the loss of faith through ignorance and vicious error need not be feared.

Another and not smaller advantage which the Church **133** earnestly seeks for her children from the Rosary is the faith- *(147)* ful regulation of their lives and their conduct in keeping with the rules and precepts of their holy religion. For if, as we all know from Holy Scripture, "faith without works is dead" (a)—because faith draws its life from charity and charity flowers forth in a profusion of holy actions—then

133a St. James 2:17.

the Christian will gain nothing for eternal life from his faith unless his life be ordered in accordance with what faith prescribes. "What shall it profit, my brethren, if a man say he hath faith, but hath not works? Shall faith be able to save him?" (b) A man of this sort will incur a much heavier rebuke from Christ the Judge than those who are, unfortunately, ignorant of the Christian faith and its teaching: they, unlike the former, who believe one thing and practice another, have some excuse or at least are less blameworthy, because they lack the light of the Gospel.

(*Savior's mysteries and Christian life.*)

A model at hand

134
(130, 136)
But lest we be dismayed by the consciousness of our native weakness and grow faint when confronted with the unattainable example which Christ, who is Man and at the same time God, has given, along with mysteries which portray Him, we have before our eyes for contemplation the mysteries of His most holy Mother.

135
(82, 113)
She was born, it is true, of the royal family of David, but she fell heir to none of the wealth and grandeur of her ancestors. She passed her life in obscurity, and in a humble town, in a home humbler still, the more content with her retirement and the poverty of her home because they left her freer to lift up her heart to God and to cling to Him closely as the Supreme Goodness for which her heart yearned.

136
(79, 82)
The Lord is with her whom He has filled with His grace and made blessed. The heavenly messenger sent to her points her out as the Virgin from whom, by the power of the Holy Ghost, the expected Savior of nations is to come forth clothed in our humanity. The more she wonders at the sublime dignity and gives thanks to the power

133b *Ibid.,* 14.

and mercy of God, the more does she, conscious of no merit
in herself, grow in humility, promptly proclaiming and
consecrating herself as the handmaid of God even while
she becomes His Mother. Her sacred promise was as sa-
credly kept with a joyous heart; henceforth she leads a
life in perpetual union with her Son Jesus, sharing with
Him His joys and sorrows.

It is thus that she will reach a height of glory granted
to no other creature, whether human or angelic, because no
one will be able to be compared to her in virtue and in merit; it is thus that she will be Queen of heaven and of earth
for she will be the invincible Queen of Martyrs..It is thus
that she will be seated in the heavenly city of God, by
the side of her Son, crowned for all eternity, because she
will drink with Him the cup overflowing with sorrow,
faithfully through all her life, most faithfully on Calvary.

137
(80,
85,
86,
101,
104)

In Mary we see how a truly good and provident God
has established for us a most suitable example for every
virtue. As we look upon her and think about her we
are not cast down as though striken by the overpowering
splendor of God's power; but, on the contrary, we are attracted by the closeness of the common nature we share
with her, and we strive with greater confidence to imitate
her (a). If we, with such powerful help, should dedicate
ourselves wholly and entirely to this undertaking, we will
be able at least to approach such great virtue and sanctity,
and, reproducing that perfect conformity of life to all God's
designs which she possessed in so marvelous a degree, we
shall follow her into heaven.

138
(82,
126,
130,
131)

138a *Ecce autem in Maria virtutis omnis exemplar vere
bonus et providens Deus constituit nobis aptissimum: eam-
que oculis et cogitatione intuentes, non animos quasi divini
numinis fulgore perstricti, despondemus, sed ex ipsa allecti
communis propinquitate naturæ, fidentius ad imitationem
enitimur.*

139
(125,
130)
    Undaunted and full of courage, let us go on with the pilgrimage we have undertaken even though the way be rough and full of obstacles. Amid the vexation and toil let us not cease to hold out suppliant hands to Mary with the words of the Church: "To thee do we send up our sighs, mourning and weeping in this valley of tears. Turn thine eyes of mercy upon us." Grant us a pure life, open for us the sure and safe way, that we may rejoice with thee in the contemplation of Jesus forever in heaven (a).

140
(34,
74,
134)
    And Mary, without having herself experienced them, yet who knows our weakness and the defects of our fallen nature, she who is the best and most devoted of mothers, how quickly and generously she will come to our aid! with what tenderness she will comfort us! with what strength support us! Travelling the road which the divine Blood of Christ and Mary's tears have consecrated, we are certain to attain without trouble to a share in her blessed glory.

(The Rosary commended.—Indulgences granted.)

141
(124,
158)
    We ask Our Christian people to bring their supplications to the altar, to pray for the Church storm-tossed and contradicted, to pray for Us, who advanced in years, worn out by vexations, in the throes of the gravest difficulties, stripped of all human security, hold fast the rudder of the Church.

142
(158)
    Every day Our hope grows greater in Mary, Our powerful and tender Mother. To Us she becomes sweeter and sweeter. If We have received from God numerous and special favors, to her We attribute with singular gratitude the joy of anticipating the near approach of the fiftieth anniversary of Our episcopal ordination.

(Thanksgiving, well wishes, blessing.)

139a *Salve Regina* and *Ave Maris Stella.*

GUARDIAN OF FAITH

Letter *Perhibenti quidem,* to the Bishops of Mexico, August 2, 1894.

We have thought it good to accede gladly to your unanimous request that We enhance with additions proper to your dioceses the office that Our illustrious Predecessor, Benedict XIV, granted in honor of the Blessed Virgin Mary of Guadalupe, sovereign patroness of your country. In fact, We know what close union exists between the cultus of the Mother of God and the birth and development of the Christian faith among Mexicans; since its beginning, as well as in its history a succession of remarkable favors have followed on the veneration of that image of Mary. We know, too, with what devotion you venerate her most august shrine of Tepeyac and what efforts you are making to restore it, to enlarge it and to give it new splendor. Countless pious crowds come on pilgrimage from every section of the Republic. These same motives led Us some years ago to direct that in Our name and authority the august image of our Queen be crowned with a golden diadem.

143
(160, 172)

We are pleased, beloved Brethren, to recall that; We have also wished to show by a special token the joy which the excellent harmony existing in the episcopal body and between clergy and people gives Us; that harmony continues to strengthen the ties uniting you with the Apostolic See.

144
(135, 160)

Since you yourselves are aware that the author and guardian of that harmony is the good and gracious Mother of God, venerated in your country under the title of Our Lady of Guadalupe, through you We exhort the Mexican people with keen affection to preserve the respect and love of the Virgin of Guadalupe, a title of glory for her and the source of most precious favors.

145
(125)
First, in regard to your Catholic faith, that excellent good surpassing all others, but in Our time the object of more attacks than are other beliefs, look upon it as certain and absolutely proven that, as long as that devotion reigns among you, that faith will remain always intact and solid and worthy of the faith of your forefathers.

Let all, therefore, venerate and love that most powerful Patroness with an ardor that grows without ceasing; may favors of every kind through her propitious intercession shower down on you and assure you of safety and peace.

THE PRACTICE OF MEDIATION

Encycl. *"Jucunda semper,"* September 8, 1894.

146
(124,
126,
146)
It is always with joyful expectation and inspired hope that We look forward to the return of the month of October. At our exhortation and by Our express order, this month has been consecrated to the Blessed Virgin, during which for some years now the devotion of her Rosary has been practiced with sedulous earnestness by the Catholic people throughout the world. Our reasons for making the exhortation we have made known more than once. For as the sad conditions affecting both the Church and civil society proved to Us the extreme necessity for signal aid from God, it was manifest to Us that that aid should be sought through the intercession of His Mother, and by the express means of the Rosary, which Christians have ever found to be of marvelous value.

147
(146,
148)
This indeed has been well proved since the very institution of the devotion, both in the vindication of our Holy Faith against the furious attacks of heresy, and in the restoration to honor of the virtues which, by reason of the corruption of the age, needed to be rekindled and sustained. And this same proof was continued in all succeeding ages,

by a never failing series of private and public benefits, the illustrious remembrance of which is everywhere perpetuated and immortalized by monuments and public institutions.

In our age, likewise, afflicted with a tempest of various evils, it is a joy to our soul to relate the beneficent influence of the Rosary. Notwithstanding all this, you yourselves, Venerable Brethren, behold with your own eyes the persistence—yea the increase—of renewing again this year Our Summons to the faithful to turn with increased ardor in prayer to Mary, the Queen of Heaven.

Moreover, the more we fix our thoughts upon the character of the Rosary, the clearer its excellence and power appear to Us. Hence, while Our wish increases that it may flourish, Our hope grows that through Our encouragement it may come to be more greatly prized, and its holy use become more extended and flourish more abundantly. **148** *(40, 135, 145, 146)*

We shall not now return to the various instructions which in past years we have given upon this subject. We shall take instead the opportunity of pointing out the particular ruling and designs of Providence, which ordain that the Rosary should have new power to instill confidence into the hearts of those who pray, and new influence to move the compassionate Heart of our Mother to comfort and generously help us.

The Mediation of Mary in the Joyful Mysteries

The recourse we have to Mary in prayer follows upon the office she continuously fills by the side of the throne of God as Mediatrix of divine grace, being by worthiness and by merit more acceptable to Him, and for that reason surpassing in power all the angels and saints in heaven. Now, this merciful office of hers appears perhaps in no other form of prayer as manifestly as it does in the Rosary. For in the Rosary the part that Mary took as our Coredemptrix is set before us, as though the facts were even **149** *(39, 40, 45, 49)* then taking place. And this affords great profit to our piety, both in the contemplation of the successive sacred mysteries, and in the prayers which we enunciate.

150
(144)
First come the joyful mysteries; the Eternal Son of God stoops to mankind, putting on its nature, with the assent of Mary who conceives Him by the Holy Ghost. Then St. John the Baptist, by a singular privilege, is sanctified in his mother's womb (a) and favored with special graces, that he may prepare the way of the Lord; and this comes to pass by the greeting of Mary, who had been inspired to visit her cousin. At last the Expected of Nations (b) comes to light, Christ the Savior. The Virgin bears Him. And when the shepherds and the Wise Men, the first fruits of the Christian faith, come with longing to His cradle, they find the young Child with Mary His Mother (c). Then, that He may offer Himself as a Victim to His heavenly Father, He desires to be taken to the Temple, and by the hands of Mary He is there "presented to the Lord" (d). And Mary, in the mysterious losing of her Son, seeks Him sorrowing and finds Him again with joy.

. . . in the Sorrowful Mysteries

151
(42,
44,
144)
And the same truth is told again in the sorrowful mysteries. In the Garden of Gethsemani, where Jesus undergoes His agony, in the judgment hall, where He is scourged, crowned with thorns, condemned to death, we do not find Mary. But she knew beforehand all these agonies; she knew and saw them. When she professed herself the handmaid of the Lord for the mother's office, and when, at the foot of the altar, she offered up her whole self with her Child Jesus—then and thereafter she took her part in the painful

150a Cf. Luke 1:31-76.
150b Cf. Gen. 49:10.
150c Matth. 2:11.
150d Luke 2:22.

expiation offered by her Son for the sins of the world. It is certain, therefore, that she suffered in the very depths of her soul with His most bitter sufferings and with His torments. Finally, it was before the eyes of Mary that the divine Sacrifice for which she had borne and nurtured the Victim was to be finished. As we contemplate Him in the last and most piteous of these mysteries, we see that "there stood by the cross of Jesus Mary His Mother" (a), who, in a miracle of love, so that she might receive us as her sons, offered generously to Divine Justice her own Son, and in her Heart died with Him, stabbed by the sword of sorrow.

And in the Glorious Mysteries

Thence the Rosary takes us on to the glorious mysteries, wherein also is revealed the mediation of the great Virgin, still more abundant in fruitfulness. She rejoices in heart over the glory of her Son, triumphant over death, and follows Him with a Mother's love in His Ascension to His eternal Kingdom. But, though worthy of heaven, she abides a while on earth, so that the infant Church may be directed and comforted by her "who penetrated, beyond all belief, into the deep secrets of divine wisdom" (a). **152**
(144)

Nevertheless, for the fulfillment of the task of human redemption there remains still the coming of the Holy Spirit, as promised by Christ. And behold, Mary is in the room; there, praying with the Apostles and entreating for them with sighs and tears, she hastens for the Church the coming of the Spirit, the Comforter, the supreme Gift of Christ, the Treasure that will never fail. And later, in a complete and permanent way, she will be able to plead our cause when she will have passed into life eternal. Therefore we behold her taken up from this valley of tears into **153**
(48,
101,
102,
117)

151a John 19:25.
152a St. Bernard. *De Duod. prærog. B.M.V.*, n. 3.

the heavenly Jerusalem amid the choirs of angels. And we honor her, glorified above all saints, crowned with stars by her Divine Son, and seated at His side, the sovereign Queen of the universe.

154
(52,
144)
If in all this series of mysteries, Venerable Brethren, are developed the counsels of God in regard to us—"counsels of wisdom and of tenderness" (a)—not less apparent is the greatness of the benefits for which we are debtors to the Virgin Mother. No one can meditate upon these without feeling a new awakening in his heart of confidence that he will certainly obtain through Mary the fullness of the mercies of God.

Riches of the Rosary

155
(46,
47,
136)
To this end vocal prayer harmonizes with the mysteries. First, as is fitting and right, comes the Lord's Prayer, addressed to Our Father in heaven. Having, with the petitions dictated by our divine Master, called upon the Father, from the throne of His Majesty, we turn our prayerful voices to Mary. Thus is confirmed that law of merciful mediation of which we have spoken, and which St. Bernardine of Siena thus expresses: "Every grace granted to man has three successive steps: By God it is communicated to Christ, from Christ it passes to the Virgin, and from the Virgin it descends to us" (a). And we, by the very form of the Rosary, do linger longest and as it were, by preference upon the last and lowest of these steps; repeating by decades the Angelic Salutation, so that with greater confidence we may thence attain to the higher degrees—that is, may rise, by means of Christ, to the divine Father.

156
(47,
For if we thus again and again greet Mary, it is precisely that our failing and defective prayers may be

154a St. Bernard, *Serm. in Nativitate B.M.V.* n. 6.
155a Serm. 6, n. 1., *in Fest.* B.M.V. a. I., c. 2.

strengthened with the necessary confidence; confidence
which rises in us in thinking that Mary more than praying
for us prays to God in our name.

    Nor can our prayers fail to ascend to Him as a sweet
savor when commended by the prayers of the Virgin. For
He, all benign, invites her: "Let thy voice sound in my
ears: for thy voice is sweet" (a). For this cause do we repeatedly celebrate those glorious titles of her ministry as
Mediatrix. Her do we greet who found favor with God (b);
who was in a signal manner filled with grace (c) by Him
so that the superabundance thereof might overflow upon all men; who was united with the Lord by the most
intimate of all bonds; who was blessed among women (d);
and who "alone took away the curse and bore the blessing" (e)—that Fruit of her womb, that happy Fruit in
which all the nations of the earth are blessed (f). Her, do
we invoke finally as Mother of God, and in virtue of a
dignity so sublime, what graces from her may we not
promise to ourselves, sinners though we are, in life and in
the agonies of death.

    A soul that shall devoutly repeat these prayers, that
shall ponder with faith these mysteries, will, without doubt,
be filled with wonder at the divine purposes of this great
Virgin and in the work of the restoration of mankind.
Doubtless this soul, moved by a warmth of love and of
confidence toward her, will desire to take refuge in her
maternal heart, as was the sweet feeling of St. Bernard:
"Remember, O most loving Virgin Mary, that never was it
known that anyone who fled to thy protection, implored
thy help and sought thy intercession, was left unaided."

*52,
126,
173)*

*157
(135,
170)*

156a Cant. 2:14.
156b Luke 1:30.
156c Luke 1:28.
156d Luke 1:28.
156e St. Thomas Aquinas, *Super Salut. angel,* n. 8.
156f Cf. Gen. 18:18.

The Rosary causes Mary to bestow her mercies upon us

158
(143,
146)

The fruits of the Rosary appear likewise and in equal measure, in the turning with mercy of the heart of the Mother of God toward us. How sweet a happiness must it be for her to see us all intent upon the task of weaving for her crowns of devout prayers and lovely praises! And if, indeed, by those prayers we desire to render to God the glory which is His due, if we protest that we seek nothing whatsoever except the fulfillment in us of His holy will; if we magnify His goodness and graciousness; if we call Him our Father; if we, being most unworthy, yet entreat of Him His best blessings—oh! how shall Mary rejoice in all these things! How shall she magnify the Lord!

There is no language so fit to lead us to the majesty of God as the language of the Lord's Prayer.

159
(40,
142,
146)

Furthermore to each of these things for which we pray—things that are righteous and ordered, and in harmony with Christian faith, hope and charity—is added a special joy for the Blessed Virgin. With our voices she seems to hear also the voice of her divine Son who with His own mouth taught us this prayer, and by His own authority commanded it, saying:"Thus therefore shall you pray" (a). And seeing how we observe that command in saying our Rosary, she will bend toward us with more loving solicitude. The mystical crowns we offer her will be welcome to her, and productive of graces to our soul.

(*Another fruit of the Rosary.—Meditation of the mysteries keeps our attention alive.*)

160
(39,
40,
143,

And yet another title of joy and of acceptation in her eyes do our crowns of prayers acquire. For every time we look once more with devotional remembrance upon these mysteries, we give her a sign of the gratitude of our hearts,

159a Matt. 6:9.

we prove to her that we cannot often enough call to   *146)*
mind the blessings of her unwearied charity in the work
of our salvation. From such recollections, which with the
frequency of love we awoke in her presence, who may
express, who may ever conceive, whatever new joys overflow her ever blessed soul, and what tender affections of
mercy, and of a mother's love arise therein?

Besides these recollections, moreover, as the Sacred   **161**
Mysteries pass by, they cause our prayers to be transformed   *(39,*
into impulses of entreaty that have an indescribable power   *80,*
over the heart of Mary. Yes, we fly to thee, we miserable   *134)*
children of Eve, Oh! holy Mother of God; to thee, we
lift our prayers, for thou, powerful and merciful, are the
Mediatrix of our salvation. Oh! by the sweetness of the
joys that came to thee from thy sweet Son Jesus, by thy
participation in His ineffable Sorrows, by the splendors of
His Glory shining in thee, we earnestly beseech thee, listen, have pity on us, hear us, unworthy though we be!

Opportunity of the Rosary

Thus the excellence of the Rosary, considered under   **162**
the double aspect we have here set forth, will convince   *(135,*
you, Venerable Brethren, of the reasons We have for Our   *146,*
unremitting eagerness to commend and to promote it. At   *147)*
the present day, and on this We have already touched—
there is a signal need of special help from heaven, particularly manifest in the many tribulations suffered by the
Church in her liberties and her rights, and also in the perils
whereby the prosperity of Christian society is fundamen-
tally threatened. So it is that it belongs to Our office to
assert once again that We place our best hope in the holy
Rosary, inasmuch as more than any other means it can
implore from God the help that We need.

It is Our ardent wish that this devotion shall be
restored to a place of honor in the city and in the village,
in the family and in the workshop, in the noble's house and

in the peasant's, that it be to all a dear devotion and a
noble sign of their faith; that it be a sure way to the gaining
of the favor of pardon.

(*Reason for praying with greater fervor.—The recent
outrages perpetrated against our Lord Jesus Christ.*)

163
(38,
47)
This is a further motive for the enkindling, in private
and in common prayer, throughout the coming month of
October, of a holy emulation in celebrating and honoring
the Mother of God, the mighty helper of Christian people,
the most glorious Queen of Heaven. For Our own part,
We confirm with all Our heart the favors and indulgences
We have already awarded in this connection.

Now may God, who in His most merciful providence
gave us this Mediatrix (a) "and decreed that all good
should come to us by the hands of Mary" (b) receive propi-
tiously our common prayers and fulfill our common hopes.

PRAYER FOR OUR ENGLISH BRETHREN

Encycl. *Amantissimæ Voluntatis,* April 14, 1895.

(*Letter to the English people on the occasion of the
anniversary of the mission of St. Augustine of Canterbury.*)

164
(32,
42,
122,
171)
O Blessed Virgin Mary, Mother of God and our most
gentle Queen and Mother, look down in mercy upon England, thy Dowry, and upon us all who greatly hope and
trust in thee. By thee it was that Jesus, Our Savior and our
hope, was given unto the world. He has given thee to us
that we may hope still more. Plead for us thy children,
whom thou didst receive and accept at the foot of the
Cross, O sorrowful Mother. Intercede for our separated
brethren, that with us in the One True Fold they may be
united to the Chief Shepherd, the Vicar of thy Son. Pray

163a St. Bernard, *De XII prærogativis B.M.V.,* n. 2.
163b St. Bernard, *Sermo in nativ.* B.M.V., n. 7.

for us all, dear Mother, that by faith fruitful in good works
we may be counted worthy to see and praise God, together
with thee in our heavenly home. Amen.

THE MOTHER OF CHRISTIAN UNITY

Encycl. *Adiutricem populi,* September 5, 1895.

The mightiest helper of the Christian people, and the **165**
most merciful is the Virgin Mother of God. How fitting it *(121,*
is to accord her honors ever increasing in splendor, and *151)*
call upon her aid with a confidence daily growing more
ardent. The abundant blessings, infinitely varied and constantly multiplying, which flow from her all over the world
for the common benefit of mankind, add fresh motives for
invoking and honoring her.

For such magnanimous favors, Catholics on their part
have not failed to return to her the tender devotion of
grateful hearts; for, if ever there was a time when love
and veneration of the Blessed Virgin were awakened to
new life and inflaming every class of society, it is in these
days so bitterly anti-religious. The clearest evidence of this
fact lies in the sodalities which have everywhere been
restored and multiplied under her patronage; in the magnificent temples erected to her august name; in the pilgrimages undertaken by throngs of devout souls to her most
venerated shrines; in the congresses whose deliberations are
devoted to the increase of her glory; in other things of a
like nature which are praiseworthy in themselves and
augur well for the future.

It is specially deserving of notice, and it gives Us the **166**
greatest pleasure to recall, that of all the forms of devotion *(142)*
to the Blessed Virgin, that most excellent method of
prayer, Mary's Rosary, is establishing itself most widely
in popular esteem and practice. This, We repeat, is a source
of great joy to Us. If We have spent so large a share of
Our activities in promoting the Rosary Devotion, We can

easily see with what benevolence the Queen of Heaven has come to Our aid when We prayed to her; and We express the confident conviction that she will continue to stand at Our side to lighten the burdens and afflictions which the days to come will bring.

To establish Christian unity

167
(148,
171)

It is mainly to extend the Kingdom of Christ that we look to the Rosary for the most effective help. On many occasions We have declared that the object which at the present time engrosses Our most earnest attention, is the reconciliation to the Church of nations which have become separated from her. We recognize, at the same time, that the realization of Our hopes must be sought chiefly in prayer and supplications addressed to Almighty God. This conviction We again affirmed not long ago, when We recommended that special prayers be offered for this intention to the Holy Ghost during the solemnities of Pentecost; a recommendation that was adopted everywhere with the greatest good will.

But in view of the importance and the difficulty of such an undertaking, and the necessity of perseverance in the practice of any virtue, it is well to recall the Apostle's apt counsel: "Be constant in prayer" (a)—counsel all the more to the point because an auspicious beginning of the enterprise will supply the best inducement to perseverance in prayer. Next October, therefore, if you and your people devoutly spend the whole month with Us in praying assiduously to the Virgin Mother of God through her Rosary and the other customary devotions, nothing could do more to further this project or be more pleasing to Us. We have the best reasons for entrusting our plans and our aspirations to her protection and the highest hopes of seeing them realized.

167a Col. 4:2.

The Source: Spiritual Motherhood

The mystery of Christ's immense love for us is revealed **168**
with dazzling brilliance in the fact that the dying Savior (29,
bequeathed His Mother to His disciple John in the memor- 32,
able testament: "Behold thy son" (a). Now in John as the 116,
Church has constantly taught, Christ designated the whole 121)
human race, and in the first rank are they who are joined
with Him by faith. It is in this sense that St. Anselm of
Canterbury states:—"What dignity, O Virgin, could be
more highly prized than to be the Mother of those to
whom Christ deigned to be Father and Brother!" (b)

With a generous heart Mary undertook and discharged
the duties of her high but laborious office, the beginnings
of which were consecrated in the Cenacle. With wonderful
care she nurtured the first Christians by her holy example,
her authoritative counsel, her sweet consolation, her fruitful
prayers. She was, in very truth, the Mother of the Church,
the Teacher and Queen of the Apostles, to whom, besides,
she confided no small part of the divine mysteries "which
she kept in her heart" (c).

It is impossible to measure the power and scope of her **169**
offices since the day she was taken up to that height of (33,
heavenly glory in the company of her Son, to which the 46,
dignity and luster of her merits entitle her. From her heav- 121)
enly abode, she began, by God's decree, to watch over the
Church, to assist and befriend us as our Mother; so that
she who was so intimately associated with the mystery of
human salvation is just as closely associated with the distribution of the graces which from all time will flow from
the Redemption (a).

168a John 19:26.
168b Or. 47, olim 46.
168c Luke 2:19, 51.
169a *Ad hæc vero dici vix potest quantum amplitudinis vir-*
tutisque tunc accesserit, cum ad fastigium cælestis gloriæ,
quod dignitatem eius claritatemque meritorum decebat, est

170
(125)
The power thus put in her hands is all but unlimited, how unerringly right, then, are Christian souls when they turn to Mary for help as though impelled by an instinct of nature, confidently sharing with her their future hopes and past achievements, their sorrows and joys, commending themselves like children to the care of a bountiful Mother. How rightly true has every nation and every liturgy without exception acclaimed her great renown, which has grown greater with the voice of each succeeding century. Among her many other titles we find her hailed as "Our Lady," our "Mediatrix," the "Reparatrix of the Whole World," "the Dispenser of all Heavenly Gifts."

Guardian of our Faith

171
(52-
80)
Since faith is the foundation, the source of the gifts of God by which man is raised above the order of nature, and is endowed with the disposition requisite for life eternal, we are in justice bound to recognize the hidden influence of Mary in obtaining the gift of faith and its salutary cultivation—of Mary who brought the "Author of Faith" (a) into this world, and who because of her own "great faith" was called "blessed." O Virgin most holy, none abounds in the knowledge of God except through thee; none, O Mother of God, attains salvation except through thee, none receives a gift from the throne of mercy except through thee" (b).

172
(52,
118,
It is no exaggeration to say that it is due chiefly to her leadership and help that the wisdom and teachings of the Gospel spread so rapidly to all the nations of the world in

apud Filium assumpta. Nam, inde, divino consilio, sic ella cœpit advigilare Ecclesiæ, sic nobis adesse et favere mater, ut quæ sacramenti humanæ redemptionis patrandi administra fuerat eademque gratiæ ex illo in omne tempus derivandæ esse pariter administra, permissa ei pæne immensa potestate.

171a Hebr. 12:1.
171b St. Germ. Constantinop, Orat. II, in Dormitione B.M.V.

spite of the most obstinate difficulties and most cruel persecutions, and brought everywhere in their train a new reign of justice and peace. This is what stirred the soul of St. Cyril of Alexandria to the following prayerful address to the Blessed Virgin: "Through you the Apostles have preached salvation to the nations ... through you the priceless Cross is everywhere honored and venerated; through you the demons have been put to rout and mankind has been summoned back to heaven; through you every misguided creature held in the thralls of idols is led to recognize the truth; through you have the faithful been brought to the laver of Holy Baptism and churches been founded among every people" (a).

122)

Nay, she has even, as this same Doctor claims upheld and given strength to the "Scepter of the orthodox faith" (b). It has been her unremitting concern to see to it that the Catholic Faith stands firmly lodged in the midst of the people, there to thrive in its fertile and undivided unity. Many and well-known are the proofs of her solicitude, manifested from time to time even in a miraculous manner.

In the times and places in which, to the Church's grief, faith languished in lethargic indifference or was tormented by the baneful scourge of heresy, our great and gracious Lady in her kindness was ever ready with her aid and comfort.

173
(83,
121,
123,
154)

Under her inspiration, strong with her might, great men were raised up—illustrious for their sanctity no less than for their apostolic spirit—to beat off the attacks of wicked adversaries and to lead souls back into the virtuous ways of Christian life, firing them with a consuming love of the things of God. One such man, an army in himself, was Dominic Guzman. Putting all his trust in our Lady's Rosary he set himself fearlessly to the accomplishment of

172a St. Cyril Alex. *Homil: contra Nestor.*
172b *Ibid.*

both these tasks with happy results. No one will fail to remark how much the merits of the venerable Fathers and
Doctors of the Church who spent their lives in the defense
and explanation of the Catholic Faith, redound to the Virgin Mother of God. For from her, the "Seat of Divine Wisdom" (a), as they themselves gratefully tell us, a strong
current of the most sublime wisdom has coursed through
their writings. And they were quick to acknowledge that
not by themselves but by her have iniquitous errors been
overcome.

174
(121-
123,
171)

Finally, princes as well as pontiffs, the guardians and
defenders of the faith—the former by waging holy wars,
the latter by the solemn decrees which they have issued—
have not hesitated to call upon the name of the Mother of
Our Lord, and have found her answer powerful and propitious.

Hence it is that the Church and the Fathers have given
expression to their joy in Mary in words whose beauty
equals their truth: "Hail, Voice of the Apostles forever
eloquent, solid foundation of the Faith, unshakeable prop
of the Church" (a). "Hail, thou, through whom we have
been enrolled as citizens of the One, Holy, Catholic and
Apostolic Church" (b); "Hail, thou, Fountain springing
forth by God's design, whose rivers flowing over in pure
and unsullied waves of orthodoxy put to flight the hosts of
error" (c). "Rejoice, because thou alone hast destroyed all
the heresies in the world" (d).

Pray to Mary for Unity

175
(35,

The unexampled part which the Virgin most admirably
played and still plays in the progress, the battles and the

173a Litanies of Our Lady.
174a From the hymn of the Greeks:
174b St. John Damasc.; *In Annunt. Dei genitricis*, n. 9.
174c St. Germ. Constantinop. *Serm. I in SS. Deip.* no. 14.
174d Office of Our Lady.

triumph of the Catholic Faith, makes it evident what God has planned for her to do. It should fill the hearts of all good people with a firm hope of obtaining those things which are now the object of our common desire. Trust Mary, implore her aid.   *121, 122)*

That the one selfsame profession of faith may unite the minds of Christian nations in peace and harmony, that the one and only bond of perfect charity may gather their hearts within its embrace—such is our prayerful hope. And may Mary by her powerful help, bring this ardently desired gift into our possession! And remembering that her only-begotten Son prayed so earnestly to His Heavenly Father for the closest union among the nations whom He has called by the One Baptism to the one inheritance of salvation bought for an infinite price, will she not, for that reason, see to it that all in his marvelous light will strive as with one mind for unity? And will it not be her wish to employ her goodness and providence to console the Spouse of Christ, the Church, through her long-sustained efforts in this enterprise, as well as to bring to full perfection the boon of unity among the members of the Christian family, which is the illustrious fruit of her motherhood?

A token that the fulfillment of these hopes may soon become a reality is to be seen in the conviction and confidence which warms the hearts of the devout. Mary will be the happy bond to draw together with strong yet gentle constraint all who love Christ, no matter where they may be, to form a nation of brothers yielding obedience to the Vicar of Christ on Earth, the Roman Pontiff, their Common Father.   **176** *(161)*

Here our mind, almost of its own accord, looks back through the annals of the Church to the illustrious examples of her ancient unity, and dwells with affectionate regard on the memories of the great Council of Ephesus. The absolute unity of faith, the participation in identical worship, which in those days linked East with West, mani-   **177** *(24, 171)* fested itself in the Council with a strength unparalleled, and shone beyond it with a radiant beauty when, after the Fathers had emphasized the dogma that the blessed Virgin is the Mother of God, the news of their procedure—spread about from the exultant populace of that most devout of cities—filled all Christendom with transports of universal joy (a).

178
(122,
169,
171)
Every motive which bolsters and increases confidence in the power of our mighty and kindhearted Virgin Mother to obtain the things we ask for, should act as a powerful incentive generating in us that fiery zeal to pray her—a zeal We would incite in every Catholic heart. Let each one weigh for himself, moreover, how fitting is this practice, and how fruitful to himself, and how acceptable and pleasing to the Blessed Virgin it is bound to be. For possessing as they do, unity of faith, Catholics thus make clear that they value this precious gift not only at its true worth, but also that they intend to hold to it with jealous tenacity. No better way is afforded of proving a fraternal feeling toward their separate brethren than to aid them by every means within their power, to recover this, the greatest of all gifts.

Such brotherly affection, truly Christian, and practiced as long as the Church can remember, has traditionally sought a special efficacy from the Mother of God, since she has been the foremost promoter of peace and unity.

179
(175)
St. Germain of Constantinople addresses this prayer to her: "Be mindful of Christians who are thy servants; commend the prayers of all; help all to realize their hopes; strengthen the faith, keep the Church in unity" (a). And to this day the Greeks beseech her in this manner: "O Virgin most pure, whose privilege it is to approach thy Son without fear of rebuff! Beseech Him, O Virgin most

177a Cf. No. 1 and 295 ff.
179a *Orat: hist. in Dormitione Deiparæ.*

holy, to grant peace to the world and to breathe into the churches of Christendom one mind and one heart, and we shall magnify thee!" (b)

The Eastern churches deserve much of our Lady

There is another special reason why Mary will be favorably disposed to grant our united prayers in behalf of the nations cut off from communion with the Church; namely the prodigious things they have done for her honor in the past, especially in the East. To them is due much of the credit for propagating and increasing devotion to her. From them have come some of the best heralds and champions of her dignity, who have wielded a mighty influence by their authority or their writings—eulogists famed for the ardor and the charm of their eloquence; "empresses well beloved of God" who imitated the Virgin Most Pure in the example of their lives, and paid honor to her with lavish generosity, temples and basilicas built to her glory with regal splendor. **180** *(161, 171)*

And We may here add a detail not foreign to Our subject, and reflecting further glory upon the Mother of God. It is common knowledge that under the changing fortunes of time, great numbers of venerable images of our Lady have been brought from the East to the West, most of them finding their way to Italy and to Rome. **181** *(121, 153)*

Our forebears received them with deepest respect and venerated them with magnificent honors; and their descendants, emulating their piety continue to cherish these images as highly sacred treasures. It is a delight for the mind to discover in this fact the approval and the favor of a mother wholly devoted to her children. For it seems to indicate that these images have been left in our midst as witnesses of the ages when the entire Christian family was held together by ties of absolute unity, and as so many

179b Men. 5 maii.

precious pledges of our common inheritance. The very sight of them must needs invite souls, as though the Virgin herself were bidding them to keep in devout remembrance those which the Catholic Church calls with loving care back to the peace and the gladness which they formerly enjoyed within her embrace.

And so, in Mary, God has given us the most zealous guardian of Christian unity. There are, of course, more ways than one to win her protection by prayer but, as for Us, we think that the best and the most effective way to her favor lies in her Rosary.

Prayer brings us closer to Mary

182
(29,
144)
We have elsewhere brought it to the attention of the devout Christian that not least among the advantages of the Rosary is the ready and easy means it puts in his hands to nurture his faith, and to keep him from ignorance of his religion and the danger of error.

The very origin of the Rosary makes that plain. When such faith is exercised by vocally repeating the "Our Father" and "Hail Mary" of the Rosary prayers, or better still, in the contemplation of the mysteries, it is evident how close we are brought to Mary. For every time we devoutly say the Rosary in supplication before her, we are once more brought face to face with the marvel of our salvation; we watch the mysteries of our Redemption as though they were unfolding before our eyes; and as one follows another, Mary stands revealed at once as God's Mother and our Mother.

183
(29,
144,
148)
The sublimity of that double dignity, the fruits of her twofold ministry appear in vivid light when in devout meditation we think of Mary's share in the Joyful, Sorrowful and Glorious Mysteries of her Son. The heart is inflamed by these reflections with a feeling of grateful love toward her, and esteeming everything beneath her, as so much worthless chaff, strives with manful purpose to prove

worthy of such a Mother and the gifts she bestows. Meditation on the mysteries of the Rosary, often repeated in the spirit of faith, cannot help but please her and move her, the fondest of mothers, to show mercy to her children.

For that reason We say that the Rosary is by far the best prayer by which to plead before her the cause of our separated brethren. To grant a favorable hearing belongs properly to her office of spiritual Mother. For Mary has not brought forth, nor could she?—those who are of Christ except in the One same Faith and in the One same Love; for "Is Christ divided" (a)? And all must live the life of Christ in an organic unity, in order "to bring forth fruit to God" (b) in the one same body.

Everyone of the multitudes, therefore, whom the mischief of calamitous events has stolen away from that unity, must be born again to Christ of that same Mother whom God has endowed with a never failing fertility to bring forth a holy people. And this, Mary, for her part, longs to do. Adorned by us with garlands of her favorite prayer, she will obtain by her entreaties help in abundance from the Spirit that quickeneth. God grant that they refuse not to comply with the burning desire of their merciful Mother, but, on the contrary, give ear, like men of good will with a proper regard for their eternal salvation, to the voice gently persuasive which calls to them: "My little children of whom I am in labor again, until Christ is formed in you" (a). **184** *(31, 35, 171)*

Knowing what power our Lady's Rosary possesses, not a few of Our Predecessors took special care to spread the devotion throughout the countries of the East—in particular Eugene IV in the Constitution "Advesperascente" issued in 1439, and later Innocent XII and Clement XI. By **185** *(142, 146)*

183a 1 Cor. 1:13.
183b Cf. Rom. 7:4.
184a Gal. 4:19.

their authority, privileges of wide extent were granted to the Order of Preachers in favor of this Project. The hoped-for results were forthcoming thanks to the energetic activity of the brethren of that Order, results to which many a bright record bear witness, although time and adversity have since raised great obstacles in the way of further progress.

(*Present devotion of the East shown by erection of a basilica of the Rosary at Patrasso.*)

"Monstra te esse Matrem"

186
(34,
169,
178)
And now, Venerable Brethren, our exhortation returns to the point from which it began. Well may all, shepherds and flocks alike, fly with fullest confidence to the protection of the Blessed Virgin, especially next month, let them not fail to call upon her name with one voice beseeching her as God's Mother, publicly and in private by praise, by prayer, by the ardor of their desire: "Show thyself our Mother" (a). May her motherly compassion keep her whole family safe from every danger, lead them in the path of genuine prosperity, above all establish them in holy unity. She looks upon Catholics of every nation with a kindly eye. Where the bond of charity joins them together she makes them more ready, more and more determined, to uphold the honor of religion which, at the same time, brings upon the state the greatest blessings.

187
(161,
171)
May she look with utmost compassion upon those great and illustrious nations which are cut off from the Church and upon the noble souls who have not forgotten their Christian duty. May she inspire in them most salutary desires, foster their holy aspirations and bring them to happy completion. In the East, may that widespread devotion to her, which the dissident nations profess, as well as the

186a *Ave Maris Stella.*

countless glorious acts of their ancestors in her honor, effectively aid them. In the West, may the memory of her beneficent patronage stand its dissidents in good stead; with surpassing kindness she has, through many ages, manifested her approval of, and has rewarded, the admirable devotion shown her among every class.

May the peoples of the East and the West, and all the others wherever they may be, profit by the suppliant voice of Catholics united in prayer, and by Our voice which will cry to Our last breath: "Show thyself a Mother."

CLOSE TO THE MEDIATOR

Encycl. *Fidentem Piumque,* September 20, 1896.

188
(120, 134, 146)
We have already had the opportunity on several occasions during Our pontificate of bearing testimony to that confidence and devotion toward the Blessed Virgin which we sustained in Our tenderest years, and have endeavored to cherish and develop all our life long. For, having come upon times of calamity for Christendom and of peril for nations, We have realized how prudent it is warmly to recommend this means of safeguarding happiness and peace which God has most mercifully granted to men through His august Mother, and which has always been celebrated in the annals of the Church. The manifold zeal of Christian people has responded to Our desires and exhortations, most particularly by showing a devotion to the Rosary, and a plentiful harvest of excellent fruits has not been wanting.

189
(136, 143, 175)
Still We can never do enough in honoring the Mother of God, who is in truth worthy of all praise, and with urging love and affection toward her, who is also the Mother of mankind, who is full of mercy, full of grace. Yea, Our soul, wearied with the cares of the apostolate, the nearer it feels the time of Our departure to be at hand,

the more earnestly and confidently do We look up to her
from whom, as from a blessed dawn, rises the day of happiness which has no sunset.

It is happiness for Us to remember, Venerable Brethren, that We have in other Letters, issued from time to
time, extolled the devotion of the Rosary, for it is in many
ways most pleasing to her in whose honor it is employed,
and most advantageous to those who properly use it. But
it is equally a happiness to be able now to insist upon and
confirm the same fact. Herein We have an excellent opportunity paternally to exhort men's minds and hearts tc an
increase of religion, and to stimulate within them the hope
of eternal reward.

The Rosary is endowed with the qualities of a true prayer

190
(143) The form of prayer We refer to has obtained the
special name of "Rosary," as though it represented by its
arrangement the sweetness of roses and the charm of a
garland. This is a most fitting way to venerate the Blessed
Virgin, who is rightly styled the "Mystical Rose" of Paradise (a), and who as Queen of the Universe shines therein
with a crown of stars. By its very name it appears to fore-
shadow and be an augury of the joys and garlands of
heaven offered by her to those who are devoted to her.

(*Nature and necessity of prayer in a general way.—
Unanimity and assiduousness.*)

191
(145, Both of these qualities are conspicuous in the Rosary.
149) For, to be brief, by repeating the same prayers we strenuously implore from Our Heavenly Father the kingdom of
His grace and glory; we again and again beseech the
Virgin Mother to aid us sinners by her prayers, both during
our whole life and especially at that last moment which is
the steppingstone to eternity. The formula of the Rosary,

190a Litany of Our Lady.

too, is excellently adapted to prayer in common, so that it
has been styled, not without reason, "The Psalter of Mary."

The old custom of our forefathers ought to be preserved or restored, whereby Christian families, whether in
town or country, used to gather piously at the close of the
day, when their labors were at an end, before an image
of our Lady, and alternately recite the Rosary. She, delighted at this faithful and unanimous homage, was ever
near them like a loving mother surrounded by her children, distributing to them the blessings of domestic peace,
the foretaste of the peace of heaven.

Considering the efficacy of public prayer, We, among **192**
other decrees which We have from time to time issued con- *(152)*
cerning the Rosary, have spoken thus: "It is our wish that
in the principal church of each diocese it should be recited
daily, and that in parish churches it should be said on
every feast day" (a). Let this be constantly and devoutly
carried out. We also see with the joy the custom extended
to other solemn occasions of public devotion and to pilgrimages to venerated shrines, the growing frequency of
which is to be commended.

This association of prayer and praise to Mary is a **193**
source at once of joy and of salvation for souls. We our- *(135,*
selves have most strongly experienced this—and Our heart *178)*
rejoices to recall it—when at certain times in Our pontificate We have been present in the Vatican Basilica, surrounded by great crowds of all classes who, united with
us in mind, voice and hope, all earnestly invoked, by the
mysteries and prayers of the Rosary, her who is the most
powerful Patroness of the Catholic name.

Mediatrix with the Mediator

Who could think or say that the confidence so strongly **194**
felt in the patronage of the Blessed Virgin is excessive. *(28,*

192a Apost. Letter *Salutaris Ille*, December 24, 1883.

33,
39,
42)
Undoubtedly the name and attributes of the absolute Mediator belong to no other than Christ; for being one Person and yet both Man and God He restored the human race to the favor of the Heavenly Father. "One Mediator of God and men, the Man Jesus Christ, Who gave Himself a redemption for all" (a).

And yet, as the Angelic Doctor teaches: "there is no reason why certain others should not be called in a certain way mediators between God and Man, that is to say in so far as they cooperate by predisposing and ministering in the union of man with God" (b). Such are the angels and saints, the prophets and priests of both Testaments, but especially has the Blessed Virgin a claim to the glory of this title. For no single individual can even be imagined who has ever contributed or ever will contribute so much toward reconciling man with God. To mankind heading for eternal ruin, she offered a Savior when she received the announcement of the mystery brought to this earth by the Angel, and in giving her consent gave it "in the name of the whole human race" (c). She is from whom Jesus is born; she is therefore truly His Mother and for this reason a worthy and acceptable "Mediatrix to the Mediator" (d).

195
(42)
As the various mysteries present themselves one after the other in the formula of the Rosary for the meditation and contemplation of men's minds, they also elucidate what we owe to Mary for our reconciliation and salvation. No one can fail to be sweetly affected when considering who appeared in the house of Elizabeth as the minister of the

194a Tim. 2:5-6.
194b *Summa Theologica.* III q. 26. a. i.
194c *Summa Theologica.* III q. 30. a. i.
194d *Nemo etenim unus cogitari quidem potest qui reconciliandis Deo hominibus parem atque illa operam vel umquam contulerit vel aliquando sit collaturus. Ipsa est "de qua natus est Jesus," vera scilicet eius Mater, ob eamdemque causam digna ac peraccepta "ad Mediatorem Mediatrix."*

divine gifts, who presented her Son to the shepherds, to the kings and to Simeon. Moreover one must remember that the blood of Christ shed for our sake, and those members in which He offers to His Father the wounds He received "as the price of our liberty," are no other than the flesh and blood of the Virgin: "The flesh of Jesus is the flesh of Mary, and however much it was exalted in the Glory of His Resurrection, nevertheless the nature of His flesh derived from Mary remained and still remains the same" (a).

(*Meditation on the Mysteries of the Rosary nourishes faith.—Everyone can recite the Rosary.—Pray for unity.*)

... For that earnest desire which We have learned from the Divine Heart of Jesus, of fostering the work of reconciliation among those who are separated from us, daily urges us more pressingly to action, and We are convinced that this reunion cannot be better prepared and strengthened than by the power of prayer. **196** *(81, 121)*

The example of Christ is before us, for in order that His disciples might be one in faith and charity, He poured forth prayer and supplication to His Father. And concerning the efficacious prayer of His most holy Mother for the same end, there is a striking testimony in the Acts of the Apostles. Therein is described the first assembly of the disciples, expecting with earnest hope and prayer, the promised fullness of the Holy Spirit. And the presence of Mary, united to them in prayer, is specially indicated: "All these were persevering with one mind in prayer with Mary the Mother of Jesus" (a).

Wherefore, as the nascent Church rightly joined itself in prayer with her as the patroness and most excellent custodian of unity, so in these times it is most opportune to do **197** *(171)*

195a St. Augustine, *De Assumpt.* B.M.V., c. 5.
196a Acts 1:14.

the same all over the Catholic World, particularly during the whole month of October, which we long ago decreed to be dedicated and consecrated, by the solemn devotion of the Rosary, to the Mother of God, in order to implore her help for the afflicted Church.

198
(122,
171)
Let, then, zeal for this prayer everywhere be rekindled, particularly for the end of holy unity. Nothing will be more agreeable and acceptable to Mary; for as she is most closely united with Christ, she especially wishes and desires that they who have received the same Baptism with Him may be united with Him and with one another in the same Faith and perfect Charity. So may the sublime mysteries of this same Faith be more deeply impressed in men's minds by means of the Rosary devotion, with the happy result that "we may imitate what they contain and obtain what they promise."

SPOUSE OF THE HOLY SPIRIT

Encycl. *Divinum illud,* May 9, 1897.

(Mission and Worship of the Holy Spirit.)

199
(57,
81)
Our mind and heart turn back to those hopes with which We began, and for the accomplishment of which We earnestly pray, and will continue to pray to the Holy Spirit. Unite, then, Venerable Brethren, your prayers with Ours, and at your exhortation let all Christian peoples add their prayers also, invoking the powerful and ever-acceptable intercession of the Blessed Virgin. You know well the intimate and wonderful relations existing between her and the Holy Spirit, so that she is justly called His Spouse. Her intercession was of great avail both in the mystery of the Incarnation and in the coming of the Holy Spirit upon the Apostles. May she continue to strengthen our prayers with her suffrages, that in the midst of all the stress and troubles of the nations, those divine prodigies may be

happily revived in the Holy Spirit, which were foretold in the words of David: "Send forth Thy Spirit and they shall be created, and Thou shalt renew the face of the earth" (a).

MARY'S IMPLORING OMNIPOTENCE

Encycl. *Augustissimæ,* September 12, 1897.

Whoever considers the height of dignity to which God has raised the most august Virgin Mary will easily perceive how important it is, both for the public and private good, that devotion to her should be assiduously practiced and daily promoted more and more.   **200**
(21,
126)

God chose her from all eternity to be the Mother of the Incarnate Word, and for that reason so eminently distinguished her among all His most beautiful works in the triple order of nature, grace and glory, that the Church justly applies to her these words:—"I came out of the Mouth of the Most High, the firstborn before all creatures" (a).

And when in the beginning of the human race, the parents of mankind fell into sin, involving their descendants in the same ruin, she was set up as the pledge of the restoration of peace and salvation.   **201**
(34)

The only-begotten Son of God at all times paid to His most holy Mother most evident marks of honor. During His private life on earth, He associated her with Himself in each of His first two miracles—the miracle of grace when, at the salutation of Mary, the infant leaped in the womb of Elizabeth; the miracle of nature when He turned water into wine at the marriage feast of Cana. And at the supreme moment of His public life, when sealing the New Testament in His precious blood, He committed her to   **202**
(27)

199a Ps. 103:30.
200a Eccl. 24:5.

His beloved Apostle in those sweet words: "Behold thy Mother!" (a)

The Pope Wishes to Honor Mary

203
(31,
133)   We, therefore, who though unworthy hold the place of Vicar of Christ upon earth, shall never cease to promote the glory of so great a Mother, as long as life endures. And since, as old age weighs heavily upon Us, We feel that life cannot now last much longer, We are constrained to repeat to all Our beloved children in Christ those last words of His upon the cross, which He left to us as a testament: "Behold thy Mother!" (a) Greatly rewarded indeed shall We be if Our exhortation succeeds in making even one of the faithful hold nothing dearer than devotion to Mary, so that those words which St. John wrote about himself may be applied to each: "the disciple took her to his own."

204
(147,
152)   As the month of October again approaches, Venerable Brethren, We would not willingly leave you without Our Letter this year, once more urging you with all possible earnestness to strive by the recitation of the Rosary to aid both yourselves individually and the Universal Church in her needs. This form of prayer appears, under the guidance of Divine Providence, to have been wonderfully developed at the close of the century for the purpose of stimulating the lagging piety of the faithful. This is witnessed in the splendid churches and much frequented sanctuaries which have been dedicated to the Mother of God.

To this Heavenly Mother we have offered the flowers of the month of May; to her we would have also fruit-bearing October dedicated with especial tenderness of devotion. It is fitting that both parts of the year should be consecrated to her who said: "My flowers are the fruit of honor and riches" (a).

202a John 19: 27.
203a John 19:27.
204a Ecclus. 24:23.

(The Rosary Brotherhood includes the advantage of prayer in common.)

The history of the Church bears testimony to the power and efficacy of this form of prayer, recording as it does the rout of the Turkish forces at the naval battle of Lepanto, and the victory gained over the same enemy in the past century at Temesvar in Hungary, and on the island of Corfu. Our predecessor Gregory XIII, established the feast of Our Lady of Victories which Clement XI later distinguished by the title of Rosary Sunday and commanded to be celebrated throughout the universal Church. From the fact that this crusade of prayer is "enrolled under the name of the Mother of God" fresh efficacy and fresh honor are thereby added to it. Hence the frequent repetition of the "Hail Mary" after each "Our Father."   **205** *(146, 148)*

Efficacy of Mary's intercession

So far is this from derogating in any way from the honor due to God (as though it indicated that we placed greater confidence in Mary's patronage than in God's power) it is rather what especially moves God and wins His mercy for us.   **206** *(126)*

We are taught by the Catholic faith that we may pray not only to God Himself, but also to the Blessed in heaven, though in a different manner. From God we ask, as from the Source of All Good, but from the saints, as from intercessors. "Prayer," says St. Thomas, "is offered to a person in two ways—one, as though to be granted by himself, another, as to be obtained through him. In the first way, we pray to God alone, because all our prayers ought to be directed to obtain grace and glory, which God alone gives, according to those words of the eighty-third Psalm: 'The Lord will give grace and glory'. But in the second way we pray to holy angels and men, not that God may learn our petition through them, but that by their prayers and merits, our prayers may be efficacious. Wherefore, it is said in the

Apocalypse: 'The smoke of the incense of the prayers of the saints ascended up before God from the hand of the angel'" (a).

207
(49,
134)
Now, of all the blessed in heaven, who can compare with the August Mother of God in obtaining grace? Who sees more clearly in the Eternal Word what troubles oppress us, what are our needs? Who is allowed more power in moving God? Who can compare with her in maternal affection? We do not pray to the blessed in the same way as to God: "for we ask the Holy Trinity to have mercy on us, but we ask all the saints to pray for us" (a). Yet our manner of praying to the Blessed Virgin has something in common with our worship of God, so that the Church even addressed to her the words with which we pray to God: "Have mercy on sinners."

208
(107,
125)
The members of the Rosary Confraternity, therefore, do exceedingly well in weaving together, as in a crown, so many salutations and prayers to Mary. For so great is her dignity, "so great her favor before God, that whosoever in his need will not have recourse to her is trying to fly without wings."

(*The Rosary continues the office of the Angels.—Commendation of the Confraternity of the Rosary by Roman Pontiffs.—Approval of the "Perpetual Rosary."*

VALUE OF CONGRESSES

Letter *Mariani cœtus,* to the Archbishop of Turin, August 2, 1898.

209
(47,
121,
From the moment We heard of it, We heartily approved the plan to summon a Marian Congress at Turin, for it is always for Us a sacred and pleasant duty to give

206a *Summa Theologia,* 2. a. 2. ae. q. 83, a. 4.
207a *Ibid.*

Our strong support to whatever nourishes and furthers   *154)*
devotion to the Blessed Virgin. It is God's will that through
her, His own Mother, we have all things; in His supreme
goodness He has constituted her the unerring support of
Christianity.

Our times demand absolutely that we turn to that
Mother of men with unabated confidence; even though for
some time menacing for the Church in Italy, the times
have grown worse during the recent disorders. How will
she, who in past ages and in wondrous ways manifested
her love and power, fail to show herself propitious in the
present trial and to bring victory and joy to the Christian
name?

(*Plan of the Congress to consecrate Italy to the Heart
of Our Lady.*)

MARIAN ACCOMPLISHMENTS OF LEO XIII

Encycl. *Diuturni temporis,* September 5, 1898.

There comes to Our mind the sweet remembrance of   **210**
the motherly protection of the august Queen of Heaven,   *(30,*
and this memory likewise We shall cherish and preserve   *138)*
perpetually, ever thanking her and proclaiming her benefits. From her, as from an abundant spring, are derived
the streams of heavenly graces. "In her hand are the treasures of the mercies of the Lord" (a). "God wills that she
be the beginning of all good things" (b). In the love of
this tender Mother, which We have constantly striven to
cherish and to increase day by day, We confidently hope
that We may end our life.

We have long desired to promote the welfare of the   **211**
human race through an increase of devotion to the Blessed   *(138,*

210a St. John Damascene, Serm. I. *de Nativitate Virginis.*
210b Cf. St. Irenaeus, *Cont. Valent.,* liv. III, 33.

176) Virgin as in a powerful citadel, and We have never ceased
to encourage the constant use of the Rosary among Christians, by publishing every year since September 1, 1883,
an Encyclical Letter on this subject (a), besides frequently issuing decrees—as is well known.

And now, since God in His merciful providence has
this year again allowed Us to see the approach of the
month of October, which We have already consecrated to
our heavenly Queen under the title of the Rosary, We
cannot refrain from again addressing you. But We shall
summarize in a few words all that We have hitherto done
for the promotion of this form of prayer. We will crown
our work by yet a new document by which our earnest
desire and zeal for this form of devotion to Mary may appear still more clearly, and the fervor of the faithful may
be stimulated more and more to the devout and constant
use of this pious practice.

(*Summary of his teachings on the Rosary and of
favors granted through this prayer.—Announcement of the
Apostolic Constitution* Ubi primum *instituting the Confraternity of the Rosary.*)

THE CONFRATERNITY OF THE ROSARY

Apost. Const. *Ubi primum*, October 2, 1898.

212   As soon as We were raised by a hidden design of
(41,   divine Providence to the exalted Chair of St. Peter, We
121,   realized that evils more numerous were overwhelming the
142)   world day by day. In view of this, We considered it the
duty of Our apostolic ministry to lay plans for the Church's
safety and to search for the best means of making her
defenses and the integrity of the Catholic faith most secure.

211a Cf. above, no. 80 ff.

With this in mind, We naturally turned to the powerful Mother of God. She was the cooperatrix in man's Redemption and always the chief and sovereign refuge of Catholics in the trials they underwent. The striking benefits which they received prove how right they were in placing their confidence in her. Among those benefits it has been proved that many were in answer to that most potent form of prayer called the Rosary, taught by the Mother of God herself and propagated by the Fathers of St. Dominic.

Sovereign Pontiffs who preceded Us decreed that **213** solemn homage should be paid to the Blessed Virgin in *(142)* that form of prayer. We Ourselves, animated by a like zeal, have treated of the excellence and efficacy of Mary's Rosary. Ever since the Kalends of September 1883, We have several times issued encyclical letters exhorting the faithful to make use publicly and in their homes of that salutary practice of devotion to the august Mother and to enroll in established confraternities in Mary's honor. Still more recently We gathered together all Our pronouncements and summarized them in a few words. At the same time We made known Our intention to issue a Constitution of the rights, privileges and indulgences which are the joy of those whose names are inscribed in that pious confraternity. And now, to finish Our work and to accede to the wishes of the Master General of the Order of Friars Preachers, We are issuing that Constitution in which the rules and the privileges conceded by former Sovereign Pontiffs are re-stated and We are determining the rules that will direct that salutary institution for all times.

(*Statutes of the Confraternity of the Rosary* [a].)

213a Among the articles of Constitution, we cite the first: "The Confraternity of the Holy Rosary is instituted with the aim of inspiring a goodly number of men united by fraternal charity to praise and pray to the Blessed Virgin

RESTORER OF THE CHRISTIAN ORDER

Apost. Letter *Parta humano generi*, September 8, 1901.

(The Blessed Virgin's favors to France; Lourdes, in the region which saw the origin of the Rosary.)

214
(25, 26, 83, 114)
The prayer which in Mary's honor St. Dominic, with God's guidance and help, was the first to compose by putting the mysteries of Redemption together in set order, has rightly been called the Rosary. For, as often as we repeat the Angel's words and greet Mary "full of grace" (a), so often in repeating that tribute of praise, do we offer to the Blessed Virgin, as it were, the fragrance of most refreshing perfume: we are reminded both of Mary's exalted dignity and the graces without number which come to her from God through the "fruit of her womb" (b); we recall the other exceptional merits by which she shared with her Son Jesus in man's Redemption. Oh! how sweet, then, to the Virgin Mary, how pleasing to her is the Angel's salutation! At the moment when Gabriel addressed it to her, she understood that by the power of the Holy Spirit she had conceived the Word of God.

and to obtain her protection by concerted prayer, making use of the pious formula of prayer from which the association itself takes its name. For this reason, seeking no gain and demanding no dues, the Confraternity accepts men of every condition and establishes no bond among them except that of recitation of Mary's Rosary. The result is that each one donates but a little to the common treasury and withdraws much of it in return. In this way, each member who, by actual or habitual means, follows the Confraternity's rules and discharges his debt of recitation of the Rosary, unites in his intentions all the members of the society, who in turn perform for him many times over the same charitable office."

214a Luke 1:28.
214b Luke 1:42.

The Modern "Albigenses"

But in our times also, under a different name and **215** under the auspices of other sects, arises astonishingly the *(123,* old Albigensian heresy, containing new enticements to error *168)* and impious doctrine; it insinuates itself anew in those regions, it infects and contaminates Christian peoples with its baleful contagion and drags them to loss and destruction. We see, and We deplore greatly the storm that has at present arisen, most of all in France, against religious communities, which by their pious and charitable works have deserved so well of Church and people.

Now, while We bewail these evils and while the Church's heavy afflictions fill Our heart with bitter sorrow, with joy We see appear, side by side with the evils, the sure signs of a better future. In fact, this is to Us such a favorable and happy omen—may the august Queen of heaven bring it to pass—that We should next October, as We said above, consecrate at Lourdes as many altars as there are mysteries of the Rosary.

(*Appeal for a new victory of Our Lady.*)

Certainly, for us nothing can be more effective in **216** winning the Virgin's favor and in meriting the most salu- *(41,* tary graces than to surround with the greatest possible *168,* honor the mysteries of our Redemption in which she not *176)* only shared but also took part, and to unfold before the world the series of those divine truths proposed for our meditation. We do not doubt that the Virgin Mary, Mother of God and the tender Mother of men, will be favorable to the wishes and the prayers that the countless crowds of Christians, gathered from every part of the world, will multiply at her shrine, and that she will add her intercession to theirs, so that the joint prayerful entreaty will, as it were, do violence to heaven and touch the God of infinite mercy. May the most powerful Virgin Mary, who at one time "by her charity cooperated in the birth of the faithful in the Church" (a), be still the instrument and guardian of our salvation. May she crush the numberless heads of the hydra which spreads havoc throughout Europe more and more; may she restore the tranquillity of peace to unquiet hearts; finally, may individuals and societies hasten to return to Jesus Christ, who "is able at all times to save those who come to God through Him" (b).

THE FIFTIETH ANNIVERSARY OF THE DEFINITION OF THE IMMACULATE CONCEPTION

Letter *Da molte parti,* to Cardinals. Vincenzio Vannutelli, Mariano Rampolla, Domenico Ferrata, Guiseppe Calasanzio Vivès y Tuto, June 26, 1903.

217
(121,
124,
137)
From many quarters requests have come to Us expressing the desire of the faithful to celebrate with extraordinary solemnities the fiftieth anniversary of the proclamation of the dogma of the Immaculate Conception of the Blessed Virgin. It is easy to imagine the great joy that such requests bring to Us. Devotion toward the Mother of God was not only one of the sweetest emotions of Our tender years but it is also one of the most powerful aids granted by Providence to the Catholic Church. In every century and in all its trials and persecutions the Church has had recourse to Mary and has always obtained from her comfort and protection. And as there is so much strife today and so much to threaten the Church, We rejoice and are full of hope in seeing that the faithful, taking advantage of the

216a St. Augustine, *De Sancta Virginitate,* cap. VI.
216b Hebr. 7:25.

occasion of this fiftieth anniversary, with trust and love unanimously wish to turn to her who is invoked as Help of Christians.

(*Appointment of a Commission of Cardinals for the celebration of the Fiftieth Anniversary.*)

THE SALVATION OF FRANCE

Letter *Præclarum publicæ*, to the Archbishop of Cambrai, July 10, 1903.

The manifestation of public piety and faith, of which the crowning of the Virgin of Dunkerque was the occasion, in addition to the joy it gave Us, has touched Us in a very special way. We saw several Bishops of France and a great crowd gather together from all parts and vie one with the other in showing the Virgin Mary every mark of reverence and veneration. We felt how strong were the ties that join those marks of veneration to devotion to Christ Jesus and His Vicar on earth. In that we find a guarantee of the safety of society more potent than are the forces of evil in their attacks that grow daily more shameless. In fact, to heal the ills of society, no remedy is more timely than recourse to her who, having given for the world's salvation the Person of her Son, delights in being hailed as the Help of Christians. To calm the floods that roar, nothing is more effective for man than to look to the divine Chair of St. Peter, from which at all times inexhaustible blessings have enriched the name of France. With good reason, then, you put your hope in God, who Himself brings abundant good out of evil; with reason you look to her who freed your fatherland, the Mother of Mercy, thanks to whom the enemies of the Catholic name, their eyes opened by divine light, will return to the bosom of the Church as to a most secure harbor of truth.

218
(170, 176)

And likewise there is nothing better to calm the troubled seas than to turn to the Divine Chair of St. Peter from which innumerable blessings have come to France.

Therefore, it is only right that you place your hopes in God—in that God who knows how to draw from evil itself an infinite abundance of good. It is only right that you turn your eyes to the Mother of Mercy, Patroness of France, so that through her intercession, illumined once and for all by supernatural light, the enemies of the Christian name may return to the Church which is the sure port of Truth.

ST. PIUS X

(1903-1914)

VICTORY OVER SATAN

Prayer *O Most Holy Virgin* composed by St. Pius X for the fiftieth anniversary of the definition of the Immaculate Conception, September 8, 1903.

Most holy Virgin, who pleased our Lord and became His Mother, Virgin Immaculate in thy body and soul, in thy faith and love, at this solemn jubilee of the promulgation of the dogma which proclaimed thee to the entire world as conceived without sin, look kindly on us unfortunate ones who implore thy powerful protection. The infernal serpent, upon whom the primeval curse was laid, continues, alas, to attack and tempt the hapless children of Eve. Ah! do thou, our blessed Mother, our Queen and Advocate, who at the first moment of thy conception didst crush the enemy's head, do thou gather together our prayers and we beseech thee (our hearts one with thine) present them before God's throne, that we may never allow ourselves to be caught in the snares laid for us, but that we may reach the portal of salvation, and that the Church and Christian society may once more chant the hymn of deliverance, of victory and of peace. Amen. **219** *(48, 51, 79-80)*

TO RESTORE EVERYTHING THROUGH MARY

Encycl. *Ad diem illum lætissimum*, February 2, 1904.

An interval of a few months will again bring around that most happy day on which, fifty years ago, Our Predecessor Pius IX, of holy memory, in the presence of a resplendent assembly of cardinals and bishops, pronounced and promulgated with the authority of the infallible teaching office of the Church, as a truth revealed by God, that the Most Blessed Virgin Mary in the first instant of her **220** *(66, 134, 137)* conception was free from all stain of original sin (a). All the world knows the feelings with which the faithful of every nation of the earth received this proclamation and manifestations of public satisfaction and joy which greeted it, for truly there has not been in the memory of man any more universal or more harmonious expression of sentiment shown toward the August Mother of God or the Vicar of Jesus Christ.

221
(66,
118,
121)
And, Venerable Brethren, why should we not hope today after the lapse of half a century, when we renew the memory of the Immaculate Virgin, that an echo of that holy joy will awaken in our minds, and that the magnificent scenes of that distant day, of faith and of love toward the August Mother of God, will be repeated? Of all this We are, indeed, made ardently desirous by the devotion, united with supreme gratitude for favors received, which We have always cherished toward the blessed Virgin; and We have a sure pledge of the fulfillment of our desires in the fervor of all Catholics, ready and willing as they are to multiply their testimonies of love and reverence for the great Mother of God. Moreover, we cannot conceal the fact that this desire of Ours is especially stimulated as by a heavenly inspiration which prompts Us to regard as not far distant the fulfillment of those great hopes, assuredly not unfounded, which the solemn promulgation of the dogma of the Immaculate Conception inspired in the mind of Pius, Our Predecessor, and of all the bishops of the world.

Blessings of the definition of 1854

222
(50,
66,
Many, it is true, lament the fact that until now these hopes have been unfulfilled, and are prone to repeat the words of Jeremias (a): We looked for peace and no good

220a Cf. above no. 31 ff.
222a Jer. 8:15.

came; for a time of healing and we behold fear. But all   *155)*
such will be certainly rebuked as men of little faith who
make no effort to penetrate the works of God or to esti-
mate them in the light of truth. For, who can number the
secret gifts of grace which God has bestowed upon His
Church through the intercession of the Blessed Virgin
throughout this period? And even prescinding from these
gifts, what is to be said of the Vatican Council so oppor-
tunely convoked; or of the dogma of papal infallibility
promulgated in time to meet the errors that were about
to arise; or, finally, of that new and unprecedented fervor
with which the faithful of all classes and of every nation
have long been wending their way hither to venerate in
person the Vicar of Christ? Surely the Providence of God
has shown itself admirably in Our two Predecessors, Pius
and Leo, who with such great holiness ruled the Church
in most turbulent times through a length of pontificate
conceded to no other before them.

Then, again, no sooner had Pius IX proclaimed as a
dogma of the Catholic Faith, the preservation of Mary from
the original stain, then the Virgin herself began in Lourdes
those wonderful manifestations, followed by the vast and
magnificent movements, which have resulted in those two
temples dedicated to the Immaculate Mother, where the
prodigies which still continue to take place through her
intercession, furnish splendid arguments against the in-
credulity of our days.

Witnesses, then, as we are of all these great benefits   **22**3
which God has granted through the benign influence of   *(135,*
the Virgin in those fifty years now about to be completed,   *154)*
why should we not believe that our salvation is nearer
than we thought; all the more so since we know from experience that, in the dispensations of Divine Providence,
when evils reach their limit, deliverance is not far distant,
"Her time is near at hand and her days shall not be pro-

longed, for the Lord will have mercy on Jacob and will yet choose out of Israel" (a).

Therefore, the hope we cherish is not a vain one, that we, too, may before long repeat: "The Lord has broken the staff of the wicked, the rod of the rulers. The whole earth is quiet and still, it is glad and hath rejoiced" (b).

224
(39,
157)
But the first and chief reason, Venerable Brethren, why the fiftieth anniversary of the Proclamation of the Dogma of the Immaculate Conception should excite a singular fervor in the souls of Christians, lies for us in that restoration of all things in Christ which we have already set forth in Our First Encyclical Letter.

For can anyone fail to see that there is no surer and more direct road than by Mary, for uniting all mankind in Christ and obtaining through Him the perfect adoption of sons, that we may be holy and immaculate in the sight of God.

Mary, foundation of our faith

225
(79,
80,
112,
122)
For, if to Mary it was truly said: "Blessed are thou, that hast believed because those things shall be accomplished that were spoken to thee by the Lord" (a); or, in other words that she would conceive and bring forth the Son of God; and if she did receive in her womb Him who is by nature Truth Himself in order that "He, generated in a new order and with a new nativity, though invisible in Himself, might become visible in our flesh" (b): the Son of God made man, being the "author and finisher" of faith (c) it surely follows that His Mother most holy should be recognized as participating in the divine mys-

223a Is. 14:1.
223b Is. 14:5 and 7
225a Luke 1:45.
225b St. Leo the Great. *Serm. II de Nativ. Domin.* c. 2.
225c Cf. Hebr. 12:2.

teries and as being in a manner the guardian of them,
and that upon her as upon a foundation, the noblest after
Christ, rises the edifice of the faith of all centuries (d).

How can we think otherwise? God could have given **226**
us the Redeemer of the Human Race, and the Founder of (23,
the Faith, in another way than through the Virgin, but 38,
since Divine Providence has been pleased that we should 59)
have the Man-God through Mary, who conceived Him by
the Holy Ghost and bore Him in her womb, it only remains
for us to receive Christ through the hands of Mary.

Hence wherever the Scriptures prophesy of the "grace
which was come in us" (a) the Redeemer of mankind is
almost invariably presented to us as united with His
Mother. The Lamb that is to rule the world will be sent—
but he will be sent from the Rock of the desert; the flower
will blossom, but it will blossom from the root of Jesse.
Adam, the father of mankind, looked to Mary crushing
the serpent's head, and he restrained the tears which the
malediction brought into his eyes; Noe thought of her
when shut up in the Ark of safety; and Abraham when
prevented from the slaying of his son; Jacob at the sight
of the ladder on which angels ascended and descended;
Moses amazed at the sight of the bush which burned, but
was not consumed; David escorting the Ark of God with
dancing and psalmody; Elias as he looked at the little
cloud that rose out of the sea. In a word, after Christ, we
find in Mary the end of the law and the fulfillment of the
figures and prophecies.

When one reflects that with her alone did Jesus spend **227**
thirty years in that family union of son and mother, surely (39,

---

225d *Opus est omnino sanctissimam eius Matrem mysteriorum
     divinorum participem ac veluti custodem agnoscere in qua,
     tamquam in fundamento post Christum nobilissimo, fidei
     sæculorum omnium extruitur ædificatio.*
226a 1 Peter 1:10.

79-
83,
122)

there is no doubt that through Mary is opened to us the surest way of knowing Christ.

Who more than His Mother could have a far-reaching knowledge of the admirable mysteries of the birth and childhood of Christ, and above all of the mystery of the Incarnation, which is the beginning and the foundation of faith? She not only "kept in her heart" (a) the events of Bethlehem and what took place in Jerusalem in the Temple of the Lord, but sharing as she did the thoughts and the secret wishes of Christ, she may be said to have lived the very life of her Son. Hence nobody ever knew Christ so profoundly as she did, and nobody can ever be more competent as a guide and teacher of the knowledge of Christ.

228
(39)

Hence it follows, as we have already pointed out, that the Blessed Virgin is more powerful than all others as a means of uniting mankind with Christ. In fact, if, as Christ said, "Now this is eternal life: That they may know Thee, the Only True God, and Jesus Christ, whom Thou hast sent" (a), and if through Mary we attain to the knowledge of Christ, through Mary also we most easily obtain that life of which Christ is the source and origin.

Mother of the members of Christ

229
(28,
47,
52)

And if we consider ever so little how many and powerful are the reasons which prompt this most holy Mother to bestow on us these precious gifts, oh, how our hopes will be expanded! For is not Mary the Mother of Christ? Then she is our Mother also. And we must in truth hold that Christ, the Word made flesh, is also the Savior of mankind. Now, as the God-Man, He had a material body like that of any other man; and as Savior of the human

227a Luke 2:19-51.
228a John 17:3.

family, He had a spiritual and mystical body, the society, namely, of those who believe in Christ. "So we, being many, are one body in Christ" (a).

Now the Blessed Virgin did not conceive the Eternal Son of God merely in order that He might be made man, taking His human nature from her, but also in order that by means of the nature assumed from her, He might be the Redeemer of men. For which reason the Angel said to the shepherds: "For this day is born to you a Savior who is Christ the Lord" (b).

Therefore, in the same holy bosom of His most chaste Mother, Christ took to Himself flesh, and united to Himself the spiritual body formed by those who were to believe in Him. Hence Mary, carrying the Savior within her, may be said to have also carried all those whose life was contained in the life of the Savior. Therefore all we who are united to Christ, and as the Apostle says, "are members of His body, of His flesh and of His bones" (a), have issued from the womb of Mary like a body united to His head. Hence, in a spiritual and mystical fashion, we are all children of Mary, and she is Mother of us all (b), "the Mother spiritually, indeed, but truly the Mother of the members of Christ who we are" (c).

230
(29,
35,
81,
114)

229a Rom. 12:5.
229b Luke 2:11.
230a Eph. 5:30.
230b *Atqui æternum Dei Filium non ideo tantum concepit Virgo ut fieret homo, humanam ex ea assumens naturam; verum etiam ut, per naturam ex ea assumptam, mortalium fieret sospitator... In uno igitur eodemque alvo castissimæ Matris et carnem Christus sibi assumpsit et "spiritale" corpus adiunxit, ex iis nempe coagmentatum "qui credituri erant in eum." Ita ut Salvatorem habens Maria in utero, illos etiam dici queat gessisse omnes, quorum vita continebat vita Salvatoris... Unde, spiritali quidem ratione ac mystica, et Mariæ filii nos dicimur, et ipsa nostrum omnium mater est.*
230c St. Aug. *De Sancte Virginitate*, c. 6.

If then the Most Blessed Virgin is the Mother at once of God and men, who can doubt that she will endeavor with all diligence to bring it about that Christ, "the head of the body, the Church" (d), will transfuse His gifts into us, His members, and above all help us know Him and "live by Him" (e).

231
(42,
44)
Moreover it was not only the glory of the Mother of God to have presented to God the Only-Begotten who was to be born of human members (a) the material by which he was prepared as a Victim for the salvation of mankind, but hers also the office of tending and nourishing that Victim, and at the appointed time of offering Him at the altar.

232
(85,
116)
Hence the ever united life and labors of the Son and the Mother which permit the application to both of the words of the Psalmist: "My life is wasted with grief and my years in sighs" (a). When the supreme hour of the Son came, beside the cross of Jesus there stood Mary, His Mother, not merely occupied in contemplating the cruel spectacle, but rejoicing that her only Son was offered for the salvation of mankind; and so entirely participating in His Passion that, if it had been possible "she would have gladly borne all the torments that her Son underwent" (b).

Mediatrix of Redemption's graces

233
(37,
39,
46,
48)
From this community of will and suffering between Christ and Mary "she merited to become most worthily the reparatrix of the lost world" (a) and dispensatrix of all the gifts that our Savior purchased for us by His death and by His blood.

230d Col. 1:18.
230e 1 John 4:9.
231a St. Bede the Venerable l. V, in Luc. XI.
232a Ps. 30:11.   2
232b St. Bonav., I Sent. d. 48, ad Litt. dub. 4.
233a Eadmer Mon., *De Excellentia Virg. Mariæ,* c. 9.

It cannot of course be denied that the dispensing of these treasures is the particular and supreme right of Jesus Christ, for they are the excllusive fruit of His death, who by His Nature is the Mediator between God and man. Nevertheless, by this union in sorrow and suffering, as We have said, which existed between the Mother and the Son, it has been allowed to the August Virgin "to be the most powerful Mediatrix and advocate of the whole world, with her Divine Son" (b).

The source, then, is Jesus Christ, "and of His fullness we have all received" (a); "from Him the whole body (being closely joined and knit together through every joint of the system according to the functioning in due measure of each single part) derives its increase to the building up of itself in love." (b) But Mary, as St. Bernard justly remarks, is the "aqueduct," or if you will, the neck by which the body is joined to the head and the head transmits to the body its power and virtue: "For she is the neck of our Head, by which He communicated to His mystical Body all spiritual gifts" (c). We are thus, it will be seen, very far from declaring the Mother of God to be the authoress of supernatural grace. Grace comes from God alone. But since she surpassed all in holiness and union with Christ, and has been associated with Christ in the work of Redemption, she, as the expression is, merits *de congruo* what Christ merits *de condigno*, and is the principal minister in the distribution of grace (d).

234
(45,
47,
72)

233b Cf. above no. 64.
234a John 1:16.
234b Eph. 4:16.
234c St. Bern. Sen.,*Quadrag. de Evangelio æterno*, Serm. X, a. 3, c. 3.
234d *Ea tamen, quoniam universis sanctitate præstat coniunctioneque cum Christo, atque a Christo ascita in humanæ salutis opus, "de congruo," ut aiunt, promeret nobis quæ Christus "de condigno" promeruit, estque princeps largiendarum gratiarum ministra.*

He sitteth at the right hand of the Majesty on high (e);
but Mary sitteth as a Queen on His right hand, the secur-
est refuge of those who are in peril, as well as the most
faithful of helpers, so that we have naught to fear or
despair of, as long as she is our guide and our patroness,
she is our defender and our protector" (f).

235
(28,
46,
79,
125)
    With these principles laid down and returning to our
subject, will it not appear to all that it is right and proper
to affirm that Mary, whom Jesus made His constant companion from the house of Nazareth to the place of Calvary,
knew, as no other knew, the secrets of His heart, distributes
as by a mother's right the treasures of His merits, and is
the surest help to the knowledge and love of Christ? They
prove it only too truly who, by their deplorable manner
of life, deceived by false teaching, or the wiles of the devil,
fancy they can dispense with the aid of the Virgin Mother.
Miserable and unhappy are they who neglect her under
pretense that thus they honor Christ. They forget that the
"Child is not found without Mary His Mother" (a).

True devotion: conversion of heart

236
(127,
128)
    Under these circumstances, Venerable Brethren, such
is the end which all the solemnities that are everywhere
being prepared in honor of the Glory and Immaculate
Conception of Mary should have in view. No homage is
more agreeable to her, none is sweeter to her than that we
should know and really love Jesus Christ.

    Let then crowds fill the churches—let solemn feasts be
celebrated and public rejoicings be made. Such manifestations are eminently suited for enlivening our faith. But unless heart and will be added, they will all be empty forms,
mere appearances of piety. At such a spectacle the Virgin,

234e Hebr. 1:3.
234f Cf. above no. 65.
235a Cf. Matt. 2:11. - Luke 2:16.

borrowing the words of Christ, would address us with the just reproach: "This people honoreth me with their lips, but their heart is far from me" (a).

For to be genuine, our piety to the Mother of God   **237** must spring from the heart. Exterior acts have neither utili-   *(136,* ty nor value if the acts of the soul have no part in them.   *139)* Now these latter can only have one object, which is that we should fully carry out what the Divine Son of Mary commands. For if true love alone has the power to unite the wills of men, it is of prime necessity that we should have one will with Mary to serve Jesus our Lord. What this most prudent Virgin said to the servants at the marriage feast of Cana she addresses also to us: Whatever He shall say to you, do ye (a). Now here is the word of Jesus Christ: If you would enter into life, keep the commandments (b).

Let then each one fully convince himself of this, that if his piety toward the Blessed Virgin does not hinder him from sinning, or does not move his will to amend an evil life, it is a deceptive and lying piety, wanting, as it is, in proper effect, and in his natural fruit.

God's sanctity demanded the Immaculate Conception

If anyone desires a confirmation of this, it may easily   **238** be found in the dogma of the Immaculate Conception of   *(61,* Mary. For prescinding from Tradition which, as well as   *68,* Scripture, is a source of truth, whence has this conviction   *123)* of the Immaculate Conception of the Virgin shown itself in every age to be so much in keeping with the Christian mind as to appear fixed and innate in the hearts of the faithful. We shrink with horror from saying, as Denis the Carthusian so well expresses it, that "this Woman who was

236a Matt. 15:8.
237a John 2:5.
237b Matt. 19:17.

to crush the head of the serpent should have been crushed by him, and that the Daughter of God should have ever been the daughter of the evil one" (a). No, to the Christian intelligence the idea is unthinkable that the flesh of Christ, holy, stainless, innocent, was formed in the womb of Mary of a flesh which had ever, if only for the briefest moment, contracted any stain. Is there not an infinite opposition between God and sin? There certainly we have the origin of the conviction common to all Christians that, before Jesus Christ, clothed in human nature, cleansed us from our sins in His blood (b), he accorded Mary the grace and special privilege of being preserved and exempted from the first moment of her conception, from all stain of original sin.

239
(58,
69,
70)
If then God has such a horror of sin as to have willed to keep the future Mother of His Son not only free from the stains which are voluntarily contracted, but, by a special favor and in prevision of the merits of Christ, from that other stain of which the sad stain is transmitted to all the children of Adam, as by a sad heritage, who can doubt that it is a duty for everyone who desires to deserve well of Mary by his homage to correct his vicious and depraved habits and subdue the passions which incite him to evil?

Devotion leads to imitation

240
(80,
116,
131)
Whoever, then, wishes—and no one ought not so to wish—that his devotion should be perfect and worthy of her, should go further, and strive to his utmost to imitate her example.

It is a divine law that those only attain everlasting happiness who have by such faithful imitation reproduced in themselves the form of the patience and sanctity of Jesus

238a Dionys. Carth. 3 *Sent.*, d. 2. q. I.
238b Cf. Apoc. 7:14.

Christ: "For whom He foreknew, He also predestinated to be made conformable to the image of His Son, that He might be the firstborn among many brethren" (a).

But so deplorable is our weakness that we are sometimes discouraged by the greatness of such an example. By the providence of God, however, another example is proposed to us, which is both as near to Christ as human nature allows, and more nearly accords with the weakness of our nature. And this is no other than that of the Mother of God: "Such was Mary," very pertinently points out St. Ambrose, "that her life is an example for all."

And therefore he rightly concludes: "Have then before your eyes the virginity and life of Mary from whom as from a mirror shines forth the brightness of chastity and the form of virtue" (b).

Now if it becomes children not to omit to imitate any of the virtues of this most blessed Mother, we yet wish that the faithful apply themselves by preference to the principal virtues which are, as it were, the nerves and fibers of the Christian life—we mean faith, hope and charity toward God and our neighbor.   **241** *(80, 116, 131)*

Although no part of the life of Mary fails to show the brilliant character of these virtues, yet they attained their highest degree of splendor at the time when she stood by her dying Son. Jesus is nailed to the Cross, and He is reproached with maledictions, "for having made Himself the Son of God" (a). But she unceasingly recognized and adored the divinity in Him. She bore His dead body to the tomb, but never for a moment doubted that He would rise again. Then the love of God with which she burned made her a partaker in the sufferings of Christ and the associate in His Passion; with Him, moreover, as if forgetful of her

240a Rom. 8:29.
240b St. Ambr., *De Virginibus, L. II. c. 2.*
241a John 19:7.

own sorrow, she prayed for the pardon of the executioners although they in their hate cried out: "His blood be upon us and upon our children" (b).

The Immaculate Conception, Bulwark of Our Faith

242
(66)
But lest it be thought that we have lost sight of Our subject, which is the Immaculate Conception, what great and opportune help will be found in it for the preservation and right development of those same virtues! What in fact is the starting point of the enemies of religion in spreading the great and grievous errors by which the faith of so many is shaken? They begin by denying that man has fallen by sin and has been cast down from his primal state. Hence they regard as mere fables original sin and the evils that are its consequence. Humanity, vitiated in its source, vitiated in its turn the whole race of man, and thus was evil introduced among men, and the necessity for a Redeemer involved. Rejecting all this it is easy to understand that no place is left for Christ, for the Church, for grace, or for anything that is above or beyond nature; in a word, the whole edifice of faith is shaken from top to bottom.

243
(66)
But let the people believe and profess that the Blessed Virgin Mary has been from the first moment of her conception preserved from all stain; and it is straightway necessary to admit both original sin and the rehabilitation of the human race by Jesus Christ, the Gospel, and the Church, and the supernatural order. Thus Rationalism and Materialism will be torn up by the roots and destroyed, and the glory of Christianity as the guardian and protector of truth shines in all its splendor.

244
(66,
84)
These days especially it is a common practice of the enemies of the faith in their efforts to destroy the Christian faith in human souls to eradicate all reverence and obedi-

241b Matt. 27:25.

ence for any authority be it ecclesiastical or civil. Here we have the origin of anarchism, than which nothing is more pernicious and destructive to both the natural and supernatural order. Now the evil which is equally fatal to society at large and to Christianity is dispelled by the dogma of the Immaculate Conception by which we are impelled to recognize in the Church that power to which not only must the will be subjected but also the mind.

It is because of such subjection of the reason that Christians sing the praise of the Mother of God: "Thou art all fair, O Mary, and the stain of original sin is not in thee" (a).

And thus once again is justified what the Church attributes to this August Virgin, that "she has exterminated all heresies in the world" (a).   **245** *(27, 42, 68)*

And if, as the Apostle declares: "Faith is the substance of things to be hoped for" (b) everyone will easily grant that our faith is confirmed and our hope aroused and strengthened by the Immaculate Conception of the Virgin. The Virgin was kept immune from all stain of original sin because she was to be the Mother of Christ, and she was the Mother of Christ that the hope of everlasting happiness might be born again in our souls.

Safeguard of Fraternal Charity

Prescinding from our charity toward God, who can contemplate the Immaculate Virgin without feeling moved to fulfill that precept which Christ called peculiarly His own, namely that of loving one another, as He loved us?   **246** *(66)*

"A great sign" thus the Apostle St. John describes a vision divinely sent him, that appeared in the heavens, "a Woman clothed with the Sun and the Moon under her feet   **247** *(48, 88,*

244a Gradual of the Mass of the Immaculate Conception.
245a Antiphon at Matins, of Our Lady's Office.
245b Hebr. 11:1.

106) and on her head a crown of twelve stars" (a). Everyone
knows that this woman signified the Virgin Mary, the stainless one who brought forth our Savior.

The Apostle continues: "And being with child, she
cried, travailing in birth, and was in. pain to be delivered" (b).

John, therefore, saw the most holy Mother of God,
already in eternal happiness, yet travailing in a mysterious
childbirth. What birth was it? Surely it was the birth of us
who, still in exile, are yet to be generated to the perfect
charity of God, and to eternal happiness. And the birth
pains show the love and desire with which the Virgin from
heaven above watches over us, and strives with unweary-
ing prayer to bring about the completion of the number
of the elect.

248   This same charity We desire that all should earnestly
(135) endeavor to attain, taking advantage of the extraordinary
feasts in honor of the Immaculate Conception of the
Blessed Virgin.

Oh, how bitterly and fiercely is Jesus Christ now being
persecuted, as well as the most holy Religion which He
founded! And how grave is the peril that threatens many
of being drawn away to abandon the Faith by the errors
that are spread broadcast: "Wherefore he that thinketh himself to stand, let him take heed lest he fall" (a), and let
all, with humble prayer and entreaty, implore of God,
through the intercession of Mary, that those who have
abandoned the truth may repent.

We know, indeed, from experience that such prayer,
born of charity and trust in the Virgin, has never been vain.

249   True, even in the future, the strife against the Church
(121, will never cease, "for there must be also heresies; that they

247a Apoc. 12:1.
247b Apoc. 12:2.
248a 1 Cor. 10:12.

also who are approved may be made manifest among   *123)*
you" (a). But neither will the Virgin ever cease to succor
us in our trials, however grave they may be, and to carry
on the fight fought by her since her conception, so that
every day we may repeat: "Today the head of the serpent
of old was crushed by her" (b).

In order that heavenly graces may help Us more   **250**
abundantly than usual during this year to honor and to   *130)*
imitate the Blessed Virgin, and that thus We may more
easily secure Our object of restoring all things in Christ,
We have determined, after the example of Our Predecessors, at the beginning of their pontificates, to grant to the
Catholic world an extraordinary indulgence in the form of
a jubilee.

(*The Encyclical then outlines the conditions required
for gaining the indulgences of the jubilee.*)

The Rainbow

We close this letter, Venerable Brethren, by manifest-   **251**
ing anew the great hope We earnestly cherish that through   *(52,*
this extraordinary gift of jubilee granted by Us under the   *66,*
auspices of the Immaculate Virgin, large numbers of those   *169)*
who are unhappily separated from Jesus Christ may return
to Him, and that love of virtue and fervor of devotion may
flourish anew among the Christian people.

Fifty years ago, when Pius IX proclaimed as an article
of Faith the Immaculate Conception of the most Blessed
Mother of Christ, there was observed, as we have already
said, a most wondrous bestowal of graces on mankind;
and with the increase of confidence in the Virgin Mother
of God, the old religious spirit of the people was everywhere greatly augmented. May we not hope for still greater
things for the future?

249a 1 Cor. 11:19.
249b Office of the Immaculate Conception.

True, we are passing through disastrous times, when we may well make our own the lamentation of the Prophet: "There is no truth, and there is no mercy, and there is no knowledge of God in the land. Cursing and lying, and killing, and theft, and adultery have overflowed" (a). Yet in the midst of this deluge of evil, the Virgin most clement rises before our eyes like a rainbow, as the arbiter of peace between God and man: "I will set my bow in the clouds, and he shall be the sign of a covenant between me and between the earth" (b). Let the storm rage and sky darken— not for that shall we be dismayed. "And the bow shall be in the clouds, and I shall see it and shall remember the everlasting covenant" (c). "And there shall no more be waters of a flood to destroy all flesh" (d). Oh, yes, if we trust as we should in Mary, now especially when we are about to celebrate, with more than usual fervor her Immaculate Conception, we shall recognize in her the Virgin most powerful "who with virginal foot did crush the head of the serpent" (e).

FRUIT OF DEVOTION TO MARY

Apost. Letter *Ad omnium instaurationem,* to Cardinal Vannutelli, November 21, 1904.

252
(136,
137,
151)

Many indeed are the undertakings which We ardently desire to maintain and to develop among the Christian people in order to restore all things in Christ. We have given first place, as We have already declared, to devotion to the august and ever Virgin Mary, Mother of God. If this devotion has taken deep roots in souls We can be sure that

251a Osee 4:1-2.
251b Gen. 9:13.
251c Gen. 9:16.
251d Gen. 9:15.
251e Cf. Gen. 3:15.

it will produce and mature every fruit of virtue and of sanctity. In fact, what is said of Divine Wisdom which penetrates men's spirits may also justly be applied to devotion to the Virgin: "All good things came to me together with her" (a).

It was this thought which induced Us to approve and encourage with every means at hand the celebrations and general rejoicing of Catholics on the occasion of the fiftieth anniversary of the dogmatic definition of the Immaculate Conception of the Virgin Mary. The Marian Congress which will be shortly held in Rome will undoubtedly serve magnificently to spread devotion to the Mother of God.

We do not wish to let this opportunity pass without praising those who zealously undertook to prepare this Congress and without exhorting those who will participate in it to bear in mind chiefly the need to study and to establish practical means of augmenting in every place devotion to Mary.

APPARITIONS AT LOURDES

Apost. Letter *Summa Deus hominum,* November 27, 1907.

Moved by unequaled pity for mankind, God never ceases to work miracles by which He confirms the truth of religion and quickens the courage of the faithful, grants them relief and heals the infirmities of their bodies. However, not to the powerful of this earth, who proud of their riches, of their human learning, and of their public offices, often despise the faith and attack it with all their might, does our Lord reveal His mysteries; but rather to His dutiful children and not seldom to the little ones.

This, for example, He has done at Lourdes in France, where fifty years ago divine Mercy manifested itself visibly

253
(40, 155)

252a Wisdom 7:11.

in the person of the Virgin Mary, the Mediatrix. The Mother of God, preserved from all stain of sin, appeared several times to a girl of humble station in the Grotto called Massabielle, situated near the town, and, exhorting her as well as every one to practice penance, confirmed the heavenly vision with graces and wonders of every kind.

To perpetuate the memory of this wondrous happening, a temple sumptuously adorned was erected and honored with the title and privileges of a Minor Basilica. To it, as well as to the Grotto, have streamed at all times and from every country vast crowds imploring the aid of the Mother of Mercy and often obtaining answers to their prayers. At present that happy town possesses and with jealous care treasures that sanctuary, unique among the world's famous shrines, as a testimony to Catholic truth.

At the approach of the fiftieth anniversary of so stupendous a miracle, thanks to which devotion to the Virgin Mother of God, conceived without sin, and to her holy Rosary, has increased immeasurably, with a view to making the commemoration of that outstanding miracle more abundantly fruitful for the salvation of souls, We think We should open wide the Church's spiritual treasures, of which despite Our unworthiness the Most High has seen fit to appoint Us dispenser.

(*Appointing of a Jubilee.*)

QUEEN OF APOSTLES

Exhortation *Hærent Animo*, September 4, 1908.

(*50th Anniversary of ordination of the Holy Father. —Holiness required for the Priesthood.—Mary, Queen of Apostles.*)

254   She showed the Apostles at the happy beginning of
(50,   their priesthood how diligent they should be together in
115,   prayer, until they were clothed with virtue from on high;

and by the superabundance of her own prayers she surely   *117)*
obtained that virtue for them, at the same time increasing
and strengthening it by her counsels, all for the unlimited
fruitfulness of their apostolate.

LIVING MONSTRANCE

All. to the Franciscans, November 12, 1810.

(*Gratitude for their fidelity to the Holy See.—Exhortation to preserve the integrity of doctrine.*)

You, dear children, will guard the sanctity of your life   **255**
together with the purity and integrity of doctrine if you are   *(38,*
assiduous and careful in rendering devotion to the Queen   *46,*
of your Order, the Immaculate Mother of God. In fact, it   *126)*
is by means of her, of her who is the "mirror of justice" and
the "seat of wisdom" (a), that Almighty God ordained that
We should receive everything. When the wise men went to
Bethlehem to adore Jesus "they found on entering into the
house the Child with Mary His mother" (b). In our time
the Church is the house where Jesus and Mary receive the
newcomers. What, indeed, is Christian worship if not the
religion of Mary's Son?

If then, it is impossible to separate what God has   **256**
united, it is also certain that you cannot find Jesus except   *(24,*
with Mary and through Mary. With reason the saints called   *37,*
her "living Monstrance." She hastens to show us exiles in   *51,*
this vale of tears, Jesus, the way of salvation. Full of kind-   *52)*
ness and love, she transmits to her Son the invocations by
which we daily beseech her: "And after this our exile show
unto us the blessed fruit of thy womb, Jesus" (a). May the
Queen of Heaven, Mary our advocate, deign to continue to

255a From the Litany of Loreto.
255b Matt. 2:11.
256a Antiphon *Salve Regina.*

fulfill her motherly role on our behalf, and when sooner or later we lay aside this our mortal body, may she grant us the grace to see Jesus not as a king of awe-inspiring majesty and as a stern judge, but as the kind Savior, the smiling Friend, the merciful Brother.

(*Blessing.*)

OUR LADY OF A HAPPY DEATH

Letter *Ubere cum fructu,* to the Superior General of the Fathers of Tinchebray, April 30, 1911.

(*The 60th anniversary of the Confraternity for a Happy Death.*)

257
(*41-
44,
126,
173*)
In invoking Mary, the Mother of Sorrows, in the important business of eternal salvation, the Confraternity for a Happy Death, which We have already praised, has double grounds for being of advantage to all; first, it implores the aid of Mary, the Mother full of grace and mercy, secondly, it causes her to call to mind our Lord's Passion. The first guarantees for us throughout our lives and most of all at the moment of our last agony sure protection in the arms of the most loving of mothers; the other, the overflowing liberality of God's forgiveness. It was in the presence and under the very gaze of Mary that the divine sacrifice of our redemption was consummated; she took part in it by giving to the world and nourishing the divine Victim, she, the Queen of Martyrs (a). No title is more powerful than this in prompting her to heed the requests of those who pray to her, no argument as persuasive in inducing her to obtain from her divine Son pardon for our sins.

(*Encouragement and Blessing.*)

257a *Maria enim præsente ac spectante divinum illud sacrificium perfectum est quo redempti sumus, ejusque adeo fuit particeps ut victimam sacratissimam et peperit et aluerit, martyrum regina.*

ICONOGRAPHY

Decree of the Holy Office, January 15, 1913.

Since holy pictures representing the Blessed Virgin **258** Mary clad in priestly vestments have begun to be printed *(20)* and disseminated the eminent Cardinals Inquisitors decreed, after careful examination, that the image of the Blessed Virgin Mary clad in priestly vestments is to be condemned.

THE MESSAGE OF LOURDES

Letter *Ex omnibus locis,* to Cardinal Pignatelli, July 12, 1914.

Among the various places which have been so far chos- **259** en for the annual Catholic Congresses in honor of the Holy *(118,* Eucharist none seems more suitable than that chosen for the *120,* coming Congress—the Shrine of Lourdes. This sanctuary *121,* the Immaculate Virgin Mother of God has recently chosen, *155)* so to speak, as the seat of her wide-spread bounty.

From the beginning of Christianity the Church has experienced the continuous help of the Mother of God, help which has varied, it is true, according to changing times, but which has ever been fitting and gracious. Never did Mary wrench from her motherly heart that affection with which to her dying breath she so carefully formed the Spouse which her Son had recently redeemed by His precious Blood (a).

One might say that Mary's only occupation was to take **260** care of the Christian people,—whose condition on many oc- *(39,* casions seemed to be desperate—above all of attracting all *127,* souls to love and seek God. This was shown with extraor- *167,*

259a *Omnino eum materni animi affectum quo Sponsam filii sui, recens divino sanguine quæsitam, perstudiosa educavit usque ad extremum spiritum numquam exuit Maria.*

170) dinary evidence at the Grotto of Massabielle. There, moved
with compassion toward that human society which broke
the bonds of divine laws and consequently precipitated its
own ruin, Mary appeared and invited men to penance and
by the numerous miracles of bodily healing opened the way
to the healing of souls.

Then, as if she had finished her own part, she shows
to the wavering men of this century the Heavenly Doctor
in person, the only One who can free this world from all
the ills that torment it. It is worthy of note that in this place
of devotion to the Mother of God a singular and ardent devotion to Jesus Christ has sprung up. Even the miraculous
healings which at first took place before the statue of the
Virgin now take place more frequently during the procession of the Blessed Sacrament.

(*Greetings for France.—Sending of the Legate.*)

BENEDICT XV

(1914 - 1922)

MEDIATRIX OF PEACE

All. to the Consistory, December 24, 1915.

(*Efforts of the Pope to obtain peace.—Christmas, feast of peace.*)

The scene of Jesus' birth is complete through the presence of Mary. The faith of her believers and her children's love consider her not only God's Mother, but also the Mediatrix with God.

Mother of the Prince of peace, Mediatrix between rebellious man and the merciful God, she is the dawn of peace shining in the darkness of a world out of joint; she never ceases to implore her Son for peace although His hour is not yet come (a); she always intervenes on behalf of sorrowing humanity in the hour of danger; today she who is the mother of many orphans and our advocate in this tremendous catastrophe will most quickly hear our prayers.

In view of these considerations and the better to direct Christian thought and trust in the most powerful intercession of the Mother of God We, in answer to the requests of many children far and near, consent that they address the Blessed Virgin in the Litany of Loreto with the invocation, "Queen of Peace." And will Mary, who is Queen of a kingdom of peace and not of wars and disasters, reject the desires and prayers of her trusting children?

261
(37,
48,
50,
168,
169,
176)

On this holy night in which the prophetic promises of the golden age and of blessed times were fulfilled and on which the very Author of peace gave us the heavenly child, will she not smile on hearing the voices of innocent children called by the Episcopate and by Us to the Eucharistic Table on this lovely solemnity?

262
(46,
49,
134)

261a John 2:4.

When man has hardened his heart and hate has over-
run the earth, when fire and sword convulse the world and
make it resound with clash of arms and of wailing, when
human plans have proved misleading, and when all social
well-being is upset, faith and history point to Mary as the
only refuge, the all powerful intercessor, the Mediatrix of
all grace ... therefore, let us say with sure trust: Queen of
Peace, pray for us!

(*Conclusion.*)

QUEEN OF PEACE

Letter *Il* 27 *Aprile* 1915, to Cardinal P. Gasparri,
May 5, 1917.

(*The Pope's efforts to stop the War.*)

263
(*37,
46,
169*)
... And since all the graces which God deigns to bestow in pity upon men are dispensed through the most
holy Virgin, We urge that more than ever in this terrible
hour, the trusting petitions of her most afflicted children
be directed to the august Mother of God.

Hence we direct Your Eminence to make known to
all the bishops of the world that it is our fervent desire
that mankind turn to the Sacred Heart of Jesus—the Throne
of Grace—and that recourse to this Throne be made through
Mary. Accordingly We ordain that beginning with the first
day of June this year, there be placed in the Litany of
the Blessed Virgin the invocation: *Queen of Peace* pray
for us.... We have so authorized the Ordinaries to add it
temporarily by the decree of the Sacred Congregation of
Extraordinary Ecclesiastical Affairs by date of November 16, 1915.

264
(*169*)
From every corner of the earth—from the majestic
churches and the humble chapels; from the mansions of
the rich as well as from the huts of the poor; from
wherever dwells a faithful soul; from the bloodstained
battlefields and war swept seas, may this pious and ardent

invocation arise to Mary, the Mother of Mercy who is all-powerful in grace! To Mary may be brought each anguished cry of mothers and wives, each tear of innocent children, each longing of generous hearts! May her loving and most merciful solicitude be moved to obtain for this convulsed world the peace so greatly desired! And may the ages yet to come remember the efficacy of Mary's intercession and the greatness of her blessings to her suppliants!

(*Blessing.*)

PATRON OF A HAPPY DEATH

Letter *Inter sodalicia,* to the Association for a Happy Death, May 22, 1918.

Among the associations that promote devotion to the Blessed Virgin Mary and at the same time contribute to the spiritual interests of the faithful the association which bears the title of "Our Lady of a Happy Death," recently founded by the Fathers of Saint Mary of Tinchebray, certainly occupies a most honorable place if one considers the purpose which animates it and its already large diffusion throughout the world with abundance of fruit. **265** *(173)*

Those who take part in it, as the principles and rules of this society show, have the following aims: to venerate the Virgin of Sorrows and to do all in their power to have her honored by everyone; to offer God the merits of the prayers and sufferings of the same Virgin who stood at the foot of the cross of Jesus; trusting in these merits to obtain for themselves and for others the grace to persevere in faith and in the Christian life or at least to return to these; and, above all, to obtain the grace of a happy death in the love of Christ on whom eternal happiness depends. **266** *(173)*

The choosing and invoking of Our Lady of Sorrows as patroness of a happy death is in full conformity with Catholic Doctrine and with the pious sentiment of the **267** *(22, 41-*

44,
116,
173)
Church. It is also based on a wise and well-founded hope. In fact, according to the common teaching of the Doctors it was God's design that the Blessed Virgin Mary, apparently absent from the public life of Jesus, should assist Him when He was dying nailed to the Cross. Mary suffered and, as it were, nearly died with her suffering Son; for the salvation of mankind she renounced her mother's rights and, as far as it depended on her, offered her Son to placate divine justice; so we may well say that she with Christ redeemed mankind (a).

268
(31,
35,
41,
47,
134,
173)
Consequently, if the graces which we receive from the treasury of the Redemption are distributed, so to speak, by the hands of this sorrowful Virgin, no one can deny that the grace of a happy death must come from Mary because, in fact, it is by means of this preeminent grace that the work of Redemption reaches its fulfillment in every man. In the same way, the sorrowful Virgin was constituted by Jesus Christ as Mother of all men, and as she received them as a heritage from the infinite love of Jesus, she assumed with maternal love the duty of watching over their spiritual life,—it is evident that she cannot do other than help most devotedly her dearest adopted sons at the hour in which it is necessary to secure for them salvation and sanctity for all eternity. Thus the Church herself, in numerous prayers of the liturgy, constantly begs the Blessed Virgin Mary to grant her merciful assistance to the dying. The faithful also cherish the firm belief, supported by long experience, that all those who seek Mary's protection will be saved for all eternity.

(*Approval of the apostolate of a Happy Death.—Granting of indulgences.*)

267a *Scilicet ita cum Filio patiente et moriente passa est et pæne commortua, sic materna in Filium jura pro hominum salute abdicavit placandæque Dei justitiæ, quantum ad se pertinebat, Filium immolavit, ut dici merito queat, Ipsam cum Christo humanum genus redemisse.*

THE SCOPE OF CONGRESSES

Letter *Cohæret plane,* to the bishops of Columbia, March 21, 1919.

Your project of holding a Marian Congress in the near future fully conforms with Our desires. Of what love indeed, of what honor is not the Blessed Virgin worthy, she who was so greatly loved by God Himself as to be chosen by Him to be His own Mother! How powerful with Jesus must be the intercession of her who was raised to such a high dignity and with what bounty must she not love those who cherish her! We cannot even think of her without at the same time feeling Ourselves burn with the desire of seeing all the faithful prove how they love, honor and imitate this most loving Mother. This is why we so greatly congratulate you for your project and in it place great hopes. **269** *(21, 22, 107, 126)*

As for you, Venerable Brethren, see to it that the measures taken are not only a vapor "which appeareth for a little while" (a), that they aim not only at outward appearances, nor edify only for a day or two; but that they produce a stimulating and lasting help for furthering devotion toward the Virgin and for increasing faith and fortifying Christian morals. Who could say that the scope of these Catholic assemblies, even if there were no other result, consists only in praising the Virgin? This end is indeed holy and praiseworthy, but it is necessary that another and a superior one be added to it: it is necessary that the flowers of a tender devotion toward Maay grow as the lily and that the actions of a Christian life yield "a sweet odor and bring forth leaves in grace" (b). **270** *(151)*

(*Blessing.*)

270a James 4:15.
270b Ecclus. 39:19.

All. *Il Nous serait difficile,* to pilgrims present at the approval of the miracles for the canonization of Joan of Arc, April 6, 1919.

(Discourse of the Bishop of Orleans.)

271
(46,
47)
First of all, grateful to God and to the powerful Virgin, We must recognize that we are debtors to God alone for the two miracles attributed to Joan of Arc, the authenticity of which has today been proclaimed. And if in every miracle We must recognize the mediation of Mary by means of whom according to the divine will all graces and favors come to us, no one can deny that in one of the miracles approved by Us this mediation of the Blessed Virgin has been manifested in a very special manner.

272
(37,
46)
We think God has so disposed matters to remind the faithful that we must never forget Mary even when the miracle seems to be attributed to the intercession or the mediation of one who has been beatified or canonized. We believe that such is the lesson to be learned from the fact that Theresa Belin was completely and instantaneously cured at the Sanctuary of Lourdes. On one hand Our Lord shows us that even on this earth, which is confided to the care of His Blessed Mother, He can work miracles through the intercession of one of His servants; on the other hand, He reminds us that even in such cases it is necessary to postulate the intercession of her who the Holy Father greeted as "Mediatrix Mediatorum omnium." The eminent speaker with every good reason placed the first flower of gratitude at the foot of God's throne and at the feet of the Virgin.

(Benedict XV, Pope of Joan of Arc.—His love for France.)

EXAMPLE OF SAINT DOMINIC

Encycl. *Fausto appetente die,* June 29, 1921.

(The seventh çentenary of St. Dominic's birth.—His apostolic action distinguished for the depth of his doctrine, for his fidelity to the Holy See and his devotion to Mary.)

Saint Dominic loved Mary with a very tender and filial affection and he always placed his whole trust in her, especially so when he took in hand the Catholic cause. In the struggle against the Albigensian heretics who denied, among other truths of the Faith, the divine maternity and virginity of Mary he invoked while strenuously defending this dogma the help of the Virgin Mother with that ejaculation which he had often on his lips: "Dignare me laudare te, Virgo sacrata; da mihi virtutem contra hostes tuos" (a). **273** *(20, 87)*

It is easy to understand with what kindness the Queen of heaven responded to the devotion of her servant from the fact that she used him as her means to teach the holy Rosary to the Church. This sweet prayer being both vocal and mental (the meditation of the principal mysteries of religion accompanied by the recitation of five Our Fathers and five decades of Hail Marys) is most suitable to nourish souls and encourage them to practice virtue. **274** *(142)*

St. Dominic was inspired to ask his disciples while preaching God's word to impress often this form of prayer, of whose efficacy he was well aware, on the souls of their listeners. He knew well that while on one hand Mary is all powerful with her divine Son who grants all graces to mankind through her, on the other hand she is by nature so good and so merciful that inclined to aid spontaneously those who suffer she is absolutely incapable of refusing her help to those who invoke her. The Church is in the habit **275** *(46, 48)*

273a Antiphon from the Office of the Blessed Virgin.

of greeting the Virgin as *Mother of grace and Mother of mercy* and so she has always shown herself, especially when we have recourse to her by means of the Holy Rosary. For this reason the Roman Pontiffs have never neglected the opportunity to praise the efficacy of the Marian Rosary and to enrich it with a veritable treasure of indulgences.

(*May the Order of Preachers be faithful to this tradition.*)

PIUS XI

(1922-1939)

FRANCE, THE KINGDOM OF MARY

Apost. Letter, *Galliam Ecclesiæ filiam,* March 2, 1922.

The Roman Pontiffs, Our Predecessors, have during **276** the centuries ever showered on France, justly called the *(159)* first daughter of the Church, special signs of their paternal affection. Our Predecessor of holy memory, Pope Benedict XV, who took the spiritual cause of France deeply to heart thought of giving to that nation, noble among all, a singular proof of his benevolence.

In fact, when Our Venerable Brethren, the Cardinals, Archbishops, and Bishops of France with unanimous consent recently sent to him, by the hands of Our venerable Brother Stanislaus Touchet, bishop of Orleans, ardent and fervent petitions that he would proclaim the Virgin Mary, assumed into heaven, as principal Patroness of the French nation and St. Joan, the Maid of Orleans, as second patroness, Our Predecessor intended to answer graciously those pious requests. Overtaken by death, he could not carry out his intention. But We who have been raised by divine grace to the Sublime Chair of the Prince of the Apostles are pleased and glad to carry out the plan of Our deeply-mourned Predecessor and We decree with Our full Authority what for France can become the source of good fortune, prosperity and happiness.

Devotion of France

It is certain, according to an old adage, that "the **277** kingdom of France" has been called "the kingdom of Mary." *(64,* France has deserved the title. From the early centuries of *159,* the Church down to the present day, Ireneus, and Eucherius *175)* of Lyons, Hilary of Poitiers and Anselm, who went from France to England as archbishop, Bernard of Clairvaux,

Francis de Sales and numerous other holy Doctors have exalted Mary and helped to promote and spread throughout France devotion to the Virgin Mother of God. From the 13th century in the University of the Sorbonne, Paris, it has been historically proved that the Virgin was proclaimed immaculately conceived.

278
(152,
159)
Even the sacred monuments wonderfully bear witness to the people's ancient devotion to the Blessed Virgin. Thirty-four cathedrals enjoy the title of the Virgin Mother of God. Among these the most celebrated are: those of Rheims, Paris, Amiens, Chartres, Coutances and Rouen. Great numbers of faithful who come yearly from distant places to Marian shrines clearly show what devotion to the Mother of God can do among the people and many times during the year the Basilica of Lourdes, huge as it is, seems incapable of holding the countless throngs of pilgrims.

The Virgin Mother of God in person, before God treasurer of all graces, by her repeated apparitions seemed to approve and confirm the devotion of the French people.

279
(132,
159)
Moreover, the nation's responsible leaders have for a long time gloried in strengthening and defending this devotion to the Virgin. Converted to the Christian faith, Clovis hastened to erect on the ruins of a druid temple the Church called Notre Dame, which his son, Childebert, completed. Several churches were dedicated to Mary by Charlemagne. The Dukes of Normandy proclaimed Mary Queen of the nation. St. Louis, the King, daily recited with devotion the Office of the Blessed Virgin. Louis XI in fulfillment of his vow built a church to Our Lady at Cléry. Finally, Louis XIII consecrated the kingdom of France to Mary and ordered that annually on the feast of the Assumption of the Virgin solemn celebrations should be held in every diocese of France. We know that those solemn functions are still held every year.

Our Lady and Joan of Arc

With regard to the Maid of Orleans, whom Our Prede-   **280**
cessor raised to the supreme honor of sainthood, no one *(159,*
can deny that it was through the influence of the Virgin   *175)*
Mary that she received and accomplished the mission of
saving France. First, it was under the patronage of Our
Lady of Bermont, then under that of Our Lady of Orleans,
and finally under that of Our Lady of Rheims that she
undertook so great an enterprise with the courage of a man,
that she remained intrepid in the face of drawn swords
and spotless amid the corruption of the camps, that she
freed her country from extreme danger and reestablished
the fortunes of France. It was at the promptings of her
heavenly voices that on her glorious standard she added
Mary's name to that of Jesus, true King of France. Tied
to the stake and enveloped in flames, her soul soared up
to heaven as she uttered in a loud cry the names of Jesus
and Mary. Having experienced the manifest help of the
Maid of Orleans in time of a terrible scourge, may France
now enjoy the favor of this second heavenly patroness!
This is what the people requested, what Our Predecessor
desired, and what now pleases Us.

Having, therefore, taken advice of our Venerable
Brethren, the Cardinals of the Holy Roman Church in
charge of Rites, We declare, *motu proprio,* for the present
and in perpetuity, with certain knowledge and after mature
deliberation in the fullness of Our apostolic power, and
We confirm that the Virgin Mary Mother of God, under
the title of her Assumption into heaven, has been lawfully
chosen after God, as principal Patroness of all France, with
all the privileges and honors that that noble title and
dignity demand.

(*Joan of Arc, secondary Patroness.*)

SABBATINE PRIVILEGE

Letter *Petis tu quidem,* to Father Elias Magennis, Superior General of the Carmelites, March 18, 1922.

(*Sixth centenary of the Sabbatine Privilege.—The Confraternities of Our Lady of Mt. Carmel.*)

281
(128,
136,
173)

You ask Us to recommend—at the closing of the sixth centennial commemorating the universal diffusion in the Church of the "Sabbatine Privilege"—to the faithful throughout the Catholic world the devotion to Our Lady of Mount Carmel, and the sodalities for lay people, which take their name from the Virgin herself. We willingly do so with this Letter. In fact, with this attestation of devotion We wish to draw down upon us the good will of the great Mother of God, whom We have greatly loved since our infancy, and thus place under her care the beginning of Our Pontificate.

We do not deem it necessary to be lengthy in recommending the sodalities which the Virgin herself recommends with her liberality, and which Our Predecessors enriched with many favors, and which the zealous devotion of the Carmelite Fathers have diffused everywhere with such copious fruits. Instead We believe it more opportune to exhort those enrolled in these sodalities to observe, with persevering fervor, the conditions required to gain the various indulgences granted and above all those most important indulgences which are called "sabbatine." The Virgin, in fact, has a predilection for those who love her, nor can anyone rightfully hope to have her assistance at the point of death if, during life, he did not merit this assistance both by avoiding sin, as well as by doing that which would honor her (a).

(*Blessing.*)

281a *Diligentes enim se diligit Virgo, nec quisquam sperare jure potest se eam habiturum adjutricem in morte, nisi in vita eius inierit gratiam tum abstinendo a culpa, tum quidpiam præstando quod cedat in eiusdem honorem.*

PATRON OF THE DYING

Apost. Letter *Explorata res est,* February 2, 1923.

(Apostolate of a happy death.)

He will not taste death forever, who in his dying **282** moments has recourse to the Blessed Virgin Mary. This *(29,* opinion of the Doctors of the Church, which agrees with *32,* the mind of Christian people, is confirmed by constant *52,* experience and is based above all on the fact that the *173)* sorrowful Virgin took part with Jesus Christ in the work of the Redemption. She was constituted Mother of men, who were confided to her as a testimony of divine love. She took them to herself as sons and she lovingly protects them.

It is useless to delay long over this point, since Our Predecessor Benedict XV, of happy memory, explained it sufficiently in his apostolic Letter *Inter Sodalicia,* of May 22, 1918 (a).

RETURN OF THE EASTERN CHURCHES

Encycl. *Ecclesiam Dei,* November 12, 1923.

(The third centenary of St. Josaphat, apostle of unity.)

Another link in the reestablishment of unity with the **283** Eastern Slavic peoples lies in their singular love of and *(125,* devotion to the august Virgin Mother of God. By means *159,* of this devotion they distinguish themselves from a great *171)* number of heretics and are near to us. St. Josaphat was particularly noted for his devotion to the Virgin and he placed all his trust in her to favor the work of unity. He was also accustomed to venerate, according to the use of the Orientals, a small icon of the Mother of God

282a Cf. above N. 265 ff.

which the monks of St. Basil and the faithful of both
rites here in Rome venerate with marked devotion in the
church of Saints Sergius and Bacchus under the title of
Queen of Pasture-lands, del Pascolo. Let us, therefore, invoke under this special title, the most lovable Mother and
pray her to guide our wandering brethren to the pastures
of salvation, where St. Peter, always living in his successor,
the Vicar of the Eternal Shepherd, feeds and governs all
the lambs and sheep of Christ's flock.

BERNADETTE'S MISSION

All. following the decree of heroicity, November 18, 1923.

283 bis
(66,
173)

Bernadette's name is intimately connected with these
miracles. It has been said: "*Qui venit in solem, colorabitur,*
he who comes into the sun, will take on its color" (a).
It is not possible that Bernadette failed to take on the aspect
of Mary, so close was she to the Immaculate Virgin. She was
called to be the Virgin's first confidant, to guard her designs
as Queen and Mother, to represent her before the Catholic
Church, to communicate her wishes and commands. Therefore it was natural for Mary to prepare her for those momentous offices and to make her all the more deserving
of them. We have seen how such a preparation was made
in Mary, but in an incomparable manner. The Angel who
drew near her to announce that she was the Mother of God
found her full of grace and greeted her: "Hail, full of grace!"

(*Our mission is to cooperate with God in our neighbor's salvation.*)

283a Seneca, epist. 108, 4.

FRUITS OF MARIAN DEVOTION

Encycl. *Quas Primas,* December 11, 1925.

(*Christ's triumph.—His royalty.—Feast of Christ the King.—Teaching value of liturgical feasts.*)

But more fruitful still were the feasts instituted in honor of the Blessed Virgin. In consequence of these men increased not only in their devotion to the Mother of God as an ever-present advocate but also in their love of her as the mother bequeathed to them by their Redeemer. Not least among the blessings which have followed from the public and liturgical honors paid to the Blessed Virgin and the saints is the perfect and perpetual immunity of the Church from error and heresy. **284** *(126, 136)*

(*Hopes of new triumphs.*)

PROTECTRESS OF THE MISSIONS

Encycl. *Rerum Ecclesiæ,* February 28, 1926.

(*The missions.—Duty of Bishops.—Recruiting of missionaries.—Practical directives.*)

May Mary, Queen of the Apostles, who on Calvary took to her mother's heart the care of all humanity, deign to second our undertakings; may she love with an equal tenderness all those who do not know that they have been redeemed by Jesus Christ and all those who happily enjoy the fruits of that Redemption! **285** *(31, 40, 172)*

CHARTRES, CITY OF MARY

Letter *Cum feliciter,* to Cardinal Dubois, May 18, 1927.

As the custom of organizing religious Congresses to promote the Catholic Faith has so happily spread, it is very **286** *(125,*

159,   opportune that similar congresses be organized to preserve
168)   the people's devotion to the Mother of God. As always,
        but especially in the perils and difficulties of Our times, the
        Christian people certainly need the powerful help of Mary.

        From the beginning of Our Pontificate, We always
        fastened Our gaze and Our heart on the most sweet Virgin
        as the hope of men's salvation, and We never ceased to
        exhort all the faithful to promote devotion to her as often
        as the occasion arose.

        It was, therefore, with great joy that We learned of
        the Marian Congress to be held in Chartres on the occasion
        of the ninth century of the construction of the celebrated
        crypt in honor of the august Mother of God. On that occa-
        sion an excellent project was suggested—the calling of the
        Congress of Chartres. This project is all the more excellent
        since throughout Gaul Chartres was considered as the city
        of Mary, and the faithful were accustomed to go on pil-
        grimages from every part of Gaul to her sacred temple.
        The testimonies, kept among you, of the ancient devotion
        to your heavenly Patroness are so numerous and so illustri-
        ous that an ecclesiastical writer rightly declared: "The
        kingdom of France is the kingdom of Mary."

        (*Appointment of Legate.*)

MARY REPARATRIX

Encycl. *Miserentissimus Redemptor*, May 8, 1928.

(*Consecration to the Sacred Heart of Jesus and offering
of honorable amends in reparation.—Their opportuneness;
their fruits; practices.*)

287   May the most gracious Mother of God, who gave us Je-
(37,   sus as Redeemer, who reared Him, and at the foot of the
48)   Cross offered Him as Victim, who by her mysterious union
         with Christ and by her matchless grace rightly merits the
         name Reparatrix, deign to smile upon Our wishes and Our

undertakings. Trusting in her intercession with Christ our Lord, who though sole Mediator between God and man, wished however to make His Mother the advocate for sinners and the dispenser and mediatrix of His grace, from the bottom of Our heart as a token of heavenly favor and of Our fatherly solicitude We heartily impart to you and to all the faithful entrusted to your care Our Apostolic Benediction.

SALVATION OF CHRISTIANITY

Letter *Cum valde,* to Cardinal Esteban, February 20, 1929.

We are truly delighted with those Congresses which **288** increase devotion to the Blessed Sacrament all over the *(121,* world. We are just as pleased when Congresses are held *129,* in various places to excite daily greater devotion to the *168,* august mother of God. Who is ignorant of the powerful *177)* help that the Virgin Mother of God gives to the Christian people when difficulties of every kind arise on every side and when cruel wars make havoc of all that is Catholic? It is no wonder then that the Catholic Church at all times places her trust first in God and then in the powerful Virgin, bestows all honors on her and entreats her with many prayers.

From whom can we expect the salvation of the Christian people today if not from her of whom it is written that whosoever shall find her shall find life, and shall have salvation from the Lord? (a)

(*Cardinal delegated to preside over the Congress.*)

288a Prov. 8:35.

THE XV CENTENARY OF THE COUNCIL
OF EPHESUS

Letter *Ephesinam Synodum,* to Cardinal Sincero, December 25, 1930.

289
(24)
We are all aware that after the Council of Nicea the Council of Ephesus was the most celebrated of the Ecumenical Councils. The first defined and solemnly decreed against Arius the Divinity of Jesus Christ; the second defined and decreed against Nestorius the dogma of the Hypostatic Union and the divine Maternity of Mary. The universal Church, therefore, which five years ago commemorated the Council of Nicea, will shortly, as is fitting, celebrate in the most suitable way possible the fifteenth centenary of the Council of Ephesus.

290
(154)
Ancient historians narrate that Our Predecessor of holy memory, Celestine I, in the case against the Nestorian heresy, not only chose as his Vicar Cyril, the irresistible Patriarch of Alexandria, but that he also sent in 431, in the office of legates to the Council which was to be held at Ephesus, in the presence of Emperor Theodosius II, the bishops Arcadius and Projectus and with them the priest Philip, giving them the following instructions: "The authority of the Apostolic See must be protected. We command it. . . . If questions for debate arise, you should be judges of the opinions put forth, but do not allow yours to be discussed."

291
(20)
From this it follows that the Roman Pontiff had already taken up arms against the Nestorian heresy even before the Council pronounced sentence against it. Indeed, in the first session over which Cyril of Alexandria, as Vicar of Pope Celestine presided, when they decreed that "Mary was the true Mother of God," the Fathers of the Council declared that they had passed sentence against Nestorius according to the Canons and the letter of their most holy

Father and protector Celestine. Thus, in this text the primacy of the Roman Pontiff is at the same time clearly demonstrated.

We are told that while the bishops ardently defended the dignity of the Mother of God against Nestorius, the people of Ephesus crowded before the hall where the Council was held. When, toward evening, after a long and lively discussion the doors opened and it was solemnly decreed that "Mary was true Mother of God" the devotion of the people was so great that on hearing it they acclaimed the Fathers with an outpouring of joy, and, organizing a procession with blazing torches as signs of faith, they accompanied the bishops to their dwellings. Today, after many centuries all the Christian people manifest the liveliest devotion towards Mary. Thus is fully verified the prophecy of the Virgin Mary herself: "Behold from now on all the generations shall call me blessed" (a). **292** *(20, 154)*

Therefore as it is Our desire that the whole Catholic world which so much enjoys the motherly aid of the Virgin should commemorate the Council of Ephesus, We ordain by this letter, Venerable Brethren, that inasmuch as under Our authority you direct the affairs of the Oriental Church, and exercise your zeal in promoting them, do all in your power to make known in the East this Council and all that relates to it. To that end you will convoke a Council made up of men of ability, who, under your presidency, shall decide on the most suitable means to commemorate worthily this anniversary; and also choose talented persons who in their learned writings and by means of their discourses shall pay tribute to this happy event. **293** *(34, 171)*

We trust that Marian devotion will receive new vigor from this, and that at the same time the Orientals, through the triumph of Mary, the thoughtful Mother of all, will fi- **294** *(154, 171)*

292a Luke 1:48.

nally return to the bosom of the Roman Church, whose pre-eminence the Council of Ephesus among others of history's examples so clearly attests.

(*Blessing.*)

DOGMA OF THE DIVINE MATERNITY

Encycl. *Lux Veritatis*, December 25, 1931.

(*Celebration of the Centenary of the Council of Ephesus.*)

295   Considering this event and all the facts and circumstances connected with it as the celebration draws to a close, and the sacred season when the Blessed Virgin Mary brought forth for us the Savior, recurs, We, by the Apostolic Office which We hold from on high, deem it proper to communicate by this Encyclical Letter on this most important matter.

We cherish the good hope that not only will our words be pleasing and useful to you and yours, but also, that if the many who are separated from the Apostolic See, brothers and sons most dear to Us, being moved by the quest of truth, reflect and ponder on them, they cannot help being led by history as the teacher of life, and affected by the desire at least of one fold and one Shepherd to embrace the true faith which is ever kept sound and entire in the Roman Church.

296   In the process which the Fathers of the Council of
(46) Ephesus followed, in opposing the Nestorian heresy and conducting the Council, three dogmas of the Catholic religion, which We shall treat principally, shine forth with brilliance in the eyes of all; namely that the person of Jesus Christ is one and divine; that the blessed Virgin Mary should be acknowledged and venerated by everyone as really and truly the Mother of God; and that when matters

of faith or morals are concerned the Roman Pontiff has from on high an authority which is supreme, above all others and subject to none.

(*History of Nestorius.*)

Repercussion of errors about Christ

To appreciate the matter properly it will help to touch **297** briefly on the principal points of the Nestorian heresy. *(20)* This highly elated man, claiming that there were two complete *hypostases*, the human of Jesus, and the divine of the Word, meeting in one common *prosopo*, as he termed it, denied the marvelous and substantial union of the two natures, which we call hypostatic, and asserted that the only-begotten Word of God was not made man, but was in human flesh only by indwelling, by good pleasure, and by virtue of operating in it; that therefore he should be called not God, but *Theophoron*, or God-bearer, in much the same manner as prophets and other holy men, owing to the divine grace imparted to them, might be called God-bearing.

From these perverse fabrications of Nestorius it was easy to recognize in Christ two persons: one divine, the other human. It followed necessarily that the Blessed Virgin is not truly the Mother of God, *Theotokos*, but Mother rather of the man Christ, *Christotocon*, or at most *Theodochon*, that is the recipient of God.

(*Saint Cyril, defender of the dogma.—The Ephesus Council and Roman primacy.—The doctrine of hypostatic union and its consequences.*)

Faith of the Church

From this principle of Catholic doctrine which We **298** have treated thus far, there necessarily follows the dogma *(24)* of the divine motherhood which we attribute to the Blessed Virgin Mary, as Cyril reminds us, "not that the nature or

divinity of the Word took its origin or beginning from the
Holy Virgin, but in this sense that He derived from her
His sacred body, perfected by an intelligent soul, to which
the Word of God was hypostatically united, and by which
He was born according to the flesh" (a).

299
(20,
24,
26)
If the. Son of the Blessed Virgin Mary is God, certainly she who bore Him should rightly and deservingly
be called Mother of God. If the person of Jesus Christ
is one and divine, surely Mary is not only mother of
Christ, but should be called *Deipara*, "*Theotokos*" (a).

300
(76,
126)
Her, who was proclaimed by Elizabeth, her relative,
"Mother of my Lord" (a), who is acknowledged by the
martyr Ignatius to have brought forth God, her from
whom Tertullian says: "God was born," we can all venerate
as the beloved Mother of God, whom the Eternal Godhead
favored with fullness of grace and honored with so much
dignity.

301
(26,
56)
Moreover, no one can reject this truth handed down
from the first ages of the Church, namely, that the Blessed Virgin Mary gave to Jesus Christ a body, but did not
generate the Word of the heavenly Father; for Cyril in his
day rightly and clearly answers that just as all other women in whose womb is engendered our earthly composite
are called and really are mothers, so she by reason of the
unique personality of her Son, likewise acquired divine
maternity.

302
(20,
Rightly therefore the impious opinion of Nestorius,
which the Bishop of Rome, guided by the Holy Spirit,

298a Mansi, IV, 891.
299a *Enimvero, si Filius beatæ Mariæ Virginis Deus est, illa
pro certo, quæ eum genuit, Dei mater iure est meritoque
appelanda; si una est Jesu Christi persona, eaque divina,
procul dubio Maria non Christi hominis Genitrix tantummodo, sed Deipara, seu Theotocos vocari ab omnibus debet.*
300a Luke 1:43.

had condemned the year before, was again solemnly repro-
bated by the Council of Ephesus.

123)

So great was the devotion of the people of Ephesus
to the Virgin as *Deipara*, and so intense their love that,
on hearing the judgment of the Fathers of the Council,
they acclaimed them with an outpouring of joy, and forming ranks with blazing torches they accompanied them to
their homes. Surely she, the great *Parens Dei*, smiling
sweetly from heaven, on that remarkable spectacle, took
care of her children of Ephesus and all the faithful of
Christ in the Catholic world who were disturbed by the
treachery of the Nestorian heresy, with maternal heart
and ever ready assistance.

The source of Mary's privileges

From this dogma of the divine maternity, as from a
hidden spring of gushing water, flows the singular grace
of Mary and, after God, her great dignity. Indeed as
Aquinas nobly writes: "The Blessed Virgin, as Mother of
God, has a certain infinite dignity from the infinite Good
Who is God" (a).

303
(26,
27,
76,
77)

Cornelius a Lapide develops and explains this more
fully: "The Blessed Virgin is Mother of God, and therefore
by far excels all the angels, even the seraphim and cherubim.
She is Mother of God, therefore most pure and holy; so
much so that under God no greater purity can be imagined.
She is Mother of God, and therefore whatever privilege
has been granted to any of the saints in the order of sanctifying grace she surpasses all" (a).

304
(27,
72,
76)

Justification of Devotion to Mary

Why, therefore, should so many innovators and non-
Catholics bitterly condemn our devotion to the Blessed

305
(27,

303a *Summa Theologica* III, q. xxv a. 6.
304a Com. on Matt. 1:6.

127,
130,
139)
Virgin, as *Deipara*, as if we took away a worship due to God alone? Do they not know or consider attentively that nothing can be more pleasing to Christ Jesus, who certainly loves His Mother with a boundless love, than that we should venerate her, love her ardently and, by imitating her most holy example, endeavor to obtain her powerful patronage?

306
(123
170,
172)
Here we cannot pass over in silence what is of great comfort to Us, the fact that at the present time some of the innovators know better the dignity of the Virgin, as *Deipara*, and are drawn and disposed to reverence and honor her diligently. Whenever this proceeds from a serious and sincere conscience, and not with the motive of winning the favor of Catholics, as we have found in some places, We trust that through the works and prayers of all good people, and the intercession of the Blessed Virgin, these may be at length brought back to the fold of Jesus Christ, and in this way to Us who, though unworthy, act in His place on earth and exercise His authority.

The Mother of Christ's brethren

307
(29)
We feel, Venerable Brethren, that we should mention another role of the motherhood of Mary, which is still more pleasant and delightful. Since she brought forth the Redeemer of the human race and of all of us, whom the Lord Christ has willed to regard as brothers, she is our most beloved Mother.

Our Predecessor of happy memory, Leo XIII, wrote: "Such a one as God gave us, in whom, as He chose her for Mother of His Only-Begotten, He implanted a maternal heart, capable of nothing but love and forgiveness; such by His own acts Jesus Christ manifested her, since He was subject and of His own accord obedient to her as a son to a mother; such He proclaimed her from the cross when

He entrusted the whole human race, through the disciple
John, to be cared for and cherished by her; finally she
accepted this with complete dedication when, assuming
with great courage the vast responsibility of the heritage
left by her divine Son, she began at once to discharge
maternal duties to all" (a).

Mary is our refuge

Wherefore let us be drawn to her by a certain power-   **308**
ful impulse and let us trust to her confidently all that is   *(52,*
ours—joys, if we rejoice—woes, if we are in trial; hopes,   *121,*
if we endeavor to rise to nobler things. If the church falls   *167,*
into difficult times, if faith wanes, and charity grows cold, *168,*
if morals, private and public, deteriorate, if any danger   *173)*
threatens the Catholic cause or civil society, let us have
recourse to her begging help from heaven; in the supreme
trial of death, when all hope, all help, is gone, let us lift
up our eyes in tears and trembling, imploring through her
pardon from her Son and eternal joy in heaven.

With more ardent effort therefore in the present needs   **309**
under which we labor, let all go to her, and with supplica- *(168)*
tion beg earnestly "that, by interceding with her Son, the
erring nations may return to Christ's principles and precepts, on which the foundation of public welfare rests,
and through which desirable peace and true happiness
flourish in abundance. From her also let them more
earnestly pray for what all should have most at heart,
that Holy Mother the Church may have liberty and the
fruit of it in tranquillity, a liberty which it will use for
the sole purpose of attaining the highest interests of mankind, and from which harm has never come to individuals
or states, but rather always many and great benefits" (a).

307a Cf. above no. 114.
309a Encycl. *Octobri mense*, Sept. 22, 1891.

The pledge of Christian unity

310   Under the auspices of the heavenly Queen, we desire
(123, all to beg for a very special favor of the greatest impor-
161) tance, namely that she, who is loved and venerated with
such ardent piety by the people of the East, may not permit
that they should be unhappily wandering and still separated
from the unity of the Church and thus from her Son,
whose Vicar on earth We are. May they return to the
Common Father whose judgment the Fathers of the Council of Ephesus accepted so reverently and whom they all
acclaimed as "Guardian of the Faith." May all return to
Us who cherish a paternal kindness for all, and who repeat
as Our own those gracious words with which Cyril appealed
to Nestorius: "May the peace of the Church be preserved
and may the bond of love and unity remain unbroken
among the priests of God!" (a)

311   Would, moreover, the happiest of days might dawn
(171) when the Virgin Mother of God, whose image so exquisitely
fashioned in mosaic under our Predecessor Sixtus III in
the Liberian Basilica—and restored by Us to its original
beauty—would see the separated children returning to venerate her with Us, with one mind and one faith! That
would certainly be our greatest possible joy.

A model for family life

312   We deem it auspicious that we are celebrating Our
(131, tenth anniversary; We who have defended the dignity and
164) sanctity of chaste marriage against the assault of all manner of fallacy (a), and who have solemnly championed the
sacred rights of the Catholic Church in the instruction of
youth, and set forth, and explained the manner in which
it is to be imparted and the principles to which it should

310a Mansi, IV, 891.
312a Encycl. *Casti Connubii,* December 31, 1930.

conform (b). The directions We have given on both subjects are in accordance with the exalted exemplar of the divine maternity and of the family of Nazareth.

As our Predecessor of happy memory, Leo XIII, says: **313** "In Joseph fathers of families have the most beautiful model of fatherly attention and providence; in the most holy Virgin Mother of God the most extraordinary pattern of love, modesty, perfect submission, and fidelity; in Jesus, who as Son of the household was subject to them, a Divine Exemplar of obedience to admire, worship, and imitate" (a).

In a special manner it is opportune that those mothers **314** of our day who, wearied of childbearing or of the matri- *(80,* monial bond, have neglected or violated the obligation *131,* they assumed, should look and meditate intently upon *163)* Mary, who ennobled the sacred responsibility of motherhood to the highest degree.

This inspires the hope that with the grace received through the Queen of Heaven, they may become ashamed of the dishonor branded on the great sacrament of matrimony and be happily moved, as far as possible, to attain to her wonderfully exalted virtues.

If all these things would result as We counsel, if do- **315** mestic society—the principle and foundation of all human *(141)* relationships—should revert to the most exalted standard of this holiness, we could in time provide a remedy for our dangerous evil conditions.

May it so happen that "the peace of God which surpasseth all understanding" (a) keep the minds and the hearts of all and, with all our minds and forces united, may the longed for Kingdom of Christ be established!

312b Encycl. *Divini Illius Magistri,* December 31, 1929.
313a Letter *Neminem fugit,* January 14, 1892.
315a Cf. Phil. 4:7.

316   We shall not conclude this Letter without proclaiming
(141) something that will surely please you greatly. We desire
that this centenary shall have a liturgical memorial, which
will help to revive piety toward the Great Mother of God
among clergy and people. Wherefore We have directed
the Supreme Congregation of Sacred Rites to issue a Mass
and Office of the Divine Maternity to be celebrated by the
universal Church.

QUEEN AND MOTHER

Letter *Sollemne semper,* to Cardinal I. Schuster,
August 15, 1932.

317   In times of dangers and difficulties it was always the
(46, custom of Catholics to take refuge in Mary and to find re-
100, pose in her motherly heart. In fact, the Mother of God,
107) minister of heavenly graces, was placed at the zenith of
power and of glory in heaven to give the help of her patronage to men searching their way on earth among many
fatigues and dangers.

(*The fifth centenary of Our Lady of Caravagio, whose
patronage defended Italy from heresy.*)

THE MIRACLES OF LOURDES

Letter *Auspicatus profecto,* to Cardinal Binet, January 28, 1933.

318   We received the news of happy omen and we are
(155) glad that the annual feast of the Mother of God will be
celebrated with special solemnity at the Grotto of Lourdes
during the coming month of February on the occasion of
the seventy-fifth anniversary of the apparitions of the Immaculate Virgin in that place.

We think it is a providential design of God that it
happens at the approach of the Holy Year recently pro-

mulgated by Us with the aim of honoring the Divine Redemption with special devotion. This best of omens should
come from the Mother of God herself.

In fact, the august Virgin, conceived without original   **319**
sin, was chosen to be the Mother of Christ in order to be   *(22,*
associated with Him in the Redemption of mankind. For   *28,*
that reason she was adorned with such abundant grace and   *76,*
such great power in her Son's sight that neither human nor   *107)*
angelic nature can ever acquire a like grace or power.

It was, therefore, an excellent plan to commemorate
solemnly and with special magnificence the many marvellous graces that the most generous Virgin was pleased
for many years to grant the Christian people at the Grotto
of Lourdes. These celebrations will increase all the more
men's confidence in Mary and she will obtain from Jesus
Christ many other favors.

If bodily miseries and infirmities which await God's   **320**
healing are innumerable, more numerous still are the sick-   *(168,*
nesses and infirmities of the soul which need to be healed   *170)*
by heaven.

Who does not feel great sorrow at the thought that
many souls redeemed by the Blood of Jesus Christ are carried away by the storms of this corrupt world and cast into
eternal ruin?

We can never be sufficiently careful or zealous in preserving the devotion and piety of the people toward the
Queen of Heaven; there is nothing sweeter and more efficacious amidst the difficulties of this life than to raise suppliant hands to this most gracious Mother, unceasingly invoking her aid, and offering her the pious aspirations of
our souls.

(*Commissioning of Legate.*)

QUEEN OF ALL SAINTS

All. to pilgrims present at the reading of the decree *de tuto,* for the canonization of Blessed Antida Thouret, August 15, 1933.

(*Mary, "Queen of Saints," but not of a temporal kingdom.*)

321
(106,
175)
Hers is rather a queenship in the making of saints. By this we mean that in the particular case of saints we may in a general way apply what the Church teaches about God's entire creative act considered in its immensity and universality. In the making of saints we may say that Mary acts with God in raising them up, in forming them, and in crowning them.

Mary raises up saints

322
(52,
136,
168,
175)
Before all else Mary raises up saints. All holy souls turn to her who shines at the dawn of every saintly life. It is always through her intervention that in very early life each one of those who will one day add to the treasury of the Church's sanctity gives evidence of becoming a saint (a).

We may say that even prescinding from those holy beginnings it is always Mary that through her special station in glory and holiness truly inspires and raises up saints; at every stage in life the thought of her fills one with thoughts of sanctity.

This is also the case with that sanctity which we may call non-official, or that ordinary goodness of daily Christian life to which all are called. The thought and contemplation of Mary not only gives rise to that purity of life which is a man's highest distinction, but the thought and contempla-

---

322a *Si può dire, che, anche prescindendo da questi santi inizi, è sempre Maria che, per il suo posto speciale nella gloria e nella santità, è vera ispiratrice e suscitatrice di santi, poichè in tutti gli stadi della vita il pensiero di Maria è un pensiero ispiratore di santità.*

tion of her are furthermore the safeguard of those souls who struggle against temptation to evil and to those who are called to higher perfection.

True, the formation to sanctity is exclusively God's **323** work, because there can be no sanctity without an abundant *(47,* outpouring of God's grace. Mary herself is all holy in as *49,* much as she is "gratia plena." God alone.gives grace accord- *73)* ing to the measure which in His infinite wisdom He fore- sees. But, though that grace comes from God, it is given through Mary, our advocate and mediatrix, since motherly affection on the one hand finds response in filial devotion on the other.

With the renowned poet, then, the interpreter of Chris- tianity through the ages, We may say of Mary: "He who desires grace and fails to have recourse to thee is like one trying to fly without wings" (a). God gives grace; Mary obtains and distributes it.

(*The life of Jesus, Model of all sanctity.*)

Mary crowns saints

Mary not only raises up saints, but she also crowns **324** them. She leads them to final perseverance and eternal *(100,* glory. The Church invites us to pray to her and to invoke *136)* her with the words: "mortis hora suscipe," receive us at the hour of death (a). It is good to know that Mary not only welcomes souls which death brings to her, but that she herself in turn presents them to receive the crown of glory merited through her aid.

Our Lady's death

We must of necessity wish that the youth of today, ex- **325** posed as they are to many dangers, should make devotion *(31,*

323a Dante, *Paradiso,* 33, 14, 15.
324a Little Office of Our Lady. Hymn at Compline, 2nd stanza.

32,   to Mary the predominant thought of their whole life. By
41,   persevering prayer let us make Mary our daily Mediatrix,
43)   our true Advocate. In this way we may hope that she herself, assumed into heavenly glory, will be our advocate before divine goodness and mercy at the hour of our passing,
an hour which she also experienced, for she made the same
journey, not however possessing the grace of God's first creation, but that of Redemption which did not confer bodily
immortality in the strict sense of the term. (a)

(*Congratulations to the family of the new saint.*)

THE COREDEMPTRIX

All. to pilgrims from Vicenza, November 30, 1933.

(*Greetings to pilgrims assembled in Rome for the Jubilee of the Redemption.*)

326   These pilgrims were sent to Rome and recommended
(31,   by our Lady of Monteberico, Patroness of your region and
32,   venerated in a famous sanctuary. They were, therefore, sent
41,   by the Virgin herself to enrich themselves with the treas-
43)   ures of the Holy Year of the Redemption in which she
herself took great part.

From the nature of His work the Redeemer ought to
have associated His Mother with His work. For this reason
We invoke her under the title of Coredemptrix. She gave
us the Savior, she accompanied Him in the work of Redemption as far as the Cross itself, sharing with Him the
sorrows of the agony and of the death in which Jesus consummated the Redemption of mankind. And immediately

---

325a *Sicchè possiamo sperare che Ella, assunta nella gloria
del Cielo, nell'ora del nostro trapasso che fu pure il Suo,—
poichè Ella pure fece questo passo essendo in Lei non la
grazia di creazione ma la grazia di redenzione, la quale
non conferiva immortalità vera e propria,—possa Ella essere
nostra Avvocata pressso la divina bontà e misericordia.*

beneath the Cross, at the last moments of His life, she was proclaimed by the Redeemer our Mother, the Mother of the whole universe. "Ecce filius tuus," He said of St. John who represented all of us, and in the person of the same Apostle the other words: "Ecce Mater tua" (a) were addressed to each one of us.

The faithful people of Vicenza have, therefore, come to celebrate with Us not only the nineteenth centenary of the Redemption but also that of the universal Motherhood of Mary, officially and solemnly proclaimed by the very words of the Son of God at the particularly solemn moment of His death. They have come also to render this tribute of devotion to the Virgin, Mother of all men, whom they may truly and proudly say is in a very special way their Mother. **327** *(31, 34)*

(*Encouragement to pray to and imitate Mary.*)

BERNADETTE SOUBIROUS

Apost. Letter *Maximopere lætamur*, December 8, 1933.

We rejoice that during this Holy Year We have had once again the opportunity of gathering new flowers of sanctity in the Church's garden and of offering them, all scented with heavenly perfume, for the admiration of the Catholic world. **328** *(155)*

Today, in fact, We had the great joy of decreeing a solemn increase of devotion to that child of Lourdes whom We Ourselves crowned a few years ago with the halo of the Blessed and who continues to be adorned with new and extraordinary miracles, lawfully recognized. We cannot help seeing in this a sign of God's holy Will.

As, indeed, the seventy-fifth anniversary of the apparition of the Immaculate Virgin Mother of God to this most **329** *(155,*

326a John 19:27.

175)   innocent child at the grotto of Lourdes falls exactly in this year, dedicated in a particular manner to the memory of the Divine Redemption, it seems that God Himself, Supreme Ruler of times and events, wishes to add to the happiness of this celebration. All that adds to the praise of Bernadette Soubirous redounds also to the honor of the Immaculate Virgin; for Mary loved her with such motherly affection that she entrusted her, although only a most humble shepherdess, with the task of spreading her glory and of bringing men back to penance.

The Virgin's preferences

330   "But the foolish things of the world hath God chosen,
(167,   that he may confound the wise: and the weak things of the
175)   the world hath God chosen, that he may confound the strong" (a). We may say that His most holy Mother acted in like manner. Here is a proof: the Blessed Virgin Mary, wishing to adorn in a most miraculous manner the decree by which Our Predecessor, Pius IX of happy memory, amidst universal applause, on this very day and in this very Basilica sanctioned the dogma of the Immaculate Conception, looked not to the most learned of men, but rather to a miller's daughter who lacked education and was rich only in the candor of her pure soul. Thus she spoke to the child: "I am the Immaculate Conception." When she wishes to reawaken the Catholic faith in men's hearts and lead them from their evil ways back to the true path of Christian virtue, she does not turn to men of power nor to the rich nor to those who rule the destinies of peoples, but to a humble child of whom We may well say: "Blessed are the poor in spirit: for theirs is the kingdom of heaven" (b); and "Blessed are the clean of heart: for they shall see God" (c).

330a 1 Cor. 1:27.
330b Matt. 5:3.
330c Matt. 5:8.

Moreover, beneath the gaze of the Queen of Heaven and thanks to her handmaid a triple sanctuary rises towards heaven beside the steep rock of Massabielle. Here the faithful come alone or in crowds from all parts of the world to implore divine aid. A magnificent spectacle, Venerable sons and daughters, which everyone—even those who unfortunately do not possess the light of the Catholic faith—cannot but admire.

Lourdes! the honor and glory of the Immaculate Virgin!   **331**
                                                                   (155)

Lourdes! the monument of the proved sanctity of Marie Bernadette Soubirous! How many men, already far distant from the path of Christian truth, have there returned to the bosom of Mother Church! How many already fast in the maw of vice have returned to an honorable life! How many have here felt themselves in the depths of their souls drawn to embrace the way of perfection! And finally, how many sick and infirm have, by divine grace, obtained considerable relief or complete cure!

THE FAMILY ROSARY

Letter *Inclytam ac perillustrem,* to R. P. Gillet, Master General of the Dominicans, March 6, 1934.

(*The seventh centenary of the canonization of St. Dominic.—His mission against the Albigenses.*)

Among the weapons which St. Dominic used to convert the heretics the most efficacious, as the faithful well know, was the Rosary of Mary, the practice of which, taught by the Blessed Virgin herself, has so widely spread throughout the Catholic world. How does it happen that this sweet prayer possesses such power and efficacy? Certainly from the same mysteries of the Divine Redeemer upon which one devoutly contemplates and meditates so that we may   **332**
                                                                   (120,
                                                                    168)

rightly say that the Marian Rosary contains the principles and foundation on which the very Order of Saint Dominic depends to procure the perfection of life of its own members and the salvation of other men.

333
(146,
149)
For this reason We earnestly recommend this most efficacious form of prayer which leads us to meditate upon Our Lord's fruitful Redemption and procures for us, in the highest degree, the favors of the Queen of Heaven. We ardently desire that it be devoutly continued and that the habit of the daily recitation of the Rosary in an alternating manner, so appreciated by our forefathers and by them considered sacred for the Christian family, be once again established.

COREDEMPTRIX

R. M. to the pilgrims at Lourdes, April 28, 1935.

334
(29,
40,
41)
Mother most faithful and most merciful, who as coredemptrix and partaker of thy dear Son's sorrows didst assist Him as He offered the sacrifice of our Redemption on the altar of the Cross, preserve in us and increase each day, we beseech thee, the precious fruits of our Redemption and thy compassion. O thou who art the Mother of us all, deign to enable us through purity of life, a spirit of union and harmony of hearts henceforth to enjoy without anxiety the gifts of a secure peace.

MARY MOST HOLY IN CHURCH HISTORY

Encycl. *Ingravescentibus malis,* September 29, 1937.

(*Jesus Christ, sole salvation for mankind.*)

335
(121,
123)
Anyone who studies with diligence the history of the Catholic Church will easily recognize that the true patronage of the Virgin Mother of God is linked with all the annals of Christianity.

When, in fact, widespread errors strove to rend the seamless robe of the Church and endeavored to throw the Catholic world into confusion, our fathers confidently turned to her "alone who destroys all heresies in the world" (a) and the victory won through her brought the return of more happy times.

When the impious Mohammedan power, trusting in   **336** its powerful fleet and war-hardened armies, threatened *(159)* the peoples of Europe with ruin and slavery, then—upon the suggestion of the Sovereign Pontiff—the protection of the heavenly Mother was fervently implored and the enemy was defeated and his ships sunk.

Thus the faithful of every century, both in public   **337** misfortune and in private need, turned in supplication to *(135,* the ever most benevolent Mary, that she would come   *136)* to their aid and grant help and remedy against sorrows of body and soul. And never was her most powerful aid hoped for in vain by those who besought it with pious and trustful prayer.

(*Divine assistance assured to the Church.*)

But rather, as we said in the beginning, shall We   **338** beseech God through the mediation of the Blessed Virgin,   *(37)* so acceptable to Him, since, to use the words of St. Bernard: "Such is the will of God who has wished that we should have all things through Mary" (a).

Among the various supplications with which we successfully appeal to the Virgin Mother of God, the holy Rosary, without a doubt, occupies a special and distinct place.

This prayer, which some call the "Psalter of the Virgin" or "Breviary of the Gospel and of Christian life" was described and recommended by Our Predecessor of happy memory, Leo XIII, with these emphatic words: "Very admirable is this crown interwoven with the

335a Office of Our Lady.
338a *Serm.* 1 in Nativ. B.V.M.

Angelic Salutation, which is interposed with the Lord's Prayer, and unites with it the obligation of interior meditation. It is an excellent manner of praying ... and very useful for the attainment of eternal life" (b).

(*Nature, agelessness and universal usefulness of the Rosary.*)

339
(129,
142)
And We do not wish here to pass over in silence the fact that the Blessed Virgin herself, even in our times, has solicitously recommended this manner of prayer, when she appeared and taught it to the innocent girl in the grotto of Lourdes.

Therefore why should we not hope for every grace if we supplicate our heavenly Mother in this manner with due disposition and holiness?

An invincible weapon

340
(52)
We desire very earnestly, Venerable Brethren, that the holy Rosary should be recited in a special manner in the month of October and with increased devotion both in the churches and in homes. We wish it especially this year because of the enemies of the Divine Name—that is, those who have rebelled against and denied and scorned the eternal God—spread snares for the Catholic Faith and the liberty due to the Church, and finally rebel with insane efforts against divine and human rights, to send mankind to ruin and perdition. Through efficacious recourse to the Virgin Mother of God they may be finally converted and led to penance and return to the straight path, trusting to the care and protection of Mary.

341
(123
168)
The holy Virgin who once victoriously drove the terrible sect of the Albigenses from Christian countries, now suppliantly invoked by us, will turn aside the new errors, especially those of Communism, which reminds us in many ways, in its motives and misdeeds, of the ancient ones.

338b Cf. above n. 210-211. .

And as in the times of the crusades in all Europe there was raised one voice of the people, one supplication, so it is today.

Throughout the world in the cities, and smallest villages, people who are one in courage and resoluteness eagerly implore the great Mother of God that the enemies of Christian and human civilization be overthrown and that true peace may shine on the tired and anxious hearts of men.

If then all will do this with the proper dispositions, with great faith and with fervent piety, one may hope that, as in the past, so in our day, the Blessed Virgin will obtain from her Divine Son that the fury of the present tempest will be calmed and that a splendid victory will crown this unity of Christians in prayer.   **342** *(168)*

Duty of acknowledgment and reparation

And in addressing this encyclical to you another motive impels Us. We wish that, together with Us, our many children in Christ shall unite and render thanks to the Mother of God for the good health We have happily regained.   **343** *(37, 47)*

This grace, as We have had occasion to write, We attribute to the special intercession of the virgin of Lisieux, St. Theresa of the Child Jesus. But we know likewise that every blessing that comes to Us from the Almighty God comes through the hands of Our Lady.

And lastly, as there has been launched in the public press, with rash insolence, a very grave injury to the Blessed Virgin, We cannot let this occasion pass without piously offering, together with the Episcopate and people of that nation which venerates Mary as "Queen of the kingdom of Poland" due reparation to this August Queen, and denouncing before the whole Catholic world this sacrilegious crime which was perpetrated with impunity before a civilized people.

PIUS XII

(1939-1958)

CHILDREN'S PRAYER

Letter *Quandoquidem*, to Cardinal Maglione, April 20, 1939.

(*Introduction.*)

May fathers and mothers, with pious custom, accompany their children, even to the tiniest ones, every day to their shrines of the Blessed Virgin, presenting them to her along with flowers from their gardens and fields and together with their prayers and those of their children. **344**
(162)

And how could our heavenly Mother fail to heed so many suppliant voices imploring peace for citizens, for peoples, for nations? How could she fail to heed them if with the prayers of the angels of heaven there should be added those of children whom one may call angels of this earth?

Certainly the Virgin Mother of God, moved by such prayers will offer her aid and her intercession in this moment of universal trepidation, and by inviting the favor of her divine Son, offended by so many sins, will obtain from Him liberation from present anxieties, the peace of hearts and fraternal concord among peoples.

(*Christ's love for children.*)

PATRONESS OF THE FAMILY

All. to the newly married, May 10, 1939.

We heartily welcome the newly married, who continue to come in ever greater numbers to these public audiences. Our greeting is all the more cordial as it comes to you in **345**
(150, 164)

the joy of this month of May which the devotion of Christian people has specially consecrated to the cult of the Blessed Virgin Mary.

You, dearly beloved children, called to form new families, wish undoubtedly to give them an essentially and profoundly Christian character and a sure foundation for well-being and happiness. It is by devotion to Mary that you will succeed in doing so. Mary has many titles under which she may be considered the Patroness of Christian families, and these families, in turn, have just as many reasons to hope for her special assistance.

Mary's title to this patronage

346
(82,
85,
113,
115)
Mary knew the joys and the sorrows of the family; she knew also the happy and the sad events, the fatigue of daily work, the discomforts and sadness of poverty, separation's rending of heart. But she also tasted the ineffable joys of family life, rejoicing in the purest love of a most chaste Spouse and the smiles and tenderness of a Son who was at the same time the Son of God.

347
(85,
164)
The Virgin's merciful heart sympathizes with family needs; she will shower on them that comfort which they miss in the inevitable sorrows of the present life; under her motherly care the joys of the fireside will become for them purer and more serene.

The holy Virgin not only knows from personal experience a family's heavy burdens; as a tender mother of mercy she strives to lighten the burdens.

348
(164)
Happy and truly blessed are those spouses who begin their new state of life with the intention of having filial and trustful devotion to the Mother of God, with the holy resolution of establishing their home on a solid religious foundation. Such dispositions they will pass on as a precious heritage to the dear children with whom God will see fit to bless them.

Example of Nazareth

But, beloved children, do not forget that if such   **349**
devotion is to be true and firm and consequently produce   *(80*
precious fruits and copious graces, devotion to Our Lady   *130,*
must be quickened by the imitation of the life of her   *131,*
whom it pleases Us to honor.   *163,*

The divine Mother is a most perfect model of the   *164)*
domestic virtues which must adorn the Christian married
state. In Mary you will find the purest and the most
faithful love for her most chaste spouse. Her love was made
up of sacrifices and of delicate attentions. In Mary you
will find entire and continuous dedication to needs of
family and home, of those of her spouse and, above all, of
Jesus; in her you will find humility which manifests itself
in loving submission to St. Joseph, in patient resignation to the often hard and exacting dispositions of Divine
Providence, her lovableness and charity to all who visit
the humble house of Nazareth.

Christian spouses, may your devotion to Mary form
an ever lively source of heavenly favors and of true
happiness.

"THE IMMACULATE CONCEPTION"

All. to the newly married, December 6, 1939.

We wish you to fix your gaze today on the most   **350**
gentle Virgin Mary whose feast the Church will celebrate   *(58)*
the day after tomorrow under the title of the Immaculate
Conception. It is a lovely title, the prelude to all her
other glories, a unique privilege, almost identical with
her very person: "I am," she said to St. Bernadette at the
Grotto of Massabielle, "I am the Immaculate Conception!"

(*Purity in family life.*)

Mary was immaculate from her conception so as to   **351**
become worthily the Mother of our Savior. Therefore,   *(27,*
the Church in the Liturgy, where the echo of her dogmas   *68,*

168) resound, prays to her: "O God Who by the Immaculate
Conception of the Virgin didst prepare a worthy habitation for Thy Son . . . (a)

This Immaculate Virgin, who became Mother by another unique and divine privilege, can understand your
desires and purity of intention, and the family joys to
which you aspire. The holier your union and the freer
you are from sin, the more God and His most pure
Mother will bless you until the day on which Sovereign
Goodness will forever unite in heaven those who on earth
shall have loved each other with a Christian love.

THE LESSON OF BETHLEHEM

All. to the newly married, January 3, 1940.

(*Wishes for good fortune and the blessing of children.*)

352   During the Christmas period the Church proposes for
(164) your consideration a woman and a man tenderly bent
over a new-born child. While meditating on the mystery
of Christmas, contemplate above all the spirit of Mary
and of Joseph, try and penetrate into their hearts and
make their sentiments yours. Then, notwithstanding the
infinite difference which separates the birth of Jesus, the
Incarnate Word, Son of the most holy Virgin, and the
human birth of your little one, you may trustfully take as
your models the ideal spouses, Mary and Joseph.

Look at the grotto of Bethlehem. Is it perhaps a
suitable dwelling place even for modest artisans? Why
these animals, why these bundles used for travel, why
this absolute poverty? Is this what Mary and Joseph had
dreamed of in the intimate sweetness of their home in
Nazareth for the birth of the Child Jesus? It is more
than likely that Joseph had, for many months, been col-

351a Collect of the Mass of the Immaculate Conception.

lecting some pieces of wood which he had sawn, planed, cleaned and then made into a cradle. And we may well believe that Mary, who from childhood was trained in the temple in womanly handiwork, had like every other woman about to become a mother cut, hemmed and lovingly embroidered the layette for the Desired of Nations!

The poverty of Bethlehem

**353
(115)** But now they are not in their own home; neither are they with their friends; nor are they to be found in an ordinary inn. They are in a stable. To obey the Edict of Augustus they undertook, although they knew that the greatly desired Child was about to come into the world, a painful journey in the depths of winter. They also knew that this Child, virginal fruit of the operation of the Holy Spirit, belonged to God rather than to them. Jesus Himself, twelve years later, had to remind them that the business of His heavenly Father, Sovereign over men and over things, had to come before the loving intentions, however pure and ardent, of Mary and of Joseph. This is the reason why that night in a humble and wretched grotto they knelt and adored the Newly-born lying in a hard stable, *positum in præsepio*, instead of in a beautiful cradle; wrapped in swaddling clothes, *pannis involutum*, instead of in splendid garments (a).

The shining faith of Mary and Joseph

**354
114)** Dear young spouses, you also have had and will have sweet dreams for the future of your children. Very sad are those parents who do not have such dreams! But take care that your dreams be not exclusively earthly and human! Thinking deeply before the King of Heaven, who trembled on the straw, who cried just as every man who comes into this world does—*"et primam vocem similem*

353a Cf. Luke 2:1-7.

omnibus emisi plorans" (a)—Mary and Joseph saw—in an interior light which also lit up the aspects of material realities—that the child most blessed by God is not necessarily the child born in riches and in fortunate circumstances; they understood that men's thoughts are not always in conformity with God's thoughts; they felt deeply that all that happens on earth, yesterday, today and tomorrow, is due not to mere chance or to good or bad luck, but to a long and mysterious chain of events ordained or permitted by the Providence of our heavenly Father.

(*Imitate this supernatural spirit.*)

MEDIATRIX OF PEACE

Letter *Superiore anno,* to Cardinal Luigi Maglione, April 15, 1940.

355
(168, 170) Last year, when the dark clouds obscured the horizon, and talk of armed strife, forerunner of war, held all in trepidation, We, whose paternal heart participates in the sorrows and troubles of Our children, addressed a Letter to Your Eminence. Through you, We urged the entire Catholic world to offer, during the forthcoming month of May, fervent prayers and devout aspirations to the great Mother of God, begging her to intercede with her Son, already offended by so many sins, in order that peace might be restored to the nations through the just settlement of conflicting interests and reasonable agreement among men's minds (a).

Now, inasmuch as the international situation has grown worse, and a fierce war has broken out with so much harm to mankind and intense sorrow, We cannot fail to appeal again to Our children throughout the world with the plea that they gather around the shrine of the

354a Wisdom 7:3.
355a Cf. above, no. 344.

Virgin Mother of God and on each day, during this coming month which is consecrated to her, send up to her
their fervent prayers.

(*Popes efforts for peace.*)

Mary's powerful intercession

And since, as St. Bernard declares *"It is the Will of* **356**
God that we obtain all favors through Mary" (a) let every- *(107,*
one hasten to have recourse to Mary. May all mankind bring *125,*
its petitions, sorrows and anxieties, and lay them on her *126,*
altar, beseeching her for aid and comfort. And in this pre- *129)*
sent and most grave peril, confidently following the example of our forefathers, let us not fail to do that which,
as history testifies, they did with such gratifying results in
their days of peril and fearful uncertainty.

So powerful, indeed, is the Blessed Virgin with God
and His only-begotten Son that, as Dante observes (b) anyone who desires His help and fails to have recourse to Mary
is like one trying to fly without wings. Indeed is she the
most powerful Mother of God, but also—a fact sweet to
contemplate!—our own most lovable Mother. Wherefore
let it be a joy to everyone of us to place ourselves under
her motherly protection and her help and to have complete
confidence in her maternal goodness.

Now it is Our particular wish, Beloved Son, that in **357**
this coming month of May the white legions of innocent *(133,*
children will flock again to the shrines of Our Lady and *169)*
that, through her intercession and her mediation for peace,
there may be obtained from God the eagerly desired peace
for all nations. Daily, let them assemble before the shrine
of our heavenly Mother. With bended knees and suppliant
hands let the little ones together with their prayers offer

356a St. Bernard—*Serm. in Nativitate* B.V.M.
356b Cf. *Paradiso*, 33, 13.

their flowers—these dear children who themselves are the flowers in the mystical garden of the Church.

Great is our trust in the prayers of those "whose angels in heaven always see the face of my Father" (a), whose childish faces radiate innocence, whose glistening eyes seem to reflect the splendor of heaven. We know that our divine Redeemer loves children with a special affection, and that His most holy Mother has for them a special tenderness. We know that the prayers of the innocent pierce the heavens, assuage divine justice, and obtain heavenly graces for themselves and for others.

(*Get the children to pray for peace.*)

UNIVERSAL SPIRITUAL MOTHERHOOD OF THE BLESSED VIRGIN MARY

All. to the Pilgrims from Genoa, April 21, 1940.

(*Greetings to welcome the Pilgrims.*)

358
116,
136)
On seeing you we again behold your hills and mountains, the "Figogna" with the high tower of the "Madonna della Guardia" standing on that summit to salute, as a beacon of faith, hope and love, the tall light-house of the harbor, a light to voyagers in seas smooth and rough, the image of the restlessness of human life.

The two stars of our life

Here below in the darkness of our war we need two lights, two stars: the Divine Star, who is Jesus, our Lord, who said of Himself, "Ego sum radix et genus David, stella splendida et matutina" (a); and the Star of Mary: "Maris Stella." The brilliant Morning Star is Jesus who in the hour of His supreme sufferings has made the Cross of Golgotha

357a Matt. 18:10.
358a Apoc. 22:16.

the light of men's salvation, illuminating every other beacon and sending forth its light all over the world. At the foot
of His Cross there shines the Star of Mary, the Mother of
the Crucified, and our Mother, beacon of mercy, our life,
our sweetness and our hope.

Keep your eyes, beloved sons, fixed upon those two
stars, those two beacons, while you are being assailed by
stormy waves during your earthly journey and your daily
life; look on Jesus, look on Mary with the eyes of that faith
that conquered the world and animated your fathers and
ancestors. Four and a half centuries ago, they knelt down
for the first time before the Virgin "della Guardia" and
her Divine Son; fifty years ago they renewed towards her,
with the generosity of devoted love, the magnificent homage of a sanctuary which, standing in contrast with the
lowliness of the elder one, testifies to the fact that in you
and the Genoese people the grateful and faithful piety of
your forebears, far from diminishing and failing, has ever
been increasing, becoming more ardent and more deeply
realized. In fact, are not Jesus and Mary the two sublime
loves of the Christian people? Are they not the new Adam
and the new Eve whom the Tree of the Cross unites in
pain and love to atone for the sin of our first parents in
Eden? One of them is the source and the other the channel
of grace for giving us a new birth into spiritual life and for
enabling us to reclaim our heavenly country.

*359
(47,
116,
128)*

(*Manifestations of faith of the Genoese on Mount
Figogna.*)

Columbus, devotee of Mary

Once, upon entering the harbor, the captains of the
galleys of your most serene and glorious Republic looked
towards that mountain; the ships of the Genoese Lords,
and those of Spain and France looked towards it and fired
a salute to Mary, the Star of the Sea, who after having
gone with them and preserved them from the dangers of
storms and pirates, brought them safely to shore. Captains,

*360
(160,
175)*

soldiers and sailors vied with the confraternities in marching under the standard of the "Madonna della Guardia," and triremes and caravels gloried in her title.

But by looking farther into time and space, only two years after the apparition of the Blessed Virgin on Mount Figogna you behold in the midst of the Atlantic's squalls and gales and typhoons a daring ship called the "Santa Maria," a flag ship escorted by two smaller vessels. It sailed on toward an unknown world dreamt of and divined, under the guidance of a hero. There, having disembarked on the shores of a new continent, he planted the Cross of Golgotha, and devoutly prepared the way for the wonders, the sanctuaries and the future glories of Christ and His Virgin Mother. Genoese, in Christopher Columbus hail not only the fearless navigator who overcame the contradictions of the learned as well as the tempests of the sea, but also the devoted son of Mary who, with his dream in his heart, besought the assistance of the heavenly Queen. Wandering along the shores of the Mediterranean, and finding a ship called "Maria" to board, he said good-bye to an incredulous and astounded Europe, and ventured on the dreaded ocean in search of a shore where he might kneel down before Christ, who stills the tempests, and Mary, the Star of the Sea.

(*Devotion and gratitude of the City of Genoa to the Holy Virgin Mary.*)

A love without preference

361
(36, 46, 136) To Mary, who reigns in heaven "humble yet higher than any creature," near His Throne, God grants the custody of the treasures of His manifold graces. She is, moreover, their minister and generous dispenser. She does not discriminate between noble and princely palaces and the lowly thatched cottage. If she feels at all partial it is toward the poor and miserable, the sorrowful and the unhappy, toward all who in this vale of tears shed also

their own; souls whom misfortune casts down; whom sin and remorse humiliate; whom prayer comforts, repentance regenerates, and grace makes children of Mary in likeness to her own Son.

If in her humility, as handmaid of the Lord, all generations call her, and shall call her, Blessed, the voice of our age also unites itself to the canticles of the past and future; in Mary it exalts a Mother's heart, becoming sublime in the heavenly Child that she carries in her arms and presses to her breast. He is her heart's delight and the delight of the world; from His kiss springs up that fire of love which makes her Mother of mercy and magnanimous clemency toward every child of Adam. **362** *(33, 40, 80)*

Thousands of times at her feet on the summit of Figogna and in the course of your life you have tasted the fruits of Mary's merciful kindness. From that mountain, you came down and with your eminent and beloved Shepherd—who has so eloquently recalled the glorious memories of your loyalty to this Apostolic See—you set out for the Eternal City to unite, in the beatings of your heart, love of Mary and love of Christ, while you venerate at his tomb the Prince of the Apostles, set, by Christ, as the foundation-stone of His Church.

Our Lady and St. Peter

More exalted than St. Peter, the Vicar of Christ on earth, the Mother of our Lord Jesus yet has in common with Peter, in a manner all her own, a dignity, an authority, a power which associates her with the Apostolic College as its Queen. When to her who loved Him more than did Peter, Jesus entrusted in the person of John beneath His saving Cross all men as sons, both the sheep and the lambs of a flock in part united, in part dispersed, He designated her the heavenly Shepherdess and the common Mother of all believers, and so likened her to Peter their common father and Shepherd upon earth. **363** *(29, 33, 80, 118, 120)*

364   She is the august Queen of the Church militant, the
(102,   Church suffering, and the Church triumphant; she is the
131)   Queen of saints, the possessor of every virtue, of love
         and fear, of knowledge and holy hope. For her the white
         rose of Paradise sprouted; for her began a new cycle in
         the life of man that brought to bloom in Eden's garden
         lilies and violets and every flower of sweet and won-
         drous odor.

365   While Peter has the keys of heaven, Mary has the
(52,   key to God's heart; while Peter binds and looses, Mary
120,   also binds with the chain of love and looses with the gift
125)   of pardon. While Peter is the guardian and minister of
         indulgences, Mary is the generous and wise treasurer of
         God's favors. "He who desires grace and does not have
         recourse to Mary, desires to fly without wings" (a).

366   An abundance of special graces you, O Genoese,
(34,   have received from Mary's hands. To crown your grati-
103,   tude you feel called to celebrate the remembrance of
158)   her Apparition among you several centuries ago, and to
         renew your attestation of filial homage, solemnizing at
         the same time, after fifty years, the inauguration of that
         most noteworthy Basilica consecrated to her.

         In the name of Mary, the Lady of "La Guardia," you
         came to the Eternal City, and gathered around Us to
         enable Us also to share your festal joy so that the Vicar
         of Christ might add to yours his own gratitude toward
         Mary, that most powerful and generous Protectress of
         the whole Christian People entrusted to his care.

         Mary is also the shield of the Eternal City, and if
         the Capitoline Hill is not so high as your "Figogna," it
         does not escape the eye and watchfulness of Mary, who
         from heaven embraces the whole world, and on the
         banks of the Tiber contemplates the center and metrop-
         olis of the Holy Empire of Christ, which is also her own,

365a Dante *Paradiso*, 33, 13-15.

—where Peter sends up his prayers to her, the Guardian and protectress of the sheep and lambs of Christ's unnumbered flock.

Beloved Brethren: To Mary in union with your praises **367** and prayers I send up my own in this hour in which *(107,* sadness and fear mingle with joy. It is the hour for Mary's *123,* power, mercy and watchful protection. She, beautiful, *168)* loving and splendid, can be as terrible as an army in battle array (a), and among her names she bears that of "Our Lady of Victories," reminding us of Lepanto and Vienna. In her is our hope and our peace. A storm cloud, the color of anger and of death, is overshadowing the world. In the scales of His Justice, the Lord is weighing the powerful and the nations; but the protection and merciful intercession of the Queen of Peace can bring to bear upon God's heart such force as will cause Him to alter the course of the storm, scatter the clouds, and free us from our troubles, by changing men's hearts, appeasing hatred and rancor and making peace to dawn upon us.

A TITLE DEAR TO MARY

All. to the women of Italian Catholic Action, October 6, 1940.

(*This is the hour of Catholic youth.—Example: Defence of purity is placed in devotion to the Blessed Eucharist and to Mary Most Holy.*)

When the Word wished to become flesh and be **368** born of a woman, He cast His gaze upon the most *(22,* ideally perfect of all His creatures, a young girl in the *28,* grace of her virginity. When to this grace was added by a *84,* singular miracle the grace of divine motherhood, her *100,*

367a Cf. Cant. 6:3.

136) beauty was so sublime that artists, poets and saints have aspired ardently, but always in vain, to give it adequate expression.

The Church and the angels salute her with the titles of Queen and Mother; innumerable are the titles with which the piety of the faithful has crowned her as with a diadem of a thousand jewels. But of all these titles of glory one particularly dear to her describes her perfectly, the Virgin.

May this Virgin of Virgins, Mary, Queen of the Most Holy Rosary, be your model and your strength throughout your life as young Catholic women, and especially in your Crusade for purity.

THE QUEENLY POWER OF MARY

Letter *Dum Sæculum,* to Cardinal Maglione, April 15, 1942.

(*It is necessary to pray for peace during the month of May.*)

369
(106,
107,
129)
And because we can hope for all things through Mary, We urge everyone to have recourse to her, especially during this coming month of May which is dedicated to her. First of all, let the little boys and girls, guided by their parents, hasten to Mary's shrines with their supplication for their innocent and trusting prayers cannot fail to be most acceptable to the most merciful Mother of God who is also our Mother.

As everyone well knows, as Christ Jesus is the King of kings and Lord of lords in whose hands lie the future of individuals and of nations, so is His Mother, whom the faithful honor as Queen of the World, our most powerful advocate with God.

370
(31,
50,
102,
And since the first public miracle performed by our divine Redeemer in Cana of Galilee was brought about by Mary's merciful intercession; and since her only-begotten Son, when He was about to die on the Cross,

bequeathed what was most precious to Him on this earth, *106)*
namely: His Mother whom He gave to us as our Mother;
and, in as much as, throughout the centuries, our ancestors
in the Faith always fled prayerfully and confidently to her
when threatened by public or private dangers; why should
not we, who in this day are menaced by such dire evils
and harrowing crises, entrust ourselves and all our interests
to her most efficacious intercession!

Just as all created things acknowledge and obey the
will of God, so may it be stated that Mary's Son ever attends most favorably to the petitions of His Mother, and
especially so now that she enjoys eternal happiness in heav-
en where, adorned with the glorious crown of victory Mary
is acclaimed the "Queen of Angels and of men."

Great, indeed, is her power with God, but great also is   **371**
her love for us because she is the most loving mother of *(101,*
all mankind. Therefore, with unwavering faith and fervent   *128)*
love, let everyone of us go to Mary, let everyone bring, not
only suppliant petitions, but, likewise the holy works of
penance and of charity by which Divine Justice, outraged
by so many, and such heinous sins, may be appeased.

THE STRONG VIRGIN

All. to the Children of Mary, October 25, 1942.

(*The two safeguards of the young girl: purity and
strength.*)

Pure, incomparably purer than all the angels whose   **372**
Queen she is, the Immaculate Virgin is also the Woman,   *(25,*
strong, industrious, faithfully carrying out all her duties,   *27,*
ready in any circumstance, were it even hard or dreadful,   *82,*
to fulfill them.   *83,*
From the moment the Angel Gabriel brought her the   *113,*
divine Message you behold her as the Handmaid of the   *117)*
Lord, ever keeping the eminent dignity and accomplishing

the high office to which she has been elected—as glorious Mother of Christ; as sorrowful Mother of the Redeemer at the foot of the Cross; as Mother of the suffering and miserable human race; as Help of Christians, Refuge of Sinners, Comforter of the Afflicted. Conscious of so high a dignity, and so great a right, the Virgin unhesitatingly gave the Angel her assent. And confined though she had hitherto been to the peaceful seclusion of the Temple and the solitude of her small abode at Nazareth, you now see her walking rapidly along mountainous paths, eager to visit and assist Elizabeth, her relative.

At the beginning of Christ's public life, we see her at the wedding feast of Cana, keeping watchful eye to see that nothing should be missing to the joy of the spouses and their guests; mingling with the crowd, she patiently awaits the moment when she will be able to speak to Jesus; her heart pierced with the sword of sorrow, she remains standing at the foot of the gibbet of her Divine Son; in the midst of the Apostles, she prays and prepares them to receive also the strength from on high for the diffusion of the gospel.

(*How to act in the changed situations of the modern world.*)

CONSECRATION OF WORLD TO THE IMMACULATE HEART OF MARY

R. M. for the 25th anniversary of Fatima, October 31, 1942.

373
(105,
109,
132,
141)
. . . Queen of the most holy Rosary, Help of Christians, Refuge of Mankind, triumphant in all battles for God! We, your suppliants, prostrate ourselves at your throne, confident that we shall obtain mercy and receive grace, the needed assistance and protection, during the calamities of these days, not indeed by our own merits, of which we presume nothing, but solely through the immense goodness of your maternal heart.

To you and to your Immaculate Heart, We, the com-   **374**
mon father of the vast Christian family, We, the Vicar of   *(132,*
Him to whom was given "all power in heaven and on   *141,*
earth," and from whom we have received the care of so   *169)*
many souls redeemed by His Blood; to you and to your
Immaculate Heart in this tragic hour of human history,
We commit, We entrust, We consecrate, not only the Holy
Church, the mystical body of your Jesus, which suffers
and bleeds in so many places and is afflicted in so many
ways, but also the entire world torn by violent discord,
scorched in a fire of hate, victim of its own iniquities.

Be moved to pity in the face of so many material and   **375**
moral disasters, by so many afflictions which agonize fath-   *(167,*
ers and mothers, innocent babes! Be moved to compassion   *173,*
in view of so many lives cut off in the very flowering of   *176)*
youth, so many bodies mangled by the horrible slaughter,
so many tortured and afflicted souls, so many in danger of
eternal ruin!

You, O Mother of Mercy, obtain for us peace from   **376**
God! and above all obtain those graces which can convert   *(169,*
human hearts in an instant, those graces which prepare   *170)*
for, promote and insure peace! Queen of Peace, pray for
us and grant to this war-stricken world the peace which
the nations desire: peace in the truth, in the justice and in
the charity of Christ. Grant to us a cessation of this conflict
and true peace of soul, that in the tranquillity of restored
order, the kingdom of God may be spread.

Extend your protection to unbelievers and to them   **377**
who still stand in the shadow of death. Grant to them   *(172)*
peace. May the Sun of truth dawn in their lives that they
may join with us before Him who alone is Savior of the
world and repeat these words: "Glory to God in the highest and peace on earth to men of good will" (a).

377a Luke 2:14.

378   To the peoples separated by error or discord, and es-
(121, pecially to those who profess special devotion to you and
161,   among whom there was once not a home where your ven-
171)   erated icon was not honored (today perhaps hidden and
awaiting better days), grant peace and lead them back to
the one fold of Christ under the one and true Shepherd.

379   Obtain peace and complete liberty for the Holy
(121, Church of God. Check the inundating flood of neopagan-
136,   ism and all its materialism. Arouse in the faithful the love
137)   of purity, the practice of the Christian Life, and apostolic
zeal in order that the people who serve God may increase
in merit and in number.

380   Finally, just as the Church and the entire human race
(102, were consecrated to the Heart of your Jesus, because by
132,   placing in Him every hope, It may be for them a token
141,   and pledge of victory and salvation; so, henceforth, they
176)   are perpetually consecrated to you, to your Immaculate
Heart, O Our Mother and Queen of the world, in order
that your love and protection may hasten the triumph of
the Kingdom of God. And may all peoples at peace among
themselves and with God proclaim you blessed and intone
with you throughout the entire world the eternal "Magnificat" of glory, love and adoration of the Heart of Jesus,
in whom alone they can find truth, love and peace.

MOTHER OF OUR HEAD

Encycl. *Mystici Corporis,* June 29, 1943.

(*The Church, mystical body of Christ.—Union of faithful with Christ.—To love the Church is to suffer for her.*)

381   May these Our fatherly prayers, which are surely also
(25,   yours, Venerable Brethren, find fulfillment, and all men
52,   find a true love for the Church, through the intercession of
114)   the Virgin Mother of God. Her most holy soul, more than

the souls of all God's creatures together, was filled with the divine Spirit of Jesus Christ. She, "representing the whole of humanity," gave her consent to "a spiritual marriage between the Son of God and human nature" (a).

It was she who gave miraculous birth to Christ our Lord, adorned already in her virginal womb with the dignity of Head of the Church, and so brought forth the source of all heavenly life; and it was she who presented Him, the new-born Prophet, King and Priest, to those of the Jews and Gentiles who first came to adore Him. It was in answer to her motherly prayer "in Cana of Galilee" that her Only-begotten worked the miracle by which "His disciples believed in Him" (a).   **382** *(42, 122)*

She it was who, immune from all sin, personal or inherited, and ever most closely united with her Son, offered Him on Golgotha to the Eternal Father together with the holocaust of her maternal rights and motherly love, like a new Eve, for all the children of Adam contaminated through his unhappy fall, and thus she, who was the mother of our Head according to the flesh, became by a new title of sorrow and glory the spiritual mother of all His members.   **383** *(44, 116)*

She too it was who by her most powerful intercession obtained for the new-born Church the prodigious Pentecostal outpouring of that Spirit of the divine Redeemer who had already been given on the Cross. She, finally, true Queen of Martyrs, by bearing with courageous and confident heart her immense weight of sorrows, more than all Christians, "filled up those things that are wanting of the sufferings of Christ for His Body, which is the Church" (a); and upon the mystical body of Christ, born of the broken   **384** *(45, 82, 116, 117)*

381a St. Thom., III, q. 30, a. 1.
382a John 2:11.
384a Col. 1:24.

Heart of the Savior, she bestowed that same motherly
care and fervent love with which she fostered and nurtured the suckling infant Jesus in the cradle.

385   May she, therefore, most holy Mother of all the
(29,   members of Christ, to whose Immaculate Heart We have
103)   trustingly consecrated all men, may she who now, resplendent with glory in body and soul, reigns in heaven
with her Son, use her intercession with Him so that from
that august Head abundance of grace may flow with
steady stream into all the members of His mystical body.
May she now, as in times past, keep watch and ward over
the Church with her most powerful patronage, and at
length obtain from God times more peaceful for her and
for the whole family of men.

LIBERATOR OF ROME

All. to the faithful of Rome, June 11, 1944.

386   Never perhaps as in this instant, have We so vividly
(135) and forcibly experienced a sense of Our spiritual father-
ship toward all of you, with whom, for four long years,
We have been enduring the pains and difficulties entailed
by such a cruel war.

Conscious of your sufferings, but comforted by the
spectacle of your faith that brought you as suppliants to
the feet of Mary, Mother of Divine Love, We had already
wanted to be among you to mingle our prayers with yours
in one petition.

387   And we were about to carry out our desire to support
(46,   your confidence in Mary, powerful Mediatrix with her
158)   Divine Son, but the clement Queen and Patron "whose
kindness not only gives help to him who asks, but very
often freely meets his wish before it is expressed" (a)

387a Cf. Dante Alighieri, *Paradiso*, 33, 16-18.

anticipated our wish. Hence We are here today not only to ask her heavenly favors, but above all to thank her for what has occurred, contrary to human anticipations, in the highest interest of the Eternal City and her inhabitants.

Our Immaculate Mother has once again saved Rome from the gravest imminent danger. She has inspired those in power with a particular sense of reverence and moderation, so that through the changing course of events, and even in the midst of a cruel conflict, We have experienced a safety which ought to fill Our soul with tender gratitude toward God and His most pure Mother.

(*Prayer must be accompanied with reformation of public and private morals.*)

CONSECRATION TO MARY

All. to Marian Congregations, January 21, 1945.

Beloved Sons and Daughters, a pious intention has **388** brought you here to commemorate the fiftieth anniversary *(150)* of a sweet moment of Our life, that of Our consecration to the Blessed Virgin in the Marian Congregation of the Capranica College. And Our first word in greeting you is a fervent exclamation from Our grateful heart: "Magnificate Dominum mecum et exaltemus nomen ejus simul"; Magnify the Lord with me; and let us extol His name together (a).

Consecration

Consecration to the Mother of God in the Marian **389** Congregation is a total gift of oneself, for life and for *(132)* eternity; it is not just a mere matter of form nor a gift of mere sentiment, but it is an effective gift, fulfilled in an

388a Ps. 33:4.

intensity of Christian and Marian life, in the apostolic
life, making the member of the Congregation a minister
of Mary and, as it were, her hands visible on earth through
the spontaneous flow of a superabundant interior life
which overflows in all the exterior works of deep devotion,
of worship, of charity, of zeal.

390   It is this which your first rule inculcates with partic-
(132) ular force. Each one must seriously devote himself, according to his state, to his own sanctification, dedicate himself
not in any vague way, but with ardor and in the measure
and form suitable to his state of life to the salvation and
the sanctification of others; finally, each one must coura-
geously assume the duty of defending the Church of Christ.
Such is the work of the Congregation, freely and resolutely
accepted in the act of consecration. Such is the magnificent
program laid down by the Rules.

391   In truth, these rules only express in precise terms or,
as we may say "codify" the history and the constant practice of Marian Congregations providentially instituted by
the great Company of Jesus and approved and repeatedly
given high praise by the Holy See (a).

392   All this is far removed, as you see, from the concept
(151) of a simple union of quiet piety, of a mere refuge against
the dangers that threaten weak souls and also far from the
concept of a simple union merely for external action which
is weak because artificial and which cannot even for a
brief time kindle and light a fire of straw. *Numquid potest
homo abscondere ignem in sinu suo, ut vestimenta ejus
non ardeant?* "Can anyone hide fire in his bosom without having his clothing burn?" (a) If such is true of unruly
human passion, how much more truly can it be said of
the flame of charity which the Holy Spirit enkindles and
constantly feeds.

391a See above, No. 2 ff.
392a Prov. 6:27.

At the service of Mary and of the Church

The Marian devotion of a member of our Congrega- **393**
tion cannot be merely self-interested, a piety which sees *(128,*
in the powerful Mother of God only the distributor of *139,*
benefits, and especially benefits of a temporal order; nor *151)*
can it be a devotion aimed at securing only repose, that
thinks only of removing from life the holy Cross of troubles, of struggles, of suffering; nor can it be merely a
sensible devotion of sweet consolations and enthusiastic
displays; nor finally—no matter how holy it may be—a
devotion exclusively anxious over its own spiritual advantages. A member of the Congregation, true son of Mary,
knight of the Virgin, cannot satisfy himself with a simple
service of honor; he must be at her orders in all things; he
must be the guardian, the defender of her name, of her
high prerogatives, of her cause; and he must bring to his
brethren graces and heavenly favors from their common
Mother, and fight unceasingly at the command of her who,
"cunctas hæreses sola interemit in universo mundo" (a).

He has enrolled under her banner for perpetual service; he cannot, without being unfaithful to his word,
desert and abandon his place of battle and of honor.

You have taken upon yourself to defend the Church **394**
of Jesus Christ. The Church knows it, and she depends *(128)*
upon you as in the past she relied on the members of the
Congregation who preceded you. Her expectation has not
been vain; your ancestors have nobly opened out and
marked the way. In every struggle against the plague and
the tyranny of errors and for the protection of Christian
Europe Marian Congregations fought in the first line by
means of the word, the pen and the press, in controversy,
polemics, defense; in action by bolstering the courage of
the faithful, helping confessors of the faith, cooperating
with them and aiding them in their hard and difficult

393a Antiphon of Office of B.V.M.

ministry; by keeping watch against public immorality
with methods suitable to the age, energetic and efficacious;
at times even with the sword on the frontiers of Christianity, for the defense of civilization, with Sobiesky, Charles
of Lorraine, Eugene of Savoy and many other captains, all
of them members of the Congregation like many thousands
of their soldiers.

But why seek examples in the past when in our times
in more than one nation thousands and thousands of heroic
members have fought and have fallen acclaiming and invoking Christ as King?

(*Be faithful to this heritage even in the difficulties of
this present world.—Praise of the various Congregations.—
Their cooperation with Catholic Action.*)

The Congregations are a school of sanctity

395
(136,
137,
151)
What is the intimate source of all this fruitfulness, if
not the fervent life of piety nourished with most tender and
real devotion to Mary, which according to your Rule, must
aim even at sanctity. Sanctity lies hidden in the secrecy of
your hearts. Nevertheless, it is manifested in the fruits that
it produces, in the numerous vocations which it brings
forth, in the wonderful company of the saints, of the
blessed, of martyrs who represent it in heaven.

396
(151)
Beloved Sons and Daughters, you can well make yours
St. John Eudes' devout invocation to the Virgin: "How
grateful I am to you for having admitted me to your holy
Congregation, which is a true school of virtue and devotion.... This, O Mother of grace, is one of the greatest
graces which I have received from God through your
intercession" (a).

(*Conclusion.*)

396a "*Combien vous suis-je redevable ... de m'avoir admis
en votre sainte congrégation, qui est une vraie école de*

OUR LADY OF GUADALUPE

Letter *Mater spei et gratiæ*, to Cardinal Villeneuve, September 24, 1945.

The Virgin Mother of God, Mother of hope and of **397** grace, who is honored in shrines all over the world, where *(152)* she ever graciously grants every kind of consolation to her sons and to those devoted to her, is venerated in Mexico in the age-old sanctuary of Guadalupe, on the spot where about four centuries ago she appeared to an Indian and opened an inexhaustible source of life and of salvation.

(Cardinal is designated papal Legate for the Fiftieth Anniversary of the Coronation of Our Lady of Guadalupe.)

Therefore, as you are Our representative, do all you **398** can to congratulate, on Our behalf, the Mexican people, *(128,* who have placed themselves under the protection of so *131,* august a Queen, and who have often both in adversity and *160)* in prosperity experienced her constant aid. Urgently exhort them to imitate her wonderful virtues and always to trust in her with sure hope. For, Mary enjoys such power with God, she radiates so much goodness that she can and will support us in our trials.

To obtain more easily the graces of the Mother of God, it is necessary for men to follow her example and to obey the precepts of Our Redeemer: it is Mary's greatest desire that those who received their honorable name from Jesus Christ should under the guidance of Our heavenly Mother reproduce the excellent example of the life of Jesus Christ in their public and in their private life.

(Good fruits expected for Mexico.)

vertu et de pieté. . . . Et c'est ici, o Mère de grace, une de plus grandes graces que j'ai reçues de mon Dieu par votre entremise."

R. M. to the Marian Congress in Mexico, October 12, 1945.

(The Pope recalls the coronation of Our Lady of Guadalupe as Queen of Mexico.)

399
(160) ... A homage most fitting. Who can, in fact, ignore all that that people owes to Our Lady? Who can forget the original part she took in calling it to the true Church and preserving it in the practice and purity of a faith that has been like the crucible in which its young and sturdy patriotism was tested and approved?

The Faith of the New World

400
(22,
110,
122) The most Holy Virgin was the providential instrument, chosen in the designs of our Heavenly Father, to give and present to the world His incomparable Son; to be the Mother and Queen of the Apostles who were to spread His doctrine all over the world; ever to check heresies; and also to intervene always in a wonderful manner wherever necessary in order to introduce, strengthen and defend the holy Catholic Faith. In this connection, one of her great servants, St. Cyril of Alexandria, writes as follows: "Through her the Holy Cross is known and adored all over the world; through her every creature imprisoned by the bonds of idolatrous errors comes to the knowledge of truth; through her the Apostles preached salvation to the nations" (a).

401
(160,
177) So it happened when God's hour had come for the vast regions of Anahauac. They had hardly been opened up to the world than a miracle was wrought on the shores of Lake Texaco. On poor John Diego's apron, as tradition has it, brushes not of this earth left painted a very sweet

400a St. Cyril of Alexandria, *Homil.* 4.

picture that the corrosive action of time has, in a wonderful manner, left unimpaired. The lovable Virgin was requesting a sanctuary from which she could show and pour forth all her love, compassion, help and protection over all the inhabitants of those parts, and also upon others who would invoke her and put their trust in her.

From that historic moment complete evangelization became an accomplished fact. What is more, a banner was unfurled and a rampart erected against which the fury of every tempest would shatter itself. One of the foundation pillars of the faith in Mexico and in all America was solidly established. It was as if the Cross which the frail Spanish caravels on this very day brought through stormy waves to the New Continent was entrusted to this Virgin's pure hands so that she might take it triumphantly to all those lands, plant it everywhere and then retire to her Castle Rock that overlooks ancient Tenochitlan, from there to hold sway over the New World and watch over its faith. And, as one of your poets so well expresses it: "She knew that that land would proclaim her its Queen and would faithfully preserve the deposit of that faith which is the salvation of the world."

Salvation through devotion to Mary

Today, Beloved Americans gathered at this Congress, **402** more rapidly and securely than the radio waves that carry *(136)* Our voice to you, Our thought takes Us to your midst, and once again Our soul feels comforted in contemplating your countless numbers and your boundless enthusiasm;—in seeing that at this moment more than fifty archbishops and bishops are representing with you the faith of all the peoples of America;—in receiving, in the person of Our Legate, the magnificent testimony of your filial devotion, of which We were already aware. And, in noting that the center of all this fervor continues to be your most excellent Patroness, almost seeing with Our own eyes that you continually acclaim the Virgin of Guadalupe as your Mother and Queen, We raise Our eyes to heaven and return thanks to the Author of all good because, in this love and in this faithfulness, We would see a guarantee of the preservation of your faith.

403
(123
139)
For this faith, Catholic Mexicans, your brothers and fathers fell victims to persecution, and to defend it they unflinchingly faced even death at the twofold cry of: "Long live Christ the King, Long live the Virgin of Guadalupe." "Viva Cristo Re, Viva la Vergine di Guadalupe."

Today the conditions of Church and religion have considerably improved in your fatherland, demonstrating that such prayer and steadfastness were not in vain. But now it is your duty, yours and that of all American Catholics, to remain steadfast at your post, conscious of your rights, always with head erect in front of your enemies whether those of today or those of all times, those enemies who do not care for Mary because they do not care for Jesus and who would wish to discard or ignore Jesus, thus tearing away from Mary the most excellent of her titles. Let your faithfulness rise against their rebellion. May the Virgin of Tepeyac, the Empress of America and Queen of Mexico, not have to deplore any desertions! May she be tomorrow, as she was yesterday, proud of her children!

404
(42,
52,
131,
160)
Your Congress, which gathered thousands of signatures, proclaimed her *Sedes Sapientiæ* (Seat of Wisdom). Do not forget, Catholics of Mexico, that true wisdom is that which she vouchsafed us, that which she teaches us in the name of Wisdom Incarnate.

"Hail, Most Abundant Source from which spring out the streams of Divine Wisdom, and holds back, with the purest and clearest waters of orthodoxy, the curling waves of error" (a).

404a St. Germanus of Constantinople, *Serm. I in SS Deip. Praesent.* No. 14.

Hail, O Virgin of Guadalupe! We, to whom an admirable disposition of Providence—without considering Our unworthiness—entrusted the sacred treasure of Divine Wisdom on earth for the salvation of every soul, We again today encircle thy brow with the crown which forever places under thy powerful patronage the purity and integrity of Holy Faith in Mexico and in all the American Continent; for We feel sure that as long as thou shalt be recognized as Queen and Mother, America and Mexico shall be safe.

PREPARATION OF THE DEFINITION OF THE ASSUMPTION

Encycl. *Deiparæ Virginis,* May 1, 1946.

The Christian people have never ceased to invoke and experience the Blessed Virgin Mary's assistance, and therefore they have, at all times, venerated her with ever growing devotion. **405** *(96, 138)*

And so, because love when it is true and deeply felt tends of its own nature to manifest itself through ever renewed demonstrations, the faithful have vied with one another all through the centuries in expressing at all times their ardent piety toward the Queen of Heaven. In our opinion, this is the reason why, for a long time past, numerous petitions (those received from 1840 to 1940 have been gathered in two volumes which, accompanied with suitable comments, have been recently printed), from cardinals, patriarchs, archbishops, bishops, priests, religious of both sexes, associations, universities and innumerable private persons have reached the Holy See, all begging that the bodily Assumption into heaven of the Blessed Virgin should be defined and proclaimed as a dogma of faith. And certainly no one is unaware of the fact that this was fervently requested by almost two hundred fathers in the Vatican Council (a).

405a Cf. Manse 53, 481 ff.

Consultation of the Episcopate

406
(96)
But We, who are charged with the care of defending and developing the Kingdom of Christ, have at the same time to exercise continual care and vigilance to keep away everything adverse to this Kingdom, and to support whatsoever may promote it. Therefore, from the beginning of Our Pontificate, we had to examine most carefully whether it would be lawful, convenient and useful to support with Our authority the above-mentioned petitions. We have not neglected and do not at present neglect to offer insistent prayers to God that He might clearly manifest the will of His ever-adorable goodness in this instance.

In order that We may receive the gift of heavenly light, do you, Venerable Brethren, in pious competition, unite your entreaties with Ours. But, while paternally exhorting you to do this, thus following the example of Our Predecessors, and particularly that of Pius IX when about to define the dogma of the Mother of God's Immaculate Conception (a), we earnestly beg you to inform us about the devotion of your clergy and people (taking into account their faith and piety) toward the Assumption of the most Blessed Virgin Mary. More especially We wish to know if you, Venerable Brethren, with your learning and prudence consider that the bodily Assumption of the Immaculate Blessed Virgin can be proposed and defined as a dogma of faith, and whether in addition to your own wishes this is desired by your clergy and people.

MARY'S UNIVERSAL QUEENSHIP

R. M. on the occasion of the coronation of the statue of Our Lady of Fatima, May 13, 1946.

407
(38,
Venerable Brethren and dearly beloved Sons, "Blessed be the God and Father of our Lord Jesus Christ, the Father

406a Cf. above, no. 19 ff.

of mercies and the God of all comfort, who comforteth us   *156)*
in all tribulation" (a) and with our Lord may she be
blessed whom He constituted Mother of Mercy, Queen and
our most loving Advocate, Mediatrix of His graces, Dispenser of His treasures!

When, about four years ago, in the throes of the most
terrible war that history recalls, We ascended with you
in spirit this holy mount to thank with you our Lady of
Fatima for the immense benefits which she had recently
bestowed on you, We also united with the "Magnificat"
of all the faithful Our cry of filial trust and We begged
the Immaculate Queen and Patroness of Portugal to complete what she had so wonderfully begun (b).

Your gathering here today in this Sanctuary in such a   **408**
countless throng bears witness to the fact that the Virgin   *(156,*
Lady, Immaculate Queen, to whose maternal and compas-   *159)*
sionate Heart we owe the miracle of Fatima, has heard
our requests with unhoped-for generosity.

Your ardent love, full of gratitude, led you here, and
you wished to give a tangible form to this love by symbol-
ically representing it in that precious crown, which is the
fruit of much generosity and of many sacrifices and with
which We have now crowned the miraculous statue by
means of Our Cardinal Legate.

Our Lady's protection of Portugal

Significant symbol, for, if it shows your filial love and   **409**
your gratitude to our heavenly Queen, it first of all brings   *(159)*
to your mind the most wonderful love manifested in the
innumerable benefits showered by the Virgin Mother on
the "Land of Mary most holy." Eight centuries of graces!
The first five were lived under the standard of St. Mary
of Alcabaca, of St. Mary of the Victory, of St. Mary of

407a 2 Cor. 1:3-4.
407b See above, no. 373 ff.

Belem, both in the national struggles against the Moham-
medans for the establishment of the country and in all
the adventurous heroism of the discoveries of new islands
and new continents, where your fathers travelled and
planted, with the national standard, the Cross of Christ.

The last three centuries have been passed under
the special protection of the Immaculate Virgin, whom
the restored Monarch together with the whole Nation
reunited in the "Cortes," proclaimed Patroness of his Kingdoms and Dominions. The King consecrated his crown to
her with a special tribute of submission and with an oath
to defend, even with his life, the privilege of her Immaculate Conception. "We put," said he, "great trust in the
infinite mercy of Our Lord, who through the intercession
of our Lady, Patroness and Protectress of our kingdoms
and dependencies, the Patroness of whom we have the
honor to profess ourselves vassals and tributaries, protects
and defends us from the enemy, who enlarges our territories greatly, all for the glory of Christ our God, for the
exaltation of our Holy, Catholic, Roman faith, for the
conversion of the Gentiles and the return of the heretics (a).

410   And the most faithful Virgin did not fail those who
(156) placed their hope in her. We need only reflect on these
last 30 years which are the equal of centuries because
of the crises undergone and the benefits received; We
need only stop to view this Cova da Irìa transformed into
a source of heavenly graces, of miracles in the physical
order and even more so in the moral one, miracles which
like torrents flow all over Portugal and, crossing frontiers,
extend to all the Church and to the whole world.

Portugal's gratitude

411   How withhold our thanks, or, rather, how can we
(34, worthily show our gratitude? Three hundred years ago the

409a The "Cortes" of Lisbon in 1646.

Monarch of the Restoration, as a sign of his love and of *40)*
his own and his people's gratitude, placed the royal crown
at the feet of the Immaculate, proclaiming her Queen and
Patroness. Today, all of you—all you people of Mary's land
together with the shepherds of your souls, with your Government—to the ardent prayers, to the generous sacrifices, to
the Eucharistic solemnities, to the thousand acts of homage
dictated by filial love you are adding in remembrance of
her favors a precious crown and with it encircling the brow
of our Lady of Fatima. This you are doing in that blessed
oasis, fertile ground of the supernatural, where you experience her miraculous patronage very sensibly, and where
you feel her Immaculate Heart beating with an immense
tenderness and motherly solicitude for you and for all
mankind.

Precious crown, expressive symbol of love and gratitude!

Heavenly and universal Queenship of Mary

Your own immense concourse, the fervor of your **412**
prayers, the resounding echo of your acclamations, your *(101,*
holy enthusiasm which manifests itself unrestrainably and *102,*
then the sacred rite lately concluded in this hour of the *109)*
Virgin Mother's incomparable triumph,—all this calls to
Our mind other multitudes more numerous still, other
acclamations even more ardent, other triumphs much more
divine, another hour—eternally solemn—in the never-end-
ing day of eternity, wherein the glorious Virgin, entering
triumphantly into heaven, was elevated above the hierarchies of the blessed and the angelic choirs to the throne
of the most Holy Trinity who, placing on her brow a triple
diadem of glory, presented her to the heavenly court
seated at the right hand of the immortal King of the ages
and crowned "Queen of the Universe."

And Paradise recognized that she was really worthy **413**
of receiving honor, glory and rule, because she is full of *(46,*
grace, holier, more beautiful, more exalted, incomparably *54,*

57,
73,
104)
more so than the greatest saints and angels, taken individually or all together; because, as the first-born daughter
of the Father, the perfect Mother of the Word, the beloved
Spouse of the Holy Spirit, she is related in virtue of the
Hypostatic Union to the whole Most Holy Trinity, to Him
who in Himself alone is by essence infinite Majesty, the
King of kings, Lord of lords; because she was the Mother
of the King divine, of Him to whom from His Mother's
womb the Lord God gave the throne of David and eternal
kingship in the house of Jacob (a) and who, after asserting
in His own right that all power was given to Him in
heaven and on earth (b), He, the Son of God, gave His
heavenly Mother a share in His glory, His majesty, His
kingship; because, associated as Mother and Minister to
the King of martyrs in the ineffable work of man's Redemption, she is likewise associated with Him forever,
with power so to speak infinite, in the distribution of the
graces which flow from Redemption (c).

414
(102,
106,
125)
Jesus is by nature and by conquest the King of the
eternal ages; through Him, with Him, subordinated to
Him, Mary is Queen by grace, by divine association, by
conquest, by singular election. Her Kingdom is as vast as
that of her divine Son because nothing of His dominion is
excluded (a).

For this reason the Church salutes her Sovereign and as
Queen of the angels and the saints, of patriarchs and prophets, of apostles and martyrs, of confessors and virgins;

413a Cf. Luke 1:32-33.
413b Cf. Matt. 28:18.
413c ... *associada, como Mãe e Ministra, ao Rei dos mártires
na obra inefável da humana Redenção, lhe é para sempre
associada, com cum poder quasi imenso, na distribuiçao das
graças que da Redenção derivam.*
414a *Jesus é Rei dos séculos eternos por natureza e por conquista; por Ele, com Ele, subordinadamente a Ele, Maria é
Rainha por graça, por parentesco divino, por conquista, por
singular eleição. Eo o seu reino é vasto como o de seu Filho
e Deus, pois que de seu domínio nada se exclude.*

for this reason the Church acclaims her Queen of Heaven and of earth, the glorious and most worthy Queen of the Universe: "Regina cælorum," "gloriosa Regina mundi," "Regina mundi dignissima," and she exhorts us to invoke her day and night, the mourning and weeping, of this our exile: "Hail Holy Queen, Mother of mercy, hail our life, our sweetness and our hope" (b).

And this queenship of hers is essentially motherly, used only for our good.

Significance of the event at Fatima

Is it not precisely that queenship that you are acknowledging? Are you not today proclaiming and recognizing her countless favors, the numberless graces which the motherly heart of your august Queen has showered on you? The most savage war that ever devastated the world has for four years blocked your frontiers, but, thanks to our Lady who from her throne of mercy, like a sentinel stationed on high in the center of your country, stood watch over you and your statesmen, it never crossed those frontiers. She did not permit the war to touch you, or at the most to touch you just enough to make you realize the unwonted calamities from which her protection saved you. **415 (106, 111, 156)**

You crown her Queen of Peace and of the world so that she may help the world to find peace once again and rise from its ruins. Thus that crown, the symbol of love and emblem of gratitude for the past, of faith and of submission for the present, becomes also a crown of fidelity and of hope for the future.

In crowning the image of Our Lady, you made an act of faith in her Queenship, of loyal submission to her authority, of filial and continued correspondence with her love. You did something more: you enrolled yourselves as Crusaders for the conquest and the reclamation of her

414b Antiphon *Salve Regina*.

kingdom, which is the kingdom of God; in other words
you pledged yourselves to work so that she may be loved,
venerated and served everywhere, in the family, in society, in the world.

In this decisive hour of history, in which the kingdom
of evil with infernal strategy uses every means and looses
all its forces to destroy faith and morals and the Kingdom
of God, the children of light and the children of God must
use every means and pledge themselves wholly to defend
these, if they wish to avoid more disastrous and vastly
greater ruin than the material ruin heaped up by war.

416
(168) In this struggle no one can be neutral or hesitant.
We need an enlightened, a convinced and fearless Catholicism, one that takes its inspiration from faith and is
obedient to the commandments, a Catholicism of mind
and action both in public and in private.

(*Conclusion and blessing.*)

THE SAFETY OF SOCIETY

R. M. to the National Marian Congress of Columbia.
July 19, 1946.

(*Columbia's Marian riches.*)

417
(160) Columbia, land of the Holy Virgin, Columbia, a Marian garden! Is not this one of the reasons why your country
is such a strong bulwark of our faith on the American
Continent, so that particularly in certain regions of your
land one still breathes that Christian air, healthy, genuine
and deep, which is, unfortunately, becoming ever more
rare in the vitiated atmosphere of our present world?

Apostolate in the New World

418
(122 "Great was her (Mary's) unceasing care," said our immortal Predecessor, Leo XIII, who was profoundly devoted
to Mary, "to see that the Catholic faith should be kept

firm among the peoples of the world, and flourish intact *160)* and fruitful" (a). And those who one day will want to examine thoroughly the spread and preservation of our Holy Faith in the regions colonized by your mother country, Spain, will have to recognize that to secure such plentiful fruit the Holy Spirit inspired the heroic missionaries to raise the Holy Cross with one hand and with the other to show to the peoples a picture of Our Lady, deeply grafting into them that threefold love which has resisted all storms: Love of the Blessed Eucharist, of the Holy Mother of God, and of the Sovereign Pontiff.

Under the auspices of the Virgin Mary, our Lady, in the mystery of her Immaculate Conception, the electoral College of Cundinamarca decreed absolute independence; and similarly under the special protection of the Blessed Virgin, our Lady, the Federal Congress of the United Provinces of New Granada was constituted.

The Virgin of Carmel, the patroness of seafaring peo- **419** ple who entrust their lives daily to the fluctuation of wind *(120-* and wave! From our post, as helmsman of St. Peter's bark, *121)* when we hear the storm raging and see spuming before our eyes the furious surge that would fain submerge our vessel, calmly and confidently we look up to the Virgin of Mount Carmel, "Respice Stellam, voca Mariam" (a) and beseech her not to desert Us. Although hell unceasingly renews its attacks, and the violence, audacity and fury of evil forces are ever increasing, as long as we rely on her powerful patronage we never may doubt the victory.

The safety of society

The Virgin of Carmel, the Queen of Columbia! **420** Promise her solemnly absolute fidelity to the faith of *(154,* your forefathers, the doctrine which they proclaimed as *176)*

418a Cf. above, no. 172.
419a St. Bernard, Serm. 2, *super Missus est.*

the foundation of your fatherland; to the Catholic, Apostolic and Roman religion "abundant source of heavenly blessings;" as your Liberator, the great Simon Bolivar called it in a solemn moment of your national existence. Beseech the heavenly Queen that she preserve that which, at all times, was the basis of your happiness: an ardent faith, purity of morals, sanctity of life. Ask her to continue to show herself the Mother of mankind, "Monstra te esse matrem" (a) because our poor world of today stands more than ever in need of her humility, simplicity and purity if it does not wish totally to perish in the abysses of pride, double-dealing and corruption into which it is hurling itself with giant strides.

Pray to her that she may comfort the numerous sufferers, since, as one of your poets in speaking of the Virgin of the Rocks said: "She listens to all, does not neglect anyone, protects all and comforts every one. She pities those who mourn and comforts those who weep."

We desire and beg for you the plenitude of Mary's motherly love and protection and especially her powerful mediation with her Divine Son.

A MODEL OF CHRISTIAN LIFE

Letter *Philippinas Insulas*, to the Archbishop of Manila, July 31, 1946.

(*The fruits of Christian civilization.—Freedom is in danger whenever God's authority is forgotten.*)

421
(68, 70, 130)
The order of Christian wisdom shines forth whenever we fully adhere with our minds to the Divine Truth and Commandments, and with God's help conform our habits and our actions to them.

For the attainment of such perfection the Blessed Virgin Mary shows us the way by her actions, precedes

420a Hymn *Ave Maris Stella.*

us with her example and assists us with her protection. Victorious over the devil and sin, with which she is in perpetual enmity, adorned with the splendor of every virtue, and above all with Christ's grace, she is a sterling example of the life, which the faithful should contemplate and reproduce in themselves. Tower of fortitude, Mother of Fair Love, Seat of Wisdom, she has in herself in all its integrity and effectual power the spirit of the Christian religion which the Apostle describes in these words: "For God hath not given us the spirit of fear: but of power and of love and of prudence" (a).

The Rosary, a summary of the Gospel

Through the Rosary of the Blessed Virgin Mary we have, indeed, before our eyes the mysteries of the Mother of God; we think of her with devout affection, love her, implore her protection with the loving insistence of our prayers; we meditate with ease and imitate fully the example of our Mother's life. **422** *(130, 145)*

Let the Holy Rosary be held again in very high honor among you for it is a synthesis of the whole Gospel: meditation on the mysteries of the Lord, an evening sacrifice, a garland of roses, a hymn of praise, a family prayer, a compendium of Christian life, a sure pledge of heavenly favors, a defence while we await our expected salvation. Under its guidance may the virtue of old—the most faithful guardian of right living—flourish again among you; may the hope of a better world dawn upon you, wherein united in fruitful alliance, and with true reverence toward God, Sacred Letters, studies of every kind, liberal arts, noble honesty of life, the practice of social justice and Christian happiness may revive among you.

(*Prayers for the diffusion of the Catholic Faith.*)

421a 2 Tim. 1:7.

OUR LADY OF HEALTH

Apost. Letter *Suavissima inter*, February 2, 1947.

423
(121,
167,
177)
Among the sweetest names conferred on the Blessed Virgin Mary, the name by which she is called "Our Lady of Health" excels and is widely spread among the faithful. Indeed, the Virgin Mary as a tender Mother is rightly called "Health" of bodies broken and racked by sickness not without special advantage to souls. She is "Health" not only of each one of the faithful, but of all Christian people in trials and adversities.

(*Our Lady of Health, principal patron of Monfalcone.*)

MARY'S SOVEREIGN LIBERTY

Letter *Ab Octaviensi Archidiocesi*, to Cardinal McGuigan, March 25, 1947.

(*Subject matter of the Ottawa Marian Congress: true freedom.*)

424
(74,
122)
Christ is Truth; through Him we become acquainted with hidden matters and we practice what is right.

Christ came into this world through Mary: "Truth, which is in the bosom of the Father, appeared on the earth to be enclosed in Mary's womb; Truth, which contains the world, came to earth to be carried in a Woman's arms" (a).

Because of this, true freedom proceeds from Mary. She was the freest of creatures because the holiest. Mistress of all virtues, she teaches her children and devotees the way to rid themselves of error and evil and to spend the days of this mortal life in caring for their own salvation, in doing good to others, in glorifying God more and more, and in advancing ever towards greater perfection.

424a St. Augustine, *Serm.* 185, 1.

In the name of and under the patronage of the Moth- **425**
er of God let all those who call themselves and really are *(82,*
Christians labor and struggle to safeguard liberty, the hope *130,*
and salvation of mankind, against those who trample it *131)*
under foot or alter it; above all let them conform their
own actions to those of Mary; these shine with inimitable
grace and attractive light. Who is nobler than the Mother
of God? Who is more resplendent than she whom Splendor
Himself has chosen? (a)

(*Cooperation of Canada expected for restoration of
Christian values.*)

OUR MOTHER'S HEART

Apost. Letter *Novissimo universarum*, May 1, 1947.

While the last world war was raging, while every kind **426**
of atrocity was committed on land, on sea and in the air, *(28,*
terrified men almost convinced themselves that no shred of *40,*
of goodness remained any longer in human hearts. Let *80,*
those think thus who are no longer mindful of that moth- *141)*
erly Heart, which beats with most tender love in time
with the most sweet Heart of Jesus, her Child. The tenderness of the Immaculate Heart of Mary is in a certain sense
infinite, with that infinity which the Angelic Doctor said
belonged to the Mother of God by reason of her consan-
guinity with God (a). The Melliflous Doctor declared that
the soul of the most Blessed Virgin is full of the most ardent affection. And as in the midst of a world grown
cold there was need to rekindle the fire from heaven, We
wished, on the feast of the Immaculate Conception of the
Blessed Virgin, in the year 1942, to consecrate all mankind
forever to the Immaculate Heart of Mary (b).

425a St. Ambrose, *De virginibus*, II, c. II, 7.
426a *Immaculati Mariæ cordis pietas est propemodum infini-
ta, ex illa quadam infinitate quam propter consanguinitatem
cum Deo, Deiparæ proprium esse Doctor dicit angelicus.*
426b Cf. above, no. 373 ff.

427   Since that time the faithful from all over the world
(132) have begun to approach with great confidence the throne
of Grace and at the same time the most merciful help of
Mary manifested itself more widely.

The faithful of the Diocese of Suchow in China who
attribute their safety from the dangers of war and especially from the attacks of the Japanese greatly benefited from
the abundance and sweetness of the Maternal Heart.

(*Our Lady, under the title of the Immaculate Heart,
Patroness of the Diocese of Suchow.*)

MOTHER OF GRACE

Apost. Letter *Per Christi Matrem,* May 15, 1947.

428   The grace of Christ comes to us through the Mother
(33, of Christ. She in fact "Sumens illud ave Gabrielis ore," (a)
42, who greeted her as full of grace, became at the same time
52, Mother of Christ and Mother of divine grace. The mater-
121) nal office of "Mediatrix" really began at the very moment
of her consent to the Incarnation; it was manifested for the
first time by the first sign of Christ's grace, at Cana in
Galilee; from that moment it rapidly spread down through
the ages with the growth of the Church.

(*Dante's devotion to the Virgin Mary.—Our Lady of
Montenero constituted principal Patron of Tuscany.*)

MOTHER OF THE MEMBERS OF CHRIST

R. M. to the National Marian Congress of Canada,
June 19, 1947.

(*Our Lady's role in the history of French Canada.—
Exhortation to live faithful to that Christian heritage.*)

428a Hymn *Ave, Maris Stella.*

Mother of God! What an ineffable title! The grace of the divine maternity is the key which opens up to weak, human scrutiny the untold riches of Mary's soul; as it is likewise a challenge commanding for her the utmost reverence of every creature: "She alone by her dignity trancends heaven and earth. None among created beings, visible or invisible, can compare with her in excellence. She is at once the Handmaid and Mother of God, a Virgin and yet a Mother" (a). **429** *(25, 28, 104)*

But when the young girl of Nazareth uttered her "fiat" to the message of the angel and the Word was made flesh in her womb, she became not only the Mother of God, in the physical order of nature, but also in the supernatural order of grace she became the Mother of all, who through the Holy Spirit would be made one under the headship of her Divine Son. The Mother of the Head would be the Mother of the members. The Mother of the Vine would be the Mother of the branches. **430** *(29, 114)*

(*Mary's protection over Canadian youth.*)

THE SECRET OF FATHER DE MONTFORT

All. at the canonization of Father de Montfort, July 21, 1947.

(*Greeting to the various groups of Pilgrims.*)

Finally, a word of greeting to you pilgrims who have come here from different countries. Outwardly, you are different one from the other but your love for Mary unites you and makes you see in him, whom you have come to honor, the guide who leads you to Mary and through Mary to Jesus! All the saints were undoubtedly great servants of Mary and they all lead souls to her. Grignion de Montfort is one of those saints who worked more ardently and more efficaciously to make her loved and served. **431** *(175, 176)*

429a St. John Chrysostom, *Serm. Apud Metaphast.*

(Devotion of Father de Montfort to the Holy Cross and to Our Lady.—His character.)

432
(48,
129,
170,
175)
The greatest force behind all his apostolic ministry and his great secret for attracting and giving souls to Jesus was his devotion to Mary. All his activity depended on that devotion; in it he placed all his security: and he could not have found a more efficacious weapon for his age. To the sad austerity, the somber terror, the depressing pride of Jansenism he opposed the filial, trusting, ardent, expansive and effective love of the devout servant of Mary, towards her who is the Refuge of sinners, the Mother of Divine Grace, our life, our sweetness and our hope (a). Our Advocate, placed between God and the sinner, takes it upon herself to invoke clemency of the Judge so as to temper His justice, touch the heart of the sinner and overcome his obstinacy. Convinced by his own personal experience of Mary's role, the missionary declared with a picturesque simplicity all his own that "never did a sinner resist him after he had touched his coat collar with the rosary."

The true devotion

433
(139,
175)
Moreover, it must be a sincere and loyal devotion. The author of "True Devotion to the Blessed Virgin" distinguishes in a few precise words this authentic devotion from the false and more or less superstitious devotion, which consists only in exterior practice and superficial sentiment. Such a devotion leads those who cultivate it to live as they think fit and remain in sin, presuming to receive an extraordinary grace at their last hour (a).

434
(128,
140)
The true devotion, the traditional devotion, that of the Church, the devotion, we might say, of the well-meaning Christian and Catholic, aims essentially at union with

432a From the Litany of I oreto; and the Antiphon *Hail, Holy Queen.*
433a Chapter 3.

Jesus, under the guidance of Mary. The form and practice of this devotion may vary according to time, place and personal inclination. Within the bounds of a sane and a secure doctrine, of orthodoxy and of the dignity of worship, the Church leaves her children a just margin of liberty. She is conscious that the true and perfect devotion to the Blessed Virgin is not bound up with any modes in such a manner that one of them can claim a monopoly over the others.

And for this reason, Beloved Sons and Daughters, We ardently hope that in addition to the various manifestations of devotion to the Mother of God and of men you will draw from the treasury of the writings and example of our Saint that which constitutes the basis of his Marian Devotion: his firm conviction of the most powerful intercession of Mary, his resolute will to imitate as far as possible the virtues of the Virgin of Virgins, and the vehement ardor of his love for her and for Jesus.   **435** *(126, 130, 131)*

THE MODEL OF ALL VIRTUES

R. M. to the National Marian Congress of Argentina, October 12, 1947.

(*Recalling the International Eucharistical Congress of 1934 and the Visit to the Sanctuary of Lujan, the Marian center of Argentina.*)

In common with all Christian peoples, the Argentine people know (and your present Congress has repeated it) that the cult of the Mother of God, prophesied by herself when she said: "Beatam me dicent omnes generationes" (a), is a basic element of Christian life.   **436** *(107, 125)*

In fact, who among all those who are passing through this world, carrying the burden of so many weaknesses and exposed to so many dangers, has no need of assist-

436a Luke 1:48.

ance? Listen therefore to the Doctor Eximius when he
tells you: "We have the Virgin as universal advocate in
all things, for she is more powerful in whatever necessity
than are the other saints in particular needs" (b).

437   Consequently, let us honor her, recognizing the un-
(80,   equalled splendor of her beauty, the delicacy of her
130-   goodness, and her irresistible power. For the excellency
135)   of her virtues and the incomparable dignity of her mission, let us venerate her, proclaiming her grandeur, showing her our reverence and invoking her intercession. Finally
let us imitate her without hesitation in so noble a task
since, to quote the words of a great Marian Pontiff, the
immortal Leo XIII: "God, good and provident, offers us
in Mary the most perfect model of every virtue . . . ; and
we, attracted by the affinity of common nature, undertake
with greater confidence to imitate her" (a).

Timeliness of Marian devotion

438   This poor world, as it it wished to go back twenty
(128)   centuries to the aberrations of decaying pagan society,
places upon its altars the vain idols of lust, pride, covetousness and, as a natural consequence, hatred of everything that might deny it its miserable ration of pleasure,
its paltry portion of power, or the drop that might quench
its thirst, not for water but for money.

          You, instead, at this moment, are renewing your
allegiance to her who is the symbol of all purity—"Mater
castissima"—the incarnation of the most perfect humility—
"*Ecce ancilla Domini*"—and the personification of total
self-denial; to her who is, above all possible comparison,
"*Mater pulchræ dilectionis*," the most perfect model of
charity and love.

436b Suarez, *In* 3. *am*, disp. 23. sect. 3, n. 5.
437a Leo XIII, cf. above, no. 138.

Promise Mary that you will devote yourselves with **439**
all your energies to preserving and enhancing the dignity *(136)*
and sanctity of Christian marriage, the religious education
of youth in schools, the application of the teaching of the
Church in the ordering of economic conditions and the
solution of social questions. Your close adherence to the
Church on these fundamental points of Christian civilization will today be unquestionable evidence that you have
a true and genuine love for the Blessed Virgin Mary and
her Divine Son. Promise her also, in accordance with the
spirit of the Congress, to grow everyday in devotion toward her; a growth which, if it be all that it should be,
cannot but lead you to the full realization of the principles
and standards of Christian life, without leading you into
the mistake of those who manifestly want to boast of being
Christians and at the same time support doctrines incom-
patible with Christianity.

(*Good wishes to the members of the Congress.—Prayer
to the Blessed Virgin Mary to implore peace.*)

CULTUS OF HYPERDULIA

Encycl. *Mediator Dei*, November 20, 1947.

(*The sacred Liturgy.—Eucharistic worship.—The Divine Office and the liturgical year.—Worship due to the
Saints.*)

Among the saints of heaven, the Virgin Mary, Mother   **440**
of God, is the recipient of a more exalted worship. Because *(32,*
of the function she received from God, her life is closely   *40-*
linked with the mysteries of Christ, and no one assuredly   *42,*
has followed more closely and effectively in the steps of   *78,*
the Incarnate Word; no one enjoys greater favor and   *126,*
greater power with the Sacred Heart of the Son of God   *134)*
and, through Him, with His heavenly Father. Holier
than the cherubim and the seraphim, she enjoys a glory

greater than that of the other saints because "she is full of grace" (a) and Mother of God, and by her blessed maternity has given us the Redeemer. Since she is "Mother of mercy, our life, our sweetness, and our hope" let us cry to her, "mourning and weeping in this valley of tears" (b) and place ourselves and all that is ours confidently under her patronage. She became our Mother when the Divine Redeemer was consummating the sacrifice of Himself; hence, by this title, also, we are her children. She teaches us all the virtues; she gives us her Son, and with Him all the help we need, for God "has willed that we should have everything through Mary" (c).

(*Pastoral directives.*)

THE VICTORIES OF THE IMMACULATE VIRGIN

All. to the Roman Youth of Catholic Action, December 8, 1947.

(*Directions for the present: clear principles, individual courage, harmony between religion and life.*)

441
(70,
123,
134,
136)
We are today celebrating the triumph of the Immaculate, who with her virginal heel crushed the head of the serpent. The Church thus sings her praises: "*Cunctas hæreses sola interemisti in universo mundo*" (a). Thou alone hast destroyed all heresies, all errors, all wrong systems which promise the human race to lead it to perfection, to raise it up to the heights of felicity, but, instead, plunge it into the abyss of corruption and ruin.

To the protection of this pure and strong Virgin we are entrusting you, Young Catholics of Rome, and with

440a Luke 1:28.
440b Cf. Antiphon, *Salve Regina.*
440c St. Bernard, *In Nativ.* B.V.M., 7.
441a Office of Our Lady.

you the Catholic Youth of your country, and of all countries, for you to form into line under her scepter, fight under her banner, and go forward under her guidance without fear.

She, the Seat of Wisdom, the Faithful Virgin, the Powerful Virgin, the Help of Christians and Queen of Peace will lead you safely to Victory.

"TERRIBLE AS AN ARMY"

Letter *Flagranti semper animi*, to the Polish Episcopate, January 18, 1948.

(*Poland's Resurgences throughout the course of her history.*)

Beloved Sons and Venerable Brethren, We are not surprised therefore at those matters which you thought it well to point out to Us with much kindness when you assembled not long ago at the Marian Sanctuary of Czestochowa. In fact, in that most renowned sanctuary, dedicated to the heavenly Queen of Poland, you gather almost yearly with the hope that the gracious Mother will grant you, in due time, enlightenment, counsel, and her never-failing help. This last Episcopal Conference coincides with the first anniversary of the consecration of all the Polish Nation to the Immaculate Heart of Mary. Today there is greater urgency to draw strength from and to find refuge in her Heart. **442** (82, 154)

Undoubtedly, our heavenly Mother not only shines as the morning star but is also that strong Woman who, to defend the rights of her Divine Son, so often manifests herself in the Church "terrible as an army set in battle array" (a).

(*Redouble zeal in view of future threats.*)

442a Cant. 6:3.

DEVOTION TO THE IMMACULATE
HEART OF MARY

Letter *Ex officiosis litteris*, to the Bishop of Autun, February 15, 1948.

(*The third centenary of the concession of a Mass in honor of the Immaculate Heart.*)

443
(125,
168)
We think it fitting to recall this event to the memory of the Christian people and We hope that as in the days of John Eudes so also at the present time the souls of the faithful may profit from this Mass and be stimulated and exhorted not only to promote devotion to the Virgin Mother of God and to conceive a more ardent love of her, but also to imitate the example of her virtues. Never has this devotion appeared more necessary than it does in these our present times.

A few years ago, as all will remember—when the fearful war was raging and human hope and strength appeared very uncertain and unstable in the throes of such a very grave conflict—We with prayers and supplication begging the all powerful patronage of the most pure Heart of the Virgin Mary turned to our most merciful Redeemer. And like Our Predecessor, Leo XIII of happy memory, who at the beginning of the twentieth century wished to consecrate all mankind to the most Sacred Heart of Jesus, We, as representative of the human family divinely redeemed, also wished to consecrate it solemnly to the Immaculate Heart of the Virgin Mother of God.

Although the war has almost ceased everywhere, hate has not yet died away nor have disagreements and disputes been settled. In fact, the very structure of civil society appears in great danger, and many nations and populations, still suffering with many wounds and afflicted with much destruction and disaster, scrutinize with fear the direction that this new year will take.

Therefore, do not cease to invoke divine help nor to **444**
implore the guardianship of the Blessed Virgin Mary, *(169)*
without whose help he who wishes to obtain great favors
and divine help is compared to the person who vainly
wishes to fly on high without the help of wings. For this
reason you will do well if while commemorating this
happy event you profit from such a suitable occasion and
so put yourself in a position to arouse more easily the
devotion of the people towards the most gracious Mother
of God, by pointing her out and recommending her to all
as Patroness of peace and Mediatrix of heavenly favors

(*Invocation to St. John Eudes.*)

THE PEACE OF THE WORLD

Encycl. *Auspicia quedam,* May 1, 1948.

(*Despite peoples' desire for Peace, the situation remains perilous.*)

For this reason, it was comforting for Us in past years **445**
to appeal earnestly to all—especially to the young so dear *(162)*
to Us—to crowd around the altar of the Great Mother of
God during the month of May, imploring the end of a
cruel war; so now, similarly today by means of this Letter, We invite you not to cease from this pious practice;
and further, to prayers add resolutions for Christian renewal and salutary works of penance.

Above all, speak to the Virgin Mother of God and **446**
our most tender Mother words of most heartfelt thanks *(50)*
for having obtained, through her powerful intercession,
the longed desired termination of that great world conflagration, and also for so many other graces obtained from
the Most High.

At the same time beg her, with renewed prayers, that
at long last there may shine forth, as a gift from heaven,

mutual, fraternal and complete peace among all nations, and the longed for harmony among all social classes.

Let there be an end to dissensions that redound to no one's advantage.

Let there be a just reconciliation of disputes that often sow the seeds of further misfortunes.

Let international relations, public and private, be fittingly strengthened.

Let religion, the inspirer of all virtues, enjoy the liberty to which she is entitled.

And let men set about their peaceful work of abundant production for the common welfare—with justice their guide and charity their motive.

Conditions and Intentions of Prayer

447
(128,
150)
But you are aware, Venerable Brethren, that our prayers are most readily welcomed by the most Blessed Virgin when they are not merely fleeting and empty words, but the outpouring of hearts adorned with the required virtues.

See to it, then, as your apostolic zeal will suggest, that these prayers in common during the month of May are matched by a corresponding reform and revival of Christian conduct.

For only from Christian virtues may we hope to see the course of history take its proper, orderly direction, and men empowered not only to achieve prosperity in this world with God's help but also to enjoy, with the infusion of sanctifying grace, unending happiness in heaven.

448
(150)
But there is another special reason today which brings affliction and keen anxiety to our hearts. We mean to refer to the holy places of Palestine, which have long been disturbed.

Indeed, if there exists any place that ought to be most dear to every cultured person, surely it is Palestine, where, from the dawn of antiquity, such great light of

truth shone for all men, where the Word of God made
flesh announced, through the angels' choir, peace to all
men; where finally Christ hanging on the cross acquired
salvation for all minkind, with arms outstretched, as if He
were inviting all nations to fraternal harmony; and where
He consecrated His precept of charity with the shedding
of His Blood.

We desire, therefore, Venerable Brethren, that supplications be poured forth to the most holy Virgin for this
request: that the situation in Palestine may at long last
be settled justly and thereby concord and peace be also
happily established.

Consecrate ourselves to the Immaculate Heart

We place great confidence in the most powerful **449**
patronage of our heavenly Mother—a patronage which *(108,*
during this month dedicated to her, innocent children es- *134)*
pecially will implore in a holy crusade of prayer.

It will be precisely your task to invite and stimulate
them with all diligence—not only children but also fathers
and mothers who, in great numbers, should give them
leadership and example.

We know well that We have never appealed in vain **450**
to the ardent zeal which inflames your hearts. That is why *(168-*
We seem to enjoy already the sight of a great multitude *170)*
of children, of men and women, crowding the churches to
beg from the great Mother of God all the graces and favors of which we stand in need.

May she, who has given us Jesus, obtain for us that
all those who have wandered from the path of truth may
straightway return to Him moved by salutary contrition.

May she obtain for us—she is our kindest Mother,
who has shown herself always, in the face of every danger, our powerful helper and channel of grace—may she
obtain for us, We say, that even in the midst of the grav-

est need surrounding us a just solution may be found for disputes, and that a firm and free peace will finally dawn resplendent for the Church and for all nations.

451
(37,
132)
Some years ago, as all will remember, while the late war was still raging, when human means showed themselves to be uncertain and inadequate to that terrible conflagration, We addressed our fervent prayers to the all-merciful Redeemer, invoking the powerful patronage of the Immaculate Heart of Mary.

And even as Our Predecessor of immortal memory, Leo XIII, at the dawn of the twentieth century saw fit to consecrate the whole human race to the Most Sacred Heart of Jesus, so We have likewise, as the representative of the whole human family which He redeemed (a), desired to dedicate it in turn to the Immaculate Heart of the Virgin Mary.

It is Our wish, consequently, that wherever the opportunity suggests itself, this consecration be made in the various dioceses, as well as in each of the parishes and families. And we are confident that abundant blessings and favors from heaven will surge forth from this private and public consecration.

THE SCAPULAR OF MOUNT CARMEL

Letter *Neminem profecto,* to the Superior General of the Carmelites, February 11, 1950.

452
(136)
No one is ignorant how much love of the Virgin Mother of God helps to quicken Catholic faith and improve morals, more especially through those forms of devotion which enlighten men's minds with heavenly doctrine, and incite their wills to practice Christian virtues. Among such forms of devotion the one first to be

451a Cf. above, no. 373 ff.

recorded is that of the Sacred Scapular of the Carmelites, which, adapting itself through its simplicity to the character of every one, is largely diffused among the faithful and produces many good fruits.

For this reason We have been glad to hear that as the Seventh Centenary of the institution of this scapular of the divine Mother of Mount Carmel approaches, the Carmelite brethren (calced and discalced) have decided to hold solemn celebrations in honor of the Blessed Virgin Mary. We, who have always nourished an ardent love toward the Holy Mother of God and since our early childhood have been admitted into the Confraternity of the said Scapular, do heartily recommend this devout project, and We confidently hope that, with God's favor, it will produce abundant spiritual fruits. Indeed, this is not a small matter; it is a question of the attainment of eternal life in virtue of the most Blessed Virgin's promise; therefore, it is an extremely important project, on which it behooves all concerned to proceed with prudence.   **453** *(150, 158)*

As a Marian vestment, the Sacred Scapular is certainly a sign and guarantee of the protection of the Mother of God. However, let not those who wear it think that they can in sloth and indolence of spirit attain eternal life, for the Apostle thus openly admonishes: "Work out your salvation in fear and trembling" (a). Therefore, all Carmelites—(whether in cloisters of the first or second order, in the regular or secular third order, or in the confraternities) who belong, by a special particular bond of love, to the family that honors itself with the name of the most Blessed Virgin should recognize in this badge of the said Virgin a pattern of humility and chastity; in the very form of the vestment itself they should recognize an epitome of modesty and simplicity; above all they should see in the vestment itself, which they wear day and night, an eloquent expression of the prayers with which they ask for   **454** *(50, 131, 150)*

454a Phil. 2:12.

divine assistance; finally they should recognize in it an invitation to that consecration to the Immaculate Heart of the Virgin Mary which We recently earnestly recommended.

On her part, the most holy Mother will not fail to intercede with God that her children who in purgatory are expiating their sins may, at the earliest possible moment, reach the Eternal Fatherland in accordance with the so-called Sabattine Privilege (b).

A MARIAN CENTURY

Letter *Cum audiverimus Romam,* to the Superior General of the Jesuits, April 15, 1950.

(*History of Marian congregations; their object, sanctity, deep formation ...*)

455
(131, 154)
... Finally must be given a total and constant obedience and homage to Christ our Lord and His Church, under the leadership and example of the most Blessed Virgin Mary. In that we recognize the happiest omen of our century, a century which may well be called "Marian," because it has experienced the effective protection and powerful patronage of the Mother of God.

(*Invitation to expand Marian sodalities.—One should be particularly watchful about inner formation.*)

456
(125)
This sound spiritual formation and its consequent Apostolic activity must be of an outstandingly Marian character; for this inclination of the mind to honor and love the most Blessed Virgin, which has ever been professed by your sodalities, must be always and everywhere the distinctive and obvious feature of true faith and doctrine.

(*Sodalities should be established in every quarter.*)

454b See above, no. 281 ff.

MARIAN HERITAGE

All. on the canonization of St. Joan of France, May 28, 1950. **457** *(125)*

(*The great number of French pilgrims testify to the faith of this nation.—It is necessary to imitate St. Joan.*)

... The deep penetration of Joan of France into the life of the Blessed Mother of God, her total consecration to Mary, the resplendent reflection of Marian sentiments and virtues in her life and in her Order of the Annunciation give in our days to her example and rules the appearance of a new message to France. In the difficult spiritual struggles of our times wherein believers in Christ and those who deny Him are confused in the multitude, devotion to the Mother of God is an infallible touchstone for distinguishing the one from the other.

Catholics of France, your history so entirely interwoven with Mary's graces and favors compels you, in a very special way, to watch over the integrity and purity of your Marian inheritance. Defend it against those who have broken the bonds with your ancient and glorious traditions, by your courageous perseverance in the pursuit of your most sacred interests and the example of your respect for just laws and the legitimate order of the State. **458** *(123, 159)*

You are about to leave these scenes where you witnessed the triumph of your Saint; you are about to return to your country which, so many times, has felt the effects of the Blessed Virgin Mary's powerful intercession and protection. Let the desire of your hearts, then, the ardent prayer of your souls ascend to the blue and luminous heavens: "Holy Mary, make us strong in the struggle against thy enemies." *Virgo, Sacrata, da mihi virtutem contra hostes tuos* (a).

(*Part which women took in the story of France; their mission at the present time.*)

458a Office of Our Lady.

THE MYSTERY OF MARY IN OUR TIMES

Letter *Multiples et fécondes,* to the Marian Congress at Rennes, June 30, 1950.

459
(151) Every year, numerous and fruitful assemblies of French Catholics gather around their pastors to study and bring into force the conditions most adapted for the expansion of Christian life and doctrine. The Marian Congress, according to a happy tradition, has become one of the most persistent manifestations of these assemblies, and We rejoice in knowing that on your invitation, impressive multitudes will reunite in the Breton capital, in order to increase by prayer and study their devotion to the Virgin Mary.

460
(132) With a full heart, We address to all Our paternal wishes for the spiritual success of these assemblies, and We pray God to bless your work whose sole theme, the Assumption of the most holy Virgin, is dear, for many motives, to the heart of all our children. Is it not, moreover, in the halo of this glorious Assumption that a memorable consecration has proclaimed the Mother of God, "Queen and Patroness of France?

Doctrinal foundations of the devotion

461
(128, Above all, it is your will that this Marian devotion be
130, anchored to the most solid and certain foundations. We
154) could do no other than encourage you in this attempt at reflecting on theological doctrine. For some years now, the manifestations of the devotion to Mary have assumed, among the faithful, a renewed fervor and We indeed have seen the precious fruits of grace in France as in other countries. But when the Christian people allows itself to be carried by the upsurge of filial confidence, it is necessary for them also to nourish their piety with the solid sustenance of truth. This is the particular task of a Congress such as yours and of the many conferences which shall

take place at it. The competence of the teachers, who shall open to all the doctrinal richness of the faith of our fathers, together with the docility of the faithful to the traditional teachings of the Church are the surest guarantees of the religious tone and supernatural fruitfulness of these magnificent ceremonies. *De Maria numquam satis!* . . . St. Bernard used to say. No one can ever fully understand the providential design of God concerning Mary; no one can ever dedicate himself too much to shedding due light on the shining example of the Virgin of the Annunciation or of Calvary!

The mystery of Mary in our times

Especially at the present time, against arrogant and pagan doctrines which are extolling the greatness of man to the detriment of God's sovereign rights and His merciful designs, Marian devotion must be to the Christian conscience the efficacious reminder of the absolute preeminence of God in our life, and of the general obedience it requires from us. Does not the Mother of the Incarnate Word in all her mysteries celebrate the most splendid triumph of the Savior's love in a mere creature? To those who with disordered minds and confused passions seek, doubt, rebel, or become discouraged, We present Mary, "The Blessed among women," all filled with humility, purity and charity in the radiancy of that grace which she was given through the foreseen merits of her Son. Let us remember the secret of this Virgin to whom God did great things because her life was a continuous assent to the mysteries of salvation being carried out in her. And when an ancient and venerable tradition urges believers to celebrate the glorious Assumption of the Mother of God, the "Magnificat" of their gratitude should be united to that of this Holy Virgin, their Mother, who was the first to be filled with the plenitude of the fruits of the Redemption and Resurrection which Jesus Christ acquired with His blood to the glory of God the Father.

462
(69,
79,
136,
168)

Prayer and action

463   Thus anchored upon faith, Marian devotion will
(108, freely increase in hope and filial confidence. And hence
128, it is that We are, in this holy year, renewing to all the
137, invitation which we have already addressed to them in
159) the solemn consecration of the world to the Immaculate
Heart of Mary. Since it has pleased God, in His mercy,
to put into Mary's maternal hands such power of intercession (of which our French children have so many times
experienced the fullness and the charm), let no one
cease to implore her assistance for this wounded and
sinful world. The Virgin Mary cannot turn a deaf ear
to the cry of her children, if such cry comes not only
from their lips, not only from a superficial and passing
intention, but from a pledge of effectual reform and of
a necessary renovation of spirit in individual and family,
in civic and social, in national and international circles.

In these times, when in many souls inward renewal
is already operating (which is what We desire as one
of the first fruits of the Jubilee), but in which also un-
easiness oppresses the heart of so many, we like to think
that the Rennes Congress will give a new impetus to
Marian devotion in France, and that it will also mean
an enrichment of Christian life in your dear fatherland.

MARY, MOTHER OF PRIESTS

Exhortation *Menti nostræ*, to the entire Clergy, September 23, 1950.

(*The model of the priest in modern times.—The means
of perfection.*)

464   Inasmuch as priests can be called by a very special
(37, title, sons of the Virgin Mary, they will never cease to
165) love her with an ardent piety, invoke her with perfect
confidence, and frequently implore her strong protec-

tion. So that every day, as the Church herself recommends, they will recite the holy rosary, which, by proposing for our meditation the mysteries of the Redeemer, leads us "to Jesus through Mary."

(*Sanctity of Priesthood.—Formation of young clerics.— Adaptation.*)

When you meet very serious difficulties in the path of holiness and the exercise of your ministry, turn your eyes and your mind trustfully to her who is the Mother of the Eternal Priest and therefore the loving Mother of all Catholic priests. You are well aware of the goodness of this Mother. In many regions you have been the humble instruments of the mercy of the Immaculate Heart of Mary in wonderfully reviving the faith and charity of the Christian people.   **465** *(24 165)*

Our Lady loves everyone with a most tender love, but she has a particular predilection for priests who are the living image of Jesus Christ. Take comfort in the thought of the love of the Divine Mother for each of you and you will find the labors of your sanctification and priestly ministry much easier.   **466** *(50, 165)*

To the Beloved Mother of God, mediatrix of heavenly graces, We entrust the priests of the whole world in order that, through her intercession, God will vouchsafe a generous outpouring of His Spirit which will move all ministers of the altar to holiness and, through their ministry, will spiritually renew the face of the earth.

TRUTH OF MARY'S ASSUMPTION

All. to the Consistory, October 30, 1950.

You well know the reason for which We have convoked this Sacred Consistory today. It is an event which will fill Us, you, and the whole Catholic world with   **467** *(97, 162)* unspeakable joy. On the first of November, the feast of All Saints, the radiant brow of the Queen of Heaven and the beloved Mother of God will be wreathed with new splendor, when, under divine inspiration and assistance, We shall solemnly define and decree Her bodily assumption into heaven.

468
(92,
94,
96)
With the authority which the Divine Redeemer transmitted to the Prince of the Apostles and to his successors, We have the intention of ordaining and defining what, from the earliest days, the Church piously believes and honors, what the Holy Fathers have elaborated and brought to a clearer light through the centuries, and what the faithful of all classes everywhere have earnestly requested and implored by innumerable documents— namely, that Mary, the virgin Mother of God was assumed, body and soul, into the glory of heaven.

Preliminary consultations

469
(95,
96)
Before taking this resolution We deemed it opportune, as you are aware, to entrust the study of the matter to experts. They, at Our command, assembled all the requests which had been addressed to the Holy See on the matter and examined them with all attention, so that there might emerge in the clearest possible manner what the Sacred Magisterium and the entire Catholic Church held should be believed on this point of doctrine.

Furthermore, at Our bidding, they studied with the greatest diligence all the attestations, indications and references in the common faith of the Church, as well as lastly in the writings of the Fathers and the theologians and with the admirable harmony of this with other revealed truths.

470
(96)
We also sent letters to all the bishops requesting them to state, not only their own opinion, but also the thought and desire of the clergy and faithful.

In a wonderful and almost unanimous chorus, the voices of the shepherds and of the faithful from every part of the world reached Us, professing the same faith, and requesting the same things, as supremely desired by all. We judged then that there was no reason for further delay, and We decided to proceed to the definition of the dogma. **471** *(92, 96)*

If it is true that the entire Catholic Church cannot deceive or be deceived, the Divine Redeemer, who is truth Himself having promised to the Apostles: "And behold I am with you all days even unto the consummation of the world" (a) it follows that this truth firmly believed by the whole shepherds and by the people has been defined by God, and can be defined by Our supreme authority. **472** *(92, 96)*

Results hoped for from the definition

Nor is it without the will of Divine Providence that this happy event should coincide with the holy year which is now drawing to a close. It seems that to all and especially to those who from all parts of the earth came to this beloved city to purify their souls and renew their ,life in Christian practice, the Blessed Virgin, resplendent on her throne as with a new light, stretched forth her maternal arms exhorting them to climb with courage the heights of virtue so that, at the end of their earthly exile, they may come to the enjoyment of supreme happiness in their heavenly home. **473** *(96, 97)*

May the sublime Mother of God take under her watchful protection the innumerable multitudes, whom, with unspeakable joy, We have seen giving proof of fervent faith and ardent piety, as they throng not only the house of the Common Father and the immense Basilica of St. Peter, but also the square of St. Peter and the adjoining streets, and may she obtain for them the heavenly inspir- **474** *(137, 154)*

472a Matt. 28:20.

ation and those gifts whereby they, illuminated and strengthened, may tend more readily to Christian perfection.

475
(99,
170)
Further, we nourish the great hope that the beloved Mother of God, crowned with new glory on earth, may contemplate with loving gaze, and bind to herself those who languish in spiritual apathy, or loathfully dally in the snares of vice, or who, having lost the straight way of truth, do not recognize that sublime dignity of hers with which the privilege of her bodily assumption into heaven is strictly connected.

476
(122,
134)
May our most benign Mother, assumed to the glory of heaven, lead to that divine light, which descends only from on high, the entire human race which, in many places, is still enveloped in the darkness of error, tormented by cruel chastisements, and afflicted by grave dangers; may she obtain for them those supernal consolations which restore and raise up the soul of man, even if prostrate with frightful sufferings.

477
(169,
178)
May she obtain from her Divine Son that peace, which is based, as on a most solid foundation, on the tranquillity of right order, on the just treatment of citizens and peoples, and on the liberty and dignity due to all, may finally return to shine among the nations and peoples at present divided to the common detriment.

478
(120,
121)
May she above all defend, with her most powerful patronage, the Catholic Church, which in not a few parts of the world is either little known or is charged with false accusations and calumnies, or oppressed by unjust persecutions, and may she lead back to the unity of the Church all the erring and the wayward.

479
(33,
96)
May you, Venerable Brethren, and with you the entire Christian people, strive to obtain all these things from the heavenly Mother by fervent prayer.

But now, although, as We have said, the answers of the bishops of all parts of the world have reached Us on this matter, We desired nevertheless that you likewise manifest your opinion to this august assembly.

Is it your good pleasure, Venerable Brethren, that we proclaim and define, as a dogma revealed by God, the bodily assumption of the Blessed Virgin into heaven?

(*After receiving the opinion of those present, the Holy Father went on as follows.*)

We greatly rejoice that all of you, as with one thought **480** and one voice, assent to that which We ourselves think *(95)* fitting and desire; because by this admirable agreement of the cardinals and bishops with the Roman Pontiff there emerges still more clearly what the holy Church believes, teaches, and desires in this matter.

You will nevertheless kindly continue to implore **481** God with unceasing prayer, so that, by His favor and *(97)* inspiration, that which all ardently await may happily come to pass; and may this event redound to the holy name of God, to the benefit of the Christian religion, to the glory of the most Blessed Virgin, and may it be for all a new incentive to devotion towards her.

THE DOGMA OF THE ASSUMPTION

Apost. Const. *Munificentissimus Deus,* November 1, 1950.

The most bountiful God, who is Almighty, the plan **482** of whose Providence rests upon wisdom and love, tempers, *(36,* in the secret purpose of His own mind the sorrows of *138,* peoples and of individual men by means of joys that He *168)* interposes in their lives from time to time, in such a way that, under different conditions and in different ways, all things may work together unto good for those who love Him.

Now, just like the present age, Our pontificate is weighed down by ever so many cares, anxieties, and troubles, by reason of very severe calamities that have taken place and by reason of the fact that many have strayed away from truth and virtue. Nevertheless We are greatly consoled to see that, while the Catholic Faith is being professed publicly and vigorously, piety towards the Virgin Mother of God is flourishing and daily growing more fervent, and that almost everywhere on earth it is showing indications of a better and holier life. Thus, while the Blessed Virgin is fulfilling in the most affectionate manner her maternal duties on behalf of those redeemed by the blood of Christ, the minds and the hearts of her children are being vigorously aroused to a more assiduous consideration of her prerogatives.

483
(21,
53,
94)

Actually God, who from all eternity regards Mary with a most favorable and unique affection has, "when the fullness of time came," (a) put the plan of His providence into effect in such a way that all the privileges and prerogatives He had granted to her in His sovereign generosity were to shine forth in her in a kind of perfect harmony. And, although the Church has always recognized this supreme generosity and the perfect harmony of graces and has daily studied them more and more throughout the course of the centuries, still it is in our own age that the privilege of the bodily Assumption into heaven of Mary, the Virgin Mother of God, has certainly shone forth more clearly.

Connection with the Immaculate Conception

484
(68,
99)

That privilege has shone forth in new radiance since Our Predecessor of immortal memory, Pius IX, solemnly proclaimed the dogma of the loving Mother of God's Immaculate Conception (a). These two privileges are most

483a Gal. 4:4.
484a Cf. above, no. 31 ff.

closely bound to one another. Christ overcame sin and death by His own death, and one who through Baptism has been born again in a supernatural way has conquered sin and death through the same Christ. Yet, according to the general rule, God does not will to grant to the just the full effect of the victory over death until the end of time has come. And so it is that the bodies of even the just are corrupted after death, and only on the last day will they be joined, each to its own glorious soul.

Now God has willed that the Blessed Virgin Mary **485** should be exempted from this general rule. She, by an en- *(68,* tirely unique privilege, completely overcame sin by her *70,* Immaculate Conception, and as a result she was not *90,* subject to the law of remaining in the corruption of the *98)* grave, and she did not have to wait until the end of time for the redemption of her body (a).

Preparation of the definition

Thus, when it was solemnly proclaimed that Mary, **486** the Virgin Mother of God, was from the very beginning *(66)* free from the taint of original sin, the minds of the faithful were filled with a stronger hope that the day might soon come when the dogma of the Virgin Mary's bodily Assumption into heaven would also be defined by the Church's supreme teaching authority.

Actually it was seen that not only individual Catho- **487** lics, but also those who could speak for nations or ecclesi- *(94,* astical provinces, and even a considerable number of the *96)* Fathers of the Vatican Council, urgently petitioned the Apostolic See to this effect (a).

485a *Quæ quidem, singulari prorsus privilegio, immaculata conceptione sua peccatum devicit, atque adeo legi illi permanendi in sepulcri corruptione obnoxia non fuit, neque corporis sui redemptionem usque in finem temporum exspectare debuit.*
487a Cf. Mansi, 53, 481.

488
(94)
During the course of time such postulations and petitions did not decrease but rather grew continually in number and in urgency. In this cause there were pious crusades of prayer. Many outstanding theologians eagerly and zealously carried out investigations on this subject either privately or in public ecclesiastical institutions and in other schools where the sacred disciplines are taught. Marian Congresses, both national and international in scope, have been held in many parts of the Catholic world. These studies and investigations have brought out into even clearer light the fact that the dogma of the Virgin Mary's Assumption into heaven is contained in the deposit of Christian faith entrusted to the Church. They have resulted in many more petitions, begging and urging the Apostolic See that this truth be solemnly defined.

489
(95)
In this pious striving, the faithful have been associated in a wonderful way with their own holy Bishops, who have sent petitions of this kind, truly remarkable in number, to this See of Blessed Peter. Consequently, when We were elevated to the throne of the supreme pontificate, petitions of this sort had already been addressed by the thousands from every part of the world and from every class of people, from our Beloved Sons the Cardinals of the Sacred College, from our Venerable Brethren, Archbishops and Bishops, from dioceses and from parishes.

490
(96)
Consequently, while We sent up earnest prayers to God that He might grant to Our mind the light of the Holy Ghost to enable Us to make a decision on this most serious subject, We issued special orders in which We commanded that, by corporate effort, more advanced inquiries into this matter should be begun and that, in the meantime, all the petitions about the Assumption of the Blessed Virgin Mary into heaven which had been sent to this Apostolic See from the time of Pius IX, Our Predeces-

sor of happy memory, down to our own days should be
gathered together and carefully evaluated.

And, since We were dealing with a matter of such **491**
great moment and of such importance, We considered it *(95,*
opportune to ask all Our venerable brethren in the epis- *96)*
copate directly and authoritatively that each of them
should make known to Us his mind in a formal statement.
Hence, on May 1, 1946, We gave them Our letter "Deiparæ Virginis Mariæ" (a), a letter in which these words are
contained: "Do you, Venerable Brethren, in your outstanding wisdom and prudence, judge that the bodily
Assumption of the Blessed Virgin can be proposed and
defined as a dogma of faith? Do you, with your clergy
and people, desire it?"

The ordinary teaching authority of the Church

But those whom "the Holy Ghost has placed as **492**
bishops to rule the Church of God" (a) gave an almost *(96)*
unanimous affirmative response to both these questions.
This "outstanding agreement of the Catholic prelates and
the faithful" (b), affirming that the bodily Assumption of
God's Mother into heaven can be defined as a dogma of
faith, since it shows us the concordant teaching of the
Church's ordinary doctrinal authority and the concordant
faith of the Christian people which the same doctrinal

491a Cf. above, No. 405-406.
429a Cf. Acts 20:28.
492b *Hæc "singulars catholicorum Antistitum et fidelium con-
   spiratio," qui Dei Matris autumant corpoream in Cælum
   Assumptionem ut fidei dogma definiri posse, cum concordem
   Nobis præbeat ordinarii Ecclesiæ magisterii doctrinam
   concordemque christiani populi fidem—quam idem magisterium sustinet ac dirigit—idcirco per semet ipsam ac ratione
   omnino certa ab omnibusque erroribus immuni manifestat
   eiusmodi privilegium veritatem esse a Deo revelatam in
   eoque contentam divino deposito, quod Christus tradidit
   Sponsæ suæ fideliter custodiendum et infallibiliter declaran-*
   dum. Cf. Vatican Council, *De fide catholica*, Chap. 4.

authority sustains and directs, thus by itself and in an entirely certain and infallible way, manifests this privilege as a truth revealed by God and contained in that divine deposit which Christ has delivered to His Spouse to be guarded faithfully and to be taught infallibly (c). Certainly this teaching authority of the Church, not by any merely human effort but under the protection of the Spirit of Truth, and therefore absolutely without error, carries out the commission entrusted to it, that of preserving the revealed truths pure and entire throughout every age, in such a way that it presents them undefiled, adding nothing to them and taking nothing away from them. For, as the Vatican Council teaches, "the Holy Ghost was not promised to the successors of Peter in such a way that, by His revelation, they might manifest new doctrine, but so that, by His assistance, they might guard as sacred and might faithfully propose the revelation delivered through the Apostles, or the deposit of faith."

493
(90,
92,
100)   Thus, from the universal agreement of the Church's ordinary teaching authority we have a certain and firm proof, demonstrating that the Blessed Virgin Mary's bodily Assumption into heaven—which surely no faculty of the human mind could know by its own natural powers, as far as the heavenly glorification of the virginal body of the loving Mother of God is concerned—is a truth that has been revealed by God and consequently something that must be firmly and faithfully believed by all children of the Church (a). For, as the Vatican Council asserts, "all

492c Constit. *de Ecclesia Christi*, Denz. 1836.

493a *Itaque ex ordinarii Ecclesiæ magisterii universali consensu certum ac firmum sumitur argumentum, quo comprobatur corpoream beatæ Virginis Mariæ in Cælum Assumptionem—quam quidem, quod celestem ipsam "glorificationem" virginalis corporis almæ Dei Matris, nulla humanæ mentis facultas naturalibus suis viribus cognoscere poterat— veritatem esse a Deo revelatam, ideoque ab omnibus Ecclesiæ filiis firmiter fideliterque credendam.*

those things are to be believed by divine and Catholic faith
which are contained in the written word of God or in
tradition, and which are proposed by the Church, either
in solemn judgment or in its ordinary and universal
teaching office, as divinely revealed truths which must be
believed" (b).

Testimonies from the faith of the Church

Various testimonies, indications, and signs of this   **494**
common belief of the Church are evident from remote   *(95)*
times down through the course of the centuries; and this
same belief becomes more clearly manifest from day
to day.

Christ's faithful, through the teaching and the lead-   **495**
ership of their pastors, have learned from the sacred books *(76,*
that the Virgin Mary, throughout the course of her earthly   *85,*
pilgrimage, led a life troubled by cares, hardships, and   *89,*
sorrows, and that, moreover, what the holy old man Sim-   *95,*
eon had foretold actually came to pass, that is, that a   *116)*
terribly sharp sword had pierced her heart as she stood
under the cross of her divine Son, our Redeemer. In the
same way, it was not difficult for them to admit that the
great Mother of God, like her only-begotten Son, had
actually passed from this life. But this in no way prevented them from believing and from professing openly
that her sacred body had never been subject to the corruption of the tomb, and that the august tabernacle of
the Divine Word had never been reduced to dust and
ashes. Actually, enlightened by divine grace and moved
by affection for her, God's Mother and our own dearest
Mother, they have contemplated in an ever clearer light
the wonderful harmony and order of those privileges
which the most provident God has lavished upon this loving
associate of our Redeemer, privileges which reach such

493b Constit. *de fide catholica* c. 3, Denz. 1792.

an exalted plane that, except for her, nothing created by God other than the human nature of Jesus Christ has ever reached this level.

496
(93,
95,
144)

The innumerable temples which have been dedicated to the Virgin Mary assumed into heaven clearly attest this faith. So do those sacred images, exposed therein for the veneration of the faithful, which bring this unique triumph of the Blessed Virgin before the eyes of all men. Moreover, cities, dioceses, and individual regions have been placed under the special patronage and guardianship of the Virgin Mother of God assumed into heaven. In the same way, religious institutes, with the approval of the Church, have been founded and have taken their name from this privilege. Nor can We pass over in silence the fact that in the Rosary of Mary, the recitation of which this Apostolic See so urgently recommends, there is one mystery proposed for pious meditation which, as all know, deals with the Blessed Virgin's Assumption into heaven.

The liturgical argument

497
(93,
141)

This belief of the sacred Pastors and of Christ's faithful is universally manifested still more splendidly by the fact that, since ancient times, there have been both in the East and in the West solemn liturgical offices commemorating this privilege. The holy Fathers and Doctors of the Church have never failed to draw enlightenment from this fact since, as everyone knows, the sacred liturgy, "because it is the profession, subject to the supreme teaching authority within the Church, of heavenly truths, can supply proofs and testimonies of no small value for deciding a particular point of Christian doctrine" (a).

498
(28,
89.

In the liturgical books which deal with the feast either of the Dormition or of the Assumption of the Blessed Virgin there are expressions that agree in testifying

497a The encyclical *Mediator Dei.*

that, when the Virgin Mother of God passed from this
earthly exile to heaven, what happened to her sacred body
was, by the decree of divine providence, in keeping with
the dignity of the Mother of the Word Incarnate, and with
the other privileges she had been accorded. Thus, to cite
an illustrious example, this is set forth in that Sacramentary which Adrian I, Our Predecessor of immortal memory,
sent to the Emperor Charlemagne. These words are found
in this volume, "Venerable to us, O Lord, is the festivity
of this day on which the holy Mother of God suffered temporal death, but still could not be kept down by the bonds
of death, who has begotten Thy Son Our Lord incarnate
from herself" (a). 93, 99)

What is here indicated in that sobriety characteristic
of the Roman liturgy is presented more clearly and completely in other ancient liturgical books. To take one as
an example, the Gallican Sacramentary designates this
privilege of Mary's as "an ineffable mystery all the more
worthy of praise as the Virgin's Assumption is something
unique among men." And, in the Byzantine liturgy, not
only is the Virgin Mary's bodily Assumption connected,
time and time again, with the dignity of the Mother of God,
but also with the other privileges, and in particular with
the virginal motherhood granted her by a singular decree
of God's providence. "God, the King of the universe, has
granted thee favors that surpass nature. As He kept thee
a virgin in childbirth, thus He has kept thy body incorrupt
in the tomb and has glorified it by His divine act of
transferring it from the tomb" (a). **499** (88, 93, 99)

The fact that the Apostolic See, which has inherited
the function entrusted to the Prince of the Apostles, the
function of confirming the brethren in the faith, has by
its own authority, made the celebration of this feast ever **500** (93, 141)

498a *Sacramentarium Gregorianum.*
499a *Menæi totius anni.*

more solemn, has certainly and effectively moved the attentive minds of the faithful to appreciate always more completely the magnitude of the mystery it commemorates. So it was that the feast of the Assumption was elevated from the rank which it had occupied from the beginning among the other Marian feasts to be classed among the more solemn celebrations of the entire liturgical cycle. And, when Our Predecessor St. Sergius I prescribed what is known as the litany, or the stational procession, to be held on four Marian feasts, he specified, together, the feasts of the Nativity, the Annunciation, the Purification, and the Dormition of the Virgin Mary (a). Again, St. Leo IV saw to it that the feast, which was already being celebrated under the title of the Assumption of the Blessed Mother of God, should be observed in even a more solemn way when he ordered a vigil to be held on the day before it and prescribed prayers to be recited after it until the octave day. When this had been done, he decided to take part himself in the celebration, in the midst of a great multitude of the faithful. Moreover, the fact that a holy fast had been ordered from ancient times for the day prior to the feast is made very evident by what Our Predecessor St. Nicholas I testifies in treating of the principal fasts which "the Holy Roman Church has observed for a long time, and still observes" (b).

The voice of the fathers of the Church

501
(93,
94,
100)
However, since the liturgy of the Church does not engender the Catholic faith, but rather springs from it, in such a way that the practices of the sacred worship proceed from the Faith as the fruit comes from the tree, it follows that the holy Fathers and the great Doctors, in the homilies and sermons they gave the people on this feast day, did not draw their teaching from the feast itself

500a *Liber Pontificalis.*
500b *Responsa Nicolai I ad consulta Bulgarorum.*

as from a primary source, but rather they spoke of this doctrine as something already known and accepted by Christ's faithful. They presented it more clearly. They offered more profound explanations of its meaning and nature, bringing out into sharper light the fact that this feast shows, not only that the dead body of the Blessed Virgin Mary remained incorrupt, but that she gained a triumph out of death, her heavenly glorification after the example of her only-begotten Son, Jesus Christ: truths that the liturgical books had frequently touched upon concisely and briefly.

Thus St. John Damascene, an outstanding herald of this traditional truth, spoke out with powerful eloquence when he compared the bodily Assumption of the loving Mother of God with her other prerogatives and privileges. "It was fitting that she, who had kept her virginity intact in childbirth, should keep her own body free from all corruption even after death. It was fitting that she, who had carried the Creator as a child at her breast, should dwell in the divine tabernacles. It was fitting that the spouse, whom the Father had taken to Himself, should live in the divine mansions. It was fitting that she, who had seen her Son upon the Cross and who had thereby received into her heart the sword of sorrow which she had escaped in the act of giving birth to Him, should look upon Him as He sits with the Father. It was fitting that God's Mother should possess what belongs to her Son, and that she should be honored by every creature as the Mother and as the Handmaid of God" (a).
**502
(28,
88,
99,
116)**

These words of St. John Damascene agree perfectly with what others have taught on this same subject. Statements no less clear and accurate are to be found in sermons delivered by Fathers of an earlier time or of the same period, particularly on the occasion of this feast. And so, to
**503
(74,
94,
99)**

502a *In Dormit.* B.V.M. hom. 11, 14.

cite some other examples, St. Germanus of Constantinople considered the fact that the body of Mary, the Virgin Mother of God, was incorrupt and had been taken up into heaven to be in keeping, not only with her divine motherhood, but also with the special holiness of her virginal body. "Thou art she who, as it is written, appearest in beauty, and thy virginal body is all holy, all chaste, entirely the dwelling place of God, so that it is henceforth completely exempt from dissolution into dust. Though still human, it is changed into the heavenly life of incorruptibility, truly living and glorious, undamaged and sharing in perfect life" (a). And another very ancient writer asserts: "As the most glorious Mother of Christ, our Savior and God and the giver of life and immortality, has been endowed with life by Him, she has received an eternal incorruptibility of the body together with Him who has raised her up from the tomb and has taken her up to Himself in a way known only to Him" (b).

Scrutiny by scholastic theologians

504
(93,
99)
When this liturgical feast was being celebrated ever more widely and with ever increasing devotion and piety, the Bishops of the Church and its preachers in continually greater numbers considered it their duty openly and clearly to explain the mystery that the feast commemorates, and to explain how it is intimately connected with the other revealed truths.

505
(27,
73,
91,
98)
Among the scholastic theologians there have not been lacking those who, wishing to inquire more profoundly into divinely revealed truths and desirous of showing the harmony that exists between what is termed the theological demonstration and the Catholic faith, have always con-

503a *In S. Dei Generic. dormit. serm.* 1.
503b *Encomium in Dormitionem B.M.V.* attributed to St. Modestus of Jerusalem, no. 14.

sidered it worthy of note that this privilege of the Virgin Mary's Assumption is in wonderful accord with those divine truths given us in Holy Scripture.

When they go on to explain this point, they adduce various proofs to throw light on this privilege of Mary. As the first element of these demonstrations, they insist upon the fact that, out of filial love for His Mother, Jesus Christ has willed that she be assumed into heaven. They base the strength of their proofs on the incomparable dignity of her divine motherhood and of all those prerogatives which follow from it. These include her exalted holiness, entirely surpassing the sanctity of all men and of the angels, the intimate union of Mary with her Son, and the affection of preeminent love which the Son has for His most worthy Mother.

Often there are theologians and preachers who, following in the footsteps of the holy Fathers, have been rather free in their use of events and expressions taken from Sacred Scripture to explain their belief in the Assumption. Thus, to mention only a few of the texts rather frequently cited in this fashion, some have employed the words of the Psalmist: "Arise, O Lord, into thy resting place: thou and the ark, which thou hast sanctified" (a), and have looked upon the Ark of the Covenant, built of incorruptible wood and placed in the Lord's temple, as a type of the most pure body of the Virgin Mary, preserved and exempted from all the corruption of the tomb and raised up to such glory in heaven. Treating of this subject, they also describe her as the Queen, entering triumphantly into the royal halls of heaven and sitting at the right hand of the divine Redeemer. Likewise they mention the Spouse of the Canticles "that goeth up by the desert, as a pillar of smoke of aromatical spices, of myrrh and frankincense" to be crowned (b). These are proposed as de-

506
(91,
101)

506a Ps. 131:8.
506b Cant. 3:6.

picting that heavenly Queen and heavenly Spouse who
has been lifted up to the courts of heaven with the
divine Bridegroom.

507
(75,
78,
91,
98)
Moreover, the scholastic Doctors have recognized the
Assumption of the Virgin Mother of God as something
signified, not only in various figures of the Old Testament,
but also in that Woman clothed with the Sun, whom John
the Apostle contemplated on the island of Patmos (a).
Similarly they have given special attention to these words
of the New Testament: "Hail, full of grace, the Lord is with
thee, blessed art thou amongst women" (b), since they saw,
in the mystery of the Assumption, the fulfillment of that
most perfect grace granted to the Blessed Virgin and the
special blessing that countered the curse of Eve.

508
(82,
98)
Thus, during the earliest period of scholastic theology,
that most pious man, Amadeus, Bishop of Lausanne, held
that the Virgin Mary's flesh had remained incorrupt—for
it is wrong to believe that her body has seen corruption—
because it was really united again to her soul and, together
with it, crowned with great glory in the heavenly courts.
"For she was full of grace and blessed among women. She
alone merited to conceive the true God of true God, whom
as a virgin, she brought forth, to whom as a virgin she gave
milk, fondling Him in her lap, and in all things she waited
upon Him with loving care" (a).

509
(98,
101)
Among the holy writers who at that time employed
statements and various images and analogies of Sacred
Scripture to illustrate and to confirm the doctrine of the
Assumption, which was piously believed, the Evangelical
Doctor St. Anthony of Padua holds a special place. On the
feast day of the Assumption, while explaining the Prophet's

507a Cf. Apoc. 12:1 ff.
507b Luke 1: 28.
508a *De Beatæ Virginis Obitu, cælum. Exaltatione ad Filii*
Dexteram.

words: "I will glorify the place of my feet" (a), he stated it as certain that the divine Redeemer had bedecked with supreme glory His most beloved Mother from whom He had received human flesh. He asserts that "you have here a clear statement that the Blessed Virgin has been assumed in her body, where was the place of the Lord's feet. Hence it is that the holy Psalmist writes: 'Arise, O Lord, into thy resting place: thou and the ark which thou has sanctified.'" And he asserts that, just as Jesus Christ has risen from the death over which He triumphed and has ascended to the right hand of the Father, so likewise the ark of His sanctification "has risen up, since on this day the Virgin Mother has been taken up to her heavenly dwelling" (b).

When, during the middle ages, scholastic theology **510** was especially flourishing, St. Albert the Great who, to *(98)* establish this teaching, had gathered together many proofs from Sacred Scripture, from the statements of older writers, and finally from the liturgy and from what is known as theological reasoning, concluded in this way: "From these proofs and authorities and from many others, it is manifest that the most blessed Mother of God has been assumed above the choirs of angels. And this we believe in every way to be true" (a). And, in a sermon which he delivered on the sacred day of the Blessed Virgin Mary's Annunciation, explaining the words "Hail, Full of grace"— words used by the angel who addressed her—the Universal Doctor compared the Blessed Virgin with Eve and stated clearly and incisively that she was exempted from the fourfold curse that had been laid upon Eve (b).

Following the footsteps of his distinguished teacher, **511** the Angelic Doctor, despite the fact that he never dealt *(94)*

509a Is. 60:13.
509b *In Assumptione B. Mariæ Virginis sermo.*
510a Mariale, q. 132.
510b Cf. *Serm. in Annunt.* B.M.V.

directly with this question, nevertheless, whenever he touched upon it, always held together with the Catholic Church, that Mary's body had been assumed into heaven along with her soul.

512
(88,
98-
100)
Along with many others, the Seraphic Doctor held the same views. He considered it as entirely certain that, as God had preserved the most holy Virgin Mary from the violation of her virginal purity and integrity in conceiving and in childbirth, He would never have permitted her body to have been resolved into dust and ashes. Explaining these words of Sacred Scriptures: "Who is this that cometh up from the desert, flowing with delights, leaning upon her beloved" (a), and applying them in a kind of accommodated sense to the Blessed Virgin, he reasons thus: "From this we can see that she is there bodily . . . her blessedness would not have been complete unless she were there as a person. The soul is not a person, but the soul joined to the body is a person. It is manifest that she is there in soul and in body. Otherwise she would not possess her complete beatitude" (b).

And later doctors

513
(98)
In the fifteenth century, during a later period of scholastic theology, St. Bernardine of Siena collected and diligently evaluated all that the medieval theologians had said and taught on this question. He was not content with setting down the principal considerations which these writers of an earlier day had already expressed, but he added others of his own. The likeness between God's Mother and her divine Son, in the way of the nobility and dignity of body and of soul—a likeness that forbids us to think of the heavenly Queen as being separated from the heavenly King—makes it entirely imperative that Mary

512a Cant. 8:5.
512b *De Assumptione B. Mariæ Virginis,* sermo 1.

"should be only where Christ is" (a). Moreover, it is reasonable and fitting that not only the soul and body of a man, but also the soul and body of a woman should have obtained heavenly glory. Finally, since the Church has never looked for the bodily relics of the Blessed Virgin nor proposed them for the veneration of the people, we have a proof on the order of a sensible experience.

The above mentioned teachings of the holy Fathers and of the Doctors have been in common use during more recent times. Gathering together the testimonies of the Christians of earlier days, St. Robert Bellarmine exclaimed: "And who, I ask, could believe that the ark of holiness, the dwelling place of the Word of God, the temple of the Holy Ghost, could be reduced to ruin? My soul is filled with horror at the thought that this virginal flesh which had begotten God, had brought Him into the world, had nourished and carried Him, could have been turned into ashes or given over to be food for worms" (a). **514** *(88, 98)*

In like manner St. Francis of Sales, after asserting that it is wrong to doubt that Jesus Christ has Himself observed, in the most perfect way, the divine commandment by which children are ordered to honor their parents, asks this question: "What son would not bring his mother back to life and would not bring her into paradise after her death if he could?" (a) And St. Alphonsus writes that "Jesus did not wish to have the body of Mary corrupted after death, since it would have redounded to His own dishonor to have her virginal flesh, from which He Himself had assumed flesh, reduced to dust" (b). **515** *(98)*

Once the mystery which is commemorated in this feast had been placed in its proper light, there were not **516** *(90,*

513a *In Assumptione B. Mariæ Virginis*, sermo II.
514a *Conciones habitæ Lovanii*, d. 40, *De Assumptione*.
515a Sermon for the feast of the Assumption.
515b The Glories of Mary, Part 2, d. I.

94,   lacking teachers who, instead of dealing with the theo-
95)   logical reasonings that show why it is fitting and right to
       believe the bodily Assumption of the Blessed Virgin Mary
       into heaven, chose to focus their mind and attention on the
       faith of the Church itself, which is the Mystical Body of
       Christ without stain or wrinkle and is called by the Apos-
       tle "the pillar and ground of truth" (a). Relying on this
       common faith, they considered the teaching opposed to the
       doctrine of Our Lady's Assumption as temerarious, if not
       heretical. Thus, like not a few others, St. Peter Canisius,
       after he had declared that the very word "Assumption"
       signifies the glorification, not only of the soul but also of
       the body, and that the Church has venerated and has
       solemnly celebrated this mystery of Mary's Assumption for
       many centuries, adds these words of warning: "This teach-
       ing has already been accepted for some centuries, it has
       been held as certain in the minds of the pious people,
       and it has been taught to the entire Church in such a
       way that those who deny that Mary's body has been as-
       sumed into heaven are not to be listened to patiently but
       are everywhere to be denounced as over-contentious or
       rash men, and as imbued with a spirit that is heretical
       rather than Catholic" (b).

517   At the same time the great Suarez was professing
(64,   in the field of Mariology the norm that "keeping in mind
65,   the standards of propriety, and when there is no contra-
96)   diction or repugnance on the part of Scripture, the
       mysteries of grace which God has wrought in the Virgin
       must be measured, not by the ordinary laws, but by the
       divine omnipotence" (a). Supported by the common faith of
       the entire Church on the subject of the mystery of the
       Assumption, he could conclude that this mystery was to

       516a 1 Tim. 3:15.
       516b *De Marie Virgine.*
       517a Suarez. *In tertiam Partem* D. Thomæ, q. 27, a. 2, disp. 3,
            sec. 5, no. 31.

be believed with the same firmness of assent as that given to the Immaculate Conception of the Blessed Virgin. Thus he already held that such truths could be defined.

By title of "Socia Christi"

All these proofs and considerations of the holy Fathers and the theologians are based upon the Sacred Writings as their ultimate foundation. These set the loving Mother of God as it were before our very eyes as most intimately joined to her divine Son and as always sharing His lot. Consequently it seems impossible to think of her, the one who conceived Christ, brought Him forth, nursed Him with her milk, held Him in her arms, and clasped Him to her breast, as being apart from Him in body, even though not in soul, after this earthly life (a). Since our Redeemer is the Son of Mary, He could not do otherwise, as the perfect observer of God's law, than to honor, not only His eternal Father, but also His most beloved Mother. And, since it was within His power to grant her this great honor, to preserve her from the corruption of the tomb, we must believe that He really acted in this way.

518
(91, 98)

. . . of the new Eve

We must remember especially that, since the second century, the Virgin Mary has been designated by the holy Fathers as the new Eve, who, although subject to the new Adam, is most intimately associated with Him in that struggle against the infernal foe which, as foretold in the *protoevangelium*, would finally result in that most complete victory over the sin and death which are always mentioned together in the writings of the Apostle of the

519
(91, 98, 129)

518a *Quamobrem quasi impossibile videtur eam cernere, quæ Christum concepit, peperit, suo lacte aluit, eumque inter ulnas habuit pectorique obstrinxit suo, ab eodem post terrestrem hanc vitam, etsi non anima, corpore tamen separatam.*

Gentiles. Consequently, just as the glorious resurrection of Christ was an essential part and the final sign of this victory, so that struggle which was common to the Blessed Virgin and her divine Son should be brought to a close by the glorification of her virginal body (a), for the same Apostle says: "when this mortal thing hath put on immortality, then shall come to pass the saying that is written: Death is swallowed up in victory" (b).

520
(23, 28, 98-103)
Hence the revered Mother of God, from all eternity joined in a hidden way with Jesus Christ in one and the same decree of predestination, immaculate in her conception, a most perfect virgin in her divine motherhood, the noble associate of the divine Redeemer who has won a complete triumph over sin and its consequences, finally obtained, as the supreme culmination of her privileges, that she should be preserved free from the corruption of the tomb and that, like her own Son, having overcome death, she might be taken up body and soul to the glory of heaven where, as Queen, she sits in splendor at the right hand of her Son, the immortal King of the Ages.

521
(90-102, 123)
Since the Universal Church, within which dwells the Spirit of Truth who infallibly directs it towards an ever more perfect knowledge of the revealed truths, · has expressed its own belief many times over the course of the centuries, and since the Bishops of the entire world are almost unanimously petitioning that the truth of the bodily Assumption of the Blessed Virgin Mary into heaven should be defined as a dogma of divine and Catholic faith—this truth which is based on the Sacred Writings, which is thoroughly rooted in the minds of the faithful, which has been approved in ecclesiastical worship from the most re-

519a *Quamobrem, sicut gloriosa Christi anastasis essentialis pars fuit ac postremum huius victoriæ tropæum, ita beatæ Virginis commune cum Filio suo certamen virginei corporis "glorificatione" concludendum erat*...
519b 1 Cor. 15:54.

Oct 18. 1961

Grade; my blessing;
they have done for
our quite my little
note for me;
Faithly
father ♥

+

SALVE ii spes nostra, 139

Regina: vita dulcedo MADE IN SPAIN

Salve

mote times, which is completely in harmony with the other revealed truths, and which has been expounded and explained magnificently in the work, the science, and the wisdom of the theologians—We believe that the moment appointed in the plan of divine providence for the solemn proclamation of this outstanding privilege of the Virgin Mary has already arrived.

Hoped-for results

We, who have placed Our pontificate under the special patronage of the most holy Virgin, to whom We have had recourse so often in times of grave trouble, We who have consecrated the entire human race to her Immaculate Heart in public ceremonies, and who have time and time again experienced her powerful protection, are confident that this solemn proclamation and definition of the Assumption will contribute in no small way to the advantage of human society, since it redounds to the glory of the Most Blessed Trinity, to which the Blessed Mother of God is bound by such singular bonds. It is to be hoped that all the faithful will be stirred up to a stronger piety towards their heavenly Mother, and that the souls of all those who glory in the Christian name may be moved by the desire of sharing in the unity of Jesus Christ's Mystical Body and of increasing their love for her who shows her motherly heart to all the members of this august Body. And so we may hope that those who meditate upon the glorious example Mary offers us may be more and more convinced of the value of a human life entirely devoted to carrying out the heavenly Father's will and to bringing good to others. Thus, while the illusory teachings of materialism and the corruption of morals that follows from these teachings threaten to extinguish the light of virtue and to ruin the lives of men by exciting discord among them, in this magnificent way all may see clearly to what a lofty goal our bodies and souls are destined. Finally it is our

522
(29,
34,
97)

hope that belief in Mary's bodily Assumption into heaven
will make our belief in our own resurrection stronger and
render it more effective.

523
(96,
97)
We rejoice greatly that this solemn event falls, according to the design of God's providence, during this Holy
Year, so that We are able, while the great Jubilee is being
observed, to adorn the brow of God's Virgin Mother with
this brilliant gem, and to leave a monument more enduring than bronze of Our own most fervent love for the
Mother of God.

Definition

524
(90,
96,
97)
For which reason, after We have poured forth prayers
of supplication again and again to God, and have invoked
the light of the Spirit of Truth, for the glory of Almighty
God who has lavished His special affection upon the
Virgin Mary, for the honor of her Son, the immortal King
of the Ages and the Victor over sin and death, for the
increase of the glory of that same august Mother, and for
the joy and exultation of the entire Church; by the authority of Our Lord Jesus Christ, of the Blessed Apostles Peter
and Paul, and by Our own authority, We pronounce, declare, and define it to be a divinely revealed dogma: that
the Immaculate Mother of God, the ever Virgin Mary,
having completed the course of her earthly life, was assumed body and soul into heavenly glory (a).

525
(20)
Hence if anyone, which God forbid, should dare
willfully to deny or to call into doubt that which We have
defined, let him know that he has fallen away completely
from the divine and Catholic Faith.

(*Usual concluding sentences.*)

524a ... *pronuntiamus, declaramus et definimus divinitus
revelatum dogma esse: Immaculatam Deiparam semper
Virginem Mariam, expleto terrestris vitæ cursu, fuisse corpore et anima ad cælestem gloriam assumptam.*

FRUITS OF THE DEFINITION

All. to the faithful, assembled in St. Peter's Square, November 1, 1950.

Venerable Brethren and dear Sons and daughters assembled in Our presence, and all of you who are listening to Us in this holy city of Rome and in every part of the Catholic world: **526** *(97, 99)*

Moved as We are by the proclamation of the Assumption in body and soul of the most Blessed Virgin to heaven as a dogma of faith, exulting with the joy that fills the hearts of all believers whose most fervent wishes have thus been gratified, We feel an overwhelming desire to offer, together with you, a hymn of thanksgiving to the loving Providence of God who willed to reserve for you the happiness of this day, and to reserve for Us the joy of encircling the brow of Mary, the Mother of Jesus, and our Mother, with the brilliant diadem that crowns her singular prerogatives.

Through God's inscrutable design upon the men of the present generation so greatly distressed and sorrowful, misled and deceived, but also happily anxious to recover a great good lost, behold, we discover a corner of heaven, a gleam of dazzling splendor which gives promise of a blessed life where Mary, Queen and Mother, sits enthroned beside the Sun of Justice. **527** *(96, 102)*

A memorable day

This day to which we have long looked forward is at last ours. Ours is the voice of centuries, We would rather say the voice of eternity, which with the assistance of the Holy Spirit has solemnly defined this most high privilege of our heavenly Mother. Yours is the clamor of centuries which today bursts forth in the vastness of this venerable place already sacred to the glories of Christian- **528** ity, the spiritual crossroads for all the peoples, now converted into an altar for your overflowing devotion.

529
(152) As if shaken by your heart-throbs and by the shouts that rise to your lips, the very stones of this patriarchal basilica are vibrating, and together with them it seems that the innumerable ancient sanctuaries, erected everywhere in honor of the Virgin of the Assumption, are exulting with secret tremors, monuments as they are of a unique faith and the earthly pedestals of the glorious celestial throne of the Queen of the Universe.

530
(129) On this joyful day it is not possible that from this rending of heaven, together with the surge of exulting angels, a torrent of graces should fail to descend upon the souls of men, fruitfully renewing sanctity. Therefore, to so excelling a creature let us raise our eyes confidently from this earth, in our time, among our generation. To all let us cry "Lift up your hearts!"

The lesson of this day

531
(22,
82,
107) To the innumerable anxious and distressed souls (a dismal heritage of a disturbed and turbulent time) who, oppressed but not resigned, no longer believe that life is good and accept it only because they can do naught else, the humble, devout Virgin of Nazareth, now glorious in heaven, will open up a nobler perspective and encourage them to think of the sublime destiny and mission to which she was raised who, chosen by God to be the Mother of the Incarnate Word, unhesitatingly took God's word to heart.

532
(82,
87,
100) And you who are particularly near to Our heart, who are the constant care of Our days, the solicitude of Our every hour; you, the poor, the sick, the refugees, the prisoners, the persecuted; arms deprived of work and limbs deprived of shelter; sufferers of every kind and of every country; you to whom the earthly sojourn appears to offer only tears and privations despite all efforts that are made,

and must be made, to come to your help, raise up your eyes to her who, before you, traversed the ways of poverty, contempt, exile and pain, whose soul was pierced with the sword of sorrow at the foot of the cross, and whose eyes now contemplate, steadily, the Light Eternal.

To this world devoid of peace, tortured by mutual distrust, divisions, quarrels and hatreds, because it has allowed faith to grow weak and the sense of love and brotherhood in Christ to spend itself, We beg with all Our powers that she who is assumed into heaven will bring about a return of warm affection and love to the hearts of men. **533 (50)**

We ceaselessly recall that nothing must ever make us forget the reality, and the consciousness that we are, all of us, sons of the same Mother Mary, who lives in heaven, who is the bond of union for the Mystical Body of Christ, and who as the new Eve, and the new Mother of the living, desires to lead all men to the truth and the grace of her divine Son. **534 (39, 121)**

And now, kneeling, let us devoutly pray!

Prayer to Our Lady of the Assumption

O Immaculate Virgin, Mother of God and Mother of men, we believe with all the fervor of our faith in your triumphal Assumption both in body and in soul into heaven where you are acclaimed as Queen by all the choirs of angels and all the legions of saints; we unite with them to praise and bless the Lord who has exalted you above all other pure creatures and to offer you the tribute of our devotion and our love. **535 (100, 102)**

We know that your gaze, which on earth watched over the humble and suffering humanity of Jesus, in heaven is filled with the vision of that humanity glorified and with the vision of uncreated Wisdom, and that the joy of your soul in the direct contemplation of the adorable **536 (39, 131, 136)**

Trinity causes your heart to throb with overwhelming tenderness; and we, poor sinners whose body weighs down the flight of the soul, beg you to purify our hearts so that, while we remain below, we may learn to see God and God alone in the beauties of His creatures.

537
(31,
133-
135)
We trust that your merciful eyes may deign to gaze down upon our miseries and anguish, upon our struggles and our weaknesses; that your countenance may smile upon our joys and our victories; that you may hear the voice of Jesus saying to you of each one of us, as He once said to you of His Beloved Disciple: "Behold thy son," and we who call upon you as our Mother, we, like John, take you as the guide, strength and consolation of our mortal life.

538
(85,
120)
We are inspired by the certainty that your eyes, which wept over the earth crimsoned by the blood of Jesus, are yet turned toward this world racked by wars and persecutions, the oppression of the just and the weak. From the shadows of this vale of tears, we seek in you heavenly assistance, tender mercy, comfort for our aching hearts, and help in the trials of Church and country.

539
(100,
136)
We believe finally that in the glory where you reign, clothed with the sun and crowned with stars, you are, after Jesus, the joy and gladness of all the angels and the saints, and from this earth, over which we tread as pilgrims, comforted by our faith in the future resurrection, we look to you our life, our sweetness, our hope; draw us onward with the sweetness of your voice, so that one day, after our exile, you may show us Jesus, the blessed fruit of your womb. O clement, O loving, O sweet Virgin Mary. Amen.

OUR LADY AND PIUS XII

All. to the Portugal Pilgrims, June 4, 1951.

(*The Pope's thanks for the gift in commemoration of his episcopal consecration, May 13, 1917.*)

This happy day, so important in Our life, was pre-   **540**
paring by the secret design of Providence (and without *(123,*
our suspecting it) another day even more important on   *158)*
which the Lord would burden our shoulders with the
government of the Universal Church. On that very day
there occurred on the heights of Fatima the first apparition of the glorious Queen of the Most Holy Rosary, as
if the most Merciful Mother wished to tell Us that in the
stormy times through which Our Pontificate was to pass,
during one of the greatest crises in world history, we
would always be surrounded, protected and guided by the
watchful eye and motherly heart of her who in all God's
wars is our Lady of Victory.

We are aware that this is the deepest conviction of
yourselves and of all those you represent. For this reason
you wished to manifest it in the marble of the altar consecrated to the Virgin of Fatima. Is it not true that We
more than experienced, that we have perceptibly felt the
evident protection of the Virgin, not only in the wonders
which the Pilgrim Lady has liberally lavished on all the
world, but by her having allowed Us to consecrate the
world to her Immaculate Heart, and define her glorious
Assumption? (a)

(*Obligation of Portuguese to respond to the Virgin's
favors.*)

OUR LADY OF POLAND

Letter *Cum iam lustri abeat*, to the Polish Bishops,
September 1, 1951.

Five years have now elapsed since you, Venerable   **541**
Brethren, solemnly consecrated your faithful and all your   *(129)*
nation to the Immaculate Heart of the Blessed Virgin Mary.

540a Cf. above, nos. 373 and 482.

Prompted by the intense love we nourish for Poland, ever strong and faithful, we reveal to you what, for some time past, has been the subject of our considerations, in order to revive the confidence which you then placed in the Mother of God and Mother of men and to keep you dauntless in this difficult hour.

(*Bishops who died during the last five years.*)

The Polish people's love for Mary

542
(159)
... Well-tried by adversity, as good soldiers of Christ, lift up your eyes, never becoming downhearted, to the mountain from which, in due time, help will come to you; to the mountain which your forefathers named Clear, upon which the Mother of God, your Queen, made her abode, where her image smiles maternally on the crowds of suppliants.

543
(97,
159)
As We are well aware of your burning devotion to the Virgin Mother of God, We imagine how great must have been your sorrow at not being able to be present in Rome when, for the glory of Almighty God and the honor of Christ, to increase the honor due to His Mother, and to overwhelm the whole Church with joy, We have sanctioned the dogma of Mary assumed into heaven. Meanwhile, I was consumed with a burning desire to see you here, justly exultant over such an event; for We knew well that your noble nation, already for a thousand years past, has been united by the strongest of bonds to the Mother of God assumed into heaven, and that you burn with an ardor for her that can hardly be equalled.

In fact, as soon as the mystery of the Cross was preached in your parts, the people of Poland with very sweet affectionate respect straightway venerated as their own Mother and the Mother of their fatherland the most high Mother of God. The first sacred temple built at Gniezno, by the illustrious Prince Mieszko, with the approval of Our Predecessor John XIII, was consecrated in

honor of the Blessed Mary's Assumption; that sanctuary
became the head and mother of countless other churches
with the same title.

Testimony of the nation's history

Courage, then! God will be propitious to the strong,   **544**
and the Mother of God, your Queen, will not deprive   *(159)*
of her patronage the people under her protection. The
heavenly Mother and Patroness whom you for a long succession of centuries, with the ardent sweetness of loving
children, have been addressing in the most lovely hymn
"Bogurodzica—Dziewica" (Deipara—Virgin), will after the
dark tempests, lead the Polish nation safely into the harbor
of peace. Recall how often through the years with the
obvious assistance of the Blessed Virgin, Mother of the
Redeemer, your people won brilliant victories. The echo
has not yet faded of that Clear Mountain battle, in which
a few monks and eager knights of Mary compelled the
enemy host to raise the siege of the sacred Mount and
to abandon Polish territory. To the same heavenly Queen,
on Clear Mountain, the illustrious John Sobieski, whose
eminent valor freed Christianity from the attacks of its old
enemies, confided himself. Later, as if foreseeing the impending calamities that would befall Poland, the Polish
bishops set a golden crown on the miraculous Clear
Mountain statue, a crown received from Our Predecessor
Clement XI, and during those tempestuous times they entrusted the tottering kingdom to the protection of God's
Mother.

The august Virgin of the Assumption,—besought with   **545**
earnest prayers,—gave to your resurgent fatherland, again *(159)*
threatened with serious misfortune, wonderful assistance
against the efforts of the ungodly, of which assistance Our
Predecessor Pius XI of happy memory was himself a witness. We Ourselves, while the recent war was raging,
learned from clear indications the high degree of ardent

devotion and confidence maintained by the Polish people toward the Mother of God. Among the smoking ruins of the Monastery of Monte Cassino, once victory had been obtained, they erected an altar adorned with the image of the most Blessed Virgin. At the risk of their own lives they preserved from fire and destruction the Holy House of Loreto, struck by incendiary bombs. And We then conferred on those very sturdy soldiers, defenders of Mary's Sanctuary, the insignia of the Pontifical Orders.

Poland's future

546
(122,
159)
The struggle is still raging: "For our wrestling is no against flesh and blood: but against principalities and powers, against the rulers of the world of this darkness, against the spirits of wickedness in the high places" (a).

You are still enduring heavy attacks from the enemy; but the Mother of Mercy, the sure cause of salvation, is watching over you, and your hopes shall in no wise be disappointed. She, the powerful Virgin and Conqueror of the infernal hosts, will procure for you splendid victories, and keep for you intact the priceless treasure of faith which you received from your forebears. This Virgin is truly worthy of the praises you sing in your hymn: *"Thou art terrible to the enemy, as an army in battle array; be the refuge and haven of Christians."* Renowned Poland can and ought most justly confide herself to her secure patronage, and place in her the confidence and hope of a better future in order that thus strengthened and invigorated, you may: *"Live, praising the name of the Lord. And let not the mouths be closed that sing His praise!"* (b)

546a Eph. 6:12.
546b Esther 13:17.

THE MOST BEAUTIFUL PRAYER

Encycl. *Ingruentium malorum*, September 15, 1951.

Ever since We were raised, by the design of Divine **547** Providence, to the Supreme Chair of Peter, We have never *(96,* ceased in the face of approaching evils, to entrust to the *154)* most powerful protection of the Mother of God the destiny of the human family, and, to this end, as you know, We have from time to time written letters of exhortation.

You know, Venerable Brethren, with what zeal and with what spontaneous and unanimous approval the Christian people everywhere have answered Our invitation. It has been magnificently testified many times by the great demonstration of faith and love toward the august Queen of heaven, and, above all, by that manifestation of universal joy which, last year, Our eyes had the pleasure to behold when, in St. Peter's Square, surrounded by an immense multitude of the faithful, We solemnly proclaimed the Assumption into heaven of the Virgin Mary, body and soul.

The recollection of these things comes back pleasantly to Us and encourages Us to trust firmly in Divine Mercy. However, at present, we do not lack reasons for profound sorrow which torment and sadden Our paternal heart.

Sad conditions of our times

You know well, Venerable Brethren, the calamitous **548** conditions of our times. Fraternal harmony among nations, shattered for so long a time, has not yet been reestablished everywhere. On the contrary, here and there, we see souls upset by hatred and rivalry, while threats of new bloody conflicts still hover over the peoples. To this, one must add the violent storm of persecution, which, in many parts of the world has been unleashed against the Church, depriving it of its liberty, saddening it very

cruelly with calumnies and miseries of all kinds, and
making the blood of martyrs flow again and again.

549   To what and to how many snares are the souls of so
many of Our sons submitted in those areas to make them
reject the Faith of their fathers; and to make them break
most wretchedly the bond of union which links them to
this Apostolic See! Nor can we pass over in silence a new
crime to which, with utmost sorrow, We want earnestly
to draw not only your attention, but the attention of the
clergy, of parents, and even of public authorities. We
refer to the iniquitous campaign that the impious lead
everywhere to harm the shining souls of children. Not
even the age of innocents has been spared for, alas, there
are not lacking those who boldly dare to snatch from the
mystical garden of the Church even the most beautiful
flowers, which constitute the hope of religion and society.
Considering this, one cannot be surprised if peoples groan
under the weight of divine punishment and live under the
fear of even greater calamities.

The remedy of prayer

550
(52,   However, consideration of a situation so fraught with
134,   dangers must not depress your souls, Venerable Brethren.
168)   Instead, mindful of that divine teaching: "Ask and it shall
be given to you; seek and you shall find; knock and it shall
be opened to you" (a), fly with greater confidence to the
Mother of God. There the Christian people have always
sought chief refuge in the hour of danger, because "she
has been constituted the cause of salvation for the whole
human race" (b).

551   Therefore, We look forward with joyful expectation
(142.   and revived hope to the coming month of October, during

550a Luke 11:9.
550b St. Irenaeus. *Adv. hær.*, 3, 22.

which the faithful are accustomed to flock in larger num- *146)*
bers to the churches to raise their supplications to Mary
by means of the Holy Rosary.

O Venerable Brethren, We desire that this year this
prayer should be offered with such greater fervor of heart
as is demanded by the increased urgency of the need. We
well know the Rosary's powerful efficacy to obtain the
maternal aid of the Virgin. By no means is there only one
way to pray to obtain this aid. However, we consider the
Holy Rosary the most convenient and most fruitful means,
as is clearly suggested by the very origin of this practice,
heavenly rather than human, and by its nature.

What prayers are better adapted and more beautiful **552**
than the Lord's Prayer and the Angelic Salutation, which *(128,*
are the flowers with which this mystical crown is formed? *130,*
With meditation on the sacred mysteries added to the *144-*
vocal prayers, there emerges another very great advantage, *147)*
so that all, even the most simple and least educated, have
in this a prompt and easy way to nourish and preserve
their own faith.

And truly, from the frequent meditation on the mysteries, the soul little by little and imperceptibly draws
and absorbs the virtues they contain, and is wondrously
enkindled with a longing for things immortal, and becomes
strongly and easily impelled to follow the path which
Christ Himself and His Mother have followed. The recitation of identical formulas, repeated so many times,
rather than rendering the prayer sterile and boring, has,
on the contrary, the admirable quality of infusing confidence in him who prays, and brings to bear a gentle
compulsion on the motherly heart of Mary.

Let it be your particular care, O Venerable Brethren, **553**
that the faithful, on the occasion of the coming month of
October, should use this most fruitful form of prayer with
the utmost possible zeal, and that it become always more
esteemed and more diligently recited.

Through your efforts the Christian people should be led to understand the dignity, the power and the excellence of the Rosary.

The Family Rosary

554
(147,
149)
But it is above all in the bosom of the family that We desire the custom of the holy Rosary to be everywhere adopted, religiously preserved, and ever more intensely practiced. In vain is a remedy sought for the wavering fate of civil life if the family, the principle and foundation of human community, is not fashioned after the pattern of the Gospel.

To undertake such a difficult task We affirm that the custom of the family recitation of the holy Rosary is a most efficacious means. What a sweet sight, most pleasing to God, when at eventide the Christian home resounds with the frequent repetition of praises in honor of the August Queen of Heaven!

Then the Rosary, recited in common, assembles before the image of the Virgin, in an admirable union of hearts, the parents and their children who come back from their daily work. It unites them piously with those absent and those dead. It links all more tightly in a sweet bond of love, with the most holy Virgin who, like a loving Mother, in the circle of her children, will be there bestowing upon them an abundance of the gifts of concord and family peace.

555
(144,
147,
149)
Then the house of the Christian family like that of Nazareth will become an earthly abode of sanctity, and, so to speak, a sacred temple where the holy Rosary will not only be the particular prayer which every day rises to heaven in an odor of sweetness, but will also form the most efficacious school of discipline and Christian virtue. This meditation on the divine mysteries of the Redemption will teach the adults to live, admiring daily the shining examples of Jesus and Mary, and to draw from these examples comfort in adversity, striving toward

those heavenly treasures "where neither thief draws near nor moth destroys" (a). This meditation will bring to the knowledge of the little ones the main truths of the Christian faith, making love for the Redeemer blossom almost spontaneously in their innocent hearts, while, seeing their parents kneeling before the Majesty of God, they will learn from their very early years how great before the throne of God is the value of prayers said in common.

The power of the Rosary

We do not hesitate to affirm again publicly that We put great confidence in the holy Rosary for the healing of evils which afflict our times. Not with force, not with arms, not with human power, but with divine help obtained through the means of this prayer, strong like David with his sling, the Church undaunted shall be able to confront the infernal enemy, repeating to him the words of the young shepherd: "Thou comest to me with a sword, and a spear, and with a shield; but I come to thee in the name of the Lord of Hosts, the God of armies ... and all this assembly shall know that the Lord saveth not with sword and spear, for this is His battle, and He will deliver you into our hands" (a).   **556** *(148)*

For this reason, We earnestly desire, Venerable Brethren, that all the faithful, following your example, and your exhortation, should respond solicitously to our paternal exhortation, uniting their hearts and their voices with the same ardor of charity. If the evil and the assaults of the wicked increase, so likewise must the piety of all good people increase and become more vigorous. Let them strive to obtain from our most beloved Mother, especially through this form of prayer, that better times may quickly return for the Church and society.   **557** *143,* *169)*

555a Luke 12:33.
556a 1 Kings 17:45-47.

Intentions

558
(48)   May the very powerful Mother of God, moved by the prayers of so many of her sons, obtain from her only Son—let us all beseech her—that those who have miserably wandered from the path of truth and virtue may, with new fervor, find it again; that hatred and rivalry, which are the sources of discord and every kind of mishap, may be put aside, and that a true, just and genuine peace may shine again upon individuals, families, peoples and nations. And finally may she obtain that, after the rights of the Church have been secured in accord with justice, its beneficent influence may penetrate without obstacle the hearts of men, the social classes, the avenues of public life so as to join people among themselves in brotherhood and lead them to that prosperity which regulates, preserves and coordinates the rights and duties of all without harming anyone, and which daily makes for greater and greater friendship and collaboration.

559
(168)   Venerable Brethren, and beloved ones, while you entwine new flowers of supplication by reciting your Rosary, do not forget those who languish miserably in prison camps, jails and concentration camps. There are among them, as you know, also bishops dismissed from their Sees solely for having heroically defended the sacred rights of God and the Church. There are sons, fathers and mothers, wrested from their homes and compelled to lead unhappy lives far away in unknown lands and strange climates.

Just as we love them with a special charity and embrace them with the love of a father, so must you with a brotherly love, which the Christian religion nourishes and enkindles, join with Us before the altar of the Virgin Mother of God and recommend them to her motherly heart. She doubtless will, with exquisite sweetness, revive in their hearts the hope of eternal reward and, We firmly believe, will not fail to hasten the end of so much sorrow.

(*Make the Pope's wishes known.*)

OUR LADY'S PEACE MESSAGE

R. M. to the Fatima Pilgrims, October 13, 1951.

Venerable Brethren and beloved children: *"Magnificat anima mea Dominum!"* These words come spontaneously to Our lips to give expression to Our soul's overwhelming feelings in the historic moment of these solemnities over which in the person of Our worthy Carinal Legate We are presiding. These solemnities are like a magnificent hymn of thanksgiving for the inestimable benefit of the Holy Year extended to the whole world, which your enlightened devotion wished to send up to the Lord, there, on the privileged mountain of Fatima, chosen by the Virgin Mother to be a throne of her mercies and an inexhaustible source of graces and miracles.

560
(156)

Fruits of the Jubilee

Last year in the unforgettable and solemn hour when, in the Basilica of the Prince of the Apostles, We closed the Holy Door, it seemed to Us that We were beholding the Angel of the Lord who, having left from this door twelve months earlier, had been going throughout the world inviting men of good will to come to seek peace and renew their supernatural life in this salutary font of the Jubilee, prepared in the heart of the Eternal city.

561
(170)

Today, the end of the Jubilee extended to the whole world, another vision, no less comforting, fills Our spirit. Not only the Angel of the Lord, but the Queen of Angels herself goes forth in the form of her miraculous images from the most famous sanctuaries of the Christian world, notably from that of Fatima. And as she goes along, God's blessings are pouring down, and miracles of grace are so multiplying that We can hardly believe Our eyes. Not only are the good and obedient children of the Church redoubling their fervor, but the prodigal sons also, overcome with a longing for maternal tenderness, are return-

562
(170)

ing to their Father's House. Still others, enshrouded in the
darkness of error and scattered among countries upon
which the light of the Gospel has hardly begun to dawn,
await her visit, to vie as it were with the faithful here.

563   Under the maternal eye of the heavenly Pilgrim no
(137, conflict of nationality or race, no diversity of territory can
176) separate, no clash of interests provoke, but rather men
everywhere experience the joy of brotherhood.

564   Such a unique and singularly impressive spectacle
(135) causes Us to cherish the highest hopes. Is it not perhaps
because thereby the most gracious "Regina Mundi" wishes
to show us that she takes this Holy Year under her special
protection?

That is the reason why at the same time as we willingly agree to preside in spirit over these solemnities. We
intend thereby to entrust the Holy Year to her, certain
that Our prayers to her Immaculate Heart will be acceptable to the Lord, and that in her blessed hands the fruits
of the Jubilee will reach maturity and by those hands be
preserved, blessed and multiplied.

Our Lady's peace message

565   There is no doubt that the world is longing for peace
(164, and, despite what has been done, it is still sighing for it,
169, fearing to see it depart once again.
176)   The Pilgrim Lady keeps repeating that we must desire peace and shows us the means of obtaining it from
heaven; for very little faith can be placed in human means.

When, with particular insistence, she impresses upon
us the need for saying the family Rosary, she seems to
say that the secret of peace at home consists in the imitation of the Holy Family. When she exhorts us to be mindful of our neighbor's interests as if they were our own, to
the extent of our praying and making sacrifices for his
spiritual and temporal welfare, she points out the really
efficacious means of restoring harmony in the social order.

And when, with a sorrowful, motherly voice, she **566** entreats us to bring about a general and sincere return to *(50,* a more Christian life, is not she repeating thereby that it *168,* is only upon peace with God and upon the observance of *169)* justice and the eternal law that the peace of the whole world can be securely based? For in the end, "unless God builds the house, they labor in vain that build it" (a).

Let us continue to work untiringly with every means at our disposal for the true welfare of the great human family, place our hopes above all in the powerful inter- cession of Our Lady, imploring her unceasingly to hasten the hour in which from one end of the earth to the other the divine message may be realized: "Glory be to God and Peace to men of good will" (b).

MARY'S IRRESISTIBLE VOICE

All. to the faithful of Rome, February 10, 1952.

(*Anxiety over the world going to destruction.*)

To acquaint you with Our anxiety We have selected **567** the feast that takes place tomorrow of the Blessed Virgin *(40,* of Lourdes, as it commemorates the wonderful apparitions *155,* which were, nearly 100 years ago, in a century of ration- *158)* alist confusion and religious decay, the merciful answer of God and His heavenly Mother to men's rebellion, an irresistible reminder of the supernatural, and the first step towards a steady religious recovery.

What Christian heart, however indifferent or forget- ful, could resist Mary's voice? Certainly not the hearts of Romans, of you who have as inheritance handed down for so many centuries, together with the faith of the martyrs, a filial love for Mary. At her holy statues you invoke her with loving titles and lapidary eloquence: "*Salus Populi*

566a Ps. 126:1.
566b Luke 2:14.

Romani," "*Portus Romanæ Securitatis*" and with the more recent "*Mother of Divine Love,*" all of which are monu-ments of your constant Marian devotion, or, to put it better, the sweet echoes of a long history of proven interventions of the Blessed Virgin at times of public calamities that shook these old ramparts of Rome, ever saved through her intercession.

(*In the present perils it is necessary to have recourse to the goodness of God and the mercifulness of Mary.*)

MARY, THE GLORY OF WOMAN

R. M. to the Marian Congress of the Union of South Africa, May 4, 1952.

(*Happy proximity of Easter to the month consecrated to Mary.*)

568
(24,
85,
114,
139)

But mark the words of St. Augustine, the illustrious African Doctor of the Church: "The Lord has risen," he says, "in that nature He took from you. He could not rise, had He not been dead; nor could He have died but for his having a body of flesh" (a). Now from whom did He receive that body of flesh? "Oh, Queen of Heaven, rejoice," the Church answers that question in her thrice daily chant, "Oh, Queen of Heaven, rejoice, because He, whom thou didst carry in thy womb, has risen as He said" (b). Yes, dearly beloved, in the loving providence of God, it was Mary's "be it done unto me according to thy word" (c) that made possible the passion and death and resurrection of the divine Redeemer of the world. That is why we dare not separate the Mother from the Son. His death on Golgotha was her martyrdom; His triumph is her exaltation.

568a *Enarr. in Ps.* 129, no. 7.
568b Antiphon *Regina cæli.*
568c Luke 1:38.

The witness of three centuries confirms the fact, as the learned Cardinal Newman pointedly observes, that "Catholics who have honored the Mother still worship the Son; while those who have now ceased to confess the Son, began by scoffing at the Mother" (d). With all the ardor of your faith, then, be quick at all times to offer to the Virgin Mother the homage of your gratitude, your love and loyalty.

The Virgin Mother! What a blessed vision of virginal **569** purity and gentle motherhood these words unveil. Is there *(74,* any wonder that the beauty, the charm, the holiness of *82,* the peerless Virgin Mother has left behind her in the *121)* Church militant the sweetest memories "like to choice myrrh" (a) and a mighty influence, that not only lifted woman from her especial degradation, but gave her the impetus to become the latent force that would give renewed and refined vitality to civilization?

Woman accepted the challenge. The home and civil society have felt the quickening pulse of a life purified by woman's love and holiness. Holiness and all that it implies of courage, self-restraint, patient endurance, kindliness, modesty and unworldliness, how gracefully it becomes a woman! It is the source of her greatest power for good.

And thrice blessed is the family circle, where a woman's gentle rule and high ideals point the way of sanctity to those who reverence her beyond all else on earth.

One result of this first Marian Congress in your cherished land will be, We trust, that the women of the Union of South Africa will form the high resolve to be worthy clients of the Virgin Mother of God.

(*Praise for the Oblates of Mary Immaculate for the work accomplished in South Africa.*)

568d *Discourses to Mixed Congregations, Discourse* XVII.
569a Eccli. 24:20.

THE FIRST MARIAN CONGREGATION

All. to the Children of Mary, May 22, 1952.

(*Welcome greetings.*)

570
(117,
118,
165)
The day of this audience appears to Us particularly suitable for speaking to you, even briefly. As a matter of fact, in one sense We may say that the first Congregation was formed on the very day of the Ascension. We like to think that the Blessed Virgin was not absent from the Mount of Olives when her Divine Son, for the last time on earth, blessed His disciples and ascended into heaven. Who became at that time the soul of the first gathering of the faithful, if not Jesus' Mother? We know that she was in the "Cenacle" during the days of expectancy and prayer which culminated in the glorious Advent of the Holy Spirit. Her presence was for the apostles and disciples an incentive to a better love of Jesus. She was for them the Mother of Good Counsel, the Mother of true and sound piety.

571
(129,
133)
And We also, at this moment, feel the presence here of Our dear Mother Mary in whom, after Jesus, we confidently place all Our hopes. She is present in the midst of you as the Mother of a family, who with her glance embraces her dear children and presses them to her heart; she is present beside Us, as a heavenly guide, so that, through Our exhortation, your Christian life may take new nourishment and your work in this world gain new impetus.

(*Privileges and duties of the members of the Congregation.—Formation and interior life prepare for Catholic Action.*)

MOTHER OF PRIESTS

All. at the beatification of Antonio Maria Pucci, "Servite" of Mary, June 21, 1952.

(*Life and virtue of Blessed Antonio.*)

... We could not, however, conclude these few words **572** without pointing out the very large part which devotion *(165)* to the Blessed Virgin Mary had in the life of the newly beatified. From the very outset he had wanted to consecrate himself to God through the hands of Mary in the Order of her faithful Servants, and his first address as a parish priest was to place himself and his people under the protection of Our Lady of Sorrows. His industrious zeal promoted her cult, caused it to penetrate into daily life, and renewed it so intensely that Viareggio became preeminently the city of Our Lady of Sorrows.

We Ourselves, Venerable Brethren and Beloved Sons, are so greatly convinced that the Heavenly Queen is, for priests, a Mother, the guardian of chastity, a guide in the difficulties of life, the source of the most abundant graces (as We, for instance, set forth in the Exhortation "Menti Nostræ" [a] to the Clergy of the Catholic world), that We earnestly urge you to imitate Blessed Antonio Maria Pucci, and to seek near the Mother of Jesus strength to realize the sublime ideal of sanctity which the priestly state demands.

(*Exhortation to religious and priestly holiness under the patronage of the newly beatified.*)

CONVERSION OF RUSSIA

Apost. Letter *Sacro vergente anno*, to the People of Russia, July 7, 1952.

(*Attempts made to maintain good relations with Russia.—Impartiality of Pius XII.—Certainty that the Russian people will return to the faith, which even those who have gone astray yet keep alive in their hearts.*)

572a Cf. above, no. 464.

573
(159)

... We know—and the knowledge has filled Our heart with hope and with deepest comfort—that you love and honor the Virgin Mother of God with ardent affection, and that you venerate her sacred images. It is known that in the Kremlin itself there was constructed a church—today unfortunately no longer being used for divine worship—dedicated to Our Lady assumed into heaven; and this is a most clear testimony of the affectionate devotion which your forebears had, and you have, for the beloved Mother of God.

574
(40,
107,
129,
135)

Now we are well aware that the hope of salvation can never be absent whenever hearts are turned with sincere and ardent piety to the most holy Mother of God. Though attempts be made by men, no matter how powerful or impious to extirpate the Christian religion and Christian virtue from the minds of the citizens, and though Satan himself may strive with every means to foster this sacrilegious struggle, as it is described in the words of the Apostle of the Gentiles: "For our wrestling is not against flesh and blood, but against the principalities and the powers, against the rulers of the world of this darkness, against the spirits of wickedness in the high places" (a)—yet notwithstanding, when Mary interposes her powerful protection, the gates of hell cannot prevail.

She, in fact, is the most loving and most powerful Mother of God, and of us all, and never was it heard that anyone has had suppliant recourse to her and has not experienced her most efficacious protection. Continue, therefore, as you have been doing, to venerate her with fervent piety, and to love her ardently and to invoke her with these words which you have been accustomed to address to her: "To you alone has it been given, O most holy and most pure Mother of God, unfailingly to have your petitions ever answered" (b).

574a   Eph. 6:12.
574b   *Acath. Festi Patrocinii SS. Dei Genetricis;* K. 3.

Plea for peace

May our most loving Mother be pleased to look with **575** clemency also upon those who are organizing the ranks *(159)* of militant atheists and upon those who are collaborating in promoting such activities; may she deign to obtain for their minds that light which comes from God and direct their hearts through divine grace unto salvation.

(Consecration of Russia to the Immaculate Heart.)

In order that Our and your prayers be more readily **576** answered, and to give you an especial attestation of Our *(132)* particular affection, therefore, just as not many years ago We consecrated the entire world to the Immaculate Heart of the Virgin Mother of God, in a most special way, so now We dedicate and consecrate all the peoples of Russia to that same Immaculate Heart, in confident assurance that through the most powerful protection of the Virgin Mary, there may, at the earliest moment, be happily realized the hopes and desires which We, together with you and with all those of upright intention, have for the attainment of true peace, of fraternal concord, and of rightful liberty for all: In the first place for the Church, so that through the mediation of the prayer which We raise to heaven, in union with you and with all Christian peoples, the saving Kingdom of Christ, which is "a Kingdom of truth and of life, a Kingdom of sanctity and of grace, a Kingdom of justice, of love and of peace" (a), may triumph and be firmly established in every part of the world.

And with suppliant appeal we pray the same most **577** loving Mother that she may assist every one of you in the *(136)* present sad circumstances and obtain from her divine Son heavenly light for your minds, and for your souls that virtue and fortitude by which, with God's grace, you may be able to overcome impiety and error.

576a Preface of Christ the King.

"RESPICE STELLAM"

Encycl. *Doctor Mellifluus*, May 24, 1953.

*(The eighth centenary of the death of St. Bernard.—
Predominating merits and qualities of the Saint.)*

578
(22,
47,
175)
To this warm love of Jesus Christ was joined a most
sweet and tender devotion towards His glorious Mother,
whose motherly love he repaid with the affection of a
child, and whom he jealously honored. So great was his
confidence in her most powerful intercession, that he did
not hesitate to write: "It is the will of God that we should
have nothing which has not passed through the hands of
Mary" (a). Likewise: "Such is the will of God, who would
have us obtain everything through the hands of Mary" (b).

579
(88)
And here it is well, Venerable Brethren, to bid you
all consider a page in praise of Mary than which there is
perhaps none more beautiful, more moving, more apt to
excite love for her, more useful to stir devotion and to
inspire imitation of her virtuous example: "Mary . . . is
interpreted to mean 'Star of the Sea.' This admirably befits
the Virgin Mother. There is indeed a wonderful appro-
priateness in this comparison of her with a star, because
as a star sends out its rays without harm to itself, so did
the Virgin bring forth her Child without injury to her
integrity. And as the ray does not diminish the brightness
of the star, so neither did the Child born of her tarnish
the beauty of Mary's virginity.

580
(122,
133)
"She is therefore the glorious star, which, as the
prophet said, arose out of Jacob, whose ray enlightens the
whole earth, whose splendor shines out for all to see in
heaven and reaches even unto hell. . . . She, I say, is that
shining and brilliant star, so much needed, set in place
above life's great and spacious sea, glittering with merits,

578a *In vigil. Nat. Domini*, Serm. III, 10.
578b *Serm. in Nat. Mariæ*, 7.

all aglow with examples for our imitation. Oh, whosoever thou art that perceiveth thyself during this mortal existence to be rather drifting in treacherous waters, at the mercy of the winds and the waves, than walking on firm ground, turn not away thine eyes from the splendor of this guiding star, unless thou wish to be submerged by the storm! When the storms of temptation burst upon thee, when thou seest thyself driven upon the rocks of tribulation, look at the star, call upon Mary.

"When buffeted by the billows of pride, or ambition, **581** or hatred, or jealousy, look at the star, call upon Mary. *(128,* Should anger, or avarice, or fleshly desire violently assail *(130,* the frail vessel of thy soul, look at the star, call upon *136,* Mary. If troubled on account of the heinousness of thy *167)* sins, distressed at the filthy state of thy conscience, and terrified at the thought of the awful judgment to come, thou art beginning to sink into the bottomless gulf of sadness and to be swallowed in the abyss of despair, then think of Mary. In dangers, in doubts, in difficulties, think of Mary, call upon Mary. Let not her name leave thy lips, never suffer it to leave thy heart. And that thou mayest more surely obtain the assistance of her prayer, see that thou dost walk in her footsteps. With her for guide, thou shalt never go astray; whilst invoking her, thou shalt never lose heart; so long as she is in thy mind, thou shalt not be deceived; whilst she holds thy hand, thou canst not fall; under her protection, thou hast nothing to fear; if she walks before thee, thou shalt not grow weary; if she shows thee favor, thou shalt reach the goal" (a).

We can think of no better way to conclude this En- **582** cyclical Letter than in the words of the "Doctor Mellifluus" *(154)* to invite all to be more and more devout to the loving Mother of God, and each in his respective state in life to strive to imitate her exalted virtues. If at the beginning of

581a *Hom.* II *super "Missus est,"* 17.

the twelfth century grave dangers threatened the Church
and human society, the perils besetting our own age are
hardly less formidable.

(*The lessening of faith brings about the corruption
of morals.*)

583   Therefore, as the Doctor of Clairvaux sought and ob-
(169) tained from the Virgin Mother Mary help for the troubles
of his times, let us all through the same great devotion
and prayer so strive to move our divine Mother, that she
will obtain from God timely relief from these grave evils
which are either already upon us or may yet befall, and
that she, who is at once kind and most powerful, will, by
the help of God, grant that the true, lasting, and fruitful
peace of the Church may at last dawn on all nations and
peoples.   (*Conclusion.*)

THE MARIAN YEAR

Encycl. *Fulgens Corona*, September 8, 1953.

The Definition of the Immaculate Conception

584   The radiant crown of glory, with which the most pure
(66, brow of the Virgin Mother was encircled by God, seems
101) to Us to shine more brilliantly, as We recall to mind the
day on which, one hundred years ago, Our Predecessor of
happy memory, Pius IX, surrounded by a vast retinue of
cardinals and bishops, with infallible apostolic authority,
defined, pronounced, and solemnly sanctioned "that the
doctrine which holds that the most blessed Virgin Mary
at the first moment of her conception was, by a singular
grace and privilege of the omnipotent God, in virtue of
the merits of Jesus Christ, Savior of the human race, preserved from all stain of original sin, is revealed by God,
and therefore to be firmly and resolutely believed by all
the faithful" (a).

584a Cf. above, no. 62.

The entire Catholic world received with joy the pro-
nouncement of the Pontiff, so long and anxiously awaited.
Devotion of the faithful to the Virgin Mother of God was
stirred up and increased, and this naturally led to a great
improvement in Christian morality. Furthermore, studies
were undertaken with new enthusiasm, which gave due
prominence to the dignity and sanctity of the Mother
of God.

585
(18,
66,
137)

Lourdes, confirmation of the definition of 1854

However, it seems that the Blessed Virgin Mary herself wished to confirm by some special sign the definition
which the Vicar of her Divine Son on earth had pronounced amid the applause of the whole Church. For
indeed four years had not yet elapsed when, in a French
town at the foot of the Pyrenees, the Virgin Mother,
youthful and benign in appearance, clothed in a shining
white garment, covered with a white mantle and girded
with a hanging blue cord, showed herself to a simple and
innocent girl at the Grotto of Massabielle.

586
(66,
155)

And to this same girl earnestly inquiring the name
of her with whose vision she was favored, with eyes raised
to heaven and sweetly smiling, she replied "I am the Immaculate Conception."

This was properly interpreted by the faithful who
from all nations, and almost countless in number, flocked
in pious pilgrimage to the Grotto of Lourdes, aroused
their faith, enkindled their devotion, and strove to conform their lives to the Christian precept. There also miraculous favors were granted them, which excited the
admiration of all, and confirmed that the Catholic religion
is the only one given approval by God.

587
(155)

In a special manner was its significance grasped by
the Roman Pontiffs, and when, in the space of a few years,

588
(155)

the devotion of clergy and people had raised there a wonderful church, they enriched it with spiritual favors and generous gifts.

Dogma of the Immaculate Conception

589
(61,
66)
    When Our Predecessor decreed in the Apostolic Letter that this tenet of Christian doctrine was to be firmly and faithfully believed by all the faithful, he was merely carefully conserving and sanctioning with his authority the teaching of the Fathers and of the whole Church from its earliest day down through the centuries.

Scriptural basis

590
(59,
63,
68,
70)
    In the first place, the foundation of this doctrine is revealed in Sacred Scripture, where we are told that God, the Creator of all things, after the sad fall of Adam, addressed the serpent, the tempter and corrupter, in these words, which not a few Fathers, Doctors of the Church, and many approved interpreters applied to the Virgin Mother of God: "I will put enmities between thee and the woman, and thy seed and her seed" (a).

    Now, if at any time the Blessed Mary were destitute of divine grace even for the briefest moment, because of contamination in her conception by the hereditary stain of sin, there would not have come between her and the serpent that perpetual enmity spoken of from earliest tradition down to the time of the solemn definition of the Immaculate Conception, but rather a certain subjection.

591
(59)
    Moreover, since the same holy Virgin is saluted full of grace and "blessed among women" (a), by these words, as Catholic tradition has always interpreted, it is plainly indicated that "by this singular and solemn salutation, otherwise never heard of, it is shown that the Mother of God was the abode of all divine graces, adorned with

590a Gen. 3:15.
591a Luke 1:28.

all the gifts of the Holy Spirit, yea, the treasury well nigh infinite, an abyss inexhaustible, of these gifts, so that she was never subject to the one accursed" (b).

The teaching of the Fathers

This doctrine, unanimously received in the early **592** Church, has been handed down clearly enough by the *(63,* Fathers who claimed for the Blessed Virgin such titles *68)* as: "Lily among thorns, Land Wholly Intact; Immaculate; Always Blessed; Free from All Contagion of Sin; Unfading Tree; Fountain ever Clear; the One and Only Daughter not of Death, but of Life; Offspring not of Wrath but of Grace; Unimpaired and Ever Unimpaired; Holy and Stranger to All Stain of Sin; More Comely than Comeliness itself; More Holy Than Sanctity; Alone, Holy Who, Excepting God, Is Higher Than All; By Nature More Beautiful, More Graceful and More Holy Than the Cherubim and Seraphim Themselves and the Whole Host of Angels" (a).

If these praises of the Blessed Virgin be given the **593** careful consideration they deserve, who will dare to *(87)* doubt that she, who was purer than the angels, and at all times pure, was at any moment, even for the briefest instant not free from every stain of sin? Deservedly, therefore, St. Ephrem addresses her Divine Son in these words: "Really and truly Thou and Thy Mother are alone entirely beautiful" (a).

From these words it is clearly apparent that there is only one among holy men and women about whom it can be said that the question of sin does not even arise, and also that she obtained this singular privilege, never granted to anyone else, because she was raised to the dignity of Mother of God.

591b Cf. above, no. 49.
592a Cf. above, no. 51, 54.
593a *Carmina Nisibena.*

Agreement of Theologians

594
(24-
27,
68,
72,
77)

This high office which the Council of Ephesus solemnly declared and sanctioned against the heresy of Nestorius—an office than which nothing greater can be imagined—demands the fullness of divine grace and a soul immune from stain since it requires the greatest dignity and sanctity after Christ. Yea, indeed, from this sublime office of the Mother of God, seem to flow as it were from a most limpid hidden source, all the privileges and graces with which her soul and life were adorned in such extraordinary manner and measure.

For as Aquinas correctly states: "The Blessed Virgin, because she is the Mother of God, has a certain infinite dignity from the infinite Good, which is God" (a). And a distinguished writer develops and explains this in these words: "The Blessed Virgin is the Mother of God; therefore, she is the purest and most holy, so that under God a greater purity cannot be understood" (b).

595
(21,
25-
27,
68)

And again, if we consider the matter with attention, and especially if we consider the burning and sweet love which Almighty God had, and has, for the Mother of His only-begotten Son, for what reason can we even think that she was, even for the briefest moment of time, subject to sin and destitute of divine grace? Almighty God could certainly, by virtue of the merits of the Redeemer, bestow on her this singular privilege; that therefore He did not do so we cannot even suppose. It was fitting that Jesus Christ should have such a Mother as would be worthy of Him as far as possible; and she would not have been worthy if, contaminated by the hereditary stain even for the first moment only of her conception, she had been subject to the abominable power of Satan.

594a Cf. *Summa Theologica*, I, q. 25, art. 6 ad. 4.
594b Cornelius a Lapide, in Matt. 1:16.

Nor can it be asserted that the Redemption by Christ **596**
was on this account lessened, as if it did not extend to *(69)*
the whole race of Adam; and that, therefore, something
was taken away from the office and dignity of the divine
Redeemer. For if we carefully and thoroughly consider
the matter, we easily perceive that Christ the Lord in a
certain most perfect manner really redeemed His Mother,
since it was by virtue of His merits that she was preserved
by God immune from all stain of original sin.

Wherefore the infinite dignity of Jesus Christ and
His office of universal redemption is not diminished or
lowered by this tenet of doctrine; rather it is greatly
increased.

Non-Catholics and Reformers are therefore mistaken, **597**
when, because of this pretext they find fault with, or dis- *(127)*
approve of, our devotion to the Virgin Mother of God, as
if it took something from the worship due to God alone
and to Jesus Christ. The contrary is true, because any
honor or veneration which we may give to our heavenly
Mother undoubtedly redounds to the glory of her Divine
Son, not only because all graces and all gifts, even the
highest, flow from Him as from their primary source, but
also because "the glory of children are their fathers" (a).

Universal belief

Wherefore, right from ancient Church times, this **598**
tenet of doctrine both among pastors and in the minds *(17,*
and hearts of the people became daily more illustrious *62)*
and more widespread. The writings of the Fathers bear
witness to it; the Councils and the Acts of the Roman
Pontiffs declare it; and finally the ancient liturgies, in
whose Sacred Books this feast is mentioned as traditional,
testify to it.

597a Prov. 17:6.

599
(62,
161)
         And even among all the communities of Oriental
Christians, which long since have broken away from the
unity of the Catholic Church, there were not wanting,
nor are there wanting those who, although animated by
prejudices and wrong opinions, have embraced this doctrine and celebrated annually the solemnity of the Immaculate Conception, which would undoubtedly not be so
had they not received this doctrine from ancient times,
before they were cut off from the one fold.

600
         It is, therefore, a pleasure, a full century having
passed since the Pontiff of immortal memory, Pius IX,
solemnly sanctioned this singular privilege of the Virgin
Mother of God, to summarize the whole doctrinal position
and conclude in these words of the same Pontiff, asserting
that this doctrine "vouched for in Sacred Scripture according to the interpretation of the Fathers, is handed down
by them in so many of their important writings, is expressed and celebrated in so many illustrious monuments
of renowned antiquity, and proposed and confirmed by the
greatest and highest decision of the Church" (a) so that to
pastors and faithful there is nothing "more sweet, nothing
dearer than to honor, venerate, invoke, and praise with
ardent affection the Mother of God conceived without
stain of original sin" (b).

Accord between Immaculate Conception
and Assumption

601
(66,
68,
96)
         But that most precious gem, with which one hundred
years ago the sacred diadem of the Blessed Virgin was
adorned, seems to Us today to shine with brighter light,
since by Divine Providence it was given to Us, toward the
close of the Jubilee Year of 1950—and gratefully do We
recall it—to define that the Mother of God was assumed

600a Cf. above, no. 56.
600b *Ibid.*

body and soul into heaven, and thus to satisfy the wishes
of the faithful, which had been more urgently expressed
after the solemn definition of the Immaculate Conception.
For then, as We Ourselves wrote in the Apostolic Letter
Munificentissimus Deus, "the faithful were moved by a
certain more ardent hope that the dogma also of the corporal Assumption of the Virgin Mary into heaven should
be defined as soon as possible by the supreme magisterium
of the Church" (a).

Henceforth, it seems that the faithful can with greater
and better reason turn their minds and hearts to the mystery of the Immaculate Conception. For the two dogmas
are intimately connected in close bond. And now that the
Assumption of the Virgin Mary into heaven has been
promulgated and shown in its true light—that is, as the
crowning and complement of the prior privilege bestowed upon her—there emerge more fully and more
clearly the wonderful wisdom and harmony of the divine
plan, by which God wishes the most Blessed Virgin Mary
to be free from all stain of original sin. **602** *(68, 98- 99)*

And so these two very singular privileges, bestowed
upon the Virgin Mother of God, stand out in most splendid light as the beginning and as the end of her earthly
journey, for the greatest possible glorification of her virgin
body is the complement, at once appropriate and marvelous, of the absolute innocence of her soul, which was free
from all stain; and just as she took part in the struggle of
her only-begotten Son with the wicked serpent of hell,
so also she shared in His glorious triumph over sin and its
sad consequences. **603** *(59, 70, 74, 90, 98- 101)*

How to celebrate the Marian Year

Yet this centenary celebration should not only serve
to revive Catholic Faith and earnest devotion to the **604** *(67)*

601a Cf. above, no. 486.

Mother of God in the souls of all, but Christians should also, in as far as possible, conform their lives to the example of the same Virgin.

605
(32, 116)
Such as all mothers are deeply affected when they perceive that the countenance of their children reflects a characteristic likeness to their own, so also our most sweet Mother wishes for nothing more, never rejoices more than when she sees those whom, under the cross of her Son she has adopted as children in His stead, portray the lineaments and ornaments of her soul in thought, word and deed.

606
(130)
But if this devotion is not to consist of mere words, is not to be a counterfeit coin of religion, or the weak and transitory affection of a moment, but is to be something sincere, true and efficacious, it is necessary that each of us should, according to his condition of life, avail of it for the acquisition of virtue. The commemoration of the mystery of the most holy Virgin, conceived immaculate and immune of all stain of original sin, should, in the first place, urge us to that innocence and integrity of life which flees from and abhors even the slightest stain of sin.

607
(82, 104, 131, 136)
And it seems to Us that the Blessed Virgin who, throughout the whole course of her life, both in joys, which affected her deeply, as well as in distress and atrocious suffering, through which she is the Queen of Martyrs, never departed from the precepts and example of her own Divine Son; it seems to us, We say, that she repeats to each of us those words, with which she addressed the servers at the wedding feast of Cana, pointing as it were to Jesus Christ: "Whatsoever He shall say to you, do ye" (a).

608
(136)
This same exhortation, understood, of course, in a wider sense, she seems to repeat to us all today, when it is evident that the root of all evil by which men are harshly

607a John 2:5.

and violently afflicted and peoples and nations straitened, has its origin in this especially, that many people have forsaken Him "the fountain of living water and have dug for themselves cisterns, broken cisterns, that can hold no water" (a) They have forsaken Him who is "the Way and the Truth and the Life."

If, therefore, there has been a wandering, there must be a return to the straight path.   **609** *(34)*

If the darkness of error has clouded minds, it must be dispersed immediately by the light of truth.

If death—death in the true sense—has seized upon souls, eagerly and energetically must life be taken hold of. We mean that heavenly life, which knows no ending, since it comes forth from Jesus Christ; which, if we faithfully and confidently pursue in this mortal exile, we shall surely enjoy forever with Him in the happiness of the eternal home.

This is what she teaches us, to this the Blessed Virgin Mary exhorts us, our most sweet Mother who, with true charity, loves us more than any earthly mother.

(*The present evils point to the timeliness of returning to Jesus Christ.*)

Program of Marian Year

Without doubt all these principles of Christianity, which the Virgin Mother of God incites us to follow with eagerness and with energy, can be entirely and lastingly productive only when actually put into practice.   **610** *(136)*

Taking this into consideration We invite everyone of you, Venerable Brethren, by reason of the office that you exercise, to exhort the clergy and people committed to you to celebrate the Marian Year which We proclaim to be held throughout the whole world from the month of December next until the same month of the coming year.   **611** *(157)*

608a   Jer. 2:13.

612
(157)   At that date just a century will have elapsed since the Virgin Mother of God, amid the applause of the entire Christian people, shone with a new brilliance, when, as We have said, Our Predecessor of immortal memory solemnly decreed and defined that she was absolutely free from all stain of original sin.

Confidently do We trust that this Marian celebration may bring forth those most desired and salutary fruits which all of us long for.

613
(17-
19,
(151)   But to facilitate matters and make the project more successful, We desire that in each diocese there be held for this purpose appropriate sermons and discourses, by means of which this tenet of Christian doctrine may be more clearly explained so that the faith of the people may be increased and their devotion to the Virgin Mother of God become daily more ardent, and that thenceforth all may take upon themselves to follow in the footsteps of our Heavenly Mother, willingly and with promptitude.

614
(152)   And since in all cities, towns and villages, wherever the Christian religion thrives, there is a shrine or an altar in which the sacred image of the Blessed Virgin is enshrined for the devotion of the Christian people, We desire, Venerable Brethren, that the faithful should assemble there in great numbers and should offer to our most sweet Mother not only private, but also public supplications with one voice and with one mind.

At Lourdes

615
(152)   But where, as is the case in almost all dioceses, there exists a church in which the Virgin Mother of God is venerated with more intense devotion, here on stated days let pilgrims gather in great numbers and publicly and in the open give glorious expression to their common faith and to their common love toward the Virgin most holy.

We have no doubt that this will be done in an especial manner at the grotto of Lourdes, where there is such ardent devotion to the Blessed Virgin Mother conceived without stain of sin.

At Rome

But let this holy city of Rome be the first to give the example, this city which from the earliest Christian era venerated the heavenly Mother, its Patroness, with a special devotion.

616
(158)

As all know, there are many sacred edifices here in which she is presented for the devotion of the Roman people; but the greatest, without doubt, is the Liberian Basilica, in which the mosaics of Our Predecessor of pious memory still glisten, an outstanding monument to the divine maternity of the Virgin Mary, and in which the "Salvation of the Roman People" (Salus Populi Romani) benignly smiles.

Here especially let the suppliant citizens flock, and before that most sacred image let all put forth pious prayers, imploring especially that Rome, which is the principal city of the Catholic world, may also give the lead in faith, in piety and in sanctity.

(*Intentions for the Marian Year: Renewal of Christian life, the persecuted Church, Our separate Brethren, World Peace.*)

PRAYER FOR THE MARIAN YEAR

Prayer, *O Immaculate Virgin,* composed by Pius XII, November 21, 1953.

Enraptured by the splendor of your heavenly beauty and impelled by the anxieties of the world, we cast ourselves into your arms, O Immaculate Mother of Jesus and our Mother, Mary, confident of finding in your most loving heart the satisfaction of our ardent desires, and a safe harbor from the tempests which beset us on every side.

617
(22,
29,
134)

618
(76,
102)
Though dejected by our faults and overwhelmed by infinite misery, we admire and praise the unequalled richness of sublime gifts with which God has filled you, above every other creature, from the first moment of your Conception until the day on which, after your Assumption into heaven, He crowned you Queen of the Universe.

619
(122,
123)
O crystal Fountain of Faith, bathe our minds with the eternal truths! O fragrant Lily of all holiness, captivate our hearts with your heavenly perfume! O Conqueror of evil and death, fill us with a deep horror of sin which makes the soul detestable to God and a slave of hell!

620
(84,
134)
O well-beloved of God, hear the ardent cry which rises up from every heart in this year dedicated to you. Bend tenderly over our aching wounds. Convert the wicked, dry the tears of the afflicted and oppressed, comfort the poor and the humble, quench hatreds, assuage the hard ways of men, safeguard the flower of purity in youth, protect the Holy Church, make all men feel the attraction of Christian goodness. In your name, which sounds ever in the music of heaven, may they recognize that they are brothers, and that all nations are members of one family, upon which may there shine forth the sun of a universal and sincere peace.

Receive, O most sweet Mother, our humble supplications, and above all obtain for us that, one day, happy with you, we may repeat before your throne that hymn which today is sung on earth around your altars: You are all beautiful, O Mary! You are the glory, you are the joy, you are the honor of our people! Amen.

A PICTURE OF THE BLESSED VIRGIN

R. M. to the Italian Catholic Action, December 8, 1953.

621
(134)
We intensely desire to speak familiarly to you as a father speaks to his own children, taking part in their

joys, confiding his worries to them, and sharing with them his wishes.

Since this day on which exactly a hundred years ago Our glorious Predecessor Pius IX, in virtue of his infallible power, added another gem to the crown of our common Mother by proclaiming her Immaculate (a) is also the feast of our Mother, We have before Our eyes the holy Virgin's image. On this day We invite you to gaze on her until you feel her charm, to imitate her and feel her protection and support. We have as guide the Sacred Liturgy which does not tire of calling her: *pulchra ut luna,* fair as the moon; *electa ut sol,* bright as the sun; terrible as an army set in battle array, *terribilis ut castrorum acies ordinata* (b).

Mary's beauty

Above all, Beloved Sons and Daughters, look at Mary: "beautiful as the moon" "pulchra ut luna." It is a way of expressing her exalted beauty. How beautiful the Blessed Virgin must be! How often have we been struck by the beauty of an angelic countenance, by the charm of an infant's smile, by the fascination of a pure glance! Surely in His own Mother's countenance God has gathered together all the splendors of His divine artistry. Mary's glance! Mary's smile! Mary's sweetness! The majesty of Mary, Queen of heaven and of earth! As the moon shines resplendent in the dark heavens, so is Mary's beauty set apart from all other beauties, which are but shadows beside her. Mary is the most beautiful of all God's creatures. You know, beloved Sons and Daughters, how easily human beauty, which is like the shadow of a flower, enraptures and exalts a kind heart. What would it ever do before the beauty of Mary, if it could gaze on it unveiled, face to face? This is why Dante Alighieri saw in Paradise, in the midst of "more than a million

622
(84)

621a Cf. above, no. 31 ff.
621b Office of the Assumption.

rejoicing angels . . . a beauty beaming which was a joy in the eyes of all the other saints!" Mary! (a)

623
(84,
100)

But that countenance reveals more than mere natural beauty. God by a miracle of His almighty power has poured into her soul the fullness of His riches; He has made pass into Mary's glance something of His own super-human and divine dignity. A ray of beauty from God shines in His Mother's eyes. Do you not think that Jesus' countenance, that countenance which the angels adore, must have reproduced in some way the lines of Mary's countenance? For every son's countenance mirrors his mother's. *Pulchra ut luna.* Blessed is he who can see you, Mother of our Lord, who can find his happiness with you; may we be able, Mary, to remain with you, in your house to serve you forever.

Mary's Splendor

624
(30,
39,
42,
46)

But the Church does not compare Mary solely to the moon; again making use of Sacred Scripture she uses a more vivid figure when exclaiming: "O Mary, thou art bright as the sun" (*Electa ut sol*) (a).

Sunlight is far different from moonlight; it is light that warms and vivifies. The moon shines upon the Polar icefields, but the icefields remain compact and barren just as darkness and frost endure on moonlit winter nights. Moonlight does not give warmth nor bring life. The sun is the source of light, warmth and life. Now Mary, beautiful as the moon, shines brightly as the sun and irradiates life-giving warmth. Whenever we speak of her, or speak to her, let us not forget that she is really our Mother, for through her we received divine life. She gave us Jesus, Himself the Source of grace. Mary is the Mediatrix and Dispenser of graces.

622a   *Canto* XXXI, 130-133.
624a   Canticle of Canticles 6:9.

Electa ut sol. Under the sun's light and warmth, plants   **625**
grow on the earth and bear fruit; under the influence and   *(52,*
with the help of Mary, that other Sun, good thoughts fructi- *104,*
fy in souls. Perhaps, already at this moment, you are filled *106)*
with the glory that emanates from the Immaculate Virgin,
the Mother of divine grace, the Mediatrix of all graces.
Oh! could We but have the voice of St. Bernard who never
tired of praising, of singing, and of exulting before the
Virgin's throne! Oh, that we had the tongues of angels to
enable us to tell the beauty and grandeur of their Queen!

Beloved sons and daughters, think over the story of   **626**
your own lives. Do you not notice therein a pattern of   *(47,*
graces received from God? You are then able to add the   *52)*
thought, "Mary took a part in the granting of such graces."
Flowers bloomed and fruits ripened in my life thanks to the
warming influence of the Woman who is "bright as the Sun."
    Have you been praying this morning? Well, the grace
which urged you to accomplish an act of such exquisite
piety was, perhaps, a special grace from Mary, a grace
that came to you through her.
    At the moment you are listening to Our Message in
honor of the Virgin. Have a few words of it perhaps entered more deeply into your hearts, stirring in them good
sentiments and a yearning for fervor? This also is a grace
that came to your souls through Mary's intercession, with
the light from Mary, that heavenly Sun.

Are you hoping one day to reach Paradise through   **627**
the grace of perseverance to the last moment of your   *(52)*
lives? Are you trusting to die in the grace of God? This
grace also will come to you, as those devoted to Mary,
through a smile of hers, as a ray from that Sun.

Mary's Strength

But the Church takes another figure from Holy Scrip-   **628**
ture and applies it to the Virgin. Mary is, in herself,   *(82,*

123) beautiful as the Moon. She shines like the sun and radiates beams of light, but against the "enemy" she is also strong and terrible like an army in battle-array, "Acies ordinata."

In this day of exultation and joy God knows how we should like to forget the harshness of the times we are experiencing. But the dangers threatening the whole human race are so great that we must never, so to speak, forbear to utter our cry of warning. The "enemy" is pressing against the Church's gates and is threatening souls. And here is another timely view of Mary, of her strength in conflict.

629
(59,
70,
82)

Already after Adam's pitiful act, the first mention of Mary, according to not a few of the holy Fathers and doctors, tells us of the enmity between her and the serpent, the enemy of God and man. As necessary as it is for her to be faithful to God, so necessary is it that she be victorious over the devil. Preserved from all stain, Mary crushed the head of the tempting and corrupting serpent. Whenever one draws near Mary, the serpent flees, even as, when the sun rises, darkness disappears. Where Mary is, Satan is not; where the Sun is, the dark is powerless.

Imitate those characteristics of Our Lady

630
(79-
80,
130)

Beloved sons and daughters of Catholic Action, oh, if that threefold splendor of Mary could become your light! If the three figures taken from Holy Scripture were to apply in reality to each of you and to the whole Association!

First of all we desire that you, as sons and daughters of Mary, should try to reproduce in your own souls her superhuman beauty. To that end you should like her keep perfectly united to Jesus. Let Jesus be in you, and be yourselves in Him to the end that your lives may be fused with His life. Let the splendors of the faith prevail in your minds; may you, like her, see things, judge them and speak of them according to God. And, as far as possible, let your own hearts aspire to the integrity of her heart which shared nought with others, but kept its warmth, its life and love for God. With the eyes of the mind, with the ardor of your hearts, cultivate absolute devotion to God. Sons and daughters of Mary, you should bear in your souls the features of your heavenly Mother. Through this gloomy and muddied world you must send streams of light and the sweet odor of purity undefiled.

Secondly, we should wish you to be like the sun that warms and vivifies the persons and things around you. Everywhere let your presence be conspicuous for the fire of your charity. The devil has deluged the world with hate. Be instant in rekindling love! So many people are still bad because, up till now, they have not been sufficiently loved. Vivify everything that comes under the influx of your rays. Be like Mary, be with her the means of life to souls that are dying of hunger and cold, that, if stirred by your words and incited by your examples, might return to their Father's House.   **631** *(39, 133)*

Finally, apply also to yourselves the third figure of Mary: be strong against the "enemy." Here it is a matter not only of spiritual advantage for each of you but of your cooperation for the good of souls. All Catholic Action which must be, in its members, beautiful as the moon and vivifying as the sun, must contrive to be as strong against the "enemy," as an army in battle-array. This family gathering takes an aspect of a "mustering of forces" of the leading lay contingent of the great Catholic army of Italy.   **632** *(131, 165)*

(*Victory is certain, but we must be prepared for any struggle. To unite for spiritual restoration of Italy under the Bishops' leadership. Appeal to the little ones to pray.*)

And now, we kneel and recite with you a prayer. Let us join in making sweet assault on our heavenly Mother.   **633** *(52)*

O Virgin fair as the moon, the delight of heaven, on whose countenance the blessed gaze and the angels see themselves reflected, make us, your children, like unto you, and let our souls receive a ray of your beauty, which does not fade with the years but shines forth in eternity.

634 O Mary, Sun of heaven, reawaken life where there is
(122) death and enlighten spirits sunk in darkness. Reflected on the countenances of your children, grant us a reflection of your light and fervor.

635 O Mary, strong as an army, grant victory to our le-
(80, gions. We are so weak, and our enemy rages in his pride.
82, Yet, under your banner we feel sure of conquering him;
136) he knows the force of your foot; he fears the majesty of your glance. Save us, O Mary, fair as the moon, bright as the sun, strong as an army in battle array, supported not by hate but by the flame of love. Amen.

SUFFER WITH MARY

R. M. to the Sick, February 14, 1954.

(*Since the opening of the Marian Year, the Pope has thought of the sick.*)

636 The Mother of God, indeed, bends over you with lov-
(167) ing tenderness, eager to dry the tears of the afflicted who run to her maternal bosom as to a secure haven in the storm. So also the Vicar of Christ relies upon you, the precious jewels of God's Church and her powerful source of spiritual energy, to obtain in this holy year the many sorely needed blessings mentioned in Our Encyclical "Fulgens Corona" (a) for the good of humanity and of the Church herself.

636a Cf. above, no. 584.

We wish, in all tenderness, to whisper to each of you, **637**
"Soul in anguish, why do you rebel? Let the rays of light *(85,*
which come from the Cross of Jesus fall on the dark my- *116,*
stery of suffering. What evil had He done? Look! Over *167)*
your bed, in the hospital ward, perhaps there is a picture
of the Madonna. What evil did she do? And so, tortur~d
soul, oppressed by trouble, listen: Jesus and His Mother
certainly did not suffer through their own fault, but voluntarily and in full conformity with the divine design.
Have you ever wondered why?"

(*Suffering that purifies.—Do not rebel.*)

Even the misfortunes of the innocent, therefore, are a **638**
mysterious manifestation of the divine glory. Lest you be *(43,*
wearied by long reflections, look at the Holy and Immacu- *85,*
late Mother: she holds in her lap the lifeless body of her *116)*
Divine Son. Could you possibly imagine that the Sorrowful
Mother would murmur against God? That she would ask
the reasons for such suffering? We would not have been
redeemed, if that Mother had not seen her Son die in torment, and there would not have been for us any possibility
of salvation.

(*Fruitfulness of Christian Suffering.*)

TEACHER OF VIRGINITY

Encycl. *Sacra Virginitas*, March 25, 1954.

(*Merits and privileges of virginity consecrated to
God.—Arduous virtue but possible.*)

The best way to protect and foster an unsullied and **639**
perfect chastity, as proven by experience time and again *(132,*
throughout the course of centuries, is solid and fervent de- *136,*
votion to the Virgin Mother of God. In a manner, all other *166)*
helps are contained in this devotion. There is no doubt
that whoever is sincerely and earnestly stirred by this devotion is well inspired to be always on the watch, to pray

without ceasing, to receive the Sacraments of Penance and the Holy Eucharist. Therefore, as a father, We exhort all priests, religious men and women, to entrust themselves to the special protection of the holy Mother of God, who is the Virgin of virgins, the "teacher of virginity," as Ambrose says (a), and the most powerful Mother of those in particular who have vowed and consecrated themselves to the service of God.

640   That virginity owes its origin to Mary is the testimony
(136, of Athanasius (a), and Augustine clearly teaches that "The
166)   dignity of virginity began with the Mother of the Lord" (b). Pursuing the ideas of Athanasius, Ambrose holds up the life of the Virgin Mary as the model of virgins. "Imitate her, my daughter ... ! Let Mary's life be for you like the portrayal of virginity, for from her, as though from a mirror, is reflected the beauty of chastity and the ideal of virtue. See in her the pattern of your life, for in her, as in a model, her goodness plainly shows what you should correct, what you should copy and what preserve.... She mirrors virginity. For such was Mary, that her life alone suffices for the instruction of all.... Therefore, let holy Mary guide your way of life" (c). "Her grace was so great, that it not only preserved in her the grace of virginity, but bestowed the grace of chastity upon those upon whom she gazed" (d). How true is the saying of Ambrose, "Oh, the richness of the virginity of Mary!" (e) Because of this richness, it will be of great use for religious men and women, and for priests of our day, to contemplate the virginity of Mary, in order that they may more faithfully and perfectly practise the chastity of their calling.

639a *De institutione virginis,* c. 6. n. 46.
640a Cf. *De virginitate.*
640b *Serm.* 51, c. 16, n. 26.
640c St. Ambrose, *De virginibus* 1. 2, c. 2, n. 6, 15; c. 3, n. 19.
640d St. Ambrose, *De institutione virginis,* c. 14, n. 87.
640e Ibid, 1. 2, c. 2, n. 6, 15.

But it is not enough, beloved sons and daughters, to **641** meditate on the virtues of the Blessed Virgin Mary: with *(132,* absolute confidence fly to her, and obey the counsel of *166)* St. Bernard, "Let us seek grace, and seek it through Mary" (a). In a special way entrust to her, during the Marian Year, the care of your spiritual life and perfection, imitating the example of Jerome, who asserted, "My virginity is dedicated in Mary and to Christ" (b).

(*Problem of vocations.—Exhortations.*)

MARY, FORTRESS OF THE CHURCH

R. M. to the Swiss Catholics, May 16, 1954.

(*Introduction.*)

But the beauty of the city bathed by the River Sarine **642** is today far surpassed by the magnificence of her to whom *(52,* your meeting is dedicated, Mary, Virgin conceived with- *122)* out stain and Mother of God. Her shining splendor is light and strength. It is a light which illumines the richness and depth of the truths of Christian faith. It is a force which overflows into the will and the heart and makes them capable of translating that faith into action, even to the last detail.

When We proclaimed the Marian Year to mark the **643** centenary of the definition of the Immaculate Conception, *(122,* We did so precisely with the intention and hope of seeing *168)* that living faith, through the powerful intercession of Mary, grow and strengthen itself in the Church herself and in her sons and daughters as a dam against the rising tide of materialism.

(*The duty of Catholics in the modern world.—Responsibility of leaders.*)

641a *Sermo de aquæductu,* n. 8.
641b Epist. 22, n. 18.

644   Give also to your brothers and sisters the example of
(137)   a genuine love for the Church. Where there is love for
Mary, there is love for the Church. Wherever there is
devotion to the Church, there is also devotion to Mary.
The one implies and stimulates the other.

(*Christian optimism.—The pope entrusts the Swiss
people to Mary.*)

CHILDREN OF MARY

All. to the Children of Mary, July 17, 1954.

645   In the Encyclical "Fulgens Corona," by which We
(101, proclaimed the Marian Year now in progress, We asked
130)   that the year be marked by a more attentive study by all
the faithful of Mary's prerogatives with a view to imitating her better and praying to her even more. We also
invited them to take part in festivals, congresses and
pilgrimages organized in honor of the Mother of God (a).
Now you, dear Children, have fulfilled Our desires to the
letter, with an eagerness and haste which brings joy to
Our heart and makes Us prophesy the richest results for
your international Association—for your different groups
and for each among you.

646   Who is better prepared than you to understand fully
(46,   the deep meaning of these events? Are you not by special
134,   title children of the Immaculate, by individual consecra-
151)   tion long thought about, often renewed, and loyally prac-
tised? For this reason the year must mark a notable date
in your history. The canonization of St. Catherine Labouré
seven years ago coincided providentially with the centenary of your Association. Even as its foundation served as a
prelude to the definition of the dogma of the Immaculate
Conception by inflaming with intense devotion souls moved
by this great Marian privilege, so, too, the pilgrimage
which you are making today at Rome should, We fervently

645a Cf. above, no. 610 ff.

hope, stimulate your warm piety and the generous spirit of your apostolic labors. We know that this is the chief interest of your directors and of the organizers of your groups. Through these means, even as in the past through the voice of her faithful servant Catherine Labouré, Mary wishes, We believe, to renew her invitation to fervent souls and to make them turn their gaze and their hearts towards her hands of grace, from which rays of light never cease to shine: "O Mary conceived without sin, pray for us who have recourse to thee."

Privileges of the Immaculate

And so, dear children of Mary Immaculate, may you put into this invocation, diffused through the whole Christian world by the Miraculous Medal, all the love and all the trust which your heavenly patron deserves. Mary is in truth the mother of all Christians; but the supernatural origin of your Association, the way you have applied yourselves to searching deeper into the grandeur of her privileges, and the love which marks your consecration to her, are all so many ties to unite you to the Immaculate in a particular way. Let your reverence for her be truly alive. Never fear to exalt her too much—she shines forth in eternity as the masterpiece of God, the most marvelous of creatures, the mirror most resplendent of the divine perfections. That she might become the Mother of God she received from her divine Son all the gifts of nature and of grace. That is why devotion to the Virgin, at least when correctly understood, far from subtracting from the glory of God, leads us rather directly back to that Author of all good who has willed her to be so great and so pure. Have great trust in the intercession of the most holy Virgin and ask her with all urgency to help you hold fast to your promise.

647
(19,
22,
27,
126-
129,
133)

(*Obligations imposed by difficulties of the modern world.*)

Docility to Our Lady

648
(30-
33,
42,
48,
108,
116)
    Whatever kind of life God has in store for you, act from this day forward, with the help of the most Blessed Virgin, in keeping with that noble status which you assumed at Baptism. Mary, our Mother, will make us understand this divine sonship which gives man not merely the name of a child of God but also its reality, and she will make us love its obligations. Jesus Himself from His Cross on high ratified by means of a symbolic and efficacious gift the spiritual motherhood of Mary toward men when He pronounced the memorable words: "Woman, behold thy son" (a). He thus entrusted all Christians, in the person of the beloved disciple, to the most Blessed Virgin. The "Fiat" of the Incarnation, her collaboration in the work of her Son, the intensity of the sufferings endured during the Passion, and this death of the soul which she experienced on Calvary, had opened the heart of Mary to the universal love of humanity, and the decision of her Divine Son impressed the seal of omnipotence on her motherhood of grace. Henceforth, she consecrated that immense power of intercession with Jesus which her title of Mother confers on her to saving those whom Jesus points out to her from the heights of heaven, saying to her once again, "Woman, behold thy children."

649
(39,
131)
    Dear Children, ask the Immaculate Virgin to obtain for you a childlike spirit toward God. May she teach you to pray as she prays in her Magnificat, her face turned toward the Almighty with gratitude and joy. May she teach you docility, as she did at Cana when she advised the servants to do all that her divine Son might tell them. Last of all, may she obtain for you a far-reaching fraternal and apostolic charity, as she obtained it by her prayer in the midst of the first Christians gathered at the Cenacle.

648a John 19:26.

MARY'S VIRTUES

R. M. to Pilgrims at the Shrine of St. Anne of Auray, July 26, 1954.

At the moment when the Venerable and worthy **650** Cardinal-Archbishop of Rennes is getting ready to read the act of consecration which will renew your gift of yourselves, your families, your sick, your schools, your parishes, to the Immaculate Heart of Mary, the Father of all the faithful is following this great action with close attention and now comes to encourage you and bless you. If We may repeat the words which Our holy Predecessor, Pius X, addressed to Cardinal Labouré in 1906, We would like to tell you, on this solemn occasion, that "in the midst of the violence of which the Catholic faith is the object," it is from you in particular that "We expect ... the greatest part of our joy."

Devotion of Bretons

Brittany, We know well, has always been a land of **651** Mary, and such it wishes to remain. The signs of your *(152,* devotion to the most Blessed Virgin are innumerable. How *153)* many churches in your dioceses are dedicated to her! How many crowned Virgins receive the homage of your daily prayers at the shrines of your countryside! How many in your families have received the name of Mary at Baptism! All of you, carry this blessed name of the Mother of God in your hearts! Honor it by your piety, honor it even more by your life!

May today's solemn consecration be for you a bulwark **652** against temptations, a motive for confidence in prayer, a *(82,* stimulus in the daily battle in the service of God. Anyone *132,* who has been consecrated to Mary belongs to her in a *136)* special way. He has become, as it were, a shrine of the most Blessed Virgin: the thought of Mary helps him to drive out vigorously all evil thoughts. Love of Mary gives

him the courage to undertake great things, to conquer
human respect, to shake off egoism, to serve and to obey
patiently. With his interior gaze fixed steadily on her, he
falls in love with the purity, the humility, the charity,
with which the soul of the Virgin was resplendent. He
develops a hatred for sin, he battles against it in himself,
and wages war on it with all his powers. When he sees
the Immaculate One crush the infernal serpent at her feet,
when he contemplates the Mother of God lifting her divine Son in her arms, his will can no longer take pleasure
in evil. On the contrary, he is proud to belong to Jesus
and Mary, and he knows that Mary is urging him to do
all that Jesus commands or desires.

653   Therefore, place yourselves with confidence under
(134) the mantle which with motherly arms she spreads out to
take in all her children. May all the sons of Brittany find
themselves united under her patronage; may they be her
court and her guard of honor, and always and everywhere
may they show themselves worthy sons of such a Mother.

654   In your history examples of extraordinary and fruitful
(132, devotion to Mary are not lacking. We will cite but one,
175) undoubtedly the most remarkable,—that of St. Louis Marie
Grignion de Montfort, whom We had the happiness of
elevating to the supreme honors of the Church on July 20,
1947. The next day, while receiving numerous pilgrims
from Brittany, the Vendée, and from the city of Poitiers,
who had come to Rome on that occasion, We declared:
"Assuredly, all of the saints have been great servants of
Mary and all have brought souls to her. He (Saint Louis
Marie) is without doubt one of those who have worked
ardently and most effectively to make her loved and
served" (a). Today, addressing Ourselves to all those who
intend to make their consecration to the Immaculate Heart
of Mary an important and permanent act, We say, "In

654a Cf. above, no. 431.

imitation of St. Louis Marie Grignion de Montfort and all
of the saints of Brittany, make Mary loved and served."

Virtues of Mary

That supposes before all else that you yourselves will
practice Mary's virtues: the charm of her Immaculate
Heart; her recollection and spirit of prayer, of which the
Gospel speaks when it twice recalls that she kept in her
heart the memory of the graces of God and of the actions
of the Child Jesus (a); the love of God, humble, ardent
and joyous, which shines forth in the Magnificat; the love
of others as well, of all, her relatives, her friends, all men—
that incomparable charity which makes her fly to the
service of her cousin Elizabeth as soon as she learns of
her approaching motherhood, which makes her attentive
to the plight of the bridal couple when the wine begins
to fail at the marriage feast of Cana, which at the end
unites her so sorrowfully and so profoundly to the sufferings of her divine Son for the salvation of the human race.
Yes, the most Blessed Virgin, whose station was so humble,
of whom the Gospel reports so few things, almost all of
whose life was filled with silence—the Blessed Virgin has
seen God accomplish in her the greatest works, without
losing that astonishing modesty which fills one with admiration. And that is why she remains the model for all
Christians. With the Savior Himself, she remained hidden
at Nazareth, united to Him in sweetness and humility, in
the accomplishment of daily duty and domestic labors, in
patience and prayer. We know of no miracle she performed, no extraordinary action, but she loved God with
all her heart, all her soul, all her mind, and all her strength.
This is the first commandment. And she loved her neighbor as herself. "There is no other commandment greater
than these" (b).

655
(80-
82,
113-
115,
131)

655a Luke 2:19; 2:51.
655b Mark 12:30-31.

Marian Sodalities

656   Nevertheless, the faithful who feel a special devotion
(151) toward the most Blessed Virgin often want to put their
lives at her service and to join with others in spreading
devotion to her. For centuries, the Church has had Associations placed under the patronage of Mary, which have
played a providential role, often praised by Our Predecessors and by Ourselves, in the personal sanctification of
many Christians and the exercise of apostolic zeal. We
would like to speak, among other things, of the Marian
Congregations, which We have called Catholic Action
in the spirit of the most Blessed Virgin. Their nature and
spirit is defined by the Apostolic Constitution *Bis sæculari*
of September 27, 1948 (a). We have learned with joy that
they are being promoted ardently in Brittany, and We
hope that they may find in that land of the Virgin a fertile
terrain, from which will spring forth legions of fervent
apostolic souls. Why should they not accomplish there in
dear Brittany, whose ancestral faith has known such
brilliant ages and such ardent revivals, that which they
have already achieved in the most diversified and widely-
scattered nations of Christianity?

657   You would be surprised, dear sons and daughters of
(72, Brittany, if today, on this feast of St. Anne, and here at
84, Auray, where she is venerated in a manner so moving,

656a Article 8 says: Associations of this kind are called
Marian, not only because they take their name from the
Blessed Virgin, but most of all because each and every
member professes special devotion to the Mother of God
and consecrates himself or herself, not of course under
pain of sin, to work most seriously for one's own Christian perfection and eternal salvation and to that of others
under the standard of the Blessed Virgin Mary; by virtue
of that consecration the member is attached forever to the
service of the Blessed Virgin Mary, unless he or she is ex-
pelled for some unworthy action or through instability he
or she leaves the association. ASS. 40, 393.

We should fail to remember her whom you justly call   *175)*
the Good Mother. Love her well, this good St. Anne. Continue to place your homes under her protection. By bringing Mary into the world, she gave humanity the most
marvelous of creatures, the holiest of women, the master-
work of God. Is not this reason for you to love her and
honor her in a particular way?

FILIAL OBLIGATIONS

R. M. to Brazilian Marian Congress, September 7, 1954.

(Our Lady's place in Brazil's history.)

You have wisely chosen to study Mary's incomparable   **658**
splendors, embodied in the dogmas of her Immaculate   *(10,*
Conception, her divine Maternity and her glorious As-   *136)*
sumption into Heaven.

Thus, the Congress will contribute to make your piety
ever more enlightened and conscious and, as a result, your
love purer, your gratitude deeper, your trust in your
August Queen and Patroness and Mother, who has always
enriched you with so many proofs of her love, firmer. But
it will also serve to make you better acquainted with the
duties which are imposed by your filial obedience, so that
your enthusiasm will not weaken nor the fruits vanish
with the last echoes of the celebrations.

All of you, who are on your knees at the feet of the   **659**
Immaculate Queen and Patroness of Brazil, have sworn to   *(110-*
her redoubled fidelity and love, and therefore it is urgent   *111,*
that you rise up as sworn champions of her maternal sov-   *131,*
ereignty, pledged to take no rest until you see her ruling   *176)*
as sovereign over everything and everyone. First, over
yourselves, in your own life and activities, as loving children who are proud to imitate their Mother's virtues; then
around you, over your families, over your social classes
and your associations and over all private and public ac-

tivities; so that your great Nation may show itself worthy
of its heavenly Queen and Patroness, making itself outstanding in this great Crusade for a better world, which
should be the fruit of the Marian Year, and with all the
more valor and zeal, because then the greater will be the
influence which you can exercise in the whole Continent
and in the Assembly of Nations.

OUR LADY'S MESSAGE TO MODERN SOCIETY

Letter *La piedad del pueblo,* to the Marian Congress
of Bolivia, August 13, 1954.

660
(70,
75,
76,
80)
The devotion of the people of Bolivia toward the
most Blessed Virgin Mary has gathered in your historical
city of Sucre the faithful of your nation, presided over by
their prelates, for the purpose of celebrating, in this Year
consecrated to Mary, the Second National Marian Congress, thus solemnly to do homage to the Queen of Heaven.

Ever since We expressed the wish of commemorating
the definition of the Immaculate Conception of the Blessed Virgin Mary We have been exhorting Our children to
consider the greatness of this privilege, which bears witness to the fact that the Mother of Jesus was at all times
full of grace, and the model of the highest virtues, in order that, attracted by the splendor of such eminent beauty,
they should themselves seek to imitate her faithfully.

Thus this Congress, which has been summoned with
a view to stimulating devotion toward the Holy Virgin in
your dear country, is an answer to Our paternal appeal
and a cause of deep satisfaction to Us; for in it We see
the promise of the fruits that will be gathered from this
Holy Year.

Esteem for our divine sonship

661
(82,
131)
The dogma of the Immaculate Conception presenting
us Mary as exempt from original sin and as having at no
time fallen a victim to sin is a loving invitation for us to

follow, as far as possible, that high example by keeping our souls always pure. Once regenerated in baptismal waters, it becomes immaculately white, but by evil doing it wanders far from the straight path and becomes stained again. If the fault be serious the soul loses God's grace and deserves eternal punishment. Is there a greater misfortune than this?

The essential matter for a Christian is not to offend God, not to commit sin, to act in such a way that the soul at all times lives in God's grace.

True sons and daughters of Mary strive to resemble such a holy Mother, and for that purpose they must struggle against their passions, against the world's temptations, against everything that might lead them to sin.

In this way they will show their appreciation for the great gift that makes them God's children and will constantly lead a fervent Christian life.

Restoration of the family

Now, if sin is the cause of such ill to individuals, its consequences are still worse when committed in the bosom of the family. One of the greatest needs of the world at the moment is the restoration to the home of the sacred and Christian character which it held among our peoples in other ages. Conjugal fidelity, family peace and mutual help of the spouses, and the religious education of the children are the basis for happiness in domestic society. Sins against these three things produce enormous evils. Mary, in the life of Nazareth, is a model of family virtues: all must learn from her the standards of life to which they are obliged. In other times, families came together at the close of day to honor the Queen of Heaven by the recitation of the Holy Rosary. The devotional life of the family and the piety inculcated in the children fostered vocations to the priesthood and to the religious life. The way in which setbacks and sufferings were borne taught the

662
(82,
164)

Christian spirit of sacrifice. If Mary is imitated, the family will be the nursery of virtues, and peace will always reign therein.

Integrity of Faith

663
(122,
123,
136)
In the world of today, full of snares and dangers, many are boldly struggling to disseminate error among the faithful. A daring propaganda, open or secret, is infiltrating among Catholics with the aim of alienating them from the loyalty due to Christ and to the true Church, and of eradicating the faith from their souls as well. And unfortunately, besides those who valiantly defend its beliefs, some are to be found who abandon them. How these defections must hurt the heart of Mary! She who has given us the author of our Redemption, Jesus Christ, will watch over the firmness of the faith of the faithful and will enlighten them so that they may recognize the enemy's snares.

(*Confide these intentions to Our Lady.*)

UNIQUE SANCTITY OF MARY

R. M. to the Canadian Marian Congress, August 15, 1954.

(*Role of Our Lady in the history of French Canada.*)

664
(72,
79-
80,
166)
Lift up your hearts, then, beloved children, and let Canada from coast to coast and even to the frozen fields of the North echo the praise and prayer that rise from grateful, loving hearts to swell the chorus of three centuries in veneration of her whom the dying Christ gave you for Mother. Lift your eyes for a moment from this earth laden with sin to contemplate the purity of Mary's life; turn for a brief space from the weaknesses of human nature and recall that the Virgin has never wavered in her burning love of God, has never weakened her complete union with Christ Jesus. Her Son's holiness was unthinkably beyond and above that of His Mother; but her growth in holiness

so far surpasses all other created holiness as to reach un-
approachable heights of splendor before the dazzled gaze
of saints and angels.

Oh, sinless, pure, grace-filled soul! When will men   **665**
learn to value the gifts of this passing world at their true   *(70)*
worth; to understand that Truth is a more precious possession than wealth; that a soul sanctified by God's love
is a greater treasure than empires; that a world at enmity
with God has lost its right to hope for lasting peace, because justice without God has a hollow ring?

Oh, Mary, Virgin Mother of God and our Mother,   **666**
accept the homage of affection and veneration which the   *(136)*
Congress of Trois-Riviéres brings to your throne in the
name of all the faithful of Canada. Show them always the
path that leads to union with your Divine Son; protect
them against the evil spirits that lurk along the way, so
that one day they may join their Mother and the whole
court of heaven in adoration of the one true God forever.

(*Conclusion.*)

DEMANDS OF CONSECRATION TO MARY

R. M. to the Belgian Marian Congress, September 5,
1954.

The miraculous statues that on this day have passed   **667**
over the square of Koekelberg in triumphant procession
are eloquent testimony that Belgium is a Marian land.
Most of them have received your homage for many centuries, while others have appeared recently as a renewed
indication of Mary's living presence among you. But
whether old or new, unhesitatingly you bring to them all
your trust; you lay before them your difficulties, your sufferings and your hopes. Bound intimately to the life of your
people, these statues shared with you many difficulties and
agonies; they have been present at the magnificent expan-

sion and astounding accomplishments of Catholicism in your country. Each day, you pour forth your prayers at their feet, gain the courage to carry on a patient struggle against all forms of evil, and receive the good things of body and soul and those thousands of kindnesses which a Mother never ceases to shower on her children.

668
(76,
126,
154)
Thus you have good reason to come in pilgrimage from all parts of Belgium to a site that you consider a sanctuary of your faith and in national homage to gather there your most famous statues, representatives of the other countless images scattered everywhere in your churches, your chapels, along the roads, in your homes. The different titles by which you invoke Mary illustrate the infinite richness and unlimited goodness of the Creature without stain, the Immaculate Virgin and Mother of God, whom the world will never cease to praise and whose goodness it will never exhaust.

The demands of consecration

669
(132)
As proof of your gratitude, you wish to make an act of consecration to this glorious sovereign. Weigh well, dear sons and daughters, the full importance of this act and the obligations it involves. By putting under Mary's mantle your personal, family, and national activities, you ask her protection and her aid in all your undertakings. But you also promise her to avoid anything that could displease her and to conform your whole life to her direction and her desires. A Mother's love can make the most severe demands on her children, when their good is at stake. She will not tolerate the family's honor to be harmed by their conduct. Indeed she longs for them to perform brilliant deeds that she may rejoice with them over their success and merits.

Mary expects you, heirs of a long tradition of fidelity in the service of Christ, to carry on at the present time the age-old struggle that divides good from evil.

Demand of fidelity

First of all, she asks you to remain firm in faith. Even if you do not have to suffer open persecution, as is, alas, the lot of so many in other countries, you must defend yourselves against a materialism which little by little is invading society, its institutions and its activities. With many, this materialism reveals itself in the search for a comfortable life, fully secure for the morrow, but a life closed to supernatural realities, to all appeal to devotion, and incapable of grasping the needs—at times the crying needs—of other social classes or other peoples. It is so easy to forget that temporal well-being is not the principal end of human life and that there are other riches infinitely more precious and lasting, those of divine charity, which make man forgetful of self in order to give himself to God and His work. The Blessed Virgin's role is to let men glimpse a reflection of heaven among all the cares that chain them to this earth and to remind them untiringly that the sufferings of this world are not worthy to be compared with the glory that God is preparing for His children.

670
(132, 136, 168)

Family sanctification

Consecration to Mary will sanctify your homes. Who better than the Blessed Virgin can preserve the intimacy and fervor of family affections and elevate them by communicating to them the purity of that completely faithful love of which God has made her the custodian? Who inspires mothers with the courage and patience necessary to take care of the countless family needs, to train their children in piety, to defend them against the snares which a paganized world constantly lays under their feet? It is in the bosom of the family, through constant daily contact, that the image of the parents is impressed on the souls of the children, that the experience of Christian life is transmitted. It is there that a viligant and tender presence is needed; one might say that there is the chosen place

671
(111, 115, 164)

where the Mother of Jesus continues the work that was
hers *par excellence,* the motherly care of the Son of God,
which is now prolonged in the members of His Church.
May Mary reign in your homes, not only because you have
placed her image or statue there but also because you
often pray to her together, come to her for her advice and
practice her virtues.

Source of vocations

672
(80,
131,
137)
It is not to be wondered at if, in hearts especially
devoted to her, the Queen of Virgins awakens the desire
to imitate the perfection of her love for Christ and men.
Following the counsels of the divine Master, young men
and women leave their homes and endeavor by a life of
prayer, renunciation and charity to call down on souls the
graces of salvation and also to show them the way by
word and example. We especially remember, not without
emotion, Belgium's magnificent missionary efforts, and all
the religious Congregations which, at the price of heavy
sacrifices, proclaim Christ's message in Africa and in many
other parts of the world. Maintain this glorious tradition
which bears witness to the vitality of your Catholicism and
does honor to the Church and her divine Head!

Apostolic zeal

673
(137)
The Blessed Virgin also inspires the lay apostolate in
its diverse forms, in particular those of Marian associations and Catholic Action groups. For souls desirous of
living out the teaching of Jesus more sincerely and more
fully, for those who burn to make it known to others, in
particular to their fellow workers, for him who wishes to
restore the order of justice and charity in social institutions
and to bring to the temporal social order a reflection of the
perfect harmony that unites the children of God, the Virgin Mary obtains the grace of the apostolate. She puts on
their lips words that convince without hurting and she animates them with a wise zeal and a humble, patient,

devoted affection, without which the apostle runs the risk of growing tired very quickly. Nourished by a deeper understanding and more lively affection for their Sovereign and their Patroness, the Marian associations will redouble their supernatural ardor in their prayers, mortifications and conquering ardor, which is fitting to those who care little for their own personal advantage and have only in mind an ever greater fidelity in fulfilling their obligation to Mary.

Mary leads to the Eucharist

You have wished to conclude this Marian day by assisting at Holy Mass and receiving Holy Communion. You could not more effectively confirm the promises made to the Blessed Virgin. Mary has no other desire but to lead men to Christ and to introduce them to the heart of the central mystery of Christianity, that of the Redemption. She continues to give to the Church the Son she brought into the world in Palestine. If she loves to see her children assembled for a stirring manifestation of faith and love, it is to lead them together to the mystical Bread, symbol of unity, of peace and of the eternal joy of heaven.

674
(39, 52, 119)

May Jesus, through Mary, continue to reign over your nation, your homes and in the depths of your souls. May He raise among you an ever more numerous and more ardent group of apostles, priests, religious and laity. May He maintain in your country the Christian spirit in all its generosity and an ever more fervent devotion toward the Blessed Virgin. May you in all truth be able to repeat to her enthusiastically the words of the beautiful hymn: "Among us, be thou Queen!"

675
(52, 125)

QUEENSHIP OF MARY

Encycl. *Ad cœli Reginam*, October 11, 1954.

676
(101-
106,
154,
168)
The Christian people have had recourse to the Queen of Heaven since the early days of the Church. To her they addressed humble prayers and devout hymns of praise in their joys and still more in their trials and dangers. Never was there a lessening of confidence in the Mother of the Divine King Jesus Christ, and never did that faith weaken, which teaches us that the Virgin Mary Mother of God is supreme in her motherly care of the world, just as she is crowned with glory in the happiness of heaven.

677
(129,
168)
In our own times what calamities We have seen! Cities and towns and villages have been reduced to ruins; the evil passions of men have passed all bounds, like a flood of evil, and caused fearful havoc. At times there has been no justice, and enticement to evil has triumphed everywhere. We are filled with grief at this alarming state of affairs, and therefore We have recourse with confidence to Mary Our Queen. To her We make known not only Our devotion but that of all those who glory in the name of Christian.

Devotion of His Holiness Pope Pius XII to Mary

678
(96,
104,
154,
157)
We recall with pleasure the following events:

On the first of November 1950, the Holy Year, We proclaimed the dogma of the Assumption of the Blessed Virgin Mary into heaven (a), where, present in body and soul, amid the choirs of angels and saints, she reigns with her only-begotten Son. On that day We were surrounded by an immense multitude of Cardinals, Bishops, priests, and faithful people who had come from all over the world.

One hundred years have now gone by since Pope Pius IX defined that the Mother of God was conceived

678a Cf. above no. 482 ff.

without any stain of original sin. To mark that event We proclaimed Our Lady's Year (b) now in progress, and it is a great consolation to Us to see devotion to the Virgin Mother of God everywhere revived and her principal churches throughout the world thronged with pilgrims. Especially do We rejoice to see the multitudes which flock to the Church of St. Mary Major in Rome, to show plainly their faith and their warm love of our heavenly Mother.

It is well known how We take every opportunity to exhort all the faithful to love their kind and powerful Mother with a great and tender love, as children should. This We do when We receive the faithful in public audiences, and when We broadcast messages to those at a distance. And here We single out for special mention the message We broadcast to the people of Portugal on the occasion when the miraculous image of the Virgin Mary which is venerated at Fatima (a) was crowned with a golden crown. We called that broadcast the Message of the "Royalty of Mary." **679** *(156, 158)*

And now to crown these many examples of Our devotion to the great Mother of God, which the Christian people have so eagerly followed; to bring Our Lady's Year now ending to a happy and successful conclusion; and to give a willing assent to the numerous requests addressed to Us from all over the world; We have decided to institute the liturgical feast of the Blessed Virgin Mary the Queen. **680** *(141)*

Our intention in this letter is not to propose a new truth for the belief of the faithful, for the title of Queen and the reasons which justify the royal dignity of Mary have always been known and have been handed down in the ancient documents of the Church and in the sacred liturgical books. We simply wish to go over again these **681** *(105, 138)*

678b Cf. above no. 584 ff.
679a Cf. above no. 407 ff.

ancient documents, which recount the praises of our heavenly Mother, thus to foster an increased devotion to her
for the spiritual gain of all the faithful.

Faith in the Queenship of Mary

682   The woman whose Son is the Son of the Most High
(27,   who "will reign in the house of Jacob forever" (a), "the
77,   Prince of Peace" (b), "the King of kings and Lord of
104) lords" (c), this woman has received from God singular
privileges of grace above all other creatures; this has been
the belief of the Christian people from the earliest times,
and because of the close relationship between Mother
and Child, it was easy for them to acknowledge the Mother
of God as Queen of all.

Homage of the Fathers

683   It is not surprising then that ancient writers in the
(26,   Church, relying on the words of the Archangel Gabriel,
104, who foretold that Mary's Son would reign forever, and
105) on the words of Elizabeth reverently greeting her as
"Mother of my Lord," should call Mary "Mother of the
King," "Mother of the Lord" (a), thus making it clear that
she received special and outstanding excellence from the
royal status of her Son.

684   So St. Ephrem, with a poet's fervor, represents our
(101, Lady as saying, "Let heaven hold me in its embrace, for
105) I am more honored than heaven. Heaven was not your
Mother, but you made heaven your throne, and the Mother
of the King is far more worthy of honor and veneration
than his throne" (a). And in another place he thus addresses
her "Empress, Maiden and Mistress, Queen and Lady,

682a Luke 1:32.
682b Isa. 9:6.
682c Apoc. 19:16.
683a Cf. Luke 1:32-33.
684a Hymn de B. Maria.

guard and protect me, lest Satan, the author of ruin, rejoice over me and the wicked enemy triumph over me" (b).

St. Gregory Nazianzen calls Mary "Mother of the King   **685**
of the whole Universe," "Virgin Mother who gave birth to   *(104,*
the King of the whole world" (a). Prudentius says Mary   *105)*
was filled with wonder that "she should be the Mother of
the God-Man who is King over all" (b).

This royal dignity of the Blessed Virgin Mary is clear-   **686**
ly taught by those writers who call her Mistress, Ruler,   *(105)*
Queen. In a sermon ascribed to Origen, Mary is not only
called by Elizabeth "Mother of my Lord" but also "You
are my Sovereign Lady" (a).

St. Jerome teaches the same when speaking of the   **687**
various meanings of the name Mary and says, "In the   *(105)*
Syrian language Mary means Lady" (a), and after him
St. Peter Chryologus: "Mary in Hebrew means Lady, and
the angel calls her Lady, so that the Mother of God should
be free from all fear, since the authority of her Son made
her our Lady in fact and in name" (b).

St. Epiphanius, Bishop of Constantinople, writing to   **688**
Pope St. Hormisdas, says that prayers should be said to   *(105)*
maintain the unity of the Church "through the grace of
the holy and undivided Trinity and the intercession of our
Lady Mary, the holy and glorious Virgin Mother of
God" (a). Another writer of the same time turns to the
Blessed Virgin, seated at the right hand of God, and asks
her to pray for us, calling her "most holy Mother of God
and Mistress of mortal men" (b).

684b *Oratio ad S. Dei Matrem.*
685a *Poëmata dogmatica,* 18, 58.
685b *Dittochæum,* 27 PL
686a *Hom. in S. Lucam hom.* 7.
687a *Liber de nominibus hebræis* PL XXIII, 886.
687b *Sermo* 142, *De Annuntiatione* B.V.M.
688a *Relatio Epiphani Ep. Constantin.*
688b Inter opera S. Modesti, *Encomium in Dormit.*

689   St. Andrew of Crete often ascribes the dignity of
(105) Queen to the Virgin Mary; he writes: "Today God Himself,
who took human form from the womb of His ever Virgin
Mother, takes her out of this world as Queen of the human
race". And again, "Queen of the whole human race in
name and, in fact, placed above all that is under God" (a).

(690   St. Germanus addresses the humble Virgin in these
(105) words: "Be seated, Lady, it is fitting that you should sit
in the highest place, for you are Queen, glorious above all
kings", and he calls her "Mistress of the inhabitants of
the earth" (a).

St. John Damascene calls her "Queen, Lady, Mistress" (b), and "Mistress over all creatures" (c). And by one
ancient writer of the Western Church, she is called "Blessed Queen," "Queen forever beside her Son, the King,"
whose "head is adorned with a golden crown" (d).

Finally, St. Ildephonsus of Toledo gathers together all
the titles of honor in this salutation, "My Lady, my Mistress, holding sway over me, Mother of my Lord...
Mistress among servants, Queen among sisters" (e).

The Popes and Theologians

691   It is from these and innumerable other ancient proofs
(105) that theologians have drawn their doctrine acclaiming the
Blessed Virgin Queen of all created things, Queen of the
world, and Mistress of all.

The Supreme Shepherds of the Church have always
thought it their duty to foster the devotion of the Christian
people to our Heavenly Mother and Queen. Not to men-

689a *Homilia II, III in Dormitionem Sanctissimæ Deiparæ.*
690a *In Præsentationem Ss.mae Deiparæ,* 1, 2.
690b *Homilia I in Dormitionem B.M.V.*
690c *De fide orthodoxa,* 4, 14.
690d *De laudibus Mariæ* PL 283 A.
690e *De virginitate perpetua B.M.V.*–PL 96, 58 AD.

tion the documents of recent Popes, let Us recall the following: in the seventh century, Our Predecessor St. Martin I, called Mary "Our Glorious Lady ever Virgin" (a), and St. Agatho, in a synodal letter, read to the Fathers of the Sixth General Council, says she is "Our Sovereign Lady, really and truly Mother of God" (b). And in the eighth century, Gregory II, in a letter to the Patriarch St. Germanus, read in the Seventh General Council with the acclaim of all the Fathers, calls her "Sovereign Mistress of all and true Mother of God," and again "Mistress of all Christians" (c).

We may well recall the following also: Our Predecessor Sixtus IV, in the Apostolic Letter in which he approves the doctrine of the Immaculate Conception of the Blessed Virgin, begins with these words, in which Mary is called the "Queen ever watchful who intercedes with the King, her Son." And Benedict XIV calls her "Queen of heaven and earth to whom the King of kings has in some measure committed His empire" (a). **692** *(28, 103-104)*

St. Alphonsus Liguori, gathering together all the testimonies of former times, writes: "Because the Virgin Mary was raised to the sublime dignity of being the Mother of the King of kings, the Church has rightly given her the title of Queen" (a). **693** *(105)*

Praise by the Liturgy

The Sacred Liturgy, which gives a true picture of the traditional belief of the Christian people, has never ceased in East and West to sing the praises of our Heavenly Queen. **694** *(105, 141)*

691a *Epist.* 14.
691b *Epist.* 3.
691c *Epist.* 20.
692a Cf. above, no. 2 ff.
693a The Glories of Mary, p. 1, c. 1.

695
(104-
105)
"O Mother of God, today you are taken up to heaven in the chariots of the Cherubim, the Seraphim wait on you, the multitudes of the heavenly host bow down before you" (a). "O just and blessed (Joseph) because you are of royal descent, you are chosen above all others to be the spouse of the pure Queen, who will give birth in a wonderful manner to Jesus the King" (b). "I will sing a hymn to the Queen Mother, and I will draw near to her with joy, and gladly will I celebrate her wonders.... O Lady, we cannot praise you as you deserve, because you gave birth to Christ the King, and you are exalted above the Seraphim.... Hail, O Queen of the world, Hail, O Mary, Mistress of us all" (c).

696
(105)
"O Mary, center of the whole world ... you are greater than the Cherubim and the six-winged Seraphim.... Heaven and earth are filled with your holiness and glory" (a).

697
(105)
The Latin Church joins in with the sweet sounding "*Salve Regina*" (Hail, Holy Queen), and the delightful antiphons "*Ave Regina Cœlorum*" (Hail, Queen of Heaven), "*Regina cœli lætare*" (Queen of heaven, rejoice), and the others which are said on the feasts of the Blessed Virgin Mary: "The Queen stands at your right hand in a vesture of gold." "Heaven and earth acclaim thee mighty Queen." "Today the Virgin Mary has ascended to heaven: rejoice, because she reigns with Christ forever" (a).

698
(105,
141,
145)
To these must be added the Litany of Our Lady, in which the faithful are daily invited to invoke her as Queen. In the fifth glorious mystery of the Rosary—Mary's mystical crown—the faithful have now for many centuries meditated on her royal sway over heaven and earth.

695a Armenian Liturgy, hymn at Matins of Assumption.
695b From *Menæo*, Byzantine Liturgy.
695c *Ibid*. Hymn Acathist.
696a *Anaphora* B.M.V.
697a Feast of the Assumption.

Christian art

Sacred art, founded on Christian principles, faithfully **699** expresses the simple and spontaneous piety of the faithful. *(105)* Ever since the Council of Ephesus it has pictured Mary as Queen and Empress, seated on a royal throne, adorned with royal emblems, crowned with a diadem, surrounded by angels and saints, and dominating, not only the forces of nature but also the evil influence of Satan. Pictures and images of the Blessed Virgin Mary have always given expression to her royal dignity and have been noted for their artistic workmanship and beauty. What could be more expressive than the picture of our divine Redeemer Himself placing on His Mother's brow a crown of glory!

The Popes have encouraged this devotion of the **700** people and have often crowned with their own hands, *(105)* or by means of their delegates, famous images of the Virgin Mother of God.

Mary's titles to Queenship: her Motherhood

From ancient documents, handed down in the Church, **701** and from the sacred liturgy, it is clear that the chief reason *(24,* for the royal dignity of Mary is her divine Motherhood. *104,* The Gospel, speaking of the Son to be conceived by the *114)* Virgin, says: "He shall be called the Son of the Most High and the Lord God shall give unto Him the throne of David His Father, and He shall reign in the house of Jacob forever, and of His kingdom there shall be no end" (a), and, again, Mary is called "Mother of the Lord" (b). Hence it is easy to conclude that Mary is herself Queen, since she gave birth to a Son, who at the very moment of His conception, by reason of the hypostatic union of His human

701a Luke 1:32-33.
701b Luke 1:43.

nature with the Word (c), was even as man King and Lord of all things.

702
(104) St. John Damascene, therefore, can rightly say: "She became Mistress of all creation when she became Mother of the Creator" (a). And we can also say that the first to proclaim the royal office of Mary was the heavenly messenger, the Archangel Gabriel.

Her Co-redemption

703
(41,
104) But the Blessed Virgin Mary is to be called Queen not only on account of her divine Motherhood but also because by the will of God she had a great part in the work of our salvation.

"What thought," says Pius XI, "could give us greater joy and consolation than this, that Christ is our King not only by natural right but by the right He won over us as our Redeemer. Would that all of us who forget our Savior would remember 'you were not redeemed with corruptible things such as gold or silver ... but with the precious blood of Christ as of a lamb unspotted and undefiled'. We are no longer our own, since Christ has bought us with a great price" (a).

704
(42,
45,
52,
104) Now in this work of Redemption the Blessed Virgin Mary was closely associated with Christ, and so the sacred liturgy sings: "Holy Mary, Queen of heaven and Mistress of the world, stood in sorrow at the cross of our Lord Jesus Christ" (a). Wherefore, according to a devout disciple of St. Anselm in the Middle Ages, "Just as ... God by His power creating all things is Father and Lord

701c ... *Inde facile eruitur ipsam quoque esse Reginam, quippe quæ Filium genuerit, qui eodem momento quo conceptus est, propter hypostaticam humanæ naturæ cum Verbo unionem, Rex etiam ut homo, erat et rerum omnium Dominus.*
702a *De fide orthodoxa,* 1. 4, c. 14.
703a *Quas primas,* December 11, 1925.
704a Feast of the Seven Dolors of the B.V.M., *Tractus.*

of all, so the Blessed Virgin Mary restoring all things by her merits is Mother and Mistress of all; for God is Lord of all things because by His command He gave them their nature, and Mary is Mistress of all things because she restored them to their original dignity by the grace which she merited" (b). For "Just as Christ, because He redeemed us, is by a special title our King and our Lord, so too is Blessed Mary (our Queen and our Mistress) because of the unique way in which she cooperated in our redemption. She provided her very substance for His body, she offered Him willingly for us, and she took a unique part in our salvation by desiring it, praying for it, and so obtaining it" (c).

From these considerations we can conclude as follows: Mary in the work of redemption was by God's will joined with Jesus Christ, the cause of salvation, in much the same way as Eve was joined with Adam, the cause of death. Hence it can be said that the work of our salvation was brought about by a "restoration" (St. Irenaeus) in which the human race, just as it was doomed to death by a virgin, was saved by a virgin.

705
(13-
14,
22,
28,
39,
44,
104)

Moreover, she was chosen to be the Mother of Christ "in order to have part with Him in the redemption of the human race" (a).

"She it was, who, free from all stain of personal or original sin, always most closely united with her Son, offered Him up to the Eternal Father on Calvary, along with the sacrifice of her own claims as His mother and of her own mother love, thus acting as a new Eve on behalf of all Adam's children, ruined by his unhappy fall" (b).

From this we conclude that just as Christ, the new Adam, is our King not only because He is the Son of God, but also because He is our Redeemer, so also in a

704b Eadmero, *De excellentia Virginis Mariæ.*
704c *De mysteriis vitæ Christi,* disp. 22, sect. 2.
705a Cf. above, no. 319.
705b Cf. above, no. 383.

somewhat similar manner the Blessed Virgin is Queen not only as Mother of God, but also because she was associated as the second Eve with the new Adam (c).

706
(12-
13,
46,
49,
101-
108)
Jesus Christ alone, God and Man, is King in the strict, full and absolute sense; but Mary shares in His royal dignity in a secondary way, dependent on the sovereignty of her Son. She is Mother of the Christ God and is His associate in the work of redemption, in His conflict with the enemy, and in His complete victory. It is from this union with Christ the King that she reaches a height of splendor unequalled in all creation. From this she has her royal power to distribute the treasures of the kingdom of the Divine Redeemer. From this union with Christ, her motherly intercession with her Son and with the Father has a power that never fails.

Queenship of excellence

707
(23,
26)
It is certain, therefore, that most holy Mary is raised by her dignity above all creation and that she comes first after her Son. "You are far above all creation... what can be more sublime than this joy, O Virgin Mary? What can be more excellent than this grace which you alone have received from God?" (St. Sophronius) (a) To these praises St. Germanus adds his tribute: "Your honor and dignity surpass all creation; the angels take second place to you in excellence" (b). And St. John Damascene goes so far as to say: "Immeasurable is the difference between the servants of God and the Mother of God" (c).

705c *Inde procul dubio concludere licet, quemadmodum Christus, novus Adam, non tantum quia Dei Filius est, Rex dici debet, sed etiam quia Redemptor est noster, ita quodam analogiæ modo, Beatissimam Virginem esse Reginam non tantummodo quia mater Dei est, verum etiam quod nova veluti Heva cum novo Adam consociata fuit.*
707a *In Annuntiationem* B.M.V.
707b *Hom. 2 in Dormitionem* B.M.V.
707c *Hom. 1 in Dormitionem* B.M.V.

To understand this supreme degree of excellence **708** which raises the Mother of God above all creation, it is *(68,* a help to note that from the first moment of her concep- *75)* tion she was filled with an abundance of grace far beyond that of all the saints. Hence Pope Pius IX wrote that Almighty God "placed her far above all the angels and all the saints, and so filled her with every heavenly grace taken from His own divine treasury, that she was always free from all stain of sin, all beautiful and perfect, possessing such a fullness of innocence and holiness to be found nowhere outside of God, and which no one but God can comprehend" (a).

Queenship of efficiency

The Blessed Virgin has not only been given the high- **709** est degree of excellence and perfection after Christ, but also *(11,* she shares in the power which her Son and our Redeemer *47,* exercises over the minds and wills of men (a). For if the *108,* Word of God, through the human nature assumed by Him, *116)* works miracles and gives grace, if He uses Sacraments and uses His saints as instruments for the salvation of souls, why should He not use His Blessed Mother's office and activity to give us the gifts of Redemption? "She has a mother's care for us, she is active in the affairs of our salvation, she is concerned for the whole human race; she has been made Queen of heaven and earth by God, exalted above all the choirs of angels and all the saints. Standing at the right hand of her only-begotten Son, our Lord Jesus Christ, she pleads strongly for us with a mother's prayers, and what she seeks she finds, nor can she ask in vain" (b).

708a Cf. above, no. 31.
709a *Præterea Beata Virgo non solummodo supremum, post Christum, excellentiæ ac perfectionis gradum obtinuit, verum etiam aliquam illius efficacitatis participationem, qua eius Filius ac Redemptor noster in mentes et in voluntates hominum regnare iure meritoque dicitur.*
709b Cf. above, no 65.

Pope Leo XIII proclaimed that almost unlimited power was given to the Blessed Virgin Mary in distributing graces (c), and St. Pius X added that Mary undertakes this office "as by a mother's right" (d).

710
(102)
Therefore, let all the faithful rejoice to be subject to the authority of the Virgin Mother of God, whose power is a Queen's, and whose love is a Mother's.

711
(20)
Theologians and preachers must take care, in all these questions relating to Our Lady, to avoid deviating from sound doctrine, lest they fall into a twofold error: let them avoid unfounded opinions expressed in words which go beyond the truth; and let them avoid too narrow an outlook in considering the singularly sublime and almost divine dignity of the Mother of God, which, the Angelic Doctor teaches, must be ascribed to her "on God's account, for He is the infinite Good" (a).

712
(4,
18)
However, in this as in all other points of Christian Doctrine, everyone has "an all-embracing standard of truth ready to hand" in the living, teaching Authority of the Church, which Christ set up "to make clear and explain in detail what was left obscure and only implicitly contained in the deposit of faith" (a).

Feast of Mary the Queen

713
(105)
We have now gathered evidence from all sides to show that the Virgin Mother of God is preeminent with a royal dignity. The monuments of Christian antiquity, the liturgical prayers, the religious sense of the Christian people, the works of art, all speak as one. We have shown that the theological arguments resting on the deposit of divine faith serve only to confirm the same truth. All

709c Cf. above, no. 169.
709d Cf. above, no. 235.
711a *Summa theol.* 1, q. 25, a. 6, ad 4.
712a Encycl. *Humani generis.*

these testimonies unite into one swelling symphony to extol the very summit of the royal dignity of the Mother of God and of men, who has all creation beneath her "as she is raised above the choirs of angels to the kingdom of heaven" (a).

We are convinced, after due consideration, that the Church will benefit greatly if this truth, so clearly proved, is made to shine before all men by being held up like a bright light. Therefore, by Our Apostolic Authority We decree and institute the feast of Mary the Queen, which is to be celebrated throughout the whole world every year on the 31st of the month of May. We also order that the consecration of the human race to the Immaculate Heart of the Blessed Virgin be renewed on that day, and We have great confidence that it will usher in a happy era of Christian peace and the triumph of religion. **714** *(111, 141, 169)*

Recognition of her rule

And now let everyone, with more confidence than ever before, approach the throne of mercy and grace of Mary, our Queen and Mother. Let them ask for help in adversity, for light in darkness, for comfort in mourning and weeping. But most of all, let them strive to break away from the slavery of sin and profess an unchangeable obedience to their Queen and a tender devotion to their Mother. Let her churches be thronged with crowds of people to celebrate her feasts; let her rosary beads be in the hands of all, and gather the faithful together in churches, in homes, in hospitals and prisons, in small groups or large crowds, to recite her praises. Let the name of Mary be held in honor: it is sweeter than honey and more precious than jewels. It is a name adorned with majesty and venerable with a mother's charm; it is a name never to be cursed— only a foul mind would think of such a thing; it is a name only to be spoken with the greatest respect. **715** *(132, 134, 141)*

713a Office of the Assumption.

716   Let all strive to imitate the sublime virtues of our
(36,   heavenly Queen and most loving Mother, each in his own
128,   way working to make his dispositions and his conduct like
131)   hers. The result will be that all Christians, by honoring and
imitating our Queen and Mother, will feel that they are
indeed brothers. Thus will they grow tired of envy and
greed, promote social concord, respect the rights of the
weak, and love peace. Let no one think he is a child of
Mary, and sure of her most powerful protection, unless he
shows himself gentle and chaste and just after her example,
and contributes to true brotherhood, not merely by re-
fraining from injuring others, but by positively helping
and consoling them.

Fruits of that recognition

717   In certain countries of the world, men and women
(121,   are unjustly persecuted for the name of Christ, and de-
167)   prived of the freedom due to them by right divine and
human, and no complaints and no protests, however
justified, have availed to end the evil. May the ever Sovereign Lady of all things, who can crush all aggression
beneath her virgin foot, turn her eyes of mercy towards
her innocent and afflicted children, disperse the clouds
and still the tempest. May she grant them without delay
to enjoy full freedom to practice their religion openly, so
that being of one mind according to the Gospel teaching,
they may become shining examples of virtue in their hard
lot, and thus contribute also to the strength and progress
of their countries.

718   It is our fervent hope that the feast which We
(108,   institute by this letter, so that all may acknowledge and
125,   venerate the kindly and maternal power of the Mother of
169)   God, will greatly contribute to the cause of peace, daily
disturbed by vexing problems. Is she not God's rainbow,
placed in the sky in the sight of God as a sign of the

covenant of peace? (a) "Look up at the rainbow, and
bless the maker of it; how fair are those bright colors that
span heaven with a ring of splendor traced by an Almighty
hand." Whoever, therefore, pays honor to the Mistress of
angels and of men—and let no one think himself exempt
from paying the tribute of a grateful and loving heart,—
let him invoke her as Queen ever at hand to obtain our
peace. Let him respect and defend peace. Peace does not
mean unpunished wrong-doing nor unbridled freedom,
but an orderly living together, guided and commanded by
the will of God. Our Lady exhorts and commands us to
protect and extend this peace.

We devoutly hope that our Queen and Mother will   **719**
hear our prayers and will grant the joy of peace to a   *(100)*
world riven with hate, and after this our exile will show
unto all of us Jesus, our peace and our joy eternal. Most
lovingly then do We give to you, Venerable Brethren,
and to your flocks, Our Apostolic Blessing as an omen of
God's almighty help and a proof of Our own love for you.

RICHES OF MARY'S HEART

R. M. to the Spanish Marian Congress, October 12,
1954.
(*Spanish sanctuaries.—The consecration of Spain to
the Immaculate Heart of Mary.*)

Most beloved children, this manifestation of your de-   **720**
votion to the most pure Heart of the Virgin Mary, seat of   *(43*
that love, of that sorrow, of those most sublime affections   *79,*
which had so great a part in our Redemption, especially   *82,*
when she kept vigil at the foot of the Cross, doubtlessly   *141)*
merits attention. This devotion is, indeed, merited by that
Heart, symbol of an interior life, whose moral perfection,
merits and virtues surpass all human conceiving. It is only

718a Cf. Gen. 9:13.

just that you should nourish and manifest this devotion, if not for any other reason, at least for that of belonging to the country of St. Anthony Mary Claret, untiring apostle of this devotion, whom We Ourselves have raised to the highest honor of the altars.

721
(128,
134,
141)
Today more than ever before that devotion is needed, because clouds are gathering on the horizon. At times it seems that darkness is blotting out the road more and more, and the boldness of the ministers of hell seems to grow greater. For these very reasons, We believe that all humanity must flee to this port of salvation (the Immaculate Heart of Mary). We have indicated this as the principal purpose of the Marian Year. Men must take refuge in this fortress, must trust in this sweet Heart which, in order to save us, asks only prayer and penance, asks only cooperation.

722
(159)
Promise it to her, most beloved sons from all parts of Spain. Promise her to live a life of piety that will become more intense, more profound and more sincere every day. Promise her to watch over that purity of morals which was always the glory of your people. Promise her never to open your doors to certain ideas and principles whose effects you already know from sad experience. Promise her not to allow the solidity of your family hearth, the cornerstone of all society, to be broken. Promise her to repress the desire for immoderate joys and greed for the goods of this world, a poison capable of destroying the most robust and healthiest of organisms. Promise her to love your brothers, first of all the humble and the needy, who are so often offended by pompous displays of luxury and pleasure! Then she will always continue to be your special protectress.

723
(132,
159)
Before your throne, therefore, O Blessed Virgin of the Pillar, let Us say, paraphrasing the words which We Ourselves pronounced on a solemn occasion, that as common father of the Christian family, as Vicar of Him to Whom

all power was given in heaven and on earth, We entrust, offer and consecrate to you, to your Immaculate Heart, not only all the multitude there present, but also the whole Spanish nation, so that your love and protection may hasten the triumphal hour of the reign of God, and all human generations, at peace among themselves and with God, may proclaim you Blessed, singing with you from one end of the earth to the other the eternal Magnificat of glory, love and gratitude to the Heart of Jesus, the sole refuge where they can find truth, life and peace.

MARY'S TEARS

R. M. to the Marian Congresses of Sicily, October 17, 1954.

(*Fidelity and Christian riches of Sicily manifested by its Marian devotion.*)

It is true that up to the present this Apostolic See has not in any way made known its judgment concerning the tears which are said to have been shed by an image of her in the humble house of some workingmen. Nevertheless, it was with lively emotion that We read the unanimous declaration of the Episcopate of Sicily of the reality of the event. Without doubt Mary is eternally happy in heaven and suffers neither pain nor sadness. And yet, she does not there remain insensible, but rather feels love and pity for the suffering human race, to which she was given as a Mother when she stood, sad and weeping, at the foot of the Cross, to which her Son was nailed. Will men understand the mysterious language of those tears? Oh, the tears of Mary! On Golgotha they were tears of compassion for her Jesus and of sadness for the sins of the world. Does she still weep for the wounds produced anew in the Mystical Body of Jesus? Or does she weep for her many sons, whose errors and sins have extinguished the life of grace and who gravely offend the divine majesty? Or are they

724
(*43,*
85,
100,
116,
170)

tears of expectation for the delayed return of her other
children, once faithful, and now led astray by mirages into
the ranks of God's enemies?

(*Lead back prodigals by fidelity to Christian life.*)

FRUITS OF DEVOTION TO MARY

R. M. to the Lebanese Marian Congress, October 18, 1954.

Under the Eastern sky

725
(57,
68,
101)
"I was exalted like a cedar in Lebanon, and as a cypress tree on Mount Zion.... Come over to me, all ye that desire me, and be filled with my fruits" (a). These words of Scripture, which the liturgy applies to the Blessed Virgin Mary, come to mind at this moment in which We have the joy of addressing you, beloved sons and daughters of the noble Lebanon nation, who have assembled in the splendor and fervor of a magnificent ceremony to celebrate with the universal Church the centenary of the definition of the dogma of the Immaculate Conception.

Yes, go to Mary, lift your hearts to her, implore the abundance of her graces with the confidence of children, that our Savior's Mother, who lived here below under the same pure and deep Eastern sky, will once again look down on your land with special satisfaction. Does not the Church herself evoke your Lebanese mountains as a particularly privileged place for praising the Virgin? It is there that the Holy Spirit contemplates her and enraptured by the splendor of her immaculate purity calls her thence to heavenly glory: "Come from Libanus, my spouse, and thou shalt be crowned" (b).

726
(151)
The rare privilege which thus joins the name of your fatherland with the cultus of the Virgin Mary creates for

725a Eccl. 24:17, 26.
725b Canticle of Canticles 4:8.

all of you the special duty of responding with still greater
faithfulness to her motherly appeals. And We are pleased
to think that the manifestations of your National Marian
Congress, over which We have desired to preside through
Our Legate, Our dear Son, the Cardinal Patriarch of
Venice, will certainly revive and increase in you a sound,
lasting and enlightened devotion toward the Immaculate
Virgin. From last May 38, hymns and prayers have continued to be sent up unceasingly in her honor from the
streets and churches during the glorious journey of the
Statue from the Sanctuary of Harissa through mountains
and vales, towns and villages. And the motherly heart of
the Virgin will have throbbed with delight at seeing so
many souls purified by the Sacraments and so many lives
again consecrated to the service of her Divine Son; she will
have been moved on beholding the fervor of the Christian
multitudes and the zeal of the whole people to take part
in her praise.

Fruits of Marian devotion

Such Marian piety is a token of hope for your dear   **727**
fatherland. Youth will derive therefrom a firm attachment   *(37,*
to the ideal of purity which Mary proposes to the human   *40,*
race wounded by sin; and by invoking the assistance of   *130,*
her who crushed the serpent's head, they will be able to   *135,*
overcome the repeated attacks of temptation.   *165)*

Fathers and mothers of families will place their homes
under her care and will wish to meditate upon the example of the Holy Family of Nazareth.

Active members of Catholic Action will look up to
Mary, who is the surest means of leading souls to Jesus,
and they will, through her intercession, implore divine
grace, without which their action would remain fruitless.

Priests above all and every consecrated soul should
bear in mind that Jesus, when about to die, entrusted His
Mother to them in the person of St. John. These will
gather round her in increased veneration, united more

than ever among the fruitful diversity of their rites by a common love for the Holy Virgin, and a common desire to promote her cultus.

And upon the social life of your fatherland the Mother of the Divine Savior will cause to shine the ideal of her Divine Son's message of charity and brotherly love, of truth and justice. She, whom all generations call blessed, is the honor of womanhood, the hope of the poor, the comfort of the afflicted and the oppressed. She is now, as in the time of King Achaz, the sign of God's mercy: "Behold a Virgin shall conceive and bear a Son" (a).

Today also, if you are attentive and faithful to her teachings, she will be a sign of salvation for your venerable Eastern Christian communities.

Devotion in the East

728
(24,
27,
63,
68)
The entire past of your ancient Christian communities confirms the long tradition of your filial piety towards the holy Virgin Mary. Was it not on Oriental land, at Ephesus, that the Church first officially proclaimed Mary's Divine Maternity, that supreme prerogative which implies in its inexhaustible richness the privileges of the Immaculate Conception celebrated in this Marian Year? The Fathers of the Eastern Church have greatly contributed on throwing light on this twofold glorious mystery, and it is to your honor never to have ceased proclaiming that the Mother of God was from the first instant of her life preserved from original sin.

(*Exhortation to fidelity under the protection of Our Lady of Lebanon.*)

727a Is. 7:14.

MARIOLOGY

R. M. to the International Mariological Congress,
October 24, 1954.

It was Our expectation when We proclaimed the **729**
celebration of this Marian Year throughout the world that *(17)*
it would produce many salutary and religious fruits. It
was Our special hope that among these fruits the year
would see a more profound study of the unique dignity of
the Mother of God, of her glorious gifts and privileges
and a clearer presentation of these to the Christian people.
Hence it was with great pleasure that We learned of the
plan to convoke a Mariological Congress here in Rome toward the end of the Marian Year. We not only approved
this project from the start, but We also showed it special
favor and endorsed it with Our blessing.

You have come, beloved children, from all parts of the
Catholic World to Rome so that, near the tomb of the
Prince of the Apostles and under the auspices of him to
whom the words "Strengthen thy brethren" (a) were addressed, you could pursue your expert and learned discus-
sions on the honor, grace and power of this great Virgin
and Mother—all in accordance with the norms of sacred
doctrine.

The basis of Mariology

Since Mariology is included in the theological studies, **730**
it must first of all be based upon the solid foundation of *(7,*
theological doctrine. The more profound the investigation, *19,*
and the more accurately the truths of Mariology are com- *136)*
pared and linked up with each other and with other
truths of sacred theology, the more necessary is this solid
foundation. This was the method employed with laudable
zeal after the solemn definition of the dogma of the Im-

729a Luke 22:32.

maculate Conception of the Blessed Virgin Mary by Our Predecessor, Pius IX, and which in our times has produced ever increasingly good results.

The magisterium

731
(4,
18,

Studies such as these are not always easy and obvious, since in pursuing them and in perfecting them what are called "positive" and "speculative" subjects are both required, each of which is governed by its own standards and laws. And the work of research even in matters of Mariology is safer and more rewarding to the extent that everyone remembers the truth that "in matters of faith and morals the immediate and universal standard of truth for every theologian" (a) is, as We have said, the Church's sacred teaching authority. For, as We explained in the Encyclical letter *Humani generis,* God has given this sacred teaching authority to His Church "to clarify and to explain things that are contained only in an obscure and, as it were, implicit way in the deposit of faith" (b). The Divine Redeemer has entrusted this deposit, to be explained and interpreted in an authentic way, to the Church's teaching authority alone. Under the mandate and guidance of the Church the theologian is assigned the great duty of investigating this deposit thoroughly, of examining well and explaining the nature and interrelations of the individual truths according to the norms of sacred doctrine.

Scripture and Tradition

732
(1,
3,
28,
88)

In doing this work the two sources of Catholic doctrine, the Scriptures and Tradition, must be carefully considered. In the books of both the Old and the New Testaments, the Sacred Scriptures tell us many glorious things about the Blessed Virgin. In fact, her magnificent

731a Encycl. *Humani generis.*
731b Ibid.

privileges and gifts, her virginal motherhood and unspotted holinesss, are expressly asserted therein. The description of the Virgin presented there in outline appears in such living colors that it almost constitutes a portrait. But the man who considers it possible to define adequately and to explain correctly the Blessed Virgin's great dignity and sublimity from the Sacred Scriptures alone, or who thinks that the same Sacred Scriptures can be explained properly without taking Catholic Tradition and the sacred teaching authority sufficiently into account is very far from the truth. On another occasion We said that "what is called positive theology cannot be considered as completely equivalent to historical science," and this certainly applies here (a).

Church's living faith

It is likewise wrong to neglect or to ignore the sacred teaching authority and the Church's life and worship, as manifested over the course of centuries, when investigating or explaining the documents of Tradition. Sometimes individual documents of antiquity when considered only by themselves give little enlightenment. But when put together and compared with the Church's liturgical life, with the faith, devotion, and piety of the Christian people—which the same teaching authority sustains and directs—they become magnificent testimonies of Catholic truth. Indeed the Church, throughout the centuries of its life, not only in teaching and defining the faith, but also in its worship and in the Catholic people's exercise of piety and devotion, is ruled and guarded by the Holy Spirit and "is infallibly directed to the knowledge of revealed truths" (a) by the same Spirit. Hence the students of Mariology, when they are investigating and considering the testimonies of past ages and of our own period, must, by all means, keep in

733
(4,
6,
18)

732a Ibid.
733a Cf. above, no. 521.

mind the perpetual and ever effective guidance of the Holy Spirit, so that they may rightly examine and express the meaning and the importance of what has been said and done.

Errors to be avoided

734
(18,
20,
69,
76,
127)
If these standards are strictly observed, Mariology will make genuine and permanent progress in inquiring ever more profoundly into the Blessed Virgin's gifts and dignity. And thus this study will go along the correct middle way, avoiding whatever falsely and intemperately goes beyond the bounds of truth, while keeping apart from those who are filled with a kind of unreasonable fear of conceding more than they ought to the Blessed Virgin, or, as they frequently say, a fear that some honor and confidence is withheld from the Divine Redeemer Himself when His Mother is honored and invoked with filial reverence.

Now the Blessed Mother of God, as a descendant of Adam, has no privilege of grace which she does not owe to her Son, the Redeemer of the human race. Consequently when we admire the Mother's eminent gifts and rightly praise them, we are admiring and praising the divinity, the goodness, the love, and the power of her Son. Whatever we may do to praise the Mother upon whom He has showered so many graces will never displease the Son.

735
(11,
26,
119)
Those gifts which the Son has bestowed upon the Mother are so great as to surpass or to equal that of the divine motherhood. Mary, as the Angelic Doctor says, has a certain infinite dignity from the infinite good that is God by the very fact that she is the Mother of God (a). Although it is true that, like ourselves, the Blessed Virgin is a member of the Church, still it is no less true that she is a unique member of Christ's Mystical Body.

736
(17,
Therefore, We ardently desire, Beloved Sons, that, keeping these norms in mind, you take up the matters you

735a Cf. *Summa Theol.* p. I, q. 25 a. 6, ad 4.

are going to deal with in your sessions and discuss and   *19)*
debate them with erudition, learning, expertness and piety.
May your united efforts bring about (and this is the desire
of everyone) the fullest increase in the praises rendered
Mary, God's Mother and ours, and in the honor paid the
Divine Redeemer who has adorned her with such great
graces and gifts.

EXERCISE OF THE ROYALTY OF MARY

All. in St. Peter's Basilica, November 1, 1954.

The marks of homage and devotion toward God's   **737**
Mother which the Catholic world has shown ever increas-   *(157)*
ingly in recent months, in public demonstrations and in
the humble undertakings of private piety, are a splendid
proof of its love for the Virgin Mary and of its faith in her
incomparable privileges. To crown all these manifestations
with a solemnity especially significant of the Marian Year,
We have wished to institute and celebrate the Feast of
the Queenship of Mary.

Feast of Mary, Queen

None of you, beloved sons and daughters, will marvel   **738**
at this or think it is a question of giving Our Lady a new   *(105)*
title. Have not faithful Christians been repeating for centuries those invocations of the Litany of Loreto which
salute Mary with the name of Queen? And does not the
recitation of the Holy Rosary, in which we piously meditate
upon the joys, sorrows and glories of God's Mother, conclude with the radiant remembrance of Mary received into
heaven by her Son and crowned by Him with a royal
diadem?

It was not Our intention to introduce anything new   **739**
but rather to have shine forth before the world's gaze a   *(141)*
truth which, in the present circumstances, is capable of

remedying its ills, of freeing it from its anguish, and of leading it toward the way of salvation which it so anxiously seeks.

More than earthly queenship

740
(102,
106,
110)
The Queenship of Mary must not be considered—and much less the Kingship of her Son—in analogy with the realities of modern political life. True, the marvels of heaven can be represented only through the ever imperfect words and expressions of human language; but this does not mean that, in order to honor Mary, one must adhere to a determined form of government or a particular political structure. Mary's Queenship is a supernal reality which at the same time penetrates men's innermost hearts and touches all that is spiritual and immortal in their very essence.

741
(28,
42,
82,
101,
169)
The origin of Mary's glories, the solemn moment which lights up her whole personality and mission, is that in which she, full of grace, replied to the Archangel Gabriel with "Fiat" ("Be it done"), expressing her consent to God's plan. Thus did she become the Mother of God and Queen, receiving the royal office of watching over the unity and peace of the human race. We have firm confidence that, through her, mankind will little by little progress along this way of salvation; she will guide the rulers of nations and the hearts of their peoples toward concord and charity.

The benefits of her Rule

742
(136,
168)
At the present hour, then, when world unity and peace, nay more, the very sources of life are endangered, what can Christians do except turn their eyes toward her whom they see vested with royal power? At one time she sheltered in her mantle the Divine Child, first-born of all creatures and of all creation (a). So now may she deign

742a Cf. Col. 1:15.

to shelter all men and all people in her watchful tenderness; may she deign, as Seat of Wisdom, to manifest the truth of the inspired words which the Church applies to her: *"Per me reges regnant, et legum conditores justa decernunt; per me principes imperant, et potentes decernunt justitiam"* —"By me kings reign and lawgivers decree just things. By me princes rule, and the mighty decree justice" (b). While the world at present struggles unceasingly to achieve unity and insure peace, the invocation of Mary's reign—surpassing all earthly means and all human plans, which are always in some way defective—is the voice of Christian faith and hope, strengthened and reinforced by divine promises and by the inexhaustible aid which Mary's rule has provided for the salvation of mankind.

Force of our Queen's exemplary soul

Yet, from the unending goodness of the most Blessed Virgin, whom We invoke today as Royal Mother of Our Lord, We also expect other benefits not less precious. Not only must she bring to nought the dark plans and wicked works of those who are enemies of a united and Christian mankind, but she has also to communicate to modern men something of her own spirit—We mean that courageous and even bold will which, in difficult circumstances and in the face of dangers and obstacles, is able unhesitatingly to make the necessary decisions and put them into effect with an unconquerable energy, so that it sweeps along in its wake the tired, the weak, the doubtful and those who no longer believe in the justice and nobility of the cause they must defend. **743** *(123)*

Who does not see how completely Mary embodied this spirit, deserving thereby the praise given to the "valiant woman"? Her "Magnificat," that canticle of joy **744** *(80, 82)*

742b Prov. 8:15-16, Common of the Feasts of Our Lady.

and of invincible confidence in the Divine Power whose works she undertook to carry out, fills her with holy daring, with a strength unknown to nature.

745
(82)
How earnestly do We wish that all those who today have the responsibility of ensuring the right and proper conduct of public affairs would imitate her example. Instead, is it not perhaps true that there is evident in their ranks at times a sort of tiredness, of resignation, of passivity, which prevents them from facing directly the arduous problems of our days with firmness and perseverance? Some of these persons, it would seem, occasionally drift with the current, instead of dominating events by sound and constructive action.

746
(82,
105)
Is it not then urgent that all the forces of life now held in reserve be mobilized, that those who are not yet fully conscious of the dangerous psychological depression into which they have fallen be aroused? Although Mary's Queenship is most appropriately symbolized by the "acies ordinata," the army set in battle array, surely no one will conceive of any warlike intentions, but only of that strength of mind which We admire in Our Lady to a heroic degree, which comes from the knowledge that one is truly striving for the establishment of God's order in the world.

747
(46,
135)
May then Our invocation to the Queenship of God's Mother obtain for men who are solicitous of their responsibilities the grace to overcome despondency and indolence at this hour when no one may allow himself a moment's rest, when, in so many countries, just freedom is oppressed, truth obscured by the machinations of lying propaganda, and the forces of evil seem to be loosed upon the earth!

Her Queenship is a service

748
(44,
The Queenship of Mary can suggest to rulers of nations attitudes and counsels corresponding to the needs

of our day. But she does not neglect others, never ceasing to pour forth upon all the peoples of the earth and upon all classes of society the abundance of her graces. After witnessing at the foot of the Cross the awful spectacle of the Passion of Our Lord, in which she had offered the most difficult sacrifice that could be asked of a Mother, she continued to lavish her maternal care upon the first Christians, adopted children. A Queen more truly than any other by her elevation of soul and her excelling divine gifts, she never ceases to bestow all the treasures of her affection and loving attention upon a humanity so much in need of compassion. The reign of Mary is far from being founded on the exaction of her rights or on a wish for haughty dominion. Her reign has only one inspiration, the total giving of herself with the highest and fullest generosity.

85, 104, 106, 118)

So it is that Mary exercises her Queenship: accepting our homage and deigning to hear even the humblest and least perfect prayers. Therefore, desiring as We do to interpret the sentiments of all Christian peoples, We raise to the most Blessed Virgin this fervent supplication:

749 *(106, 135)*

Prayer to Mary, Queen

From the depths of this vale of tears where sorrowing humanity makes weary progress—through the surges of the this sea of ours endlessly buffeted by the winds of passion —we raise our eyes to you, O most beloved Mother Mary, to be comforted by the contemplation of your glory and to hail you as Queen of heaven and earth, Queen of mankind.

750 *(102)*

With legitimate filial pride, we wish to exalt your Queenship and to recognize it as due to the sovereign excellence of your whole being, O dearest one, truly Mother of Him who is King by right, by inheritance and by conquest.

751 *(104)*

Reign, O Mother and Queen, by showing us the path of holiness and by guiding and assisting us that we may never stray from it.

752
(84,
100,
102,
106)
In the heights of heaven you exercise your primacy over the choirs of angels who acclaim you as their Sovereign, and over the legions of saints who delight in beholding your dazzling beauty. So, too, reign over the entire human race, above all by opening the path of faith to those who do not yet know your Divine Son.

753
(105,
121)
Reign over the Church, which acknowledges and extols your gentle dominion and has recourse to you as a safe refuge amid the calamities of our day. Reign especially over that part of the Church which is persecuted and oppressed; give it strength to bear adversity, constancy never to yield under unjust compulsion, light to avoid falling into the snares of the enemy, firmness to resist overt attack, and at every moment unwavering faithfulness to your kingdom.

754
(164,
176)
Reign over men's minds, that they may seek only what is true; over their wills, that they may follow solely what is good; over their hearts, that they may love nothing but what you yourself love.

755
(106,
136)
Reign over individuals and over families, as well as over societies and nations; over the assemblies of the powerful, the counsels of the wise, as over the simple aspirations of the humble.

Reign in the streets and in the squares, in the cities and the villages, in the valleys and in the mountains, in the air, on land and on the sea; and hear the pious prayers of all those who recognize that yours is a reign of mercy, in which every petition is heard, every sorrow comforted, every misfortune relieved, every infirmity healed, and in which, at a gesture from your gentle hands, from death itself there arises smiling life.

Obtain for us that all who now in every corner of the world acclaim and hail you Queen and Lady may one day in heaven enjoy the fullness of your kingdom in the vision of your Divine Son, who with the Father and the Holy Ghost, liveth and reigneth for ever and ever. Amen.

OUR LADY'S DESIRES

All. to the Cardinals and Bishops, November 2, 1954.

The consideration of the new liturgical feast of Mary, **756** Mother of God and Queen of Heaven and Earth, which *(102,* We only recently solemnly proclaimed, swells Our holy *118,* joy; for it is only fitting for her children to rejoice when *136,* they see an increase of honor given their Mother. Yet *138)* though she is Queen of all, the Blessed Virgin Mary rules over you, and your plans and undertakings, by a special title and in a more intimate way, for she has long been invoked under that singular and glorious title of Queen of the Apostles. For, being the Mother of fair love, and of fear, and of holy hope, what does she desire more eagerly and strive for more earnestly than that the authentic worship of the true God be ever more deeply implanted in souls, a more genuine charity glow in them, a pure fear of God rule their plans, a hope, solidly based on the promise of immortality, be a solace in this sad exile on earth?

TO THE SACRED HEART THROUGH THE HEART OF MARY

Letter *Cum percepimus,* to the Superior General of the Missionaries of the Sacred Heart, November 14, 1954.

(Congratulations on the centenary of the Institute.)

From the recently instituted liturgical feast of the **757** holy Virgin Mother of God, Queen of Heaven and earth, *(127)* and also from the venerable religious rite with which, in

the Roman Church dedicated to our Lady of the Sacred
Heart, you are about to set a golden crown upon her statue,
We avail Ourselves of this opportunity to exhort you,
under the guidance of so great a Lady and so powerful a
Patroness, to exert yourselves in all ways ever more deeply
to love and honor the Heart of Jesus Christ.

758
(80,
136,
141)
Certain of reaping the plentiful fruits of eternal life,
one may come near to the Heart of Jesus by honoring
religiously and devoutly His Immaculate Mother and by
paying frequent homage to her Virginal Heart, the treasure-
house of all virtues. Do, therefore, set the example of
increasing, with ever more ardent zeal, the maternal dominion of Mary, and strive diligently to make her radiant
image shine brightly in your own minds and in the example given by your own lives; may it be your special honor
to reach this height of perfection.

INVITATION TO CANA

R. M. to the National Marian Congress of India, December 8, 1956.

(*India's Marian devotion, expression of pure faith.*)

759
(26,
115,
127,
139)
Let not those without the Household of the Faith mistake for a moment the meaning, the source and the scope
of your age-old devotion to Mary.
Every flower your children lay at her feet, every song
you sing to her matchless beauty, every appeal to her power and compassion must be known for what it is, first and
finally: the expression and reflection of your personal dedication, after her example, to the living Christ; to the Divine Child whom she deserved, albeit through no merit of
her own, to bear at Bethlehem; to the Divine Teacher,
who deigned to be taught human wisdom at her holy
home in Nazareth (a); to the Divine Victim and Victor

759a Luke 2:51-52.

over sin and death, whose redemptive Sacrifice she saw completed on Calvary.

To Jesus, then, through Mary, leads the spiritual path of that authentic Marian devotion you proudly and publicly profess once more today, at the close of her historic Centenary.   **760** *(47, 52, 136)*

If you have entrusted to her maternal care and vigilance the most delicate and urgent of your family and social problems—witness the ardent resolution of your successive Marian Congresses—the light and strength you seek is not hers to give but only to procure from the Sacred Heart of her Son and Savior. She is the crystal-pure Channel, not the Fountain, of that superabundant divine grace you beg through her Immaculate Heart for home and Church and country.

Continue above all, dearly beloved, to make it clear from your deeds, especially from your corporate program for moral reform and social justice, that the devotion of men and nations to Our Lady must never be restricted to pious sentiment, however noble its motivation, however exalted its object. She is the first to insist an action to confirm your protestations of love, to complement your Christian prayer for help. Her perennial answer to every supplication rings sweetly yet sharply down the ages and across the seven seas from Cana's marriage feast: "Whatsoever He shall say to you, do ye" (a).   **761** *(128, 136-139)*

MYSTICAL ROSE

All. to a group of rose growers, May 10, 1955.

(*Creation, God's garden.—The symbolism of the rose among pagans, in the Church.*)

761a John 2:5.

762   Everywhere the rose signifies Christian joy and be-
(71, comes under this aspect an emblem of Mary, the "great
143, cause of our joy." At first the rosary represented a garden
147, of roses offered to Mary, an ornament of her image, a sym-
148) bol of her graces. Later the Virgin herself was compared
to a rose, and now Christians invoke her twice, in the
Litany of Loreto, under the symbol of the Queen of
flowers: "Mystical Rose" and "Queen of the most holy
Rosary." This last title evokes without doubt a great
victory of Christianity over the infidels but, much more
still, the shining conquests of the faith over evil and over
ignorance of religion.

When Mary appeared to St. Bernadette on the rock
of Massabielle, where the speckled rosebush grew, each
of her feet was adorned with a rose in full flower. She
whom the Church had just proclaimed the Immaculate
manifested in this way, to a poor and artless child, the
fullness of her perfections and the charm of her goodness.

763   The liturgical development of the symbol of the rose
(76, in the cult of Mary should not at all astonish us, for man
84) has instinctively chosen the most beautiful of flowers as
an offering to the most beautiful of creatures. This spontaneous gesture is repeated in various practices of piety
among the learned and the unlettered. Spiritual authors
have often treated this theme and admirably developed its
significance.

764   Gentlemen, We like to think that you find encourage-
(150) ment in your work from the mere thought that the month
of roses is and always will be the month of Mary. Thus,
while cultivating the flowers that are the adornment of
the soil so often unprofitable and difficult for men, you
are naturally led to honor the Creator, to lift your hearts
toward her who bears the beautiful title of Mystical Rose,
the honor and the joy of the human family.

"A WOMAN'S HELP"

All. to the Canadian Women's Press Club, July 2, 1955.

(*Duties of Women Journalists.*)

Your most welcome visit to Eternal Rome, ladies of the Press Club, coincides with the Church's feast of Mary's visit to Elizabeth. The ever heartening strains of her *Magnificat* reminds Us once more that the restoration of a high moral tone to the life, labor, and love of the human family through the merits of Our Lord and Savior was first and forever accomplished with the aid a woman, ever humbly alert to the responsibilities of her maternal mission among the children of men.

765
(40,
41)

May the blessing of the Son of God, through the intercession of His Immaculate Mother, attend your every personal or collective effort to respect and serve His image in your readers, and speed the coming of His Kingdom in the hearts of all His people.

THE PIETÀ

All. to a group of South Africans visiting graves in War Cemeteries, October 19, 1955.

(*Consolation in bereavement.*)

You will be visiting the monuments and hallowed shrines of Our beloved Rome; and as you enter St. Peter's Basilica, We would ask you to pause for a few moments at the first Chapel on the right. The masterpiece of Michelangelo will tell you a story of another Mother, a valiant Mother, the most perfect model of a mother's pure and ardent love that is forged in the fires of sacrifice and heroic submission to the designs of Divine Providence. It was she who stood beneath the Cross when death claimed her Son. During this month of October, the month of the Holy Rosary, the Church particularly tells over in prayerful med-

766
(33,
116,
142,
144)

itation the joys, the sorrows, the exultant glory of that
most blessed of all mothers. You have known some of her
joys, some of her sorrows. It is Our fervent prayer that
you, and the dear ones who have gone before you, may be
granted a share in her glory.

GUIDE OF APOSTLES

Letter *Quidquid Malabarensi,* to the Superior General
the Third Order of Carmelites of Malabar, October 30, 1955.

(*Zeal for the Third Order in Malabar.—Necessity for
uniting prayer to action and action to prayer.*)

767   May the Blessed Virgin Mary, the Glory of Carmel,
(*49,* whom you honor so fervently and love so ardently grant
78,   you her assistance.
165,   Never let your eyes, your minds or your souls be
168) turned away from the brightness of that Star. Look at
Mary! In dangers, difficulties, doubts, think of Mary!
Implore Mary! Let not her name depart from your lips,
nor her thought from your hearts (a).

.May this exhortation of the Mellifluous Doctor be
ever present to your minds: "By following her thou dost
not wander, praying to her thou dost not despair, thinking of her thou dost not make mistakes. If she support
thee, thou dost not fall; if she be propitious to thee, thou
reachest thy goal (b).

Therefore in your apostolic labors and the difficulties
of your ministry take refuge under her very powerful
patronage. If she beseeches her divine Son, you will experience with certainty that there is nothing which you,
sustained by divine grace, are unable to bring to a successful issue.

767a Cf. St. Bernard, Hom. 2 super "Missus est," no. 17.
767b Ibid.

POLAND'S QUEEN

Letter *Gloriosam Reginam,* to the Polish Bishops, December 8, 1955.

For a long, long time the people of Poland, with a devotion difficult to equal, have honored and venerated the glorious Queen of countless triumphs, that incomparable Woman, adorned with a crown of stars, clothed with the sun, who for us gave birth to the Sun of Justice. In return for her devoted children's testimony of their homage, that Mother of God and of men, whose bounty matches her power, has often granted graces generously to that people, in a way more clearly recognizable than the dangers among which it walked were hidden. **768** *(40, 159)*

If the whole of Polish history bears full witness to this, the issue proves it in a special way. That issue came about exactly three centuries ago, in the solemn celebrations at Christmas, and it has been immortalized by abundant documents both civil and religious.

(At the time of the Reformation, Czestochowa was the defence of freedom.—King John Casimir proclaimed Our Lady Queen of Poland.)

These facts, which merit a lasting place in our memory, show in a marvelous way that Mary, the Mother of God, is always near to afford the Polish people help in every vicissitude, especially at this time, when the Catholic faith, the infinitely precious legacy which your forefathers left you, and at the same time the strong and close union with the Apostolic See, which is your strength and your people's honor, are in danger. **769** *(122, 154)*

Through the vigilance of your heavenly benefactress and patroness, those close ties with the Roman See, the Seat of Truth, in spite of continued deceitful allures, never loosened or broke down the ages. Not only is that to the surpassing credit of the Polish people, but it is also for them a powerful incentive to resist with strong determination atheism's attempts at dissolving those ties. Atheism, alas, employs every device to devitalize and corrupt your people, a people so faithful to the Catholic religion.

(*In the struggle put your trust in God's strength.*)

770
(46,
47,
123)
Furthermore, to dispel anxiety, you must lift your eyes to the Mother of God, your Queen, in a renewal of devotion; having crushed the infernal serpent under her heel, she is the mediatrix and dispenser of reward for your every conquest. That gracious Mother will not abandon her beloved Polish people, as your renowned poet, Adam Mickiewicz sings: "They are Mary's champions; they live for her name." But they themselves, unshakable in the Catholic faith which they profess, must remember that it remains for them to imitate the fidelity and inherit the glory of their forefathers.

Under her powerful protection that glory will illumine your fatherland after the storm; it will be the golden light of a happy era and a glory that will long endure.

(*Insidious forms of present persecution.—Prayer for a glorious future.*)

MIRROR OF GOD'S SANCTITY

All. to "Catholic Relief Services," December 8, 1955.

771
(27,
58,
68-
72,
75)
Coming hither on such a festal day as this you cannot but expect to hear a word about Mary, about that precious unparalleled privilege which from the first instant of her existence flooded her soul with grace divine, making it reflect in its sheer white beauty the infinite holiness of her God, who was to become her Son. A privilege it was, indeed, that drew to her at once her Creator's love, while it emphasized the sad lot common to men born an object of God's wrath, a privilege that adds glory to the redemptive power of the divine sacrifice on Golgotha. In honoring Mary, in every thought of her, we do homage to the superabundant mercy and love of the Redeemer of

men, all of whom He wishes to draw into union with Himself through grace and His Holy Spirit.

(*Exhortation to help the poor in the spirit of faith and charity.*)

DOCILITY TO GRACE

All. to the Women's Section of UNESCO, January 26, 1956.

(*In view of the extension of modern science, necessity of deepening interior life.—Spiritual conditions of culture.*)

And how can we here omit to evoke the sweet image of the Blessed Virgin Mary? If she was worthy to give the world its Savior, was it not because she was always, from the first instant of her existence (and particularly at the time of her explicit consent to God's designs upon her), filled with the Holy Spirit, and that she agreed without hestitation to the divine intentions in her regard, and corresponded with them unreservedly? May the holy Mother of God attract and direct you by her example! May she guide your noble efforts for the restoration, among the men of today, of full moral and religious integrity, together with the sense of true values, and the will to respect and promote them. **772** *(25, 82)*

A MOTHER'S TEARS

R. M. to the faithful of Ecuador, April 22, 1956.

(*Introduction.*)

The Virgin wept. Her tears were first prophesied by St. Simeon's words (a), and later forcibly fulfilled even to the letter, in that woman who stood beneath the Cross of her Divine Son (b). Those tears obtained for us grace and salvation. **773** *(43, 120, 122,*

773a Luke 2:35.
773b John 19:25.

168)   According to the reports of witnesses, the Virgin, even in the midst of her eternal felicity, and as a sign of her motherly solicitude for her children's salvation, showed anguish and sadness to the point of appearing about to burst unrestrainedly into tears, when witnessing your nation subverted by persecution, stained with blood, and driven to extremes through sectarian hatred, to such a degree that the ancient and sacred inheritance of the faith was endangered, especially if the plan for dechristianizing the education of children should be carried through.

Who could doubt that it was that anguish and sorrow which obtained from heaven the necessary strength to restrain the power of evil and prepare this springtime of souls, the fruits of which you have now the joy to contemplate?

774   They were tears but precious tears which, beloved
(85,   sons, deserve your most sincere gratitude.
100)   They were sorrows but sorrows of which you are now enjoying the fruits, and in which you must rightly see a very special token of her maternal love.

Therefore, celebrations and rejoicing are most appropriate, as also the golden crown, if all this reminds you once more of the sublime paradox which makes of motherhood a source of tears, and converts every mother, conscious of her own mission, into a heroine of duty.

Our Mother's comfort

775   But all your homage and these splendid celebrations
(170)   would amount merely to some noise which the wind carries away, if your devout consideration did not stop for a while to think: "The Virgin wept, but is she not perhaps weeping again today, and maybe through my own fault?"

776   As a matter of fact, beloved children, with what
(85,   eyes could she, for example, behold a life of faith reduced

to a number of outward manifestations, deprived of that *135,*
inner supernatural spirit which gives value to everything, *139)*
and without which external acts are worthless?

What will be the effect upon her of seeing a heart
full of pride and arrogance, regarding the poor and
humble with contempt, and seemingly unable to do anything but appear superior to any one who dares come
into his presence?

Will she find the love due to her Divine Son, the
obedience due to the Church, the observance of God's
commandments and the Church's precepts?

The Virgin wept, beloved sons, and we should not
be truthful, as we ought to be, if we were not to tell you
that We are very much afraid that she may be weeping
still, though of course We do not doubt that you are
giving her consolation and joy by your filial piety, more
especially at this particular time.

True filial piety

It is Quito, the legendary and historical Quito, which **777**
standing on the banks of the proud Pichincha, and crowned *(128,*
with volcanic summits, seems to be slumbering and dream- *177)*
ing of glory in the serene peace of its high vale; it is
Quito, the city of the enchanting "Azucena" (whom We
Ourselves have had the peculiar satisfaction of raising to
the highest honor of the altar), which has today prepared this triumph for its sorrowful Mother, thereby paying an old debt of gratitude, in which that which counts
more than gold and precious stones—as in any filial gift—
is the heart with which it is offered.

It is a happy city for, as the Holy Spirit tells us: "He
that honoreth his mother is as one that layeth up a treasure" (a); a joyful city, and a joyful country if you be true
to what, on this solemn occasion, you have promised, because, as we said, paraphrasing the expression of a great

777a Eccl. 3:5

Doctor of the Church (b), it is right that your first thought should have been that of honoring your Mother, and thereafter should have come the intention of avoiding sin and of leading a better life. But if, some day, such intention were to be forgotten; in that case you did not really show your gratitude, and honors and praises are worth nothing.

(*Prayer to Mary on behalf of Ecuador.*)

DEVOTION TO THE HOLY HEARTS

Encycl. *Haurietis aquas,* May 15, 1956.

(*Devotion to the Sacred Heart.—Its foundations.—Its history.—Its manifestations.*)

778
(13,
37,
44,
141,
177)
That graces for the Christian family and for the whole human race may flow more abundantly from devotion to the Sacred Heart, let the faithful strive to join it closely with devotion to the Immaculate Heart of the Mother of God. By the will of God, the most Blessed Virgin Mary was inseparably joined with Christ in accomplishing the work of man's redemption, so that our salvation flows from the love of Jesus Christ and His sufferings intimately united with the love and sorrows of His Mother. It is, then, highly fitting that after due homage has been paid to the Most Sacred Heart of Jesus, Christian people who have obtained divine life from Christ through Mary manifest similar piety and the love of their grateful souls for the most loving heart of our heavenly Mother (a).

The memorable act of consecration by which We Ourselves, in the wise and loving dispositions of Divine Providence, solemnly dedicated the Church and the whole world to the Immaculate Heart of the Blessed Virgin Mary is in perfect accord with devotion to the Sacred Heart.

777b St. Augustine, *Enarr. in Ps.* 75, no. 14.
778a Cf. above, no. 373 ff.

TEACHER OF SANCTITY

Apost. Const. *Sedes Sapientiæ*, May 31, 1956.

The Seat of Wisdom, Mother of the God of all knowl- **779**
edge, and Queen of the Apostles, the most holy Virgin *(46,*
Mary, to whose veneration We have dedicated an entire *121,*
Holy Year, is rightly held to be, in a special way, the *165,*
Mother and Teacher of all who embrace the state of *166)*
acquiring perfection while striving to carry on the apostolic
warfare of Christ the High Priest. In order to devote themselves successfully to the undertaking and development of
this high vocation, which is on the one hand religious and
on the other priestly and apostolic, these individuals
stand in great need of her guidance and help. For she has
been appointed Mediatrix of all the graces which look
toward sanctification and is properly called Mother and
Queen of the Catholic priesthood and apostolate. Wherefore We earnestly implore her favor that she who obtained
divine light for Us as We drew up these norms may likewise lend gracious assistance to those whose duty it will
be to put them into effect.

(*Principles are given and General Statutes approved
which are to form and direct those called.*)

THE SAFEGUARD OF THE FAITH

All. to the pilgrims of Lichtenstein, July 27, 1956.

(*The small extent of the State compensated for by the
stupendous natural beauties and Catholic traditions.—Remain firm in the faith.*)

There exists a powerful aid to remaining faithful to **780**
the Catholic faith in any kind of society, even in that of *(136)*
our present days. You yourselves have acknowledged such
aid through a precious collection of Marian Year stamps,
which came among the gifts We received from you. This

gift is a sign of the living and authentic devotion to the Virgin Mary among you and in more than one of your neighboring regions.

Venerate her as a sacred inheritance from your fore-fathers. Be faithful to Mary! You will have no fear for your faith and your true happiness.

God grant you His grace!

MOTHER OF ORPHANS

Prayer: *Salve, O Vergine*, composed by Pius XII, August 28, 1956.

781
(100, 121, 162)
Hail, O Virgin most pure, most powerful Queen whom the human family invokes by the sweet name of Mother! We who cannot invoke an earthly mother either because we never knew her or were very soon deprived of such a sweet and necessary support, we turn to thee, certain that thou shalt be a mother to us in a special manner.

If, indeed, because of our condition, we arouse in every one feelings of pity, compassion and love, we shall awaken such feelings to a much higher degree in thee, the most loving, most tender and most merciful of all pure creatures.

O true Mother of all Orphans, we take refuge in thy Immaculate Heart, certain of receiving therein all the comfort for which our bereft hearts are yearning.

We place all our trust in thee so that thy maternal hand may guide and support us along the steep paths of this life.

782
(37, 52, 131)
Bless all those who assist or protect us in thy name; reward our benefactors and the chosen souls that devote their lives to us. Above all, be ever to us a Mother, model-ing our hearts, enlightening our minds, strengthening our wills, adorning our souls with every virtue, and keeping away from us the enemies of our God who would wish to ruin us forever!

Finally, dearest Mother, our delight and our hope, lead us to Jesus, the blessed fruit of thy womb, so that if we have not enjoyed the sweetness of a mother here below, we may hereafter, in everlasting life, enjoy thy motherly love and thy presence, together with that of thy Divine Son who lives and reigns with the Father and the Holy Spirit forever and ever. Amen!

THE SERVANT OF GOD

R. M. to the Federation of Italian Women on pilgrimage to Loreto, October 14, 1956.

(*Welcome.*)

How We would like to see all the women of Italy and of the world, with your spirit and ardor, crowd around the throne of the Virgin so that her lofty example might teach them the secret of every greatness and the best way to carry out in their own lives God's designs, which correspond to the deepest and purest aspirations of their hearts! The constant tradition of the Church in proposing Mary to Christian women as the sublime model of a Virgin and a Mother shows the high esteem that Christianity nourishes for womanhood and the immense trust which the Church herself rests in woman's power for good and in her mission on behalf of the family and of society.

783
*(131,
163,
166)*

(*The dignity of woman; her equality with man as a child of God; her proper vocation: motherhood, virginity.— The program of the Federation; interior life, social and civic action.*)

Beloved daughters, listening to Our words on the green slopes of the Shrine of Loreto, and all of you who are in the equally sacred intimacy of your own homes, We cannot say good-bye without alluding again to the spiritual presence of Mary, Blessed among women, in the hope

784
*(82,
114)*

of drawing from her maternal Heart, on concluding Our
exhortation, inspiration and a promise of efficacious
assistance.

When the Archangel Gabriel told the humble Handmaid of the Lord of the lofty mission that God had marked
out for her, her profound humility could not see anything
in herself proportionate to the grandeur of the destiny
announced to her. With the voice of a handmaid who is
ready and willing to serve but not knowing how she
could, she answered, "Quomodo fiet istud"—"How shall
this be done?" The Archangel reassured her, reminding
her of the power of the Most High and that nothing is
impossible to God (a).

(*Lesson of courage and confidence.*)

OUR LADY OF THE EMIGRANTS

R. M. to the faithful of Argentina, December 2, 1956.

785
(78)
With the splendor and magnificence of which you
are capable, most beloved children, you the Catholics of
Argentina, with that devotion and fervor with which We
are well acquainted, are preparing to receive your beloved
Mother, the Virgin Mary, whose name has, of itself, always
been sufficient to awaken your highest enthusiasm and energies. You are preparing to welcome her under her new
title, "Our Lady of the Emigrants," as a new gift from
heaven to your souls craving for peace, mercy and maternal affection, as a new opportunity of manifesting your
devotion and charity, together with all the other virtues
with which you are adorned.

786
(78,
But had not, perhaps, the Argentine nation honored
its most holy Mother already during the whole of its

784a Luke 1:34 ff.

history, from the Sanctuary of Lujan, almost at the gates 160)
of Buenos Aires, to the Virgin of the Miracle of Salta, or
our Lady of Consolation at Santiago del Estero?

Who can count the churches, chapels and hermitages
which you dedicated on your soil to the Virgin of the Holy
Rosary, not to mention the famous shrine of Our Lady of
Carmel at Cordoba and that of Our Lady of Mercy at
Cuyo, honored by your Capital itself?

Who does not know of your fervent devotion to Our
Lady of the Valley of Catamarca, and of a thousand other
titles, so numerous that it is difficult to choose among them?

(*Argentina, prepared by Divine Providence for immigration.—Present immigration movement.*)

Today, this whole immigration movement is being 787
entrusted to the gentle hands of the most loving of mothers. (100,
May "Our Lady of the Emigrants" watch over these chil- 167)
dren and through her powerful intercession obtain for them
those graces of which they stand so much in need in the
course of their difficult labors.

(*Prayer to Our Lady of the Emigrants.—Setting forth
the needs of those seeking her protection.*)

PRAYER OF PILGRIMS TO LOURDES

Prayer: *Dociles à l'invitation,* composed by Pius XII,
May 17, 1957.

Obedient to the invitation given in thine own mater- 788
nal words, O Virgin Immaculate of Lourdes, we hurry to (155,
thy feet at the humble grotto, where thou didst vouchsafe 178)
to appear to point out the way of prayer and penance to
those gone astray and to dispense the graces and wonders
of thy supreme goodness to the sick.

O gracious Queen, accept the homage and the prayers
that the peoples and the nations, caught in bitter straits,
trustingly raise to thee.

789
(37,
121,
131)

O resplendent vision of Paradise, dispel from our minds the darkness of error by the light of Faith! O mystical garden of roses, comfort the broken hearts of men with the heavenly perfume of hope! O inexhaustible fountain of saving waters, refresh with the floods of divine charity hearts that are dry.

Grant that we, thy children, may be consoled in our sorrows, protected in danger, and sustained in our struggles! May we love and serve thy dear Son Jesus in such a way that we may deserve eternal joy before thy throne in heaven above. Amen.

A PRAYER FOR CHRISTIAN WOMEN

Prayer: *O piena di grazia,* composed by Pius XII, May 26, 1957.

790
(55,
57)

O Mary, "full of grace and blessed among women" (a), stretch out the hand of thy motherly protection, we beseech thee, upon us who gather round thy queenly throne as thy handmaidens, obedient to thy command and resolved wtih thy help to bring to realization in ourselves and our sisters the ideals of truth and Christian perfecton.

Our eyes are fixed on thee in admiration, immaculate Virgin; thou who art loved by the Heavenly Father above all others! O Virgin Spouse of the Holy Spirit! Tender Mother of Jesus! Obtain for us from thy Divine Son the grace to reflect thy sublime virtues in our conduct, according to our age and condition of life.

791
(163)

Grant that we may be spotless and pure in our thoughts and in our behavior; gentle, affectionate, and sympathetic companions to our husbands; to our children solicitous, vigilant and wise mothers; prudent administrators of our homes; exemplary citizens of our dear country; faithful

790a Luke 1:28, 42.

daughters of the Church, ever ready to allow ourselves to be guided by her in thought and deed.

Help us, loving Mother, to be truly devoted to the **792** duties of our state of life; help us make our homes true *(163)* centers of spiritual life and active charity, schools where consciences will be rightly formed, gardens where every virtue will flourish. Give us thy help that in social and political life we may be patterns of deep faith, of consistent and gracious Christian practice, of incorruptible integrity, and of well-balanced judgment based upon the solid principles of religion.

Bless these our resolutions which you have inspired us to make and the trials you have helped us to bear; may we with your aid come to see their abundant fruits in time and in eternity. Amen.

CENTENARY ENCYCLICAL

Encycl. *Le pèlerinage,* to the Cardinals and bishops of France, July 2, 1957.

The pilgrimage to Lourdes, which We once had the **793** happiness of making, has left in the depths of Our heart the *(115)* most happy memories. We went there to preside, in the name of Our Predecessor, Pius XI, at the Eucharistic and Marian celebrations which closed the Jubilee Year of the Redemption. It is therefore a great pleasure to Us to learn that, on the initiative of the Bishop of Tarbes and Lourdes, the city of Mary is making ready to celebrate with all due splendor the centenary of the Apparitions of the Immaculate Virgin in the Grotto of Massabielle, and that for this purpose an international committee has been set up, under the presidency of the most Eminent Cardinal Eugene Tisserant, Dean of the Sacred College. We desire to associate Ourselves with you, dear Sons and Venerable Brethren, in thanking God for the singular favor granted to your country and for the countless graces bestowed in the course of the past century on the multitude of pilgrims. At the same time We wish to exhort all Our sons to renew in this jubilee year their confident and fervent devotion towards her who, in the words of St. Pius X, deigned to establish at Lourdes "the seat of her boundless kindness" (a).

Sanctuaries and Apparitions of Our Lady in France

794
(152,
159)
Every Christian land is a land of Mary, and there is no land redeemed by Christ's blood but loves to proclaim Mary as its Mother and Patron. This truth stands out in bold relief as we recall the history of France. The devotion to the Mother of God goes back to the time when the Gospel was first preached in the land; and among the most ancient sanctuaries of Mary, Chartres still draws many pilgrims: young men and women especially go there in their thousands. The Middle Ages, which, particularly with St. Bernard, sang the glories of Mary and honored her mysteries, saw the wonderful flowering of your cathedrals dedicated to our Lady—Le Puy, Rheims, Amiens, Paris and so many more. From far off their spires proclaim the glory of Mary Immaculate; they make it shine in the pure light of their stained-glass windows and the harmonious beauty of their statuary. Above all they bear testimony to the faith of a people which felt impelled to soar upwards and raise in the skies of France a lasting witness to its love of Mary.

795
(159)
In towns and in the countryside, on the tops of hills or on cliffs above the sea, sanctuaries dedicated to Mary, whether humble chapels or great basilicas, came gradually to spread over the land their protective shadow. Princes and shepherds, countless numbers of the faithful, in the course of centuries made their way to the shrines of the Blessed Virgin, whom they invoked under titles expressive of their confidence or their gratitude. In one place it was Notre-Dame de Miséricorde (our Lady of Mercy), de Toute

793a   Letter, July 12, 1914, cf. above, no. 259.

Aide (of All Help) or de Bon Secours (of Succor); in another Notre-Dame de la Garde (our Lady of Protection),
our Lady of Pity or of Consolation; elsewhere the pilgrim
called upon our Lady of Light, of Peace, of Joy or of
Hope; or again he invoked her as our Lady of Virtues, or
Miracles or of Victories—a veritable Litany, still incom-
plete, of titles that tell of the blessings that, in the course
of ages, the Mother of God has shed over every province
of the land of France.

Yet the nineteenth century, after the storm of the   **796**
revolution had passed, has many claims to be regarded   *(150)*
as the century of Mary's special favor. To take only one
example: everyone has heard of the "miraculous medal."
This medal, revealed in the heart of the French capital
to a humble daughter of St. Vincent de Paul—one whom
We had the joy of inscribing on the roll of the saints—and
struck with an image of "Mary conceived without sin," has
worked miracles in all parts of the world, some spiritual
and some material. A few years later, from February 11
to July 16, 1858, it pleased our Lady to grant a new favor.
In the region of the Pyrenees she appeared to a devout
and innocent girl, the child of a Christian family which
knew poverty and hard toil. To quote Our own words:
"she came to Bernadette, she entrusted her secrets to her,
made her her collaborator, the instrument of her own
maternal tenderness and of the merciful omnipotence of
her Son, to restore the world in Christ by an unmatched
outpouring of redemptive grace" (a).

Lourdes

There is no need for Us to recount to you what then   **797**
happened at Lourdes; but we are today in a better position *(155)*
to see those events in their true spiritual perspective. You

796a All. of April 28, 1935, at Lourdes: Eugenio Cardi-
    nal Pacelli.

know well, dear Sons and venerable Brethren, the amazing
way in which the message received by this child from the
Immaculate Virgin compelled acceptance by the world in
spite of ridicule, doubt and opposition. You know too how
firm and pure was the testimony she bore and how, after
being prudently tested by the episcopal authority, it was
sanctioned by that authority as early as 1862.

798   Already the crowds were gathering there, and they
(155) have never ceased to flock towards the grotto of the
Apparitions, the miraculous spring and the sanctuary
raised at Mary's request. The unending procession of the
humble, the sick, and the afflicted touches the heart,
whether it is the thousands who come on a diocesan or
a national pilgrimage or whether it is one troubled soul
who comes, unknown to anyone else, seeking the truth.
"Never in any place on earth," We have said, "will you
find a comparable procession of the suffering or such
radiant peace, serenity and joy" (a). Never, we might add,
will anyone know the sum total of the blessings that the
world owes to the help our Lady gives. "Happy the cave
in which Christ's Mother was seen! Honored those rocks
from which gushed the waters that bring life" (b).

Lourdes and the Popes

799   This hundred years of devotion to Mary has, so to
(155) speak, woven close bonds between the See of Peter and
the shrine in the Pyrenees, which it is a pleasure to Us to
recall; nor can one doubt that the Virgin Mary herself
desired it so. "What the Sovereign Pontiff at Rome defined
by his infallible teaching authority, the Immaculate Mother of God wished, it would seem, to confirm by her own

798a Ibid.
798b *O specus felix, decorate divæ Matris aspectu! Vene-
        randa rupes, unde vitales scatuere pleno gurgite lymphæ!*
        Office of the feast of the Appearance.

mouth when, a little later, she revealed herself by a celebrated Apparition in the grotto of Massabielle" (a). Not
that the infallible word of the Roman Pontiff, the authentic
interpreter of divine truth, stood in need of any confirmation from on high to gain the assent of faith from Catholics;
but it was with heartfelt gratitude that the faithful and
their pastors received from the lips of Bernadette the
heaven-sent assurance: "I am the Immaculate Conception."

Thus, it is not surprising that Our Predecessors were **800**
pleased to multiply their favors towards this sanctuary. *(155,*
Already in 1869 Pius IX, of holy memory, rejoiced that the *158)*
opposition raised against Lourdes by the malice of men
served only "to manifest with greater force the clear evidence of the fact" (a). And strong in this assurance he
heaped spiritual favors on the newly-built church and had
the statue of our Lady of Lourdes crowned. Leo XIII,
in 1892, granted the proper Office and Mass for the
feast of "the Apparition of the Blessed Virgin Mary Immaculate," which his successor was soon to extend to the
universal Church. The ancient text of Scripture would
thenceforward find a new application: "Arise my love, my
beautiful one and come: my dove in the clefts of the rock,
in the hollow places of the wall" (b).

Towards the end of his life the same great Pope **801**
personally opened and blessed the reproduction of the *(155,*
grotto of Massabielle in the Vatican gardens; and about *158)*
the same time he composed a prayer to our Lady of
Lourdes in which he asked with confidence: "that in her
power the Virgin Mother, who in times past cooperated
by her love in the birth of the faithful in the Church, may

799a Decree *de Tuto* for the canonizattion of St. Bernadette,
    July 2, 1933.
800a Letter of September 4, 1869, to Henri Lassere.
800b *Surge, amica mea, speciosa mea, et veni: columba mea
    in foraminibus petræ, in caverna maceriæ.* Cant. 2:13-14.
    Gradual for the Mass of our Lady of Lourdes.

still be the instrument and guardian of our salvation; that she may bring back tranquillity and peace to troubled hearts and hasten, in society and in the family, the return to Jesus Christ" (a).

St. Pius X: Lourdes and the Eucharist

802
(155) The fiftieth anniversary of the dogmatic definition of the Immaculate Conception gave St. Pius X the occasion to attest in a formal document the historic link between this act of the Church's teaching authority and the Appearances at Lourdes: "Hardly had Pius IX defined as of Catholic faith that Mary was exempt from original sin when the Blessed Virgin herself began to work miracles at Lourdes" (a). A little later he created the episcopal title of Lourdes, joined with that of Tarbes, and signed the introduction of the cause of Bernadette's beatification.

803
(127,
131,
155) It was this great Pope too who stressed and encouraged the union which we find at Lourdes between the worship of the Blessed Sacrament and prayer to Mary: "devotion to the Mother of God," he notes, "causes to flourish there a burning love of Christ our Lord" (a). Nor could it be otherwise. Everything in Mary leads us towards her Son, our only Savior, by whose foreseen merits she was preserved immaculate and full of grace; everything in Mary lifts up our hearts to the praise of the Holy Trinity; and blessed was Bernadette who, as she recited her rosary before the grotto, learned from the lips and the eyes of the Blessed Virgin to give glory to the Father, the Son and the Holy Ghost.

804
(155) We too are happy to associate Ourselves with this testimony of St. Pius X: "the special glory of the sanctuary

801a Brief of September 8, 1901, cf. above, no. 216.
802a Encycl., *Ad diem illum* of February 2, 1904, cf. above, no. 222.
803a Letter of July 12, 1914, cf. above, no. 222.

of Lourdes is to be found in this fact—that people from all parts are drawn by Mary to adore Jesus Christ in the Blessed Sacrament, so that this sanctuary, at once the center of devotion to Mary and the throne of the mystery of the Holy Eucharist, would seem to surpass in glory all others in the Catholic world" (a).

Benedict XV granted new indulgences to this sanc- **805** tuary, already so rich in spiritual privileges; and if the *(155)* tragic circumstances of his pontificate made it impossible for him to testify to his devotion by public acts, he none the less willed to honor the city of Mary by granting to its bishop the privilege of wearing the pallium at the place where our Lady appeared.

Pius XI, who had himself gone as a pilgrim to Lourdes, **806** carried on the work and had the joy of raising to the al- *(155)* tars her to whom our Lady had appeared, known in religion as Sister Marie Bernard, of the Congregation of Charity and Christian Instruction. In so doing he verified, in a sense, our Lady's promise to the young Bernadette "to make her happy not in this world but in the next." And from that time onwards Nevers, where the body of the Saint is enshrined, has drawn many Lourdes pilgrims desiring to learn from her how to receive fittingly our Lady's message.

A little later this illustrious Pope, who had recently **807** sent a Legate to honor the anniversary festivities of the *(155)* Apparitions, decided to close the Jubilee Year of the Redemption at the grotto of Massabielle. For there, in his own words: "The Immaculate Virgin Mary appeared many times to the Blessed Bernadette Soubirous and there she lovingly called on all men to do penance, at that same grotto where the Apparitions took place, where she poured

804a Brief of April 25, 1911.

out graces and miracles" (a). "In truth," concluded Pius XI, "this sanctuary is now rightly regarded as one of the principal sanctuaries of Mary in the whole world" (b).

Pius XII and Lourdes

808
(155)
To this chorus of praise We could not fail to add Our voice. We did so notably in Our Encyclical *Fulgens Corona* of September 8, 1953, recalling, like Our Predecessors, that "the Blessed Virgin Mary seemed to wish to confirm by a miracle the proclamation made by the Vicar of her Divine Son, to the joy of the whole Church" (a). And We recalled on this occasion how the Roman Pontiffs, realizing the importance of the pilgrimage, had never ceased to manifest their affectionate interest "by enriching it with spiritual favors and benefits."

809
(155)
The history of these hundred years, which we have just outlined, is an effective illustration of the fatherly care shown by successive Popes, of which the last act was the closing at Lourdes of the Jubilee Year of the dogma of the Immaculate Conception. But We would like especially to remind you, dear Sons and venerable Brethren, of a recent document in which We gave encouragement to that missionary apostolate which has sprung up in your beloved country. We had it at heart to call attention to "the outstanding merits that France has gained for herself over the course of centuries in the progress of the Catholic faith." And so "We turned Our mind and Our heart to Lourdes where, four years after the definition of the dogma, Mary Immaculate herself confirmed supernaturally by her Apparitions, by her words and by miracles what the supreme Teacher had declared" (a).

807a Brief of January 11, 1933.
807b Ibid.
808a Cf. above, no. 584.
809a Apost. Constit. *Omnium Ecclesiarum*, August 15, 1954.

Today We still turn towards the world-famous sanc- **810** tuary which is preparing to welcome on the banks of the *(155)* Gave the crowd of pilgrims for the centenary. And if for a century past fervent prayers, public and private, have there obtained from God, by the intercession of Mary, so many graces of healing and of conversion, We have the firmest confidence that in this jubilee year our Lady will once more respond generously to the expectations of her children. But above all We have the conviction that she is urging us all to take to heart the spiritual lessons of her Apparitions and to pledge ourselves to walk in the path she has so clearly traced out for us.

The lessons of Lourdes

These lessons, which are a faithful echo of the Gospel **811** message, manifest in striking contrast the judgment of *(155,* God as opposed to the vain wisdom of this world. In a *170)* society which was hardly aware of the evils which were eating away its very roots, which covered up its wretchedness and its injustices with a veil of brilliant and carefree prosperity, the Immaculate Virgin, whom sin had never touched, showed herself to an innocent girl. With motherly compassion she cast her eyes over this world, redeemed by the blood of her Son but where sin daily spread ruin, and uttered her urgent appeal: "Repentance, repentance, repentance." She asked also for acts expressing it: "Go and kiss the ground in penance for sinners."

But gestures were not enough; to them prayer must **812** be added: "You must pray to God for sinners." As in the *(155,* days of St. John the Baptist, as at the beginning of our *170)* Lord's ministry, the same stern command shows men the way to return to God: "Repent" (a). And no one could venture to say that in our days this appeal for a conversion of heart is no longer to the point.

812a Matt. 3:4, 17.

But the Mother of God could never come to her children without a message of pardon and of hope. Already the water was flowing at her feet: "All you that thirst, come to the waters, and you shall draw salvation from the Lord" (b). Bernadette was the first to drink at the spring, in obedience to our Lady's command; but later there would come to it all those who suffer in soul or body. "I went and washed and now I see" (c), the grateful pilgrim would be able to say, like the blind man in the Gospel. But as for the crowds who pressed around our Lord, so at Lourdes the cures of physical infirmities are at the same time acts of compassion and signs that the Son of Man has power to forgive sin. At the sacred grotto our Lady calls us to a conversion of heart and the hope of pardon. Can we turn a deaf ear to her appeal?

813
(155)
This jubilee year will be really and truly a great year if men respond by humbly recognizing their own sinfulness. The Church would rightly expect countless blessings if every pilgrim going to Lourdes—and, for that matter, every Christian united in heart to the centenary celebrations—were really to sanctify himself first of all, "not in words nor in tongue, but in deed and in truth" (a).

814
(155)
Everything there encourages us to become holy, for nowhere so much as at Lourdes does one feel the urge to prayer, self-forgetfulness and charity. No one can witness unmoved the devotion of the stretcher-bearers and the serene peace of the sick, the brotherhood which unites the faithful from different parts of the world in the same prayers, the spontaneous mutual help, the unaffected fervor of the pilgrims kneeling before the grotto. When they see all these things, ordinarily good Christians feel drawn to a life more completely given to the service of God and of

812b *Omnes sitientes, venite ad aquas, et haurietis salutem a Domino.* Office of our Lady of Lourdes.
812c John 9:11.
813a 1 John 3:18.

their brethren, the less fervent become conscious of their lukewarmness and take up again the serious practice of prayer, while hardened sinners and even unbelievers are often touched by grace. At least, if they are sincere, they do not remain quite insensible to the witness of the "multitude of believers who have but one heart and soul" (a).

Yet the experience of a few short days on a pilgrimage **815** does not generally suffice to impress indelibly on men's *(155)* hearts Mary's appeal for a genuine spiritual conversion. We therefore exhort the pastors of dioceses and all priests to rival one another in zeal to make sure that the pilgrims for the centenary benefit by an adequate preparation for their pilgrimage. In the course of the pilgrimage it must be brought home to them what they are engaged upon; and afterwards there must be a "follow-up," so that the action of grace may be deep and lasting. Every pilgrimage should have for its fruit a return to the frequentation of the sacraments, a regard for the moral law in all the circumstances of life and enrollments in Catholic Action and other good works commended by the Church. Only thus will the vast flow of pilgrims to Lourdes foreseen in 1958 bear, as our Lady herself expects, the fruits of salvation so needed by mankind in our times.

The Evils of Materialism

But though the conversion of the individual pilgrim **816** must be the first consideration, this alone is not enough. *(155)* We exhort you, dear Sons and venerable Brethren, in this jubilee year to rouse the faithful committed to your care to make a collective effort for the Christian renewal of society in response to Mary's appeal. It was the prayer of Pius XI at the time of the Marian celebrations in the Jubilee Year of the Redemption "that blinded souls should receive the light of truth and justice, that those whom

814a Acts 4:32.

error has led astray should be led back to the right path, that a just liberty should everywhere be granted to the Church and an era of peace and true prosperity drawn upon the nations" (a).

The world today has many just causes for pride and for hope; but at the same time it is subject to a terrible temptation to that materialism which Our Predecessors and We Ourselves have so often denounced.

817
(155)   It is not only the basis of that philosophy, already condemned, that underlies the politics and economic system of a portion of mankind; it is manifested also in that love of money which, in proportion to the large scale of modern enterprises, weighs heavily upon the lives of so many people. It betrays itself in the cult of the body, the excessive seeking for comfort and the shunning of any kind of austerity in life; it extends to the contempt of human life— even unborn life which it destroys before it has seen the light of day. It is present in the unbridled pursuit of pleasure which parades its shamelessness and tries to seduce souls still innocent, through literature and entertainments; it reveals itself in regardlessness for our brother's welfare, in the selfishness which crushes him and the injustice which denies him his rights. In a word it is a conception of life as regulated solely in view of material prosperity and earthly satisfactions. " 'My soul,' the rich man said, 'thou hast much goods laid up for many years. Take thy rest; eat, drink, make good cheer.' But God said to him: 'Thou fool, this night do they require thy soul of thee' " (a).

All should labor for the renewal of Christian society

818
(155)   Our Lady, with motherly love, has raised her voice to alert to its dangers a society which often denies even

816a Letter of January 10, 1935.
817a Luke 12:19-20.

the supreme rights of God and, wishing to gain the whole world at the price of its soul, runs the risk of losing it. Therefore let priests preach fearlessly to all men the great truths of salvation. There can be no lasting renewal but one founded on the irrefragable principles of faith; and it is for priests to form the consciences of a Christian people. If Mary Immaculate, having pity on our wretchedness but with clear sight of our real needs, has come to remind men that the first step is religious conversion, those who are ministers of God's word must point out with supernatural assurance to the faithful the narrow way which leads to life. They will be gentle and patient, for this is the spirit of their calling, yet without ever toning down the demands of the Gospel. They will learn in the school of Mary to live only to give Christ to the world and, if need be, to stand at the foot of the cross and await with faith the hour of Jesus.

The faithful must rally round their priests and collaborate in this effort for a renewal of Christian life. Let them ask themselves whether they could not do something more for the cause of God in that place, in those circles, where His Providence has placed them. Our thoughts turn first of all to the many souls consecrated to God and devoted to innumerable good works in the Church. The vows of religion bind them more than all others to strive till victory is gained against the uncontrolled desires for independence, riches and pleasures let loose over the world. At the call of Mary Immaculate it will be their determination to oppose the assaults of the powers of evil with the arms of prayer and penance and the victories that charity can win. **819** *(155)*

Our thoughts turn at the same time to Christian families, to adjure them to remain faithful to their irreplaceable mission in society. Let them in this jubilee year consecrate themselves to the Immaculate Heart of Mary. This act of **820** *(164)* piety will be a precious spiritual help to them in their duty of chastity and conjugal fidelity and will preserve the atmosphere of purity in the home where children are growing up. More, it will make the family, revitalized by devotion to Mary, a living cell in the social body, working from within for its regeneration.

821
(155)   Beyond the family circle, professional and civic contacts also afford to Christians who are anxious to work for the renewal of society a vast field for action. Gathering at the feet of Mary and ready to learn from her, they will first of all make a searching examination of conscience and root out from their hearts false judgments and selfishness. We have reason to fear that we are acting a lie if our love of God does not translate itself into an effective love of our brothers. Christians of all classes and nations must unite among themselves in truth and charity, laying aside mutual misunderstandings and suspicions.

822
(155)   Our complicated social structure and economic pressure sometimes put a strain on men's good will and seem to paralyze it. But if it is true, as Our Predecessors and We Ourselves have often insisted, that the possibility of social and political peace is primarily a moral question, no reform can be fruitful and no agreements enduring without a change and a purification of men's hearts. To this our Lady of Lourdes calls all men in this jubilee year.

Mary's invitations

823
(167)   And if Mary seems to choose some of her children as her favorites, singling them out for special care, it is because Jesus showed a special love for children, the poor and the sick: "Come to me, all you that labor and are burdened, and I will refresh you" (a).

823a Matt. 19:11, 18.

"Go to her," We say to those who are oppressed by   **824**
poverty and defenceless against the hardships of life and   *(167)*
the indifference of men. "Go to her," We say to those who
have inward trials to bear and to the sick and infirm, who
are received and honored at Lourdes as the suffering members of Christ. "Go to her and receive peace of mind,
strength to fulfill the duties each day brings and joy in
sacrifice." The Immaculate Virgin, who knows the secret
ways of grace in men's souls and the silent work of the
supernatural leaven in the world, knows the priceless
worth in the eyes of God of your sufferings united with
those of our Savior. They will contribute powerfully, We
are sure, towards that Christian renewal of society which
We beg God to grant by the intercession of His Mother.

May Mary, at the prayer of the sick and the humble   **825**
and of all the Lourdes pilgrims, look down upon all those   *(155,*
who still remain outside the one fold of the Church and   *171,*
upon those who are seeking and thirsting for the truth and   *172)*
lead them to the fountain of living waters. May she cast
her glance over those vast continents and territories where
Christ is so little known and so little loved and obtain for
the Church, ever young, holy and apostolic, the liberty and
the joy of responding to the expectations of mankind.

"Will you be good enough to come," the Blessed Virgin   **826**
said to Bernadette. This courteous invitation, which im-   *(155)*
poses no constraint but speaks to the heart and gently
invites us to respond freely and generously, the Mother
of God extends once more to the sons of France and to
the whole world. Christians will not turn a deaf ear to
this appeal. To all of them, as a conclusion to this letter,
We would say with St. Bernard: "In dangers, in straits, in
doubts think of Mary, call upon Mary... Following her,
you will not lose your way; praying to her, you will not
despair; thinking of her, you will not go astray; if she
holds you, you will not fall; under her protection you

need have no fear; under her guidance you will not tire;
if she be kind, you will reach your journey's end" (a).

827
(155) We are confident, dear Sons and venerable Brethren,
that Mary will hear your prayers and Ours. This we ask
of her on the feast of the Visitation, a day specially fitting to honor her who, a century ago, visited the land
of France. And while We invite you to sing to God with
the Immaculate Virgin the Magnificat of your gratitude,
We call down upon you and your flocks, upon the sanctuary of Lourdes and its pilgrims and upon all who are responsible for the centenary celebrations, the most abundant
outpouring of graces. In pledge of which, from the
bottom of Our heart, with constant and fatherly love,
We impart to you the Apostolic Blessing.

WOMAN'S IDEAL

All. to the World Union of Women's Organizations
of Catholic Action, September 29, 1957.

(*Women's advancement.—The apostolate of Truth.—
Woman's relation to God; to Christ.*)

828
(12, The union between Christ and woman has its greatest
27- charm and most perfect fulfillment in the person of the
28, Virgin Mary. "And the Word was made flesh and dwelt
41, among us" (a). It was through the Virgin Mary that God
104, assumed human nature and joined the race of the sons
112, of Adam. Her dignity as Mother of God brought singular
121) graces and extraordinary privileges upon Mary: preservation from original sin and all personal fault, the splendor

---

826a *In periculis, in angustiis, in rebus dubiis, Mariam cogita,
Mariam invoca . . . Ipsam sequens, non devias; ipsam rogans,
non desperas; ipsam cogitans, nor erras; ipsa tenente, non
corruis; ipsa protegente, non metuis; ipsa duce, non fati-
garis; ipsa propitia, pervenis. . . . Hom. II super Missus est.*
828a John 1:14.

of the virtues and the gifts of the Holy Spirit, an intimate participation in all the mysteries of the life of Christ, in His sufferings, in His death and resurrection, in the continuation of His work within the Church, and in His sovereignty over all creatures. All this she was given because she was the Mother of God, and because as such she was called upon to play a unique role in the redemption of the world.

What are the consequences of all this for you and your apostolate? First, you should derive from it a great pride in your sex. It was a woman whom the power of the Most High overshadowed; it was a woman from whom, without the cooperation of man, the Second Person of the Trinity took flesh and blood. Though life shows the depths of vice and degradation to which women may sometimes sink, Mary shows the heights to which women can rise, in Christ and through Christ, attaining a position far above all other creatures. **829 (72, 88, 163)**

What civilization or religion has ever urged women to attain such heights and such perfection? Modern humanism, laicism, Marxist propaganda, the most developed and widespread non-Christian cults offer nothing comparable to this vision, so glorious and so humble, so transcendent and yet so easily accessible!

We wanted to outline for you the ideal of womanhood as faith presents it; you find it in Mary and it can be explained by the intimacy of the bonds which united her to Christ. In the conduct of your personal life and in the exercise of your apostolate, never lose sight of her example. Let it inspire your words, your attitudes, and your efforts in the task of emphasizing the dignity of woman and the nobility of her mission. **830 (79, 130-131, 163)**

However, it is not enough simply to know Mary and her greatness. One must also draw closer to her and live in the light of her presence. It would be almost a contradiction, if a Catholic woman working in the apostolate did **831 (38, 50, 133,**

136) not foster fervent devotion for the Mother of God. Devotion to Mary will make possible in you a better understanding of Christ and a more intense union with His mysteries. You will receive Christ from the arms of His Mother and she will permit you to love and imitate Him. Pray to her that she may give you the strength to follow Him to the end with faith and ardent love! Pray to her that she may help you to lead the women of today along the road that leads to Him!

(*Woman's dependence upon the Church.—The apostolate of love.—The apostolate of action.*)

THE LOURDES JUBILEE

Apost. Const., *Primo exacto,* November 1, 1957.

832 The first century has passed since the apparitions at
(137, Lourdes of the Virgin Mary, conceived without sin. Out
155, of Our ardent devotion to her We wish Catholics in all
158) parts of the world to celebrate this anniversary in a fitting manner. We believe that the best way to do this is for all to endeavor to take as their model the lofty virtues of God's Mother and to imitate these virtues with all their strength. Holy pilgrimages will contribute to this end; for the faithful, individually or in groups, will undoubtedly come during this jubilee year to Lourdes. There, without distinction of race or nationality, but united by Christian bonds and nourished by the same strong faith and effective charity, they will raise fervent prayers to God through the most powerful intercession of the Immaculate Virgin.

The treasury of the Sacraments

833 Twenty-five years ago Our Predecessor of happy
(155) memory, Pius XI, wrote to the Bishop of Tarbes and and Lourdes (a), during similar celebrations, that there

833a Letter, *Quod tam alacri,* A.S.S. 27, 5.

was no more fitting or worthy way for Christians to celebrate these solemnities than to be cleansed in the Sacrament of Penance and take part in the Sacrifice of Calvary
renewed every day in an unbloody manner. With paternal affection We repeat this same exhortation. The Eucharist is, in fact, the center and greatest expression of the
Christian life. From it our souls draw supernatural strength
and divine grace, with the help of which we can overcome
the dangers of the present age and attain the happiness of
future life. The Sacrament of the Eucharist and the august
Sacrifice of the Altar—being gifts of such a nature that one
cannot conceive any greater, gifts that seem also to reach
the heights of the infinite love of Christ Himself and almost to exhaust His mercy—these gifts require our active
and effective love; such a love, We mean, as sustains and
influences the will, the activity and the entire course of
our life. We can, furthermore, do nothing that is more
agreeable to our most sweet Mother Mary during the
solemnities of this Jubilee Year than profit by these treasures of the divine Redemption, uniting ourselves ever
more closely to her only-begotten Son, who for all mortal
men is "the way, the truth, and the life" (b).

The message of Lourdes

The Blessed Virgin Mary, when she appeared in the   **834**
grotto of Lourdes to an innocent and unspoiled child, ex-   *(155)*
horted her, and through her all men, not only to pray but
also to perform voluntary acts of Christian penance. We
therefore desire that all Christians, in order to expiate
their sins and the sins of others, strive not only to check
and control their passions, but also to perform, whenever
possible, various voluntary acts of mortification and penance during the Jubilee Year. All must remember, moreover, that the first and most necessary acts of penance
they must perform are the work, the pains, and the

833b John 14:6.

sufferings that are an inseparable part of every man's life. These toils, these anxieties and sufferings, must be so borne by Christians that, like the hosts of the mystical sacrifice, they may become an offering in the sight of God. Thus Christians will not only make fitting reparation to God, who is offended by their sins and the sins of others; they will not only obtain from Him heavenly gifts and comforts; but those things that grieve the soul will be lightened for them, according to the comforting words of the Divine Redeemer: "Come to me, all you who labor and are burdened, and I will give you rest ... and you will find rest for your souls" (a).

(*Jubilee Indulgence granted to pilgrims.*)

MARY, MODEL OF LIFE AND ACTION

All. to Marian congregations of Italian women, April 26, 1958.

(*The Church relies on Marian congregations.*)

835   .... It is unnecessary to tell you once again with what
(*131*, hope and confidence We regard Congregations of the
151) Blessed Virgin Mary, as one of the vivid forces that for the most part silently but effectually are laboring in the Lord's vineyard.

When We stated that you were "Catholic Action" *pleno iure,* We wanted, of course, to bestow on your rules and work the acknowledgment they deserve, but, above all, We intended to pledge you to a generous and united action, in close touch with the Sacred Hierarchy.

If We were to say that you corresponded with Our intentions but poorly, We should not be fair; but, nevertheless, We do not feel We can refrain from urging you to continue along the way you have taken, that is to say, to put forth every effort to be perfect members of the Con-

834a Matt. 11:28-29.

gregation, in conformity with the demands of your rules: souls that look to Mary, as their model in life and in action: of life in the Church, and of action for the Church.

Model of life in the Church

First and foremost look to Mary as your model of life in the Church.

It is usually said that the essence of devotion to the Blessed Virgin consists first in a sentiment of respect and veneration in keeping with her dignity as Mother of God; then in a feeling of confidence in her power and goodness; and finally in a feeling of filial love, that endeavors to reciprocate in some manner her motherly love.

But veneration would not be true, confidence would not be really deep, and love would not go beyond sentiment and words, if the soul who claims to be devoted to Mary did not make it her study to imitate her virtues and reproduce in herself her life.

We are well aware that some of her qualities can be only the subject of our wonder and ecstatic admiration; for example, her Immaculate Conception, fullness of grace, virginal and divine maternity. As the royally privileged daughter of the Father, she is indeed, after Jesus, the brightest ray of His glory, the most stupendous reflection of His image, the most beautiful work from His hands. In these respects, any effort to reproduce her in us, as she actually is, would prove fruitless. She is God's masterpiece even though her beauty, like that of the Moon, is a reflected beauty: "fair as the moon" (a).

836
*(10,
72,
84,
129,
130,
133)*

However, this should certainly not prevent you from looking to Mary, and still less prevent you from imploring her assistance in the continual effort you will surely make to become clothed with at least some ray of her superhuman beauty.

837
*(133,
136)*

836a Cf. Cant. 6:9.

You must therefore learn from her to view things rightly and wholly and to live by faith. In imitation of her, proclaim that there is nothing in heaven for you except God; that you do not wish for anything on this earth save Him. Protest that your sole good is to remain united to God, to put your hopes in Him (a).

838
(82,
112,
131,
136)
To this feeling of yours, to this desire will correspond your action, this being also dedicated entirely to God, as Mary's actions were entirely dedicated to Him. Such joyful conformity with God's Will was a prerogative of hers. We desire, therefore, dear Daughters, that such an attitude and such a prerogative should become your own attitude and prerogative. Be ready, not only to comply with any order or any express call from God, but also with any sign from Him, were it only a slight whisper murmured in the depth of your soul. It should not matter to you whether God offers you joys or, on the contrary, calls you to sorrow; prepare yourselves always to maintain Mary's attitude of readiness to serve. Prepare yourselves to pronounce her "fiat." And you shall be blessed, if, chosen by the Lord to suffer with Him, to be crucified with Him, you nevertheless say your "Magnificat." In you also great things will be done by Him who is powerful "qui potens est" (a).

Model of action in behalf of the Church

839
(117-
118)
Secondly, look to Mary as a model of action on behalf of the Church. It must be well known to you when it was and how it was that Mary, from the beginning, participated intimately in the life of the Church. With Mary, the Mother of Jesus, "cum Maria matre Iesu" the Apostles were assembled, persevering with one mind in prayer "perseverantes unanimiter in orationem" (a), when the Cenacle was

837a Ps. 72:28.
838a Cf. Luke 1:49.
839a Acts 1:14.

shaken by a mighty wind, and the small community of the faithful was quickened by the Holy Spirit who filled each of them with His gifts.

Shortly afterwards, Mary could behold the first sowing and the first miraculous gathering of the Christian harvest. St. Peter spoke to the crowd and with his speech— listened to by all in their own languages—called forth the first fruits of the Church.

From that day of blessing for the young community of Jerusalem, Mary, as a most gracious Mother, has never ceased to watch over the Church of Christ. No circumstance, and more especially, no hour of anxiety or grief, has come to the Church without her feeling Mary's maternal assistance. **840** *(120- 121, 136, 170)*

Whenever it seemed that night was about to darken the world, the Blessed Virgin Mary, the Morning Star, was seen to rise in the skies. When sweat of overwhelming fatigue bathed the Church's brow, when her eyes were filled with tears, when her flesh, like the flesh of Jesus, was tortured, and even nailed to the Cross, the Church had at all times beside her Mary, the Mother of Sorrows. And in the same way as her devoted children's perseverance is due to her, so was it always she who encouraged her children who had strayed to come back, and who welcomed them with infinite tenderness.

Through her intercession the Church, when the subject of violent attacks or of base treachery, has never lacked protection. And so, the story of the Church's triumphs is the story of Mary's triumphs.

Look at Mary, beloved daughters. Thinking with the Church—as your rule prescribes (a)—let her anxieties, sorrows, hopes and joys be yours. No one of you would think that she can be a perfect member of the Congregation by **841** *(137)*

841a Rule 33.

contenting herself with attendance at Mass in a chapel, with psalms and prayers and, perhaps, an appropriate spiritual exhortation.

But neither is it right to think that you can be perfect members of the Congregation by striving only to procure for yourselves the highest degree of Christian perfection without concern for others.

You are not like that, beloved daughters. In the field of the Church—which is the world—there is so much land that needs ploughing, so many furrows to be sowed, so many plants to cultivate, so many harvests to gather. This necessarily entails that the work of every one, including you, members of the Congregation, will be active wherever the Church comes into being; where she grows and expands under suffering and groaning; where she struggles fearlessly; where she conquers and triumphs.

(*Collective action of members of the Congregations.— Organic, community character of that action.*)

THE MADONNA OF REPOSE

Prayer: *Vergine benedicta*, composed by Pius XII, June 2, 1958.

842
(50,
52,
168,
169)

Blessed Virgin who, under the title of Repose, dost remind us of the succoring pity with which thy Maternal Heart is open to thy children, hear our prayer!

Through thy powerful intercession, O Mary, may minds and hearts find repose in abandoning themselves to the Will of the Heavenly Father, in the consciousness of their frailty, in faith in divine promises, in the hope of eternal blessings, and in adhering lovingly to thy Crucified Jesus who has made our crosses His own.

If we be protected by thee, O Mary, calm amid earthly perturbation will not be an empty word. It will be repose for the strong, watchful against hostile forces; repose for the pure, away from worldly corruption. And as through thee we shall have had peace in this life, so, at the end of our pilgrimage in time, we shall enjoy peace for ever and ever. Amen!

THE LAST APPARITION TO BERNADETTE

R. M. to the Pilgrims of Lourdes, July 2, 1958.

In guarded silence, as in that of February 11, this last vision ravished the child's soul by its ethereal beauty. "Never," she said, "have I seen her so beautiful!"

After five months, the manifestations of piety from the crowds, as also, alas, men's disputes, had rendered famous that grotto in the Pyrenees. However, on the evening of July 16, 1858, the Lourdes' Apparitions terminated almost without witnesses, in contemplation and admiration of the virginal beauty of the Mother of God: "Tota pulchra es, O Maria!"

You should also know how to keep silence in your souls, dear children, and to open your minds to the contemplation of the divine splendors realized in Mary. Besides, does not this paternal exhortation—which We are addressing to you on this anniversary day—contain the spiritual lesson of the ancient and venerable tradition of Carmel, which caused to flourish, all through the centuries, wonderful contemplative vocations? In this age, greatly disturbed by so many passions and deceived by so many delusions, lift your eyes to God: they will become more clear-sighted and serene in enabling you to judge the things of the world. And whereas merciless slavery crushes the spirits of millions of men, roots out from their hearts both knowledge and love of God, and makes them bow down as slaves to earthly ambitions alone, gather in again with faith the last lesson of those apparitions of Mary, that of silent prayer in a soul docile to grace and illumined by the vision of eternal life!

(*Invitation to prayer.*)

843
(81,
84,
155)

VIRGIN, SPOUSE AND MOTHER

All. to the women of Italian Catholic Action, July 13, 1958.

(The two paths: Virginity or Marriage.)

844
(21,
88,
131)
There is a Woman,—you know it,—upon whom God willed to fix His eyes with infinite tenderness, as He had destined her to be His Mother. His all-powerful love kept her virginal glory intact, and in addition He bestowed on her the crown of a Spouse and the dignity of a Mother. Look on Mary as your model, unsurpassed and unsurpassable. Look on Mary, the Lily of the Valley, who, nevertheless, through the operation of the Holy Spirit bore fruit and gave Jesus to the world.

If you look on her and imitate her, your freshness shall remain unblemished; your perfume unaltered; and your attractiveness unchangeable.

THE MARIAN WORK OF PIUS XII

Encycl., *Meminisse juvat,* July 14, 1958.

845
(121,
158
177)
We deem it advisable to recall that when new dangers threaten the Christian people and the Church, spouse of the divine Savior, We, as Our Predecessors have done in past centuries, turn Our prayers to the Virgin Mary, most loving Mother, and We invite all the flock entrusted to Us to place themselves confidently under her protection.

While the world was assailed by a frightful war, We did everything to exhort cities, peoples and nations to peace and to recall the minds torn by contention to mutual agreement in the name of truth, of justice and of love. Nor did We restrict Ourselves to this but, seeing that We were about to exhaust human means and resources, We, with several letters of admonition, instituting a holy campaign of prayer, invoked heaven's help through the powerful intercession of the Mother of God to whose Immaculate Heart We consecrated the whole human family (a). But, if the world conflict continues, a just peace will not come nor will men find themselves united in fraternal unity.

(*The constant causes of trouble: the secularization of institutions; the persecution of the Church.*)

And since We trust so much in the protecting inter- **846** cession of the Virgin Mary, We express the ardent wish *(39,* that in every part of the earth Catholics, during the novena *121,* which usually precedes the Feast of the Assumption of *131,* the august Mother of God into heaven, should offer public *158,* prayers, particularly for the Church, which, as has already *169,* been stated, is in certain areas vexed and afflicted. *177)*

During the Holy Year, 1950, We proclaimed not without divine inspiration that the Blessed Virgin was assumed body and soul into heaven (a). We solemnly declared her Queen of Heaven and proposed her to be venerated by all under that title (b). A century after she appeared with all the richness of her graces to an innocent child at the Grotto of Lourdes, We invited the multitude of pilgrims to benefit from her maternal graces (c). We nourish the hope with certainty that she will not in any manner put aside and reject these Our wishes and the prayers of all Catholic people.

(*Invitation to join virtue to prayer.*)

If Christian morals flourish again as they did at the time of the apostles and martyrs, we can then hope with certain trust that the Blessed Virgin Mary, desirous as she is that as many of her sons as possible be preserved in virtue, will obtain for us a most benevolent fulfillment of our prayers. From the solicitous prayers directed to her

845a Cf. above, nos. 344, 355, 369, 373.
846a Cf. above, no. 482 ff.
846b Cf. above, no. 676 ff.
846c Cf. above, no. 793 ff.

by so many voices, we may also hope for more peaceful and happier times for the Church of her only-begotten Son and for the whole of human society.

RESTORATION OF THE KINGDOM OF CHRIST THROUGH MARY

R. M. to the International Marian Congress at Lourdes, September 17, 1958.

(*Word of welcome.*)

847
(134-137, 155)

Do not doubt, beloved members of the Congress, that it was Mary who, in a critical hour for mankind, wished to remind her wandering children of the true meaning of life, by showing forth her essential superabundance of grace, and her union with the other life that alone will give us true and perfect happiness.

It was she who deigned to teach men, with a mother's tenderness and instruction, the two essential means for reaching such a lofty goal: assiduous and trusting prayer and the indispensable Christian mortification sustaining it. Her supernatural prudence pointed out to men the safe road, that which passes under the care of her Son's representatives on this earth, the one that passes through the Church. Anxious to ensure the welfare of everyone, she made a strong appeal to the multitudes to flock together to drink the miraculous waters that heal both souls and bodies.

With ineffable sweetness, she wished in some way to remain among us to be our perpetual succor and sure refuge, strengthening our faith with fresh and countless wonders, sustaining our hopes with her inexhaustible and large-hearted mercy, and fanning the flame of our charity by her celestial beauty, her boundless kindness, and her blessings without number.

... Because she is today as she was a century ago, because we are sure that her solicitude and assistance will never fail us, because from this blessed Grotto, O bountiful Mother, the torrent of your maternal blessings cannot cease to descend upon the earth, no more than can the water cease to run through these valleys and the sun diffuse warmth and light, We want to proclaim strongly at the end of this Congress, which in a certain way crowns this incomparable centenary, Our conviction that the restoration of the Kingdom of Christ through Mary cannot but become a reality, as it is impossible that such a seed, thrown with so great abundance, should not yield most abundant fruit.

Evil shall not prevail

We know well how the infernal powers are endeavor- **848** ing in every way to lay waste the Blessed Virgin Mary's *(137,* inheritance, by depriving youth of its innocence and *155,* modesty; by violating the sanctity and unity of marriage; *169)* by raising social classes against one another (as if all men were not brothers); by oppressing the Church wherever they can manage to take control; and by propagating the most radical materialism. But we likewise know what thirst for light and truth men harbor in their innermost hearts; what desire to find God pervades souls, even the souls of those who cannot show any outward sign thereof without risking loss of goods and lives; We know the power of the spiritual forces that are rising on all sides, as a harbinger of a splendid springtime.

Did you not yourselves see those multitudes flocking together during this year to the holy Virgin's feet with peace and serenity such as if they were living in a world without problems, and not on the contrary on the brink of an unprecedented catastrophe?

Did you not also see them stretching out their hands to one another, and smiling fraternally as if they did not belong to nations who, yesterday, full of hatred were look-ing at each other from one trench to another? Did you not behold them, as they besieged the confessionals and knelt

down in endless lines to receive the celestial manna, praying untiringly, with arms outstretched, in front of the
grotto, or singing Mary's praises at nightfall in luminous
processions?

Did you even not see them, all of them; the faithful
full of fervor, the regenerated sinners, those privileged by
Mary's blessings or patients returning with their ills, did
you not see them reentering their homes with brows radiant with the light of God and animated with the most
fervent desire to lead a better life, a new life under the
blue mantle of her whose smile they will never forget?

Prayer to Mary

849
(48,
137,
155,
169)

It has been said that at Lourdes a window was opened
looking out towards heaven. Let us add that if through that
window it has been given us to enjoy heavenly glory in
anticipation; through it also, continually, there flows down
a torrent of light and blessings reviving confidence in the
destiny of the human race, who, though anxious to ensure
development and progress, is still more desirous of serenity
and peace.

Beloved children, do implore for the world, in this
solemn hour, all the graces which appear to you necessary
and timely—each according to the needs he is aware of—,
but ask above all that hatreds and dissensions may vanish;
that the impudent voices of covetousness and pride be reduced to silence; and that the joyful and beneficial Sun
of that Peace so greatly desired, the Peace of Christ "which
surpasses all understanding" may finally shine upon the
earth, in men's hearts, in their social and international
relations, as a natural consequence of the full application
of the Gospel! With your prayers, invoke the Kingdom of
Christ to which your most beloved Mother urges you with
her example, and for which her maternal intercession procures for you all the necessary means; does she not in

fact hold a privileged post because of the function which
Providence wished to give her in the life of the Church
and in that of each of its members?

This is why, O most sweet Mother and most powerful
Advocate, you wanted to set your spotless foot on that rock
in the Pyrenees, and to make of that unknown vale an immense sanctuary of which the clouds in heaven are the
canopy; a sanctuary where your Most Beloved Son would
be continually honored in the Sacrament of His love, received with fervor in thousands of breasts, which are
perhaps still tasting the sweetness of reconciliation, and
would be constantly invoked by the trembling lips of those
who confide to Him sufferings that nothing in the world
can remedy.

May this be your work, O Sovereign of Angels and
Queen of Peace! Do not let those triumphs remain confined within the narrow limits of your shrine, but as an
irresistible torrent flowing through the ample valleys
reaches the heights and crosses over them to fill everything with its rushing waters, so may they expand over
the whole world, purifying souls, curing ills, smoothing
over difficulties, vivifying all things in order that, through
your powerful intercession and constant assistance, the
Kingdom of Christ, "A Kingdom of Truth and Life, a Kingdom of Sanctity and Grace, a Kingdom of Love and Peace
may finally come to be!" (a)

(*Invocation to St. Bernadette.—Blessing.*)

850
*(48,
102,
137,
155)*

850a Preface of Jesus Christ, King.

JOHN XXIIII

(1958 —)

ROME AND LOURDES

All. at St. Mary Major, February 15, 1959.

(*From Venice to Lourdes, then to Rome the year was marked for the Pope by Our Lady's watchfulness over him.*)

Oh! the spectacle of the huge crowds at Lourdes, **851** which with voices loud and penetrating joined in Our *(39,* prayers of thanksgiving! How that spectacle represents the *127-* the similarity between the new construction, a marvel of *128,* modern technical skill, and the ancient basilica on the *158)* Esquiline! Both are destined to be the epitome of the beauty of all the shrines dedicated to the Mother of Jesus. The basilica at Rome and the new one at Lourdes, together both seem to cry aloud: *The Pope's house, Mary's house!* On the Esquiline, Pope Liberius, and near the Grotto of Massabielle, Pope Pius X, Pontiff and Saint!

It behooves Us for the edification of all to seize upon an outstanding trait of that association of time and circumstances. The adoring cultus of Jesus, our Savior, is the core of all devotion to His Blessed Mother. For we come to Jesus through Mary. And from the luster of St. Peter's successor, the Vicar of Christ on earth, devotion to Mary draws its inspiration and splendor.

In the fourth century on the Esquiline the temple of **852** Pope Liberius towered up to its final splendor. At Lourdes *(28-* three basilicas have risen, the first by that name called, *29,* then the Rosary Chapel, and now the third huge edifice *127,* which we have had the privilege to dedicate to St. Pius X. *152,* All three honor the name and watchful eye of Popes who *158,* summoned and trained their flocks to call on Mary in *168)* good and ill, in the joys and sorrows of our present era.

Oh! what a conjunction in history of man's faith in and love for Jesus, signalized as it is by mighty architectural triumphs beginning on the Esquiline and leading us to the underground basilica of Lourdes! Behold! the latest

testimony to the fundamental principle of Christian doctrine! Love of Christ is love of Mary. He is our Divine
Savior, she the Mother of us all. In that lies the aspiration
of every good Christian; from childhood's first word to the
last sigh of dying old age: *Holy Mary, pray for us!*

The fruit of the centennial celebration

853
(128,
152)
From all this a second thought that engages Our attention and that of every Christian is the summons it gives
for a practical application to individual lives and the lives
of the crowds of pilgrims. That summons issues from the
deposition of the daughter of Soubirous, the miller. It is a
summons to humble and trusting prayer, to the practice
of penance, to strong and solid piety,—a summons answered
in the form of pilgrimages from every part of the globe,
to venerate *"the ground which her feet trod"* (a), to follow
in the footsteps of the good and loving Mother as she
passes among her children.

A stay at Lourdes, as at any of the thousand or more
world's shrines, has for its aim not only a seemly diversion
or the satisfying of a vague, uncertain religious feeling,
but rather the recollection of eternal truths, the soul's
cleansing from sin and every other imperfection, and above
all a participation in the Eucharistic mystery and banquet.

854
(155,
157)
The Vision's instruction to Bernadette to scrape the
ground with her hands, in order to cause the miraculous
water to spring up, to eat of the bitter grass,—oh, how
they smile in pity on hearing this, the so-called free think-
ers!—the instruction to start urging the erection of a chapel,
and to accept her destiny of lacking happiness in this
world, but of being assured of joy and glory in heaven,—
all that makes up the precious deposit of doctrine and grace
required for the practice of Christian life on the part of
everyone summoned to pass from darkness into light.

853a Ps. 131:7.

In this simple reminder of Lourdes' distinctive lessons
we find the most precious fruit of the centennial celebrations.

Lessons that live

Now that a year has passed, we shall continue to
practice our devotion as good Christians, as perfect Catholics, in all that is due to the Mother of God, whose mission
from Bethlehem to Calvary was to manifest Jesus to the
world, to walk in His footsteps and to remain united with
His Apostles and disciples at all times and everywhere. His
Apostles and disciples were appointed to the grave and
momentous task of evangelizing all nations, to the difficult
mission of bringing the Gospel to the poor and pardon to
sinners: *evangelizare pauperibus, sanare contritos corde* (a).

855
(33,
39,
112,
118,
136,
165)

From Mary we should with simple hearts beg that
she obtain for us from her Divine Son Jesus even graces of
the temporal and earthly order, for everything helps and
human living needs such graces. But we should not merely
ask for these and then stop there. The aim of our earthly
pilgrimage is higher and more far-reaching; the search
for means to attain it is of an order different from the
mere satisfaction of what is near at hand and what should
not claim all our time or our whole heart.

(*Pope's duty of recalling, when necessary, the austere
lessons of discipline and penance.*)

By discipline and penance we hasten the advance of
society's welfare and we make peace secure. How true this
is! Without discipline we are not men; without penance
we cease to be Christian. At Lourdes that lesson was made
clear through the little one who *saw* and who transmitted
it to the whole world. That lesson We shall continue to
teach and preach for the spiritual profit of all and of each
one in particular.

856
(155)

855a Luke 4:18.

(*In the face of threats and actual disorders, we must pray for a revival of faith.*)

Prayer to the Virgin

857   Immaculate Mary of Lourdes, be propitious to us al-
(126, ways, under all the titles it has pleased our fathers and
154, ourselves to address thee. Immaculate Virgin, we thank
158) thee and we bless thee for all the acts of homage and
love thou hast inspired in us and hast helped us to offer
throughout this centennial year of thy Apparitions.

We shall continue to greet thee, Mary, under the titles
which are for us as well as for thee the dearest and most
blessed, as our forefathers invoked thee in the basilica of
Pope Liberius under that gleaming arch that memorializes
thy veneration and thy divine Motherhood. In that renowned sanctuary everyone calls you: "Safety of the Roman
people"—*Salus populi Romani*. Be that still, be that always,
Mary, our Queen.

858   At the end of the first world war, Our Predecessor,
(158, Benedict XV of venerated memory, took pleasure in plac-
169) ing beside thy ancient altar a white marble statue with
thy divine Child holding in His hand the olive branch of
peace; with that he decided that thou shouldst be called
and invoked as Queen of Peace (a).

We join the two titles together, Blessed Mother of
Jesus, our sweet Mother. Mary, Safety of the Roman people,
pray for us. Mary, Queen of Peace, preserve thy people
from every snare of evil and from war; make peace secure
for this city of Rome, which is thine, for our dear Italy,
for all the nations of the world, for thy Holy, Catholic
and Apostolic Church. Amen.

858a   Cf. above no. 263.

LOURDES' LASTING MESSAGE

R. M. for the closing of the Marian Year at Lourdes, February 18, 1959.

Beloved Brethren, on this occasion of the closing of the centenary of the Immaculate Virgin's Apparitions at Lourdes, We feel it incumbent on Us above all to thank our Lord for the countless graces He has been pleased to bestow on that time-honored shrine, which so often in the past We had the pleasure of visiting. **859** *(137, 155)*

This year of Jubilee was one of continuous prayer before the Grotto of Massabielle, today happily restored to the simplicity of its ancient estate. It was a year of pilgrimages more numerous and more ardent, and the wealth of religious fervor displayed affords Us a motive of consummate hope. Christians by the thousands, of every condition and nationality, united by similar faith in and love for their heavenly Mother, betook themselves to Lourdes. Were they not there as representatives of the vast Catholic family and as witnesses of a human society that yearns to live in brotherhood and peace? Blessed be our Lady, who by attracting us to her Pyrennean shrine has given the world that amazing spectacle of unity and love!

If by such public demonstrations we awaken the hidden operations of grace, our gratitude increases still more. How many minds groping in darkness discovered the light at Lourdes! How many weary or hardened hearts felt the warmth of a return to God! How many wavering wills the strength to persevere! Whether in the silence of unuttered prayer or amidst the thunderous acclamations of the Holy Eucharist or of Mary, generous souls experienced the joy of total surrender; there the sick received, if not always a cure, at least, in the offering of their pains, resignation and heart's ease, while the dying learned to surrender their lives in peace. How beautiful in God's sight is that secret story, engraved in hearts alone! It is the story of the vic- **860** *(155)*

tories of God, "who has rescued us from the power of
darkness and transferred us into the kingdom of His beloved Son, in whom we have our redemption, the remission
of our sins" (a).

Truly, "the mercies of the Lord I will sing forever" (b),
for at the hands of His divine Mother the Lord has
lavished His mercy on that city of prayer, of conversion,
of miracles.

Lourdes, Pius XII and John XXIII

861   These words of appreciation,—could We ever have
(158) thought at the opening of this Jubilee that divine Providence would afford Us the consolation of uttering them
today in the name of all Christianity? Could We have
forseen them on March 25 of last year, when We had the
privilege of consecrating the huge underground basilica of
St. Pius X—with its new architectural beauties—and the
joy of recalling in Our discourse France's Marian glories?
And, when on the same day We were celebrating the
sainted memory of the Pontiff who was Our Predecessor
in the See of Venice, We could no more imagine that We
were about to succeed him in the Apostolic See of Rome.

Beloved Brethren, We thank God for having granted
Us, a little before raising Us to the awe-inspiring pinnacle
of the Supreme Pontificate, that prayerful pause in our
Lady's presence and for having allowed Us there to drink
in abundantly, like Elias on Mt. Horeb, the strength and
peace of which We were soon to have need. That pilgrimage which We then performed, did it not have unknown
to Us a still deeper meaning? You will recall how Pope
Pius XI of illustrious memory providentially entrusted to
Cardinal Pacelli, his Secretary of State, numerous missions
to foreign lands. These formed in a way a presentation to
the world of his worthy successor. Have We not Ourselves
in the thoughtful authorization which Pius XII accorded

860a Col. 1:13-14.
860b Ps. 88:1.

Us of presiding over one of the most solemn anniversaries
of this Jubilee the right to claim a mysterious indication
of the designs of Providence, who was preparing Us for
the precious task of continuing at a later day the apostolic
labors carried on at Lourdes by Our Predecessor?

However that may be—We cannot forget it—the chief **862**
merit of this Marian Year redounds to the credit of Pope *(158)*
Pius XII. It was he who wanted to give unusual splendor
to this Jubilee and in his ardent devotion he hoped for
immense spiritual good for mankind.

Several years before he foresaw with joy the approach
of this centenary and from 1957 in an Encyclical Letter,
then an Apostolic Constitution recounted the historic ties
between the Papacy and the Pyrennean shrine. These com-
munications proposed the Jubilee intentions and invited
Catholics to the double effort of individual conversion and
society's restoration to Christ (a). From February 11, 1958,
onward, the Pope repeatedly delivered exhortations to
pilgrims to Lourdes and less than a month before his death,
in a moving radio message, he for the last time sang the
glories of the Immaculate Virgin of Massabielle and re-
iterated his love for France which has the honor of possessing so glorious a shrine (b). A short time afterwards,
that fatherly voice was stilled, and in the year dedicated to
His holy Mother, God called to Himself Mary's renowned
servant, whose pontificate will forever remain distinguished for the solemn achievements in favor of Marian
veneration which his heartfelt devotion and exalted wisdom inspired.

Message to guide our actions

Today, Beloved Brethren, We make those exhortations   **863**
Our own. Like him, we anxiously desire that Christianity *(136,*
renew itself in a concerted transport of Marian devotion, *155,*

862a Cf. above, nos. 793, 832.
862b Cf. above, nos. 842, 843, 847.

158,   for, according to the Church's teaching, that can surely and
175)   without delay lead souls to our Divine Savior, Jesus Christ.
After the example of the Pontiffs who for a century have
exhorted Catholics to give ear to the message of Lourdes,
We beg you to listen with simple heart and right mind
to the salutary warnings of God's Mother. Furthermore,
let no one be surprised at hearing the Roman Pontiffs in-
sisting on that important lesson passed on by the child of
Massabielle. Since the Pontiffs are the appointed guardians
and interpreters of divine Revelation contained in Holy
Scripture and Tradition, they also have the duty of commending to the faithful's attention—when after mature
deliberation they judge it opportune for the general good—
the supernatural lights it has pleased God to grant freely
to certain privileged souls. This they do, not to propose
new doctrines, but to guide our actions: *Non ad novam
doctrinam fidei depromendam, sed ad humanorum actuum
directionem* (a). This is the case of the Lourdes' Apparitions,
upon which excellent historical works have recently thrown
conclusive light.

864   For this closing solemnity We have purposely chosen
(155,   the feast of the saintly Bernadette. It is the anniversary of
175)   of third Apparition at which she received Mary's promise
that "she would be happy, not in this world, but in the
next." Addressing the pilgrims gathered here amid numerous religious and civil dignitaries, whom it delights Us to
greet, addressing Ourselves also to all those who are receiving Our message over the air waves, it is Our pleasure
to propose the example of that child, poor and unknown,
but privileged of God and destined to be the bearer of His
gifts. "The weak things of the world," says St. Paul, "has
God chosen to put to shame the strong, and the base
things of the world and the despised has God chosen" (a).

863a St. Thomas IIa IIæ q. 174, a. 6, ad 3.
864a 1 Cor. 1:27-28.

Model of prayer to Mary, example of humble, smiling courage, eloquent in the silence which enveloped her once her mission was fulfilled, the saintly Bernadette draws us irresistibly to Lourdes' true spiritual center, the Grotto of Massabielle. There the voice of the Mother of God never ceases to reach her children's hearts. At the same time, the child of the visions, who had the courage to leave for good that spot of indescribable meetings, reminds us that Lourdes is but a point of departure; the grace received there is a treasure which, far from burying it fruitlessly, we should make fructify for God's glory and the service of the Church.

Beloved Brethren, our age, as you know, finds itself **865** making wondrous progress in science. In view of the *(155)* unfathomed possibilities offering themselves, humanity is, as it were, reeling with fanatic pride. And behold, in contrast, from Lourdes Bernadette exhorts us to humility and prayer; without fear We Ourselves earnestly pass on that exhortation to all who today run the grave risk of being so blinded by man's power as to lose sight of true religious values. "What does it profit a man to gain the whole world, but suffer the loss of his own soul?" (a) Again, from Lourdes an exhortation to penance and charity reaches us, to detach us from riches and to teach us to share these with those who are poorer than ourselves. We likewise make that appeal at this time when millions of men are aware—sometimes, alas, with rebellion in their hearts!— of the scandalous contrast between the prosperity of some and the lack for others of the bare necessities of life.

Pray to God, therefore, with confidence, Beloved Brethren, who are listening, and continue bravely to produce in yourselves and in those about you the needed adjustments requested by Our Lady. May the saintly Marie Bernard from her wintry shrine, where her precious

865a Matt. 16:26.

reliquary ceases not to be devoutly visited, watch over the Marian pilgrimages, from now on a century old, of which she was the providential instrument and from which We still look for so many graces for France, for the Church, for the world.

(*Blessing.*)

REMINDER OF THE PLAN OF DIVINE PROVIDENCE

All. at St.-Louis-of-the-French, February 18, 1959.

(*Morning message of Lourdes, Pope's visit to their national church.—Motives of joy for French.*)

866
(155
159)
A very great reason for joy to the whole world was the visit, eighteen times repeated, of Mary, the Mother of Jesus and our Mother, to her children on this earth,—this earth, a garden of natural delights, yet to all poor mortals *weeping and wailing* throughout history also a vale of tears.

Those remarkable Apparitions of Mary in the middle of the 18th century bestow a special meed of honor on France, the land of saints and heroes, where the history of Christianity was inscribed in glowing and unforgettable pages. In the dispositions of Divine Providence, each nation has its mission; sometimes a name suffices to describe that mission. Now, when we say: "Regnum Galliæ, Regnum Mariæ," (the realm of France, Mary's realm), we proclaim to the letter the honor and love of Clovis' sons and countless descendants.

867
(155)
Certainly, the steady flow of pilgrims to the Grotto of Lourdes on French soil, originating in the Apparitions of the Immaculate Virgin—and it seems as if that flow, far from growing weaker, should grow still greater in an edifying crescendo—is a manifestation of religious fervor; at the same time it is for the whole world a gentle, insistent reminder to thoroughly Christian consciences as well

as to the less fervent. A reminder of a mysterious plan of Providence, it should, in view of the weighty problems of life and death, awaken, in each and every one, individual and collective responsibilities for the present and for the future.

Allow Us at this point to repeat some thoughts of Our radio message of this morning, sent from Rome to the whole world.   **868** *(175)*

The centenary year of the Lourdes Apparitions ends on this February 18. The liturgy dedicates this day to the cultus of the child who beheld the visions of Massabielle, Saint Marie Bernard, daughter of Soubirous, the miller. She, and she alone, received Mary's confidences and passed them on to the world. And the world—this is the great moral miracle—the world there believed, and there continues to believe.

(*The Pope repeats a portion of his morning message which may be found above, nos. 864, 865.—Invocation to his Predecessor, John XXII.*)

INDEXES

INDEXES

ABBREVIATIONS

References

AAS   *Acta Apostolicæ Sedis*, Romæ, Typographia Vaticana, 1908-1955.
Gregory, Romæ, 1900-1904.
Leo XIII, Romæ, 1881-1905.
Pius IX, Romæ.
St. Pius X, Romæ, 1905-1914.

ASS   *Acta Sanctæ Sedis*, Romæ, 1865-1908.

Aur   J. J. Bourassé, *Summa aurea de laudibus B. V. Mariæ*, Paris, Migne, 1862-1866.

Bl   *Bullarii Romani, Continuatio.*
Summorum Pontificum Benedicti XIV . . . , Pie VIII, Prati, 1845-1854.

BP   Editions of the "Bonne Presse", 5, rue Bayard, Paris. Texts and translations.
Years 1800-1878 — *Lettres Apostoliques de Pie IX, Grégoire XVI, Pie VII.*
    —   1878-1903 — *Lettres Apostoliques de Léon XIII.*
    —   1903-1914 — *Actes de S. Pie X.*
    —   1914-1922 — *Actes de Benoît XV.*
    —   1922-1939 — *Actes de Pie XI.*
    —   1939-1958 — *Actes de Pie XII.*

CD   *Catholic Documents.*

CT   *Le Canoniste contemporain* (monthly), 10, rue Cassette, Paris, 1878-1922.

CTS   *Catholic Truth Society*, London.

DC   *Documentation catholique*, Maison de la "Bonne Presse", 5, rue Bayard, Paris.

Denz.   *Denzinger.*

DR	*Discorsi e Radiomessagi di Sua Santita Pie XII*, Milano, "Vita e Pensiero", 1939-1946 — Romæ, Typographia polyglotta Vaticana, 1946-1956.
Marie	Van den Berghe, *Marie et le Sacerdoce*, Paris, Vivés, 1875.
NCWC	*National Catholic Welfare Conference*, Washington, D.C.
OR	*Osservatore Romano*, Vatican daily.
PDM	*Papal Documents on Mary*, Doheny and Kelly.
TPS	*The Pope Speaks*, Quarterly.
Univ.	*L'Univers* (daily), Paris.

Nature of Documents

All. — Allocution
Encycl. — Encyclical
Letter — Letter
Apost. Const. — Apostolic Constitution
Apost. Letter — Apostolic Letter
R. M. — Radio Message

Numbering of text

In the margin of the text or in footnotes:

The numbers in bold type indicate the division of the Pontifical text, or refer to it.
The numbers in brackets and in italics refer to the division of the Analytical Index, and facilitates the finding of texts on the same subjects.

In the indexes:

Read explanations before each index.

ALPHABETICAL INDEX

The numbers in brackets refer to the divisions of the Analytical Index; the numbers in heavy black print refer to the paragraphs of the Papal pronouncements.

Abraham: **226**.

Achaz: **727**.

Action Catholic, Mary and—: *(131)*, *(165)*.

Adam: **31, 51, 53, 226, 239, 263, 359, 362, 383, 519, 590, 595, 629, 705, 734**.

Adrian I: **698**.

Advocate, Mary our—: *(48)*.

Africa: **672**.

Agatho, St.: **691**.

Albert the Great, St.: **510**.

Albigenses: *(123)*.

Alcabaça, St. Mary of—: **409**.

Alexander VII: **38, 40**.

Alphonsus Liguori, St.: **515, 693**.

Amadeus of Lausanne: **508**.

Ambrose, St.: **240, 425, 639, 640**.

America: **401-404**.

Amiens: **278, 794**.

Anahuac: **401**.

Andrew of Crete, St.: **689**.

Angels, Mary Queen of—: *(100)*, *(102)*.

Anne, St.: **53, 650, 657**.

Annunciation: *(114)*.
  —Devotion to—: *(141)*.

Annunciation (Order of—): **657**.

Anselm, St. of Canterbury: **168, 277, 704**.

Antida Thouret, St.: **321**.

Anthony of Padua: **509**.

Anthony Mary Claret: **720**.

Anthony Mary Pucci: **572**.

Apostolate, encouraging Marian vocations: *(137)*.

Apostles, Mary and the—: *(117)*, *(118)*.
  —Mary, Queen of—: *(165)*.

Apparitions of Our Blessed Lady: *(155)* ff.

Aquaduct, mystical: **4, 23, 234, 641**.

Arcadius: **290**.

Arch of Alliance: **4, 506**.

Argentine: **436, 785**.

Arius: **289**.

Art, Christian and Mary's Queenship: *(105)*.

Ascension: *(117)*.

Associate, Mary—with Christ: see: "Socia".

Assumption: *(8)*, *(11)*, *(14)*, *(17)*, *(28)*, *(89)* ff.
  —and other truths: *(99)*.
  —devotion to—: *(141)*.
  —implicit in the fullness of grace: *(78)*.

Athanasius, St.: **640**.

Eve: **50, 161, 219, 507, 510, 705.**
—Mary most holy, new— *(9)*.
Evils present: *(168)*.

Faith, of Mary most holy: *(80)* ff.
—Mary and—: *(122)*.
—fruit of devotion to Mary most holy: *(136)*.
—fortified by the Rosary: *(147)*.
—of the Church in the Assumption: *(95)*.
Fall, original: *(23)*.
—repaired in Mary: *(58)*, *(66)*.
False devotions: *(139)*.
Family, the Rosary in—: *(149)*.
Families, Mary, protectress of—: *(164)*.
Family, royal—of Our Lady: *(113)*.
Father, Mary and the—: *(55)*.
Fathers of the Church
—teach the Assumption of Mary: *(94)*.
—the Immaculate Conception: *(63)*.
—the Queenship of Mary: *(105)*.
Fatima: *(156)*.
Ferrata, Cardinal: **217**.
Fiat of Mary most holy: *(25)*, *(119)*.
Figogna: **358-360**.
Figures, biblical: *(3)*, *(63)*.
Florence: **14**.

Fortitude of Mary most holy: *(82)*.
—Mary, teacher of—: *(131)*.
—fruit of devotion to Mary: *(136)*.
France: **214-215, 253, 262, 276-277, 286, 360, 457, 459, 463, 586, 794, 809, 827.**
—Mary, patroness of—: *(159)*.
Francis de Sales, St. **277, 515.**
Franciscans: **255**.
Free consent of Mary to the Incarnation: *(25)*, *(114)*,
Freedom—of God in the predestination of Mary: *(23)*.
—of Mary most holy: *(25)*.
—of the Church: *(177)*.
Fruits—of the definition of the Assumption: *(97)*.
—of Marian devotion: *(135)*.
—of Marian doctrine: *(19)*.
—of the Rosary: *(146-148)*.
Fullness of Grace: see Grace.

Gabriel (Arch.): **49, 118, 214, 372, 428, 430, 683, 702, 741, 784,** *(114)*.
Gaeta: **29, 58.**
Gasparri, Cardinal: **263**.
Gaul: **286**.
Genoa: **358**.
Germain of Constantinople, St.: **171, 174, 179, 404, 503, 690-691, 707.**
Gethsemane: **151**.
Gillet, R. P., O. P.: **332**.
Glory of Mary: *(100)* ff.

ANALYTICAL INDEX

PLAN OF THE ANALYTICAL INDEX

PART TWO

MARY'S LIFE

§ I. Mary's Life up to Pentecost: *(112)-(117)*.
§ II. Mary in the Church, after Pentecost: *(118)-(124)*.

PART THREE

MARIAN DEVOTION

§ I. General cult and devotion: *(125)-(139)*.
§ II. Diverse forms of Marian devotion: *(140)-(153)*.
§ III. Manifestations of Marian devotion: *(154)-(161)*.
§ IV. Mary and the diversity of human conditions: *(162)-(178)*.

ANALYTICAL INDEX

The numbers in italics between parentheses indicate the division of the present Index or refer to the division of the same;

the numbers in bold type refer to the divisions of the Papal document;

the underlined numbers refer to passages of particular importance of the Papal document;

the titles in bold capitals indicate a subject matter treated in several Papal documents already published or still to be published in a separate volume of the present collection.

INTRODUCTION

MARIAN DOCTRINE

SOURCES OF MARIAN DOCTRINE

Sacred Scripture

(1) — All the Sacred Scripture is a source of Marian doctrine: **732.**
It always presents to us Mary united in all to Jesus Christ: **518,** cf. *(12).*

Old Testament

(2) — The Old Testament announces her, after Jesus, as the end of the law and the fulfillment of the figures and prophecies: **226.**
Mary fulfills the prophecies of the Genesis: **519,**
and that of Emmanuel (of Isaias): **11;**
biblical figures and images: **226,**
the new Eve: **519,** cf. *(9),*
victorious over the serpent: **52,**
present in the thought of Noe, Ark of the Covenant: **226, 506.**

Rainbow: **251, 718,**
Cedar of Lebanon: **251, 725,**
Root of Jesse, Rock of the desert: **226,**
prefigured by Abraham, Jacob, Moses, David, Elias: **226,**
by Judith: **98.**
These types are, according to the Fathers, emblems of divine Maternity: **47.**
The prophecy of Emmanuel (of Isaias) was verified in Mary: **11.**

New Testament

(3) — The New Testament shows: that the prophecy of Isaias was verified in Mary: **11.**
Cares, hardships and sorrows of Mary: **495,**
her glorious state: in the woman of the Apocalypse: **507,**
she cried travailing in birth, the birth of us who are yet to be generated to the perfect charity of God: **247.**
Scripture is not the only source of Marian theology: **732.**

The Magisterium of the Church

(4) — The faith of the Church is the immediate basis of Marian doctrine: **516.**
The proximate standard of truth is living teaching authority of the Church: **712, 731, 733.**
It has always recognized the harmony of Marian privileges: **483, 728,**
the first of which, the divine maternity, was proclaimed at Ephesus, where the Roman primacy was affirmed: **29,** cf. *(24).*

Marian tradition in the Liturgy

(5) — The style of speech of Marian tradition has passed into the Liturgy: **55.**

which proceeds from the faith of the Church: **501,**
all tradition must be compared with the Church's liturgical life: **733,**
which gives particular proof of the relation between
the Immaculate Conception and divine maternity: **351.**

Its Antiquity

(6) — The Marian doctrine defended by the Eastern
churches: **180, 728,**
appears from the earliest times in the Church which
recognizes Mary as Mother of God: **115, 728.**
And which admits, from the most ancient times,
her original innocence: **33,**
and her singular privileges: **519, 682.**
The dogma of the divine Maternity unites the Eastern
Church and Western Church: **177, 728.**

Principles of Marian Doctrine

(7) — The foundations must be solid and theological: **730.**

Divine Maternity

(8) — Divine Maternity is the key to all Mary's prerogatives:
429.
It is the basis of all Marian privileges: **594, 682,** cf.
(27),
principle of Mary's dignity and of graces: **303, 505,**
647.
It is a unique grace: **682,**
which associates her to all the work of salvation: **82,**
motive of her corporeal Assumption: **498, 505, 507,**
cf. *(98-99),*
and foundation of her Queenship: **413, 701,** cf.
(104).

The New Eve

(9) — Mary has been designated as the innocent Eve: **519,**
534, 705.

and she is the antithesis of the disobedient Eve: **507**,
exempt from the fourfold curse of Eve: **50, 510**,
she accomplished her office at the foot of the Cross:
359, 383,

where she received the sons of Adam: **383**.
She is especially the Mother of the living: **534**.

Mary's Supreme dignity

(10) — Mary is elevated to the supreme diginity of Mother
of God: **156, 707**, cf. *(26)*,

the highest dignity of a creature: **111, 303**,

because of her link with the Hypostatic order: **413**.
Unique Dignity, almost divine: **200, 303, 505, 711**,
Head of God's work: **647, 675, 836**,

with a particular greatness and dignity: **207, 664,
683**,

which fills her more than all the other creatures:
618,

with most singular privileges: **495, 682, 828**,

where God's work is no longer carried out according
to common rules: **517**.

Her Primacy

(11) — Mary is raised above all other creatures: **10, 120, 122,
495, 592, 735, 829**.

She is the first after Christ: **707**,

being the most perfect: **368**,

the nearest to her Son: **82**,

superior to the angels: **27, 82, 304, 707, 735**,

and to the Saints: **27, 708, 735**,

the most beautiful, the most pure, the most holy: 200,
304, 505, 657, 664,

the most meritorious, the freest: **22, 424**,

the most glorified: **2, 169**.

This dignity is the basis of her power: **269**,

the cause of her Assumption and of her supreme
glory: **413, 475**,

Her permanent union with Christ

(12) — Mary is from all eternity in the decree of Christ's predestination: **31, 34, 520,**
  united with Christ by a most intimate and indissoluble bond: **46, 127, 156, 198, 518, 704, 706, 828,**
    as companion: **82, 183, 520, 705, 706,**
    inseparable: **235, 256, 568,**
    always with Him, according to the Scriptures: **127, 518,**
    following His steps: **440,**
    sharing His lot: **495, 518,**
    His life: **227,**
    partaking in all His mysteries: **183, 225, 440,**
    in His enmity against the devil: **46,**
    in His work of Redemption: **82, 127, 214, 216, 234, 282, 319, 326, 359,**
    subject to Him as Eve was to Adam: **519.**

United with Christ in every mystery

(13) — Mary is "socia" in the Annunciation and in the Purification: **151,**
    during the private life of Jesus: **227,**
    during His public life: **235,**
    in the act of Redemption: **151, 319, 413, 520-521, 704, 778,**
    at the foot of the Cross: **79, 151, 232, 241, 283, 705,**
    in His sacrifice: **69, 287,** cf. *(43-44),*
    in the union of sufferings: **137, 233, 413,**
    in His mediation: **287,** cf. *(37),*
    in the distribution of the graces of the Redemption: **234, 413,** cf. *(46), (48),*
    with her efficacious intercession: **513, 706.**
  She cannot remain corporally separated from Jesus: **518.**
  She shows His glory: **169, 706,** cf. *(101),*
    His triumph: **46, 520, 603, 706,**
    His kingdom: **137,** cf. *(103), (107),*
    His royal power: **705-706.**

Her analogy with Christ

(14) — motive of her Assumption
and of her Queenship: **413, 513, 519, 705.**

The Principle of Convenience (held by Suarez)

(15) God works in Mary all that is possible and convenient
to her dignity: **517-518, 595.**

Her solidarity with men

(16) — It is through Mary that Christ communicates with
the Mystical Body: **234, 828.**
At the Annunciation she spoke in the name of mankind: **113, 194, 381.**
she conceived Jesus in order that by means of the
nature assumed from her He might be the Redeemer of men: **229.**

Development of Marian Doctrine

Realization of this Progress

(17) — Marian studies should be ever more stimulated: **461,
613, 736,**
contemplating Mary's privileges: **482, 645, 729,**
which the Church has always investigated: the
Immaculate Conception: **483, 598, 613,**
and the Assumption: **495, 504,**
and thus acquire a greater knowledge of their
harmonies: **495.**
Doctrine and cult would reciprocally help each other
in this progress: **36 ff., 497, 504.**

Its Modalities and Conditions

(18) — This progress goes from the implicit to the explicit,
without adding anything to the revealed deposit: **45,
492, 712.**
It must unite positive and speculative discipline: **731,**
take into account the guidance of the Holy Ghost:
733,

and consider the Church's teaching authority as rule of faith: **712, 731.**
The 1950 definition added new vigor to Marian theology: **585,**
  which must be kept alive: **613, 736.**

Its Fruits

(19) — The friuts of this progress are Marian piety and grace: **461,**
  faith, devotion, imitation of Mary: **613, 645,**
  zeal: **673,**
  union with Mary: **647,**
  honor given to Christ and to Mary: **736,**
  a closer union of Mariology with theological doctrines: **730.**

Its deviations and errors

(20) — Nestorius, condemned at Ephesus, claimed Mary to be only the Mother of Christ: **292, 297, 299,**
  before the Council of Ephesus he was already condemned by the Pope: **291, 302.**
His error came from an error on the hypostatic union: **297.**
The Albigenses denied Mary's Virginity and Maternity: **273.**
The heretics who deny the Son also deny the Mother: **568.**
He who denies the Immaculate Conception is a heretic: **63,**
  he who denies the Assumption is also a heretic: **525.**
All exaggerations, minimizations and doctrinal fears must be avoided: **711, 734,**
The image of Mary presented in sacerdotal vestments is to be condemned: **258.**
It is a scandalous affair to affirm that the prophecy of Emmanuel (of Isaias) does not regard either in a literal sense, or typical sense, the Virgin and her divine Child: **11.**

PART ONE

THE MYSTERY OF MARY

CHAPTER ONE

MARY'S INTEGRAL MATERNITY

§ I. Predestination of the Mother of God

a) *The fact*

(21) — God filled Mary with His love: **2, 3, 31,**
>   and eternal affection: **483.**
>   Divine Maternity is the first effect of this love: **122, 269, 844.**
>   God inserted Mary in the plan of His Providence: **31, 157, 483,**
>>   loving her as Mother of God the Savior: **122, 595,**
>>   and bringing about its triumph: **462.**
>   This love constitutes her special election: **2, 32, 269**
>>   before all other creatures: **31, 52, 122, 200.**

b) *Its end*

(22) — God chose her among many: **2, 9, 31,**
>>   to constitute her as Mother of the Incarnate Word:
>>   **2, 114, 127, 200, 269, 319, 368, 400, 531.**
>   He wants her holy and full of grace: **31-32, 126, 647,**
>>   so that she may be "socia Redemptoris": cf. *(13)*,
>>   at the foot of the Cross: **267,** cf. *(116)*,
>>   in the glory: **200,** cf. *(100)*,
>>   mediatrix of all grace: **209, 578,**
>>   Mary help of the Church: **209,** cf. *(121)*,
>>   realization of the design of divine mercy: **115.**

c) *Its mode*

(23) — This design of giving the Redeemer through Mary
>   was perfectly free: **226.**

An identical decree predestined Christ and His Mother: **34, 520,**
> placing Mary immediately after Christ: **53, 707,** cf. *(11).*

God permitted the fall having foreseen the Incarnation, in Mary: **31.**

§ **II. Divine Maternity**

a) *The mystery*

(24) — The divine Maternity is a dogma which invests all the Catholic faith: **1, 298,**
> it was proclaimed at Ephesus: **1, 177, 289, 292, 310, 594, 728.**

Mary is the Mother of God: **114, 177, 200, 289, 299, 429,**
> thus raised above all other mothers: **127, 140,**
> because her Son is God: **299,**
> His human nature being personally united to the Word: **701.**

Mary most holy gives Christ a human body: **298, 301, 568, 829,**
> but not His soul, nor His divinity: **298, 301.**

She is true Mother of Christ: **150, 194,**
> so that the Father and the Virgin have one sole and identical Son: **32.**

She is the Mother of the eternal Priest: **465,**
> of the Christ Head: **383,**
> she is the living monstrance: **256.**

b) *Her free acceptance*

(25) — Mary freely consented to fulfill this design: **113, 381,**
> accepting it by her "fiat": **131, 150, 381, 741, 772,**
> on behalf of mankind: cf *(16).*

Conscious of the greatness of her office: **372,**
> and of the divinity of her Son: **214,**
> Mary joyfully offered herself: **131,**
> as handmaid, to be Mother: **151, 429.**

c) *Her greatness*

(26) — Divine Maternity is a supreme and infinite dignity: **111, 156, 200, 303, 372, 429, 594, 707-708, 728, 735,**
in virtue of the Hypostatic Union: **299, 413,**
of the Unique Person of the Son Jesus: **301.**
It is the highest destiny of a human creature: **111, 303, 429, 594, 707, 735,**
an infinite grace came from God through Jesus: **214,**
a unique miracle: **368,**
without the merit of any creature: **759.**
Mary must be the worthiest of Mothers: **126, 595.**

d) *Her riches and exigencies*

(27) — Divine Maternity is the reason of all Mary's gifts and riches: **304, 429, 505, 594, 647, 682, 741, 828,**
and above all of the love that Jesus bears her: **305, 505,**
of her respect: **202,**
of her Immaculate Conception: **33, 67, 245, 351, 594, 595, 728, 771,**
of her impeccability: **238, 594,**
of the fullness of grace which makes her worthy Mother of God: **50, 126, 303, 594,**
and of her perfect sanctity: **32, 304, 505, 594.**

e) *Its consequences*

(28) — Divine Maternity is a virginal maternity: **368, 429, 502, 512, 520, 569, 732, 829,**
and it is the reason of the infinite tenderness of Mary's Heart: **426,**
of her corporeal incorruptibility and of her Assumption: **502, 505, 515, 520** cf. *(98),*
of her corporeal glorification: **498,**
of her spiritual glory: **440, 741,**
of her queenship: **413, 701,** cf. *(104).*
It makes Mary the associate of the Redeemer: **82, 319, 413, 705,**
and conceives Christ as Savior: **229,**
through Mary God joined the race of the sons of Adam: **828.**

Mary has a maternal right of dispensing Christ's merits: **235, 413, 709**, cf. *(46)*.

§ **III. Spiritual Maternity**

a) *Mary Mother of men*

(29) — The Mother of God is also the mother of men: **140, 168, 182, 183, 189, 209, 216, 230, 268, 282, 307, 372, 420, 535, 541, 648, 724, 768,**
     our mother: **19, 65, 79, 116, 128, 164, 182, 186, 229, 326, 356, 440, 609, 617, 666, 716,**
     mother of all: **326, 334, 369, 430, 574,**
     always and ever known as such: **115**;
     of Christ's members: **112, 128, 129, 168, 183, 229, 230, 307, 363, 383, 385, 430, 522, 647, 671, 719,**
     mother of the living: **534.**

b) *Mother of grace*

(30) — Mary is the Mother of grace: **275,**
     as principle of grace: **126, 210, 404.**
     It is a *true* maternity: **624,**
       constituted by Mary's love for men: **648.**
     Like divine maternity, it is linked to the mystery of Christ: **183.**

c) *Dignity conferred by Christ*

(31) — Spiritual Maternity is a gift and a grace of Christ: **114, 128, 184, 268,**
     granted on Calvary: **15, 114, 168, 285, 370, 648, 724,**
     where Christianity was entrusted to Mary in the person of St. John: **79, 326, 537, 648.**
     This maternity is sealed and rendered efficacious by the omnipotence of Christ: **648.**
     It is the last Will, Christ's testament: **15, 115, 203, 268, 282, 327, 649,**
       which reveals His love for us: **168.**

takes an effective part in it: **214, 216, 257, 282, 326,**
and redeems mankind: **267, 383,**
as associate with the Redeemer: **82, 214, 234, 334, 703-705, 778,**
and is therefore co-Redemptrix: **326, 334.**

Co-redemption mediate or indirect

(42) — Mary is Mediatrix because she is Mother: **113, 194, 382,**
because she donates Christ the Savior: **164, 194, 218, 226, 287, 440, 624.**
With her free consent to the Incarnation: **113, 194, 381, 428, 648, 741,**
she donates and prepares the victim of the Sacrifice: **151, 231, 257, 440, 704.**
The body and blood of Christ were taken from Mary: **195.**
She generates the Author and the Consumer of our faith: **225.**
She donates us true Wisdom: **404,**
the source of life and benediction: **156, 624.**
She is the Mother of Christ for our salvation: **245.**
Mediatrix in the stable at Bethlehem: **195,**
at the Visitation: **150, 195, 202,**
at Cana: **202, 428.**
She accompanied Christ to the foot of the Cross in His work of Redemption: **326.**

Direct co-redemption

(43) — Mary acquires every grace because of her participation at the Cross: **268, 828,**
united to her crucified Son: **137,**
uniting her sufferings to those of her Son: **151, 161, 326, 638, 720, 778,**
and her tears: **140, 538, 724, 773.**
Because of her charity and her heart: **241, 655, 720,**
she dies with Jesus: **151, 267.**

She is, by means of this union, Reparatrix: **287**,
and cause of salvation: **550, 638**.
She redeemed men: **326**.

By means of sacrifice

(44) — Mary presents the Victim of salvation: **231, 287, 383**,
she offers Him for us to the divine Justice: **12, 151,
267, 383, 705**.
She gives herself as Mother and Mediatrix: **114**,
offers her love and her maternal rights: **267, 268,
383, 705**.
She is willingly present at the sacrifice of the Redeemer: **151, 257, 267**,
offering her sacrifice of mother: **748**.
From the Annunciation to Calvary, Mary intimately
united herself to the Sacrifice of her Son: **69**.

By merit

(45) — Mary, through her merits, takes part in the Redemption: **149, 214, 704**,
in a manner proportionate to her sanctity, and her
union with Christ: **234**.
She merits "de congruo" what Christ merited "de
condigno": **234**.
She completes the Passion of Christ more than all
other creatures: **384**.
She gathers the heritage of work which her Son left
her: **114**.
On the Cross Christ confirms this divine plan on
Mary: **114**.

c) *Mary dispenser of grace*

She takes part in the distribution of grace

(46) — Mary also fulfills her office of Mother in the Cenacle:
cf. *(117)*.
As she has been Reparatrix: **233, 268**,
she is mediatrix in the distribution of graces: **23,
114, 149, 170, 194, 233, 255, 271, 275, 287, 323**,

373, 407, 413, 450, 624, 779,
Mediatrix mediatorum omnium: 272.
Mary is minister of graces: 103, 113, 171, 234, 275,
288, 317, 428,
their dispenser: 81, 97, 155, 169, 235, 263, 287,
361, 407,
distributor: 4, 413, 624, 706, 748, 770,
treasurer: 278, 361, 365, 404, 706.
She administers them: 361,
showers them on every social class: 748,
without exception of persons: 361.
The three stages of the distribution of graces are: from
God the Father to Christ; from Christ to Mary; from
Mary to us: 155.

Mary's proper role in this distribution

(47) — Mary makes us a present of her superabundant fullness: 126, 156, 229,
she is the channel: 4, 155, 359, 709, 760,
neck channel: 234,
and not source nor creative power of grace: 234,
760.
All good comes from Mary: 163, 209, 268, 343, 578,
who intervenes in all concessions of grace: 323, 626.
God uses Mary to distribute grace: cf. *(46)*,
and to fulfill every miracle: 202, 271.
The help that she grants from heaven is more efficacious and extended: 169,
because she knows best what concerns us: 129.

d) *Mediatrix through her intercession*
Place that prayer has in Mary's mediation

(48) — Mary is mediatrix with her prayer: 13, 15, 123, 163,
222, 247, 261, 849, 850,
which upholds and substitutes our prayer: 156.
Mary intercedes on our behalf: 146, 287, 558, 647,
845,
with a unique intercession: 207,
most powerful: 275, 435, 436, 647, 648,

assiduous: **27.**
Mary is thus our advocate: **13, 153, 219, 233, 287, 323, 325, 386, 467, 432, 850,**
universal: **436.**

Privileges of Mary's prayer

(49) — Mary is heard because she is Mother, because she is full of grace, because she is united to Christ: **13, 149, 156, 706,**
her intercession is always efficacious: **26, 65, 107, 370, 387, 706, 767,**
she is in closest contact with God, sees our needs better: **207,**
she has the greatest maternal tenderness: **207,**
she enjoys the greatest favor of God: **156, 207, 208,**
she is the person united closest to Christ: **706.**
Mary has rights of possession on the Heart of Jesus: **386.**
She brings about a return of warm affection to the hearts of men: **323.**
This intercession constitutes Mary intercessor of the Omnipotent: **27, 207, 261, 269, 356, 767.**

Its fruits

(50) — They appear at Cana: **370,**
at Pentecost: **98, 199, 254, 649.**
Mary continues to have the Holy Ghost descend on Priests: **466,**
showers invisible graces on the Church: **222,** cf. *(121)*.
She works out our salvation: **126, 219, 704,**
she obtains faith for us: **230, 831, 842,**
repose and abandonment in God: **842,**
despair disappears: **18,**
she calms Our Lord: **93, 261, 367,**
she obtains His assistance: **123,**
she assures heaven: **268, 454,**
realizes human fraternity: **533,**
she worked numerous miracles at Lourdes: **222,** cf. *(155)*.

Mary is the Mediatrix of our prayers

(51) — Mary exercises her mediation with regard to our
prayers: **26, 115,**
which she presents to God: **26, 219, 256.**
She stands by them: **129, 156, 179, 199,**
renders them efficacious: **115, 116, 156, 248.**
She makes up for the unworthiness of those who
pray: **115.**
She unites herself to our prayers: **216.**

Secondary consequences of her mediation

(52) — Prayer causes Mary's bounty to flow on her sons: **633,**
makes us grow in the knowledge of God: **171, 172,
404, 625, 643, 782,**
in sanctity: **322, 626, 642, 782,**
assures sanctity: **229, 256, 268, 282, 550, 627, 704,**
builds up the Mystical Body: **247, 381,**
makes us love the Church: **381,**
grants peace and pleases God: **4, 13, 22, 52, 154, 156,
216, 251, 365, 842,**
opens Heaven: **4, 13, 140, 172, 256, 308, 627,**
puts the devil to flight, and obtains victory over
present enemies: **172, 340, 782.**

§ II. The Immaculate Conception

Privilege

(58) — Mary was conceived without original sin: **62, 239, 319, 584 ff., 771.**
   This is a unique and wonderful privilege: **238, 350, 660,**
   prelude to all other privileges of Mary: **350.**

It is contained in Sacred Scripture

(59) — The Sacred Scripture illustrates it: **61, 62, 590,**
   in the third chapter of Genesis, according to the interpretation of the Fathers and of the Liturgy: **56, 590, 603.**
   The enmity between Mary and the devil appears in it: **46, 64, 219, 226, 421, 590, 603, 629, 652.**
   The Ark of the Covenant and other Biblical figures symbolize Mary's total victory: **47.**
   The liturgy applies to Mary the origin of uncreated Wisdom: **34.**
   The absolute purity of her who is called "full of grace" appears in the Angelic Salutation: **591.**
   No passage of the Sacred Scripture is contrary to the Immaculate Conception: **44.**

Attitude of the Supreme Pontiffs before the Definition

(60) — Many Popes encouraged the doctrine of the Immaculate Conception: **28, 39, 61,**
   by favoring its veneration, by precisely declaring the object of the feast: **28, 37, 38, 39, 40, 60.**
   The interventions of Alexander VII: **40, 41, 42,**
   of Gregory XVI: **18,**
   of Pius IX: **21, 37.**

The teaching of the Church, before the Definition

(60) — Original innocence of Mary was always the object of the Church's teaching: **45, 56,**
   as a truth received from God: **33, 45.**

This truth is the object of the constant sentiment of the Church: **35, 56, 61, 238, 589, 600,**
  it is zealously defended by the Roman Church: **35, 36, 38, 39.**
The development of the doctrine declared by the Councils: **598,**
  especially by the Council of Trent: **44.**
This doctrine is propagated by the bishops: **33.**
The faithful, in agreement with their pastors, make it an object of devotion and of love: **61, 238.**

The Liturgy and the Immaculate Conception

(62) — Faith in the Immaculate Conception is manifested by veneration: **33, 37, 39, 55, 598,**
  the ancient liturgies testify to it: **598,**
  especially in the Orient: **599,**
  the Roman liturgy: **17, 20, 25, 37,**
  celebrated the Immaculate Conception: **33, 38;**
  at the time of Pius IX, this worship continued to make progress: **28.**

The Patristic Tradition

(63) — This tradition, in its complex, testifies the doctrine of the Immaculate Conception: **45, 46, 61, 590.**
The Fathers note this privilege in the Sacred Scriptures: **56,**
  in the protoevangelium: **46, 47,**
  in the prophetical symbols and biblical types: **47,**
  in the "full of grace", and in the words of Elizabeth's blessing: **49.**
They say that an all pure Mother is in conformity with divine sanctity: **53.**
For them, this privilege is required for a perfect victory over the devil: **52, 53,**
  for a perfect grace: **46, 54, 592,**
  in order to be compared to an innocent Eve: **50.**
The praises which the Fathers give to Mary imply this privilege: **51, 54, 592.**
The Oriental tradition has always proclaimed this privilege: **728.**

The Council of Trent declared that nothing could be cited from tradition against the Immaculate Conception: **44.**

The Theologians

(64) — Universities and Religious Orders are supporters of this privilege: **43.**
The Sorbonne in a particular manner: **277.**
Suarez believes that it can be defined: **517.**

Preparation for the Definition

(65) — Petitions from the hierarchy: **19, 28, 58, 59,**
princes: **28, 409,**
faithful: **16, 19, 20, 21, 25, 56, 58.**
The definition was preceded
by prayers: **25,**
by consultations and study: **20, 21, 24, 29, 57, 59,**
which favorably agreed on the definibility and on the opportune time: **30, 61,** cf. *(96).*

The definition of the dogma and its results

(66) — The canonical text of the definition: **62,**
consecrates the constant faith of the Church: **62, 589.**
It renders glory to God and to Mary most holy: **61,**
throws new light on Mary's prerogatives: **57.**
It has been the source of great good for the Church: **245, 251,**
induces us to respect and obey the Church: **221, 244,**
prepared the definition of the Pontifical Infallibility: **220, 222,**
invoked the divine reply to the apparitions at Lourdes: **222,**
where Bernadette was the confidant of the Immaculate: **283 bis,**
prepared the definition of the Assumption: **486, 566, 601.**

It gave new vigor to Marian devotion: **27, 584, 585, 726.**

It strengthens faith in the dogmas of original sin, of the Redemption, of the Church and throws light on the problem of human suffering: **242, 243, 590.**

It condemns those who deny these truths, the unbelievers, the rationalists and materialists: **66, 242, 243, 244.**

Anniversaries of the definition

(67) — The fiftieth: **220, 221,**

brings about the conversion of sinners: **251.**

The centenary enlivens faith: **604.**

Supreme reason of the Immaculate Conception

(68) — The doctrine of the Immaculate Conception is based on the relations that exist between Mary and the Most Blessed Trinity: **32, 53, 725,**

the dogma of the divine Maternity: **31-33, 66, 238, 245, 351, 594, 728, 828,**

Mary's soul reflects in its beauty the holiness of her Son: **771,**

God's continuous love for Mary: **595,**

the abundance of Mary's initial grace: **52, 660,**

her total victory over the devil and sin: **52, 238, 421, 590,**

her primacy among the Saints: **708,**

Mary's constant and total purity: **47, 592,**

the fact that this privilege was possible and convenient: **595.**

The origin of faith in this Marian privilege lies in the absolute opposition between God and sin: **238.**

It is given its proper value by the definition of the Assumption: **484, 485, 601, 602, 603.**

This privilege is in harmony with the office of "socia Redemptoris": **52, 82.**

Mary is perfectly redeemed

(69) — The privilege of the Immaculate Conception is due to the merits of Christ: **43, 62, 238, 239, 595, 596, 771.**

Mary is also a daughter of Adam: **734.**
She did not receive the grace of creation, but the grace of redemption: **325, 462, 596.**
The privilege does not consist in a seed which remained incorrupted and came down to her, as Rosmini says: **38a.**
Mary was redeemed, but in a more perfect manner: **43, 238, 462, 596.**
She exalts her redemption and thanks the Lord in the *Magnificat*: **462.**

Meaning and teaching of the privilege

(70) − The Immaculate Conception reminds the world of the esteem it must have of spiritual goods: **660, 665,**
> it points out the unhappy condition of fallen humanity: **771,**
> it exalts the elevation of mankind fulfilled by the second Adam: **31.**

The Immaculate Conception is the great sign of Mary's struggle and victory over sin: **46, 52, 239, 421, 485, 603, 629,**
> and over the devil: **32, 50, 52, 64, 421, 441, 590, 603.**

§ **III. Mary's Sanctity**

a) *The privilege*

(71) − God's work in Mary's interior life: **136,**
> ideally perfect, to make her His Mother: **54, 368,**
> and under her fully victorious: **47.**

This perfect sanctity is manifested in the Sacred Scripture and in Tradition: **46, 732.**

b) *Her sublimity*

(72) − It is a supereminent sanctity which surpasses that of every other creature: **31, 69, 234, 304, 413, 440, 505, 594, 657, 664, 829.**
> Only Jesus' sanctity is superior to this: **664,**
> of which this is a reflection: **771, 836.**

c) *Its reasons*

(73) — This sanctity is willed by God: **647,**
   Mary's relationship with the Blessed Trinity calls
   for it: **32,**
   for her divine Maternity: **31, 32, 304, 505, 828,**
   and her relationship with the hypostatic order: **413.**
   It is given by her innocence and her original
   grace: **33,**
   and by the fullness of grace which God gave
   Mary: **323.**

d) *Its consequences*

(74) — This sanctity throws its reflections on her body and
   postulates the Assumption: **503, 603.**
   It exalts the dignity of the woman: **569.**
   Shines brilliantly, with its consequences, on the
   Church: **569,** cf. *(121).*
   It is perfect liberty and total exemption from all in-
   clinations to evil: **47, 52, 140, 304, 424, 644, 828.**

e) *Original sanctity*

(75) — The Immaculate Conception (takes for granted) that
   Mary was full of grace from the first instant of her
   existence: **771.**
   Her original sanctity is already the fullness of grace:
   660, 771,
   and perfect sanctity: **33.**
   It is an original grace, superabundant, which surpasses that of all the Angels and all the Saints: **52, 54,
   126, 708.**
   It is the blessing that countered the curse of Eve: **507.**
   It is the grace of redemption and not of creation:
   cf. *(69).*

f) *Its progressive development*

(76) — Mary has always grown in her original grace: **50.**
   Her "Fiat" transformed her life of sanctity: **372.**

bringing about the perfection of the interior life: **720,**

most splendid union of divine perfections: **647.**

j) *Mary most holy and her theological virtues*

(80) — Mary has all virtues, in the highest degree, and she is the model of them: **137, 240, 314, 421, 437, 440, 655, 660, 720, 758, 828.**

Her faith is the motive of her beatitude: **171, 225, 227, 241, 630.**

Her hope is exercised, especially at the foot of the Cross: **241, 384, 744.**

She is immaculate in her faith and in her love: **219.**

Her charity towards God is ardent and continuous: **630, 635, 652, 655, 664.**

Her fraternal charity is manifested in the Visitation, at Nazareth and at Cana: **349, 655.**

Her love for the Child Jesus is love for the newborn Church: **384.**

She united her charity to the sufferings of the Crucifix: **151, 241, 655.**

At the foot of the Cross Mary loves Christ more than Peter does: **363.**

This love made Mary Mother of Mercy: **362, 408, 475, 537, 539,** cf. *(40).*

It is the condition of her spiritual maternity: **363, 672,** cf. *(31)* ff.

and it fills her with bounty: **140, 161, 275, 320, 426, 668,** cf. *(40).*

k) *The virtue of religion in Mary most holy*

(81) — Mary is also the model of prayer: **254, 843,** cf. *(49).*

This spirit of prayer is described in the Gospel: **655.**

Her prayer contributed to the Incarnation: **199.**

She asks pardon and faith for us: **230.**

She prayed for those who killed Christ: **241,**

for the unity of the Church, in the Cenacle: **196, 199,**

at the foot of the Cross she adored the Divinity: **241.**

l) *Her moral virtues*

(82) — Mary has all moral virtues: **425, 437, 660, 720,**
         purity: **313, 372, 420, 441, 640, 652, 661,**
         fortitude: **372, 384, 421, 441, 442, 628, 635, 743-
         746.**
         Divine wisdom conciliates in her justice and mercy:
         114.
         She is the perfect obedient person, obedient also to
         her Son: **50, 138, 372, 429, 455, 508, 531, 607, 741,
         772, 838.**
             she is full of humility: **2, 126, 313, 349, 372, 420,
             531, 652, 655, 784,**
             she is willingly poor, to be all God's: **135, 346, 352,
             532, 655,**
             she is faithful to God and to her own duties: **136,**
             313, 349, 372, 629, 772,
             she is silent: **655,**
             she is foreseeing (at Cana): **372, 655,**
             she is grateful (*Magnificat*): **462,**
             she possesses all domestic virtues: **313, 349, 662.**

m) *Her wisdom*

(83) — Mary is the seat of Wisdom: **68, 173, 404, 441,**
             she penetrates divine Wisdom: **152.**
         She knows Jesus and His mysteries in a most singular
         manner: **227.**
         She kept the divine mysteries in her heart: **168.**
         At the Annunciation, she is conscious of her mission:
         214, 372,
             and she knows that she conceives the Word of God:
             214.
         She knows us perfectly and our needs: **129, 140.**
         She prophesied, in the *Magnificat*, the cult which
         will be rendered to her: **436.**

n) *Her beauty*

(84) — The spiritual and corporal beauty of Mary: **53, 244,
         368, 621-623, 660, 752, 836, 843,**

it surpasses that of all other creatures: **368, 437, 622, 657, 763.**

Christ's beauty originates from her: **623, 771.**

This corporal beauty, unique, comes from the fact that Mary is Virgin and Mother: **368.**

She appeals to and deludes all other artists: she appeals to them for her perfection; she deludes them because they are not able to draw her exquisite beauty: **368.**

o) *Her sorrows, her trials, her sufferings, her joys*

(85) — Mary led a hidden life on earth: **532.**

She knew fatigue, and domestic worries: **346, 347,** anxieties, sufferings, sorrow: **137, 151, 232, 384, 495, 432, 607, 637, 720, 724, 748.**

She did not suffer through her own faults: **637,** but because of our sins: **140, 638, 655.**

She suffered, in a special manner on Calvary: **151, 241, 568, 648,** as Mother of the members of the Mystical Body: **383,** and because of our defections from faith: **663, 724.**

She has compassion on those who suffer injustice: **773.**

The tears of anxiety and of sadness which she shed in her apparitions, manifest her maternal love: **724, 774.**

Mary was joyful in accepting divine Maternity: **131,** she felt familiar joys together with sufferings: **346,** also on Calvary she experienced joy: **232.**

She received all her joys from her Son: **161.**

p) *Her merits*

(86) — By means of her virtues and merits she reached the height of glory: **22, 137, 169.**

From the first moment of her existence, the Immaculate merited all God's love: **771.**

She did not merit Divine Maternity: cf. *(26).*

She merited for us: cf. *(45).*

§ IV. Mary's Virginity

a) The "Blessed Virgin"

(87) — The name of the "Virgin" is a glorious title, which is
sufficient to designate Mary: **368, 639.**
She is purer than the Angels: **372.**
Her virginal purity is unique among the Saints: **569,
593,** cf. *(82).*
Her virginal life is a model of virtue: cf. *(131).*
Mary's perpetual virginity was denied by the Albi-
genses: **273.**

b) Virginal Mother

(88) — Mary was, at the same time, Virgin and Mother:
368, 429, 499, 520, 569, 829, 844.
She was virgin in conceiving, in bearing the child,
and always during her life: **247, 512, 514, 580.**
This virginal maternity is a motive of the Assumption: **499, 502, 512.**
The Virgin Mary is the second Eve who saves humanity: **705.**
The virginal birth of Jesus was the fulfillment of the
prophecies of Emmanuel, of Isaias: **11.**

§ V. The Assumption of Mary

a) Mary's death

(89) — The faithful admitted that Mary, following the steps
of her Son, died: **495.**
The prayer *"Veneranda"* says that Mary underwent
corporal death: **498.**
Mary died, because she did not receive the so-called
grace "of creation," but the grace of "redemption,"
which does not confer the immortality of the body:
325.
According to the Pseudo-Modesto, Mary was raised to life
by Jesus Christ: **503.**

h) *The privilege of the Assumption*

(90) — The Assumption is a privilege: **521**,
    which means not only the glorification of the soul,
    but also of Mary's body: **516, 524**,
    which means exemption from the common law of
    death: **485**,
    triumph over sin and over the consequences of sin:
    603,
    and from the corruption of the tomb: **520**.
    This privilege is noted only through faith: **493**.

c) *It is based on Sacred Scripture*

(91) — The Assumption is confirmed by Sacred Scripture:
    505, 521.
    The victory of the "Woman" preannounced in the Old
    Testament, also contains implicitly the preannounce-
    ment of the Assumption: **506, 519**.
    In the New Testament, the Assumption is contained
    in the greeting "*Gratia plena*" and "*Benedicta tu*": **507**.
    This privilege also results from the constant associa-
    tion of Mary and Jesus: **518**.
    The Assumption is also shown in the "Woman" of the
    Apocalypse: **506-507**.

d) *The teaching of the Church*

(92) — The Assumption is taught by the Church: **492, 521**,
    and is unanimously held as object of faith: **471, 535**.
    It was already believed in the first stages of the
    Church: **468, 472**,
    it is taught by the ordinary and universal Magisteri-
    um as it is revealed truth to be believed: **492-493**.
    The definibility of the Assumption is based on the
    infallibility of the Church: **472**.

e) *The Liturgy*

(93) — Liturgical cult is a proof of the Assumption: **492, 501**.
    It underlines the link that runs between the Assump-

tion and the divine and virginal Maternity: **499**, cf.
(28).
The liturgical testimonies of the Assumption are
numerous: **496-500, 504, 521.**

f) *The Fathers and Theologians*

(94) — The principal patristic testimonies in favor of the
Assumption: **501-503,**
free use of expressions taken from Scriptural texts:
506.
Theologians and spiritual authors are all in favor of
this privilege: **487, 505-517,**
their wisdom, their science, their studies develop it:
521,
they show that the Assumption is included in the
Deposit of faith: **488.**
The 20th century has thrown greater light on this
Marian privilege: **483.**

g) *The faith of Christians*

(95) — The privilege of the Assumption is dear to the faithful:
516, 521.
This is the faith of the Church: new and distinct proof
among the theological motives: **495, 516.**
It is attested by the cult of sacred images: **496,**
by the Patronage of the Assumption over dioceses
and religious Orders: **489,**
by the holy Rosary: **496,**
by petitions sent to the Pope: **405, 489,**
by the unanimous reply of bishops to the requests
of the Holy See: **480, 491,**
by Church history: **469, 494, 495.**
The opinion contrary to the Assumption was judged
temerarious for a long time: **516.**

h) *The definition*

(96) — Asked for at and after the Vatican Council: **405, 468,
487, 601,**

prepared by enquiries and studies: **406, 469, 470, 471, 479, 490,**
which came to the conclusion that it could be defined: **406, 472, 491, 492, 517,**
and considered the definition opportune: **471, 473, 521, 527,**
prepared by prayer: **406.**
It was solemnly promulgated: **524,**
 by the authority of the Pope: **468, 523.**
Precise object of the definition is the assumption of Mary both body and soul into Heaven: **468, 524.**
It was defined as a dogma of faith, revealed: **492, 524.**
Pius XII recalls this definition: **547, 678, 845.**

i) *Its fruits*

(97) — Above all God's glory: **475, 481, 522, 524, 543,**
 the honor of her Son: **524, 543,**
  the glory of Mary most holy: **473, 475, 481, 523-524, 543.**
 Numerous graces and spiritual favors: **473, 530,**
  numerous advantages for Religion: **481,**
  an increase of faith in the resurrection of the bodies: **522,**
  an increase of devotion to Mary most holy: **481, 522.**
This definition was the crowning of the definition of the Immaculate Conception: **526, 601.**
She shows the value of human life dedicated to do God's Will and to practices of charity: **522.**
It increases our desire to unite ourselves to Christ's Body: **522.**
It will benefit sinners and those erring in faith: **475.**
It brings remedy to the corruption of morals and materialism: **473, 522.**
It is a beneficial ray on the world: **467, 524, 526-527, 543.**

j) *Theological Reasons*

(98) — The definition was based on doctrinal reasons: **521.**
First of all on the divine Maternity: **505,** cf. *(28)*, *(99)*,

on the love and honor of Christ towards His Mother:
505, 515, 518;
on the Virginity of the Mother of God: **512, 514;**
on the union and likeness between Christ and His
Mother: **502, 513, 521;**
on the unity of the decree of their predestination: **518;**
on Mary's victory over sin and death: **485, 509, 603;**
on the Immaculate Conception: **602-603;**
on the fullness of grace: **507-508;**
on the blessing of Mary which excludes the curse of
Eve: **510;**
on the victory of the new Eve: **519;**
on Mary's personal perfection: **509, 512;**
It is only reasonable and fitting that not only the soul
and body of a man, but also the soul and body of a
woman should have obtained heavenly glory: **513;**
there are no relics of the body of Mary most holy on
earth: **513.**

k) *Link between the Assumption and other truths of faith*

(99) — The Assumption is linked to the other revealed
truths: **502, 504, 521.**
It is the crowning of all Mary's privileges: **498, 520,
521, 526,**
especially to the Immaculate Conception: **484, 485,
602.**
It results from the divine and virginal Maternity: **499,
502, 503, 505,**
and from the virginal integrity of Mary's body: **499,
502-503, 512,**
from the dignity which is proper to her: **475,**
from her title of beloved spouse of God the Father:
502,
and from that of Queen of Heaven: **520.**

§ **VI. Mary's Queenship and glory**

a) *Mary in Heaven*

(100) — In Heaven, Mary is perfectly happy: **370, 539, 632,
724,**

glorified also in her body: **493, 501, 512, 603, 623.**
She enjoys the vision of God and of Jesus' Humanity:
532, 536.
She is also the object of the Angels' praise: **368,
535, 752.**
She crowns the Saints: **324,**
    shows Christ to the elect: **539, 719,**
    is the happiness of the Saints who contemplate her:
    539, 752,
    and who unite themselves to her glory: **131, 140,**
    and praise her: **64.**
She is full of love and of compassion for us: **247, 371,
724, 776, 781,**
    and she does not cease to succor men: **288, 317, 748,**
    especially by means of her intercession: **385,**
    cf. *(48)* ff.

  b) *Crowned in glory*

(101) — Mary is crowned in heavenly glory: **131, 153, 169,
368, 370, 385, 412, 506, 584, 676, 738,**
    elevated next to God's throne: **22, 412, 684,**
    at the right hand of Christ the Redeemer: **65, 67,
    234, 412, 506, 520, 648, 709,**
    partakes of His glory: **131, 152, 603, 725,**
    in the highest place: **81, 137, 440, 509, 520, 535,
    706,**
    with particular dignity: **200, 683.**
This glory has its origin in the "Fiat": **741,**
    and is fully accomplished in the Assumption: **169,
    520,**
    when Mary becomes the heavenly spouse: **506.**
Her title as Mother of Christ's members, is also a
motive of glory: **383.**
This exaltation of Mary most holy is the first triumph
of Christ: **568.**

  c) *Her Queenship*

(102) — Mary is the Queen of the Universe: **65, 137, 153, 369,
380, 412, 414, 527, 529, 618, 676, 709, 756, 845.**

Sovereign of the Church militant, suffering and triumphant: 363-364.
Queen of Heaven: 65, 137, 190, 361, 506, 520, 539, 676, 740,
   of the Angels: 370, 372, 414, 535, 752, 850,
   of the Saints: 321, 364, 414, 467, 752.
Our Queen: 164, 219, 370, 527, 710, 750-751.
Queen of the Apostles: 168, 363, 400, 414, 756, cf. *(165)*.

d) *She reigns with Christ and for Christ*

(103) — Mary partakes in Christ's empire: 3, 366, 413, 414, 692, 828,
   reigning side by side with Him: 137, 385, 414, 520, 527,
   reigning for Him: 169, 414,
   for the grace and love of God: 3, 414,
   and partaking, in a finite and analogical manner, in Christ's Kingship: 706.

e) *The titles of Marian Queenship*

(104) — It is above all a Queenship of excellence: 413, 429, 707-708, 748, 751.
   She is Queen because she was born from a kingly race: 135, 695,
      because she is Mother of God: 413, 682-683, 685, 701, 702, 828,
      because she is Mother of Christ the King: 413, 683, 692, 695, 701, 751,
      because she is the associated companion of Christ the King: 413-414, 682, 705, 706,
      because she is the second Eve of the second Adam: 705,
      another title comes from the Incarnation by means of her "Fiat": 702, 741.
   She is Queen by title of conquest, as co-Redemptrix: 414, 703, 704, 828.

h) *Her power*

(107) — Mary is a powerful Mother and Queen: **114, 208, 251, 275, 356, 574.**
This power is superior to the power of all other creatures: **81, 149, 269, 288, 317, 319, 369.**
In all necessities, it is more powerful than the power of all the other Saints in each particular case: **436.**
She exercises this power with her Son and on Him: **27, 67, 82, 269, 275, 319, 256, 440,**
and by means of her Son on God's Heart: **356, 365, 367, 369, 440, 706,**
by reason of her union with God: **371, 706,**
who communicates to her almost all His power: **3.**

i) *Aspects proper to such a power*

(108) — It is a saving power: **648,**
irresistible: **26, 436,**
clement and maternal: **161, 710,**
which is exercised by means of a most efficacious patronage and protection: **26, 714,** cf. *(134).*
Power of mediation: **64, 718,** cf. *(37), (40),*
of distribution of graces: **81, 706, 709,** cf. *(46-47).*
of intercession: **369, 463, 648,** cf. *(49),*
can help the "wayfarers": **81,** cf. *(134),*
and aid all their needs: **398,** cf. *(136).*

j) *Mary's queenship is triumph and victory*

(109) — Mary is both triumphant and victorious with Christ: **373, 412, 603.**
She overcame heresy, sin, the devil: **52, 64, 245, 373, 603,** cf. *(123).*

k) *Her dominion*

(110) — She reigns over the interior life of each one of us: **322, 659, 709, 740,**
over human society: **659,**
watching over its unity and peace: **741,**
opens the path of faith to the world: **400, 752.**

l) *Her exigencies*

(111) — This kingdom calls for our faith, submission, love, our
          service in the family and in society: **415.**
          It demands our prayer and the imitation of Mary's
          virtues: **415, 659, 671.**

PART TWO

MARY'S LIFE

§ I. **Mary's life up to Pentecost**

   a) *Life with Christ*

(112) — Mary's life on earth is all linked with the mysteries of
          of Christ: **440, 828,**
              of which she is the guardian: **225,**
              she always assents to these mysteries: **462.**
          The Immaculate Conception and Assumption stand
          out at the beginning and at the end of the earthly
          life of Mary most holy: **603.**
          All Mary's actions were consecrated to God: **838.**

   b) *Before the Annunciation*

(113) — In her Immaculate Conception, Mary is the dawn of
          salvation: **53.**
          She descends from a royal family: **135.**
          She leads a hidden and laborious life at Nazareth,
          performing no extraordinary miracles: **135, 655,**
              she lives a recollected life: **372,**
              setting there the first stones of the Church: **112.**
          God, because of the respect He bears her, entrusts
          her to St. Joseph: **202,**
              who, through a true marriage, partakes in her dig-
              nity as Mother of God: **111,**
              and power: **111.**
          St. Joseph was the happiness of Mary most holy,
          and he is the object of her love: **346.**
          Mary submits herself to St. Joseph: **349.**

c) *From the Annunciation to the Crib*

(114) – The "Fiat" is the origin of the mission and glories of
Mary, Mother and Queen: **701, 741.**
Mary is conscious of conceiving the Word of God:
214,
of her place and responsibility, as Mother of the
Redeemer and Mother of men: **372.**
She promptly answers the Angel: **372,**
in the name of all Humanity: **381,** cf. *(25),*
making possible the Passion and Resurrection: **568.**
She becomes the spiritual Mother of men: **230, 430,
648,** cf. *(29)* ff.
At the Visitation, Mary manifests her fraternal charity:
372, 655.

d) *From the Crib to Calvary*

(115) – At Christmas the Child is found with Mary: **150.**
It is she who offers Him in the Temple: **150.**
She takes care of Jesus at Nazareth: **287, 671,**
she instructs Him in human wisdom: **759,**
she lives a hidden life with Him: **227, 346, 655,**
working: **346,**
she often recalls the acts of the child Jesus: **227.**
She is the auxiliatrix of the miracle at Cana: **202, 237,
382, 478,**
and there showed her vigilance and charity: **372,
655.**
During the public life of her Son, she remains near
Him: **227,**
humble and patient: **372,**
without publicly taking part in His work: **267.**

e) *During Our Lord's Passion*

(116) – Mary takes part in the agony of Gethsemani: **151.**
She is at the foot of the Cross, standing: **12, 70-71,
151, 232, 266, 372, 720, 766,**
and makes acts of faith, hope and charity: **71, 241,
358,**
without murmuring: **12, 637-638,**

calm and recollected: **75,**

she prays for those who crucified Our Lord: **241,**

her heart pierced with sorrow: **71, 372, 495, 648,**

united, through love, to the sufferings of Christ: **241, 267, 359, 828,**

Queen of Martyrs: **137, 257.**

She unites her rights and her love of a Mother to these sufferings: **267, 383, 705,**

by offering a maternal sacrifice: **151, 267, 383, 748,** cf. *(44).*

She weeps over our sins: **538, 724,**

and completes the passion for the Church: **384.**

She is entrusted to St. John: **202,** cf. *(31-32).*

Christ gives her to us: **284, 370.**

She becomes our Mother and she receives us as her children: **114, 268, 282, 358, 363, 383, 440, 605, 648, 664, 724,** cf. *(32).*

She was entrusted to the love of the Church: **2.**

This presence under the cross was in view of her future Assumption: **502.**

f) *From the Resurrection to Pentecost*

(117) – The risen Christ appears to Mary: **72,**

He consoles her and reveals to her the future triumphs of the Church: **72, 76.**

She partakes in His Resurrection: **828.**

It is very likely that Mary was present at the Ascension of Jesus into Heaven: **570.**

In the Cenacle she fulfills her office of Mother: **168,**

she prays with the Apostles and for them: **98, 153, 199, 254, 372, 384, 649, 839.**

§ II. **Mary in the Church, after Pentecost**

a) *Mary on earth, at the early stages of the Church*

(118) – After Pentecost, Mary remains on earth for the good of the new-born Church: **152, 172, 363, 839.**

She reveals God's designs to the Church, and recalls to her the truths of faith: **172, 225, 227.**

She loves the Church with the same love with which she loved the Word made flesh: **384.**

She cooperates in the birth and constitution of the Church: **216, 259, 384,**
> Queen of the Apostles: cf. *(103),*
> she helps them to spread the Gospel: **168, 172, 400,**
> she incites them to love Jesus: **570.**
She exercises her solicitude on the first Christians: **570, 748.**
She presents Christ to the Jews and to the pagans: **382.**

b) *Mary first member and Mother of the Church*

(119) — Mary is a very special member of the Church: **735, 849;**
> she is its ornament: **64,**
> she exercises an ecclesiastical role in it: **68.**
Mother of the Church: **2, 168,**
> she bore the Head of the Church in her womb: **382,**
> she always donates Him to the Church: **674.**
She receives men into the Church: **221.**

c) *Sovereign and Patroness of the Church*

(120) — Mary is Sovereign of the Church: **364.**
Higher than Peter, like unto him she has dignity, authority, magisterium: **363.**
Peter possesses the Keys of Heaven; Mary possesses God's Heart: **365.**
She is the Patroness of the Church: **187, 188, 335, 385, 419, 478.**
She protects the Church: **64, 288, 335, 366, 538, 840,**
> and exercises on it, her maternal charity: **259, 773.**

d) *Mary's action in the Church*

(121) — Mary's sanctity exercises an influence over all the Church: **209, 569.**
Mary takes part in the work fulfilled there by Christ: **828.**
She always intercedes for the Church: **9, 27, 66, 168, 222, 247, 385, 846.**

Mary never ceases to spend herself for the Church: **247, 259, 455, 840**.

She is the base, the center and the link of union between Christians: **176, 181, 186, 197, 533**.

She enrolls us in the Church: **174,**

and there strives for union in charity: **175-176, 384, 534.**

Seat of Wisdom, she illuminates Bishops, she helps them and renders all people docile to them: **68.**

Queen of apostolate, she inspires Doctors and promotes zeal of religion: **173, 186, 779,** cf. *(165)*.

She procures the dominion and extension of the Church: **64, 172, 360, 428.**

She is the stronghold, the help and the support of the Church: **64, 66, 103, 165, 169, 209, 249, 259, 423, 538, 767,**

she is its constant refuge: **82, 212, 753,**

her hope: **64, 82, 217, 288,**

her star: **358, 419.**

Mary watches over the Church: **169.**

She defends it in dangers: **22, 103, 173, 212, 217, 308, 478, 845.**

Peace comes to the Church through Mary: **22, 83, 335, 378-379, 846,**

victory: **121, 125, 717, 840,**

liberty: **424, 717, 846.**

e) *Mary and the faith of the Church*

(122) — Mary, Mother of the Author of faith, is, after Him, the base of it: **171, 178, 225.**

She is the source of faith: **172, 400, 619.**

Teacher of faith and of the knowledge of God: **227, 228, 235, 363,**

she upholds, confirms, fortifies faith: **172, 174, 179, 643,**

vigils over the integrity of the faith: **212, 663, 769, 840.**

She partakes in the doctrinal effort for the faith: **173, 175,** she enlightens us on the doctrines of faith: **227, 634, 642, 643.**

She enlightens the world: **400, 476, 580, 624, 642,** she works for the unity of the faith: **175, 198,** for the spreading of it by means of the Apostles: **173, 178, 400,** cf. *(165).*

She defends the faith, and helps it to remain forever: **173, 418, 546.**

She manifests her anguish and sorrow when persecutions put faith into danger: **773.**

She is a refuge, when faith weakens: **308.**

Through her the faith of many was ensured against the Albigenses: **119.**

She guides us to Heaven, by means of the faith: **164.**

f) *Mary overcomes error, sin and satan*   L

(123) — Mary won victory over heresies: **3, 64, 66, 67, 83, 91, 119, 173, 174, 245, 284, 335, 400, 441,**
>   Nestorianism: **302,**
>   the Albigenses: **84, 105, 119, 125, 215, 341,**
>   Rationalism: **67, 215.**

She will overcome Communism: **341.**

The East will return both to Mary and to the Pope: **310, 727,** cf. *(161).*

Diverse innovators (Protestants) return to Mary: **306.**

Mary triumphed over death and sin: **46, 83, 519, 521, 619,**
>   and over satan: **3, 22, 50, 101, 226, 238, 249, 519, 663, 770.**

She fights against the enemies of the Catholic Church: **3, 83, 94, 217, 367, 628, 743.**

Mary gives us the strength to fight against our enemies: **273, 403, 458.**

g) *The Church's attitude towards Mary most holy*

(124) — The Church loves Mary as its own Mother: **2.**

The Church unites itself to Mary in prayer: **98, 196, 197.**

It prays to Mary: **217, 365, 414,**

especially in difficult hours: **3, 82, 96, 101, 102, 107, 162, 367, 845.**

We must pray to Mary most holy for the Church: **141, 146, 356, 846.**

PART THREE

MARIAN DEVOTION

§ 1. General cult and devotion

a) *Importance and necessity*

(125) — Devotion to the Blessed Virgin Mary is fundamental in Christian life: **122, 325, 436.**

It is, at all times, necessary: **165, 208, 235, 286, 356, 365, 444, 718,**

especially in our day: **103, 367.**

It is natural to the Christian heart, and sign of orthodoxy: **115, 170, 283, 317, 456, 457, 831,**

is willed by God: **2, 235,**

approved by Christ: **675,**

and prophesied by Mary: **14, 436.**

The Church teaches us always to pray to Mary: **139, 320, 414, 725.**

b) *Cult of hyperdulia*

(126) — The nearest to God, Mary is superior to all praise: **9, 50, 165, 189, 440, 625, 647, 668,** cf. *(10)* - *(11)*.

Cult and special love of Mary have numerous motives: **432, 437, 440,**

love of God for her, superior to His love for all others: **122, 156, 300,**

Mary's dignity: **10, 122, 200,**

her divine Maternity: **129, 156, 186, 207, 255, 284, 296, 429,**

her spiritual Maternity: **116, 128, 170, 186, 284, 308, 356, 432,**

her closeness to mankind: **138,**

her office of co-Redemptrix and Mediatrix: **12, 149, 155, 257, 356,**
her intercession: **109, 146, 156, 206, 435,**
her power and her certainty of being heard: **269, 356, 435, 437,** cf. *(107)*,
her bounty and mercy: **126, 356,**
her favors bestowed in the past: **165, 742,**
her beauty, worthy of admiration: **647.**

c) *Relation between this cult and the cult which is rendered to God*

(127) — The cult rendered to Mary ascends to God her Son: **61, 305, 568, 597, 647, 734, 757, 771, 803,**
    and unites itself to the cult rendered to Christ: **236, 255, 407, 759.**
It is in close union with Eucharistic cult: **259, 418, 674, 756, 803, 823.**
It does not take away anything from the cult rendered to God: **206, 305, 597, 647, 734.**

d) *Conditions of Marian devotion*

(128) — It must be nourished by doctrine: **461,**
        it must be united to the knowledge of Christ and of His mysteries: **216,**
        faithful and docile to the Church: **244, 416, 434, 439,**
        to tradition and to Christian sense: **434,**
        animated by faith, hope, and love: **164, 236, 237, 359, 371, 539,** cf *(136)*,
        truthful and constant: **109, 174.**
It must properly dispose us to the maternal influence of Mary: **184.**
        obedient: **393, 398,**
        aim at imitating her: **581,** cf. *(130)*,
        full of humility: **109.**
It must be based on the conversion of the heart: **236, 239, 445, 447,**
        and desirous of moral reform and social justice: **281, 463, 652, 716, 722, 761, 777,**
        it must be united to holy works: **371, 394, 716, 722.**

h) *Consecration to Mary*

i) *Marian life and presence.*

j) *Patronage and protection*

She is our refuge: **64, 65, 109, 115, 161, 186, 234, 262, 550, 617, 721, 847.**

Being merciful she has pity on us: **126, 207, 367, 440, 537, 646, 715, 726.**

k) *Fruits of Marian devotion*

1. In general

(135) — Prayer to Mary honors her: **437,**

she hears in our voice, the voice of Jesus: **537.**

Filial devotion consoles her anguish during persecutions: **776.**

Devotion to Mary is the source of innumerable blessings: **7-9, 18, 115, 144, 154, 187, 223, 747.**

Mary hears those who pray to her: **81-82, 93, 97, 109, 116, 148, 157, 159, 162, 248, 275, 337, 373, 461, 564, 574, 749,**

especially if they pray to her in common: **125, 193.**

She anticipates our prayers: **126, 386.**

Our assiduous prayer makes her our daily mediatrix: **325.**

Mary remains faithful to her devotees: **157, 337, 386, 415,**

their zeal guarantees her powerful protection: **251, 319.**

This devotion is a title of glory: **144, 710.**

2. In the soul of Christians.

(136) — Devotion to Mary develops the life of sanctity: **252, 255, 322, 395, 482,**

makes our soul like unto her Son: **361, 831.**

She leads us to the integral application of the principles of Christian life: **237, 452, 610, 630-632, 722.**

She increases virtue: **252, 659, 722, 756.**

She develops faith and the integrity of doctrine: **255, 402, 452, 663, 742, 780, 837, 847,**

keeps us from errors and from heresy: **284, 400, 439, 462, 577, 663, 780,**

nourishes hope: **155, 658, 742, 756, 847.**

She enkindles love because of her beauty, her goodness, her favors: **847.**

She increases our knowledge and love of Christ and our union with Him: **165, 228, 235, 434, 608, 652, 658, 666, 756, 760, 831,**

worship of God: **536, 756,**

obedience: **237, 607, 652, 658, 761,**

humility and submission to God: **237, 432, 462, 652, 838,**

purity: **237, 322, 368, 379, 536, 639-640, 652, 727,**

fortitude and courage: **134, 395, 577, 652, 743, 760,**

gives security and victory: **18, 441, 635, 758,**

is the cause of the fruitfulness and joy of our life: **122, 780, 838,**

furnishes the remedy to difficulties and temptations: **358, 462, 574-575,**

uplifts the soul and at times the body also: **337,** cf. *(167).*

It recalls the thought of Heaven, amidst worldly matters: **670.**

It leads to final perseverance: **324, 840.**

It obtains Mary's help at the hour of death: **189, 281-282,** cf. *(173),*

prepares a great security in the sight of God: **26.**

And Mary will bestow the crown of glory on her devotees: **190, 324.**

c. Its fruits in the Church and in society

(137) — Devotion to Mary obtains graces and help for the Church: **9, 102, 217, 379, 538.**

It restores and extends the kingdom of Christ: **252, 260, 400, 847, 849, 850,**

brings about a Christian renewal: **463, 585, 832, 848,**

inspires zeal for the apostolate and enourages religious vocations: **395, 571, 656, 672-673, 841,**

obtains the light of grace which leads to perfection: **474,**

attracts souls: **432,**

shows them the sure way to the Church by means

a monopoly in favor of other practices: it permits, among the diverse forms, the liberty of choice: **434.**

a) *Mary's liturgical cult*

(141) — The first form is made up of Mary's great liturgical feasts: **500,**

The Immaculate Conception: **33, 38-39,** cf. *(62),*

The Annunciation and divine Maternity: **315-316,** cf. *(24),*

The Assumption: **497, 500,** cf. *(93),*

Mary's Queenship: **676, 680-681, 694, 698, 714-715, 718, 737, 739,** cf. *(105),*

The most pure heart of Mary: **168, 362, 373-374, 380, 408, 426, 495, 603, 617, 648, 720-721, 758, 778,**

pierced on Calvary: **532,**

The Holy Name of Mary: **715,**

Our Lady of the Rosary: **106, 120, 205, 373.**

b) *The Rosary*

1. Its institution

(142) — Devotion of the holy Rosary: **83, 96, 166,**

to which the Church consecrated the month of October: **92, 146, 551, 766,**

owes its origin to Christ: **159, 551.**

It is inspired, taught, recommended by Mary most holy: **119, 125, 166, 212, 274, 332, 339,**

recommended by Popes: **87, 89, 90, 185, 213, 275, 496,**

propagated by St. Dominic: **85, 92, 119, 173, 212, 274-275.**

2. The Rosary honors God and Mary

(143) — The Rosary glorifies God: **80, 89, 158, 205,**

honors Mary: **89, 96, 189, 190, 762,**

who wants it and is pleased with it: **100, 104, 117, 127, 129, 158, 159, 160, 184, 189, 214, 333, 557.**

3. Its fitness and utility

(144) — It is a very opportune form of devotion: **91, 99, 125, 189,**
and responds to a providential design: **121, 154,**
because it leads to the imitation of Christ and of Mary most holy: **552, 555,**
it leads us from Mary to Christ, and from Christ to the Father: **155, 182,**
by means of the meditation of the Mysteries of Jesus and of Mary: **119, 131, 150-153, 161, 182, 183, 198, 766,**
through the meditation on the Assumption and coronation of Mary: **152-153, 482, 496, 766.**

4. Excellence and Preciousness of the Rosary

(145) — The Rosary is an excellent devotion and worthy of God: **93, 158, 208,**
is a short Gospel: **422,**
which reassumes all Marian mysteries: **120,**
and bears witness to Mary's queenship: **95, 698,**
It is a perfect and an insistent prayer: **191, 552,**
in which Christ unites Himself to us: **159,**
unites to God's words, the words of the Angel and of the Church: **92, 120, 552,**
repeats the greeting to Mary: **156, 552.**
The Rosary respects the hierarchy of prayer: **191, 205.**
It unites vocal prayer to meditation: **92, 422, 552.**
It is the battle-cry of faith and the symbol of piety: **120,**
Mary's voice: **132,**
a motive of confidence: **148, 156, 158,**
the expression of Marian meditation: **149, 195.**
Leads to imitating, praying and loving Mary: **472,**
invites Mary to pray in our stead: **156.**

5. General benefits of the Rosary

(146) — This devotion is the source of many benefits: **81, 83, 96, 121, 147, 185, 188, 212, 274,**

over the Turks: **87, 88, 762.**
especially over the Albigenses: **85, 86, 119, 125,**

8. Need to propagate the Rosary

(149) — Our love for the Church urges us to spread devotion to the Rosary: **192, 204.**
Need to recite it especially in the family to obtain the grace of union among the members of the family: **191, 333, 554, 555,**
and spread the Rosary all over: **188, 192, 333,**
also in Eastern countries: **186.**

c) *Devotion of Mary's month and of the Scapular*

(150) — The month of May, consecrated to Mary, is an occasion of special devotion: **204, 345, 355, 369, 447, 448, 450, 764.**
Devotion to the scapular: **452-454,**
is a consecration and places us under Mary's protection; however it does not automatically guarantee salvation: **454.**
Devotion to the miraculous medal: **796.**

d) *Confraternities, Associations, Congresses*

(151) — Confraternities, especially the Rosary confraternity and that dedicated to the Scapular of Our Lady of Mount Carmel, famous Marian devotion: **165, 205, 281, 647, 656.**
Mary herself recommends it: **281,**
together with Marian Associations or Congregations: **7, 15, 392, 395-396, 456,**
they are recommended by the Popes: **656, 835.**
cf. The Lay Apostolate: Marian Congregations
The members of these Congregations defend Mary's greatness, and spread her graces: **393, 647, 656.**
The institution of the Children of Mary, opened the way to the definition of the Immaculate Conception: **646-647.**
Marian Congresses must not only be a manifestation of praise, but they must also bring an increase of faith,

rights of her Son: **462,**
to save the faith in calamitous times: **173, 769,**
for peace and salvation of mankind: **83, 547, 742,**
for Christian civilization: **439.**

The devotion of Christians to Mary goes back to the
first centuries, as Tertullian says: **14, 300, 676,**
then at Ephesus: **290, 294, 302,**
in the 12th century: **582,**
when Mary came to defend the Church against the
Albigenses: **105,** cf. *(123).*

This devotion is the antidote of Jansenism: **432.**

The blessings of Mary, after 1854: **223, 455, 474.**

Devotion to Mary flourishes today: **292, 362,**
and knows new hopes: **93, 120, 294, 461, 679.**

This devotion is a guarantee of future protection from
Mary: **22, 105, 455.**

Our century has absolute need of Mary's humility,
simplicity and purity: **288, 420.**

b) *Apparitions*: *at Lourdes*

(155) — Mary's apparitions at Lourdes: **215, 222, 318, 329,
586, 788, 793 ff., 827, 832, 843,**
they are an occasion of honoring Mary: **331.**

They are a reply to the definition of the Immaculate
Conception: **222, 586, 799, 808-809.**

Lourdes is the throne of Mary's bounty: **253, 259, 846,**
the center of a Christian Spring: **222, 587, 848,**
a recall to the supernatural: **328, 567, 847,**
an invitation to prayer and penance: **339, 788, 811-
812, 832-834, 843, 847,**
a cenacle of Eucharistic devotion: **260, 803, 833,
850.**

The healing of bodies is ordinate to the healing of
souls: **260, 812, 832, 847.**

These apparitions confirm the Catholic religion and
are a confutation of the unbelievers and of the rationalists: **222, 253, 567, 587.**

At Lourdes a window was opened looking out towards
Heaven: **849.**

c) *Fatima*

(156) — The miracles of Fatima: **407-408, 410,**
were the source of favors and graces: **408, 410, 560.**
Mary most holy manifests her Patronage in them: **407,
411, 415,**
and gives the message of her Queenship: **415, 679.**
These miracles are a motive of confidence in Mary:
407.
The coronation of Our Lady of Fatima is a gesture
of submission, fidelity, hope, which can assure world
peace: **415.**
It undertakes to regain Mary's Kingdom: **415.**

d) *Marian years*

(157) — A Marian year favors devotion to Mary: **611-612, 737.**
The aim of the Immaculate Conception jubilee is to
renew all things in Christ: **224, 678.**
The intentions of the 1954 Marian Year: conversion
of unbelievers; protection of youth; of Christian life
of adults; sufferings of the world; the persecuted
Church: **721.**

e) *Rome and the Popes*

(158) — Mary is the special Patroness and Protectress of Rome:
102, 366, 386, 441, 567, 616.
The Popes, in their difficulties invoke, Mary's help:
80, 174, 845.
We must pray to Mary for the Popes: **9, 18, 141.**
Pope Clement XIII expresses his devotion to Mary: **9.**
Gregory XVI: **17-18.**
Pius IX manifests devotion to and trust in Mary: **21,**
which set him free, and he therefore wishes to increase Mary's honor: **57, 64.**
Leo XIII affirms his filial piety: **122, 188, 210, 217,**
his trust: **121, 123, 142, 189,**
he is aware of the favors received from Mary and
the efficacy of devotion to her: **80, 122, 141-142,
174, 210,**

e) *Mary and Religious*

(166) — Mary is the Mother and the foundress of Religious: **779**,
protectress of their vow of chastity: **639**,
model of virgins: **639-640, 783**,
Mary takes care of their spiritual life: **641**.
The thought and life of Mary are the salvation of souls called to perfection: **322**,
The Carmelites have a particular duty to love Mary: **453**.

f) *Mary, the sick and suffering*

(167) — Mary is the health of bodies, and sometimes she heals them to cure souls: **260, 423**.
Mary is full of delicacy towards the sick: **636, 823-824**, and protects the immigrants: **787**.
Mary consoles those who suffer: **68, 275, 372, 386, 420, 531, 636, 717**.
She is their model: **532, 637-638**,
her Assumption should give them hope: **531**.
We must place our sorrows at Mary's feet: **308, 356, 375, 420**.
It is her desire to lighten the burden of their miseries and she has special love for the poor and unfortunate: **361, 372, 375, 398, 538, 823-824**.
She has, like God, the role of confusing the powerful by means of the weak: **330**.
She consoles and shares in the troubles, today as on Calvary, of those who suffer unjustly: **538, 581**.

g) *Mary and difficulties, temptations and dangers*

(168) — Mary is the refuge and the help of the Church, in her difficulties: **12, 80, 107-108, 261, 308, 317, 414, 522, 676, 842**.
In dangers, the Church has always had recourse to Mary: **83, 93, 103, 116, 288, 320, 356, 370, 547, 550, 555, 676, 767**.
Marian devotion grows in times of danger: **83, 98, 123, 557**,

where Mary's help is constant: **320, 450.**

The thought and sight of Mary are the salvation of those who struggle against the seductions of evil: **322, 351, 566.**

Mary is help and comfort in present evils: **90, 93, 116, 261, 286, 309, 332, 355, 367, 370, 442-443, 482, 550, 567, 677, 742, 753.**

The humility, purity and obedience of Mary are the antidote of present evils: **462.**

The tears of anguish and of sorrow that Mary shows obtain the strength to arrest persecution: **559, 773.**

Mary is in opposition to the return of the Albigensian heresy: **215,**

to the destructors of civilization: **341,**

to Communists: **342,**

to materialists: **643, 670,**

to the present divinization of man: **462,**

to present evil: **216, 248, 410.**

Mary will hasten the end of persecutions and will deliver us from evil: **81, 288, 309, 424, 559.**

h) *Mary and Peace*

(169) — Let us ask Mary for peace: **355, 374, 379, 386, 445-446, 448, 557,**

especially the peace and liberty of the Church: **99, 558, 846.**

Mary is the Queen of Peace: **261, 263-264, 376, 415, 718, 850.**

The acknowledgment of her Queenship will give peace to the world: **718.**

Our Lady of Peace: **367, 386; 477, 583.**

Mediatrix of Peace: **357, 718.**

Arbiter of peace between God and man: **251.**

Guide and mistress of peace: **565, 741.**

Guardian of peace: **444.**

She intercedes for peace and obtains it: **83, 261, 357, 376, 378-379, 385, 741, 842,**

she is the hope of it: **450, 566, 714,**

she exhorts peace: **718.**

She wishes us to desire and ask for peace from God: **564-565.**

She will give peace to the world: **93, 178, 344, 846,**
she will unite all the Catholic nations that draw their
fraternal love from her: **178, 186, 565, 741, 848-849.**

i) *Mary and sinners*

(170) — Mary is the Mother of fallen humanity: **372.**
Today she can still shed tears for our sins: **724, 774.**
She searches for and calls back sinners: **306, 475,**
to change their heart and cure them: **12, 320, 376,
432, 811,**
to reconciliate them and obtain pardon for them:
260, 344, 355, 812, 840.
She prayed for Christ's crucifiers: **241.**
She offered herself on Calvary for all sinners: **383.**
She leads them back to the Church and to the bishops:
68, 218, 450, 561-562.
The Rosary has particular efficacy on sinners: **432,**
who have absolute need of Mary's mediation: **114.**

j) *Mary and the Christians who are separated from the
Church*

(171) — Mary is the principal author and guardian of the unity
of the Church: **167, 178-179, 197.**
Her union with Christ makes her the link of the Bap-
tized brothers of Christ: **168, 176, 198.**
She generates the separated brethren in their return
to the Church: **184, 825,**
she prays for them: **164,**
is pleased when we pray for them: **178, 180, 198.**
Our prayer helps her to succor them: **178, 184.**
Therefore, we must pray her, like Saint Josaphat, for
the return to Christian unity: **175, 187, 283, 378,**
and entrust to Mary, Mother of faith, the hope of
this mission: **167, 175.**
Mary is the patroness of those who have returned to
the Roman unity: **187.**
Mary will lead the East to this unity: **283, 293, 310.**
Marian devotion of the Slavs, the homage and zeal of
the Orientals towards Mary, their veneration of holy
pictures will guide them in their return: **180-181, 283,
311.**

The centenary of the Council of Ephesus and the dogma of the divine Maternity will draw together the East and West: **177, 294.**

k) *Mary and the infidels*

(172) — We must also pray to Mary for the return of the Protestants: **306,**
  some of them, if they are stimulated to honor her, will return to the Pope and to the Church: **306.**
  We must ask Mary's protection over the infidels: **377, 825,**
  so that she will grant it also to those who do not know her: **285,**
  and we must remember that devotion to Mary is bound to the spreading of the faith: **143, 418.**

l) *Mary and the dying*

(173) — Our Lady of a Happy Death: **78, 257, 265-268.**
  She helps the dying at the hour of death: **257, 281, 282,**
    she exercises her office of spiritual Mother for them: **268,**
    through her help and intercession: **156,**
    she is, therefore, our refuge: **268, 308,**
    obtains for us pardon and reconciles us to Christ: **2, 56, 282, 308.**
  This assistance, verified through experience, is taught by the Doctors, who base their statement on Mary's maternal bounty, and on her participation in the Redemption: **282.**
  The prayers of the Church bear witness to it: **268.**
  Mary thus fulfills her work of redemption: **268.**
  Devotion to Mary and solicitude in pleasing her, assure her presence at the hour of death: **257, 281.**
  After death, Mary leads and helps souls to receive their reward: **324.**

m) *Mary and the souls in Purgatory*

(174) — Mary helps the souls in Purgatory by hastening their entry into Paradise—The Sabbatine Privilege: **454.**

n) *Mary and the Saints on earth*

(175) — Mary is Queen of Saints: **364,** cf. *(120).*

She exercises her Queenship of efficiency over them, she encourages, forms and crowns Saints: **322.**

All the Saints are servants of Mary and lead others to her: **431.**

Mary shines forth at the dawn of every life of sanctity, and in every step of the lives of the Saints: **322.**

Saint Joseph, as her spouse, is the nearest person to the Mother of God: **111.**

According to Mary's desire, we must unite St. Joseph to her in our prayers and trust: **110.**

We must be grateful to St. Anne because she gave us Mary: **657.**

Mary was especially honored by:

St. Germaine of Constantinople: **179,**

St. Bernard: **578,**

St. Dominic: **273, 275,**

St. Ignatius: **5-6,**

St. Josaphat: **283.**

The Saints of France who celebrated and propagated devotion to Mary: **277.**

St. Joan of Arc, who received her mission from Mary and whom Mary protected: **280.**

St. Louis Grignion de Montfort, worker at Mary's service: **431-432,**

Marian devotion was the foundation of his apostolate, his arms, his guarantee: **432,**

he taught and practiced devotion to Mary: **431-433, 435, 654,**

and propagated Consecration to Mary: **654.**

Mary chose and loved the humble Bernadette: **329-330.**

She made her her confidant, her ambassador to the Church: **283 bis.**

St. Anthony Mary Claret was the apostle of the Immaculate Heart of Mary: **720.**

Mary is the dawn of the Beatitudes to the Saints: **189.**

o) *Mary and human society*

(176) — Mary must reign over human society: **659, 717-719, 754.**

Marian devotion is to society a sign of salvation: **218**, it will lead Christ to society: **211, 216**.

Mary is the refuge of society, during danger: **261, 308, 476**.

We still believe, today, in her assistance to the world: **538**.

Love of Mary is an international link: **380, 431, 563, 832**.

Our century has, more than ever, need of the humility, simplicity and purity of Mary: **420, 727**.

Mary's victory over the Albigenses did good to all mankind: **105**.

And the same may be said of the Assumption: **522**.

p) *Mary and the Christian people*

(*177*) — Mary is the Patroness and protectress of the Christian people: **163, 288, 845**.

The re-establishment of the Church is expected from her: **98-100, 379, 717, 846**.

Marian devotion preserves the faith of the people: **417**, cf. (*122*).

Mary saves peoples: **64, 423, 727**,
when they acknowledge her as their Queen: **404**.

Mary gives her love, her compassion, her help, her defense to peoples: **401**.

Fortunate are the regions consecrated to Mary, and faithful to their promises: **727, 777**.

As the Christian people receive so much good from Mary they should pray to her: **547, 778**.

q) *Mary and the homelands*

(*178*) — Mary presides over all nations: **9**.

She protects and consoles the homeland: **538, 727**, of which she is the auxiliatrix: **193**, and salvation: **157**, accomplishes the good of every State: **186**, inspiring fraternal charity that unites them to each other: **178, 186, 477**.

Mary, Seat of Wisdom, inspires the Heads of the States: **742**.

INDEX OF QUOTATIONS

The numbers in heavy black print refer to the paragraphs of the Papal pronouncements.

HOLY SCRIPTURE

HOLY SEE AND COUNCILS

INDEX OF DOCUMENTS AND SOURCES

ALPHABETICAL INDEX OF WRITTEN DOCUMENTS

The numbers in bold type refer to the divisions of the Papal document.

CHRONOLOGICAL INDEX OF DOCUMENTS

BENEDICT XIV (1740-1758)

St. Pius X (1903-1914)

PIUS XII (1939-1958)

DAUGHTERS OF ST. PAUL

In Massachusetts
> 50 St. Paul's Ave.
> Jamaica Plain
> BOSTON 30, MASS.
> 315 Washington Street
> BOSTON 8, MASS.
> 381 Dorchester Street
> SO. BOSTON 27, MASS.
> 325 Main Street
> FITCHBURG, MASS.

In New York
> 78 Fort Place
> STATEN ISLAND 1, N. Y.
> 39 Erie Street
> BUFFALO 2, N. Y.

In Ohio
> 141 West Rayen Ave.
> YOUNGSTOWN 3, OHIO

In Texas
> 114 East Main Plaza
> SAN ANTONIO 5, TEXAS

In California
> 827 Fifth Ave.
> SAN DIEGO 1, CALIF.

In Louisiana
> 86 Bolton Ave.
> ALEXANDRIA, LA.

In Florida
> 2700 Biscayne Blvd.
> MIAMI 37, FLORIDA

In Canada
> 33 W. Notre Dame
> MONTREAL, QUEBEC, CANADA
> 134 Westmount St.
> TORONTO, ONTARIO, CANADA

In England
> 29 Beauchamp Place
> LONDON, S.W. 3, ENGLAND

In India
> 11 Baptista Road, Villa Parle.
> BOMBAY 24, INDIA

In Philippine Islands
> No. 326 Lipa City
> PHILIPPINE ISLANDS

In Australia
> 58 Abbotsford Road
> HOMEBUSH N.S.W., AUSTRALIA